SIXTH EDITION

D1239316

# SOCIOLOGY

## [ THE ESSENTIALS ]

### Margaret L. Andersen

*University of Delaware*

### Howard F. Taylor

*Princeton University*

WADSWORTH
CENGAGE Learning™

Australia • Brazil • Japan • Korea • Mexico • Singapore • Spain • United Kingdom • United States

# WADSWORTH
## CENGAGE Learning

**Sociology: The Essentials, Sixth Edition**
Margaret L. Andersen and Howard F. Taylor

Senior Publisher: Linda Schreiber

Associate Developmental Editor: Dan Moneypenny

Assistant Editor: Erin Parkins

Editorial Assistant: Rachael Krapf

Media Editor: Lauren Keyes

Marketing Manager: Andrew Keay

Marketing Assistant: Jillian Myers

Marketing Communications Manager: Laura Localio

Content Project Manager: Cheri Palmer

Creative Director: Rob Hugel

Art Director: Caryl Gorska

Print Buyer: Linda Hsu

Rights Acquisitions Account Manager, Text: Roberta Broyer

Rights Acquisitions Account Manager, Image: Don Schlotman

Production Service: TBC Project Management

Text Designer: Riezebos Holzbaur Design Group

Photo Researcher: Kelly Franz

Copy Editor: Jane Loftus

Illustrator: Macmillan Publishing Solutions

Cover Designer: Lee Friedman

Cover Image: © Vivane Moos/Corbis

Compositor: Macmillan Publishing Solutions

For product information and technology assistance, contact us at **Cengage Learning Customer & Sales Support, 1-800-354-9706.**

For permission to use material from this text or product, submit all requests online at **www.cengage.com/permissions.** Further permissions questions may be e-mailed to **permissionrequest@cengage.com.**

Library of Congress Control Number: 2009936913

International Student Edition:

ISBN-13: 978-0-495-81276-0

ISBN-10: 0-495-81276-5

**Wadsworth**
20 Davis Drive
Belmont, CA 94002-3098
USA

Cengage Learning is a leading provider of customized learning solutions with office locations around the globe, including Singapore, the United Kingdom, Australia, Mexico, Brazil, and Japan. Locate your local office at **www.cengage.com/global.**

Cengage Learning products are represented in Canada by Nelson Education, Ltd.

To learn more about Wadsworth, visit **www.cengage.com/wadsworth**

Purchase any of our products at your local college store or at our preferred online store **www.ichapters.com.**

*DEDICATION*

To Richard and Pat, with love

Printed in the United States of America
1 2 3 4 5 6 7 13 12 11 10 09

# BRIEF CONTENTS

# CONTENTS

**Chapter 7**

## Deviance and Crime 151

**PART THREE** *Social Inequalities*

## Social Class and Social Stratification 179

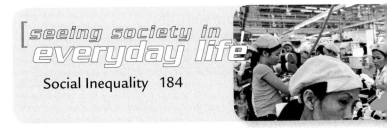

[ **seeing society in everyday life**
Social Inequality 184

[seeing society in everyday life]

Gender, Bodies, and Beauty  268

## Chapter 12

### *Sexuality* 289

## PART FOUR   Social Institutions

## Chapter 13

### *Families and Religion* 313

seeing society in everyday life

The Hurting Environment 416

# BOXES

# MAPS

# *Preface*

Studying sociology opens new ways of looking at the world. It is a perspective that is grounded in careful observation of social facts, as well as analyses of how society operates. For students and faculty alike, studying sociology can be exciting, interesting, and downright fun, even though it also deals with sobering social issues, such as inequality, racism, and crime, to name a few examples. In this book, we try to capture the excitement of the sociological perspective, while also introducing students to how sociologists do research and explain social interaction and social structure. We try to do so in a way that is engaging and accessible to undergraduate readers, while also preserving the integrity of sociological research and theory. Our experience in teaching introductory students shows us that students can appreciate the revelations of sociological research and theory if presented in a way that engages them and connects to their lives. We have kept this in mind throughout this revision and have focused on material that students can understand and apply to their own social worlds.

With each new edition, we think about the new students who will be reading the book. Although the basic perspective of sociology persists over time, the issues that new generations of learners face change. We find that keeping up with this generation is invigorating, and we hope our excitement and interest in teaching them sociology is apparent in the content and tone of the book. While we always retain a strong focus on core sociological concepts and ideas, we try to present our book in such a way that students will continue to tell us that they learn from it. As teachers and authors, one of our most rewarding moments is when a student tells us something about an insight they gained from *Sociology: The Essentials.*

We have added a particular new feature to this book with students in mind—the boxes titled **What Would They Say Now?** Each of these boxes (found in Chapters 1, 2, 7, 8, and 12) takes a very current topic of interest to students (the war in Iraq, hip-hop music, school shootings, sports and social class, sex and popular culture) and shows how the classical theorists within sociology would interpret these different subjects. We think students will find these boxes engaging and that they will "bring theory to life" in a way that shows the continuing importance of different sociological theories.

Each time we revise the book, we are also surprised by how many new topics for sociological analysis emerge and how much new research in sociology has developed, even in a short period of time. Events in the world also continue to shape the examples and explanations that we provide for our readers. Our book is known for its strong focus on sociological research and theory and for being deeply grounded in the inclusion of diversity. We have retained these focal points in the new edition.

# An Approach That Reflects the Significance of Sociology

## Diversity

With an increasingly diverse population in the United States, the study of diversity is central to our book. Unlike other introductory texts that add diversity to a preexisting approach to sociology, diversity has been part of the texture of this book since the first edition. And, with new research emerging on topics such as globalization, immigration, and changing race and ethnic patterns, diversity is just as important as ever. Indeed, the election of President Barack Obama since our last edition signals an increased interest, especially among young people, in forging a new society. Yet, social inequalities remain critical in how society is organized, how inequality shapes the experiences of different groups, and how diversity is shaping (and is shaped by) contemporary social changes. Thus, in this book, not only do we pay attention to diverse social groups, but we also maintain a core focus on the dynamics of inequality in society.

We define diversity to include the differences in experience created by social factors, including race, ethnicity, class, gender, age, religion, sexual orientation, and region of residence. We do not think of diversity as just the study of victims, although systems of disadvantage are clearly part of society. We stress the positive aspects of a diverse society, as well as its problems. We are pleased that our thorough integration of diversity has led reviewers to comment that our book provides the most comprehensive coverage of diversity of any book on the market.

## Current Theory and Research

According to readers and reviewers of this book, our presentation of current theory and research is one of its strongest features. We use the most current research throughout the book to show students the value of a sociological education. The box feature **Doing Sociological Research** showcases different research studies. We include this so that students will understand not just the concepts and procedures of research methods but also how sociologists do their work and how the questions they ask are linked to the methods of inquiry that they use. Each box begins by identifying the question asked by the researcher. Then it describes the method of research, presents the findings and conclusions, and briefly discusses the implications. These boxes also show students the diverse ways that sociologists conduct research and thus feature the rich and varied content of the discipline.

We also help students understand how different theoretical frameworks in sociology interpret different topics by including tables in every chapter that concisely compare different theoretical viewpoints, showing how each illuminates certain questions and principles. We think this comparison of theories helps students understand an important point: Starting from a different set of assumptions can change how you interpret different social phenomena.

## Critical Thinking and Debunking

We use the theme of *debunking* in the manner first developed by Peter Berger (1963) to look behind the facades of everyday life, challenging the ready-made assumptions that permeate commonsense thinking. Debunking is a way for students to develop their critical thinking, and we use the debunking theme to help students understand how society is constructed and sustained. This theme is highlighted in the **Debunking Society's Myths** feature found throughout every chapter.

In this edition, we also include a feature to help students see the relevance of sociology in their everyday lives. The box feature **See for Yourself** allows students to apply a sociological concept to an observation from their own lives, thus helping them develop their critical abilities and understand the importance of the sociological perspective.

*Critical thinking* is a term widely used but often vaguely defined. We use it to define the process by which students learn to apply sociological concepts to observable events in society. Throughout the book, we ask students to use sociological concepts to analyze and interpret the world they inhabit. This is reflected in the **Thinking Sociologically** feature that is also present in every chapter.

Because contemporary students are so strongly influenced by the media, we also encourage their critical thinking through the box feature **A Sociological Eye on the Media**. These boxes examine sociological research that challenges some of the ideas and images portrayed in the media. This not only improves students' critical thinking skills but also shows them how research can debunk these ideas and images.

## Social Change

The sociological perspective helps students see society as characterized both by constant change and social stability. How society changes and the events—both dramatic and subtle—that influence change are analyzed throughout this book. For example, the **Seeing Society in Everyday Life** photo essay in Chapter 5 discusses the impact of new technologies on social interaction, a topic that will be of special interest to students very much affected by these changes. New material added throughout on the impact of the economic recession in 2009 also shows students how their lives—seemingly individual—are greatly influenced by social structures beyond their control.

## Global Perspective

One of the main things we hope students learn in an introductory course is how broad-scale conditions influence things as seemingly individualized as everyday lives. Understanding this idea is a cornerstone of the sociological perspective and one of the main lessons learned in introductory courses. One way to see this is to help students understand how the increasingly global character of society affects day-to-day realities. Thus, we use a global perspective to examine how global changes are affecting all parts of life within the United States, as well as other parts of the world. This means more than including cross-cultural examples. It means, for example, examining phenomena such as migration and immigration or helping students understand that their own consumption habits are profoundly shaped by global interconnections. The availability of jobs, too, is another way students can learn about the impact of an international division of labor on work within the United States. Our global perspective is found in the research and examples cited throughout the book, as well as in various chapters that directly focus on the influence of globalization on particular topics, such as work, culture, and crime. The map feature **Viewing Society in Global Perspective** also brings a global perspective to the subject matter.

# New to the SIXTH Edition

We have made various changes to the sixth edition to make it current and to reflect new developments in sociological research. Taken together, these changes should make the sixth edition easier for instructors to teach and even more accessible and interesting for students.

At the suggestion of reviewers, we have added a separate chapter on sociological research methods (Chapter Three, "Doing Sociological Research"). We believe this strengthens the research focus in the book and allows instructors to give more attention to the tools of sociological inquiry. Yet, we also know that students will not grasp the importance of sociological research until they have some grounding in the interesting topics of sociology. For this reason, we have placed the research chapter as the third chapter in the book, following Chapter 1, which introduces the core sociological perspective, and Chapter 2, which discusses culture. We think this ordering of chapters will tweak students' interest in the insights of our discipline prior to learning about the tools of sociological research. Of course, instructors who would prefer introducing students to research first can simply reverse the order in which they teach the chapters.

Because of adding this new chapter, we have then combined two of the final chapters from the fifth edition. The final chapter is now "Population, the Environment, and Social Change," a chapter that now combines population, urbanization, and the environment with social change and social movements. Population expansion and change, as well as challenging changes in the physical and social environments of our society, are issues of tremendous importance, and these changes have been the causes of a number of social movements and thus social and cultural change.

*Sociology: The Essentials* is organized into five major parts: "Introducing the Sociological Imagination" (Chapter 1); "Studying Society and Social Structure" (Chapters 2 through 7); "Social Inequalities" (Chapters 8 through 12); "Social Institutions" (Chapters 13 through 15); and "Social Change" (Chapter 16).

**Part I, "Introducing the Sociological Imagination,"** introduces students to the unique perspective of sociology, differentiating it from other ways of studying society, particularly the individualistic framework students tend to assume. Within this section, **Chapter 1, "The Sociological Perspective,"** introduces students to the sociological perspective. The theme of debunking is introduced, as is the sociological imagination, as developed by C. Wright Mills. This chapter briefly reviews the development of sociology as a discipline, with a focus on the classical frameworks of sociological theory, as well as contemporary theories, such as feminist theory and postmodernism. We have added Iba B. Wells Barnett to the discussion of sociological theory, given her influence and insight on race and society in the early history of sociology. We have updated examples in this chapter, added First Lady Michelle Obama to the list of sociology majors, and included the new box, "What Would They Say Now: Classical Theorists on the War in Iraq."

In **Part II, "Studying Society and Social Structure,"** students learn some of the core concepts of sociology. It begins with the study of culture in

**Chapter 2, "Culture and the Media,"** a new title that reflects the added attention to the media, given how important the mass media are in students' lives. There is a new section on how the media are organized, something students rarely think about even while they are influenced by media images. We reorganized the chapter somewhat to include discussion of ethnocentrism and cultural relativism in the section on diversity. We include one of the new "What Would They Say Now" boxes on the topic of hip-hop—important in youth culture. We have included numerous new examples and updated graphics throughout.

**Chapter 3, "Doing Sociological Research,"** contains an updated discussion of the research process and the tools of sociological research—the survey, participant observation, controlled experiments, content analysis, historical research, and evaluation research. A new participant observation study—"A Cop in the Hood"—is included as a box. Included also are new discussions and recent participant observation studies, as well as recent studies in controlled experiments.

**Chapter 4, "Socialization and the Life Course,"** contains new material on socialization theory and research, including agents of socialization such as the media, research on children's understanding of race, and a comparison of theories of socialization. The chapter also includes discussion of aging and the life course, as well as the conversion process and "brainwashing."

**Chapter 5, "Social Interaction and Social Structure,"** emphasizes how changes in the macro-structure of society influence the microlevel of social interaction. We do this by focusing on technological changes that are now part of students' everyday lives and making the connection between changes at the societal level in the everyday realities of people's lives. The chapter also includes a discussion and comparison of newer theories about analyzing social interaction, such as dramaturgical analysis and game theory. The chapter includes new material on interaction in cyberspace, Internet dating, and an essay on how technology has affected social interaction.

In **Chapter 6, "Groups and Organizations,"** we study social groups and bureaucratic organizations, using sociology to understand the complex processes of group influence, organizational dynamics, and the bureaucratization of society. The chapter includes updates of research on juries, social networks, and the torture of Iraqi prisoners by Americans at the Abu Ghraib Prison in Iraq. New research on race, class and gender in bureaucratic organizations is included.

**Chapter 7, "Deviance and Crime,"** includes a look at the sociological theories of deviance with attention to labeling theory; corporate crime and deviance; and the effects of race, class, and gender on arrest rates. The core material is illustrated with contemporary events, such as school rampage shootings, and updates on corporate and white-collar crime, including a discussion of Ponzi schemes such as that perpetrated by Bernard Madoff. Included in this chapter is recent research on what has become *mass racialized incarceration* of Blacks and Hispanics in U.S. prisons.

In **Part III, "Social Inequalities,"** each chapter explores a particular dimension of stratification in society. Beginning with the significance of class, **Chapter 8, "Social Class and Social Stratification,"** provides an overview of basic concepts central to the study of class and social stratification. An important revision to this chapter is material on the economic crisis revealed throughout 2009, including new material on housing foreclosures, unemployment, and current material on mobility—upward and downward! There is a new "What Would They Say Now" box on sports and social class, since sports are familiar to students and a good way to reveal different theoretical analyses of how class works. Updated data on income, wealth, and poverty is included throughout.

**Chapter 9, "Global Stratification,"** follows, with a particular emphasis on understanding the significance of global stratification, the inequality that has developed among, as well as within, various nations. There is an expanded discussion of the impact of the war on poverty, given how important this topic is in current affairs. We also revised the section on globalization and social change to better analyze the impact of corporate globalization and cultural changes stemming from an increasingly global world.

**Chapter 10, "Race and Ethnicity,"** is a comprehensive review of the significance of race and ethnicity in society, plus discussion of very recent studies of effects of Latino/a immigration, of skin color gradation in both Black and Hispanic communities, and the relevance of net worth as opposed to annual income in Black communities. Included are topics such as an update on forms and types of racism, the relevance of race in the devastation caused by Hurricane Katrina, a new discussion of the combined effects of race and class, a new look at ways to attain racial equality, and speculation about the effects of the Obama presidency upon race in the United States.

**Chapter 11, "Gender,"** focuses on gender as a central concept in sociology closely linked to systems of stratification in society. The chapter links the social construction of gender to issues of homophobia, then is followed by the separate chapter on sexuality. This edition maintains a separate chapter on sexuality (Chapter 12), reflecting the increased attention in sociological research to sexuality as a component of social stratification. The new edition strengthens the discussion of violence against women, adds a discussion of the so-called mommy tax, and clarifies that sexism is both an individual belief and an institutional process.

**Chapter 12, "Sexuality,"** treats sexuality as a social construction and a dimension of social stratification and inequality. The revised chapter includes new information on teen pregnancy, sexual attitudes, and more international material on abortion, sexual activity, and contraception. New research studying the influence of abstinence-only sex education on sexual behaviors is included, as is new material on the "hooking up" phenomenon and new research on the so-called pornification of mainstream culture. There is also expanded international coverage on rape as a consequence of war and new material on sex tourism and sex trafficking.

**Part IV, "Social Institutions,"** includes three chapters, each focusing on basic institutions within society. **Chapter 13, "Families and Religion,"** maintains its inclusion of important topics in the study of families, such as interracial dating, debates about same-sex marriage, fatherhood, gender roles within families, and family violence. The section on religion includes much more research on Muslims in the United States and more material on megachurches, which are increasingly influential. There is also new material on racial–ethnic diversity and religious belief.

**Chapter 14, "Education and Health Care,"** discusses the institutions of education and health care and gives an overview of education in the United States, including recent developments in education and inequality, plus a look at health and sickness seen globally. It includes theoretical perspectives on health care and the health care crisis in America, including difficulties in access to health care by race, gender, and social class. New to this chapter is recent research and data on inequality and standardized testing, on the "cognitive elite" and the nature-versus-nurture argument, the effects of schooling and gender on income and individual mobility, and the effects of tracking in schools. The chapter also contains an update of the health care crisis in America and the issue of universal health care.

**Chapter 15, "Politics and the Economy,"** analyzes the state, power, and authority and bureaucratic government. It also contains a detailed discussion of theories of power in addition to coverage of the economy seen globally and characteristics of the labor force. This chapter has been substantially revised to reflect the presidential election of 2008 as well as to reflect the economic problems that have emerged since the last edition. There is new material on politics on the historic participation of people of color in the presidential election, as well as a discussion of youth voters. The section on the military includes updated material on women and minorities in the military, including family strains from separation, and new material on the privatization of the military. New research on sexual harassment and assault in the military is also included.

**Part V, "Social Change,"** includes **Chapter 16, "Population, the Environment, and Social Change,"** which is an all-new chapter combining population, environmental issues, social movements, and social change. Outlined are the basic demographic processes, urbanization, and theories of population growth, as well as research on pollution and depletion of the physical environment. Included is a new photo essay on the very real effects of environmental pollution, global warming, and the role of new ("green") technologies. New data are included on racial–ethnic migration and the role of environmental racism. Also addressed in this new chapter are social change and social movements, with detailed coverage on theories of social change, the causes of social change, and the nature and types of social movements. New discussions include inequality, powerlessness and the individual, as well as a broader discussion of social movements.

# Features and Pedagogical Aids

The special features of this book flow from its major themes: diversity, current theory and research, debunking and critical thinking, social change, and a global perspective. The features are also designed to help students develop critical thinking skills so that they can apply abstract concepts to observed experiences in their everyday life and learn how to interpret different theoretical paradigms and approaches to sociological research questions.

## Critical Thinking Features

The feature **Thinking Sociologically** takes concepts from each chapter and asks students to think about these concepts in relationship to something they can easily observe in an exercise or class discussion. The feature **Debunking Society's Myths** takes certain common assumptions and shows students how the sociological perspective would inform such assumptions and beliefs.

## See for Yourself

Each chapter includes a feature, **See for Yourself,** intended to provide students with the chance to apply sociological concepts and ideas to their own observations. This feature can also be used as the basis for writing exercises, helping students improve both their analytic skills and their writing skills.

## Seeing Society in Everyday Life

These photo essays help students understand concepts more clearly. Essays include "Social Interaction in an Age of Technology" in Chapter 5; "Social Inequality" in Chapter 8; "Gender, Bodies, and Beauty" in Chapter 11; and "The Hurting Environment" in Chapter 16.

## Unparalleled Integration of Web-Based Resources

Instructors will find that several technology-based teaching enhancements are integrated throughout the book, making this book the best conceived in using Internet tools for teaching and learning introductory sociology.

The *Sociology: The Essentials* companion website has a multitude of resources for students. Links to the student website are provided at the end of every chapter. On the companion website, students will find suggested readings, web links, a MicroCase® Online feature that teaches students how to research society, learning objectives, Internet exercises, quizzes, and flash cards—available at **www.cengage.com/sociology/andersen**.

In addition, **CengageNOW™,** a self-study assessment, web-based assessment, and study tool, is integrated in every chapter. (See the Supplements section later in this preface for more details on this robust study tool.)

## An Extensive and Content-Rich Map Program

We use the map feature that appears throughout the book to help students visualize some of the ideas presented, as well as to learn more about regional and international diversity. One map theme is **Mapping America's Diversity** and the other is **Viewing Society in Global Perspective.** These maps have multiple uses for instructional value, beyond instructing students about world and national geography. The maps have been designed primarily to show the differentiation by county, state, and/or country on key social facts. For example, in Chapter 4 we show the dispersion of the population under five years of age, both nationally and worldwide. Students can use this information to ask questions about how the age distribution of the population might be related to immigration, poverty, or global stratification.

We have included a critical thinking component to the maps to integrate them more effectively with the chapter material. Thus, each map includes **critical thinking questions** that ask students to interpret the map data within the context of concepts and ideas from the chapter.

## High-Interest Theme Boxes

In addition to new **What Would They Say Now?** boxes described earlier, we use three high-interest themes for the box features that embellish our focus on diversity and sociological research throughout the text. **Understanding Diversity** boxes further explore the approach to diversity taken throughout the book. In most cases, these box features provide personal narratives or other information designed to teach students about the experiences of different groups in society.

Because many are written as first-person narratives, they can invoke students' empathy toward groups other than those to which they belong—something we think is critical to teaching about diversity. We hope to show students the connections between race, class, and other social groups that they otherwise find difficult to grasp.

The box feature **Doing Sociological Research** is intended to show students the diversity of research questions that form the basis of sociological knowledge and, equally important, how the question a researcher asks influences the method used to investigate the question.

We see this as an important part of sociological research—that how one investigates a question is determined as much by the nature of the question as by allegiance to a particular research method. Some questions require a more qualitative approach, others, a more quantitative approach. In developing these box features, we ask, What is the central question sociologists are asking? How did they explore this question using sociological research methods? What did they find? and What are the implications of this research? We deliberately selected questions that show the full and diverse range of sociological theories and research methods, as well as the diversity of sociologists. Each box feature ends with **Questions to Consider** to encourage students to think further about the implications and applications of the research.

The feature **A Sociological Eye on the Media,** found in several chapters, examines some aspect of how the media influence public understanding of some of the subjects in this book. We think this is important because sociological research often debunks taken-for-granted points of view presented in the media, and we want students to be able to look at the media with a more critical eye. Because of the enormous influence of the media, we think this is increasingly important in educating students about sociology. In addition to the features just described, there is an entire set of learning aids within each chapter that promotes student mastery of the sociological concepts.

### In-Text Learning Aids

**Chapter Outlines.** A concise chapter outline at the beginning of each chapter provides students with an overview of the major topics to be covered.

**Key Terms.** Key terms and major concepts appear in bold when first introduced in the chapter. A list of the key terms is found at the end of the chapter, which makes study more effective. Definitions for the key terms are found in the glossary.

**Theory Tables.** Each chapter includes a table that summarizes different theoretical perspectives by comparing and contrasting how these theories illuminate different aspects of different subjects.

**Chapter Summary in Question-and-Answer Format.** Questions and answers highlight the major points in each chapter and provide a quick review of major concepts and themes covered in the chapter.

A **Glossary** and complete **References** for the whole text are found at the back of the book.

# Supplements

*Sociology: The Essentials,* Sixth Edition, is accompanied by a wide array of supplements prepared to create the best learning environment inside as well as outside the classroom for both the instructor and the student. All the continuing supplements for *Sociology: The Essentials,* Sixth Edition, have been thoroughly revised and updated. We invite you to take full advantage of the teaching and learning tools available to you.

## For the Instructor

**Instructor's Resource Manual.** This supplement offers the instructor brief chapter outlines, student learning objectives, ASA recommendations, key terms and people, detailed chapter lecture outlines, lecture/discussion suggestions, student activities, chapter worksheets, video suggestions, video activities, and Internet exercises. Also included is a listing of resources offered with the text, as well as an assortment of useful appendices, which include activities that help integrate ASA task force recommendations in your course.

**Test Bank.** This test bank consists of a myriad of multiple-choice, true/false, short-answer and essay questions for each chapter, all with page references to the text. Each multiple-choice item has the question type (factual, applied, or conceptual) indicated, and all test questions will be mapped to a learning objective for the chapter. All questions are also labeled as new, modified, or pick-up so instructors know if the question is new to this edition of the test bank, modified but picked up from the previous edition of the test bank, or picked up straight from the previous edition of the test bank.

**PowerLecture with JoinIn™ and ExamView® CD-ROM.** This easy-to-use, one-stop digital library and presentation tool includes the following:

- Preassembled Microsoft® PowerPoint® lecture slides with graphics from the text, making it easy for you to assemble, edit, publish, and present custom lectures for your course.

- The PowerLecture CD-ROM includes video-based polling and quiz questions that can be used with the JoinIn™ on TurningPoint® personal response system.

- PowerLecture also features ExamView® testing software, which includes all the test items from the printed Test Bank in electronic format, enabling you to create customized tests of up to 250 items that can be delivered in print or online.

**Classroom Activities for Introductory Sociology.** Made up of contributions from introductory sociology instructors from around the country, this print supplement will be offered free to adopters of Andersen/Taylor's *Sociology: The Essentials,* Sixth Edition. The booklet features classroom activities, student projects, and lecture ideas to help instructors make topics fun and interesting for students. With general teaching tactics as well as topic-focused activities, it has never been easier to find a way to integrate new ideas into your classroom.

**Introduction to Sociology Group Activities Workbook.** This supplement is both a workbook for students and a repository of ideas for instructors.

The workbook contains both in- and out-of-class group activities on activity sheets that students can complete, tear out, and turn in to the instructor. Also included are teaching ideas for video clips to anchor group discussions, maps, case studies, group quizzes, ethical debates, group questions, group project topics, and ideas for outside readings.

**Extension: Wadsworth's Sociology Reader Collection.** Create your own customized reader for your sociology class, drawing from dozens of classic and contemporary articles found on the exclusive Cengage Wadsworth TextChoice database. Using the TextChoice website (**www.TextChoice.com**) you can preview articles, select your content, and add your own original material. TextChoice will then produce your materials as a printed supplementary reader for your class.

## Classroom Presentation Tools for the Instructor

**Videos.** Adopters of *Sociology: The Essentials,* Sixth Edition, have several different video options available with the text. Please consult with your Cengage Learning sales representative to determine if you are a qualified adopter for a particular video.

**Wadsworth's Lecture Launchers for Introductory Sociology.** An exclusive offering jointly created by Cengage Wadsworth and DALLAS Tele-Learning, this video contains a collection of video highlights taken from the *Exploring Society: An Introduction to Sociology Telecourse* (formerly *The Sociological Imagination*). Each three- to six-minute video segment has been specially chosen to enhance and enliven class lectures and discussions of twenty key topics covered in the Introduction to Sociology course. Accompanying the video is a brief written description of each clip, along with suggested discussion questions to help effectively incorporate the material into the classroom. Available on VHS or DVD.

**Sociology: Core Concepts Video.** Another exclusive offering jointly created by Cengage Wadsworth and DALLAS TeleLearning, this video contains a collection of video highlights taken from the *Exploring Society: An Introduction to Sociology Telecourse* (formerly *The Sociological Imagination*). Each fifteen- to twenty-minute video segment will enhance student learning of the essential concepts in the introductory course and can be used to initiate class lectures, discussion, and review. The video covers topics such as the sociological imagination, stratification, race and ethnic relations, social change, and more. Available on VHS or DVD.

**ABC® Video Series, Volumes I–IV.** This series of videos, comprising footage from ABC broadcasts, is specially selected and arranged to accompany your introductory sociology course. The segments may be used in conjunction with Wadsworth's introductory sociology texts to help provide a real-world example to illustrate course concepts or to instigate discussion.

**Wadsworth Sociology Video Library.** Bring sociological concepts to life with videos from Wadsworth's Sociology Video Library, which includes thought-provoking offerings from *Films for the Humanities* as well as other excellent educational video sources. This extensive collection illustrates important sociological concepts covered in many sociology courses.

## Supplements for the Student

**Study Card.** This handy card provides all the important sociological concepts highlighted in Andersen/Taylor, broken down by chapter. Providing a large amount of information at a glance, this study card is an invaluable tool for a quick review.

**CengageNOW™.** This online tool provides students with a customized study plan based on a diagnostic pretest that students take after reading each chapter. The study plan provides interactive exercises, learning modules, animations, video exercises, and other resources to help students master concepts that are central to sociology. After the study plan has been reviewed, students can take a posttest to monitor their progress in mastering the chapter concepts. Instructors may bundle this product for their students with each new copy of the text for free! If your instructor did not order the free access code card to be packaged with your text, or if you have a used copy of the text, you can still obtain an access code for a nominal fee. Just visit the Cengage Wadsworth E-Commerce site at **www.ichapters.com**, where easy-to-follow instructions help you purchase your access code.

**Study Guide.** This student study tool has been significantly revised from the previous edition in order to better suit your study needs. Each chapter contains a brief chapter outline, 10–15 questions to guide your reading, key terms and key people matching exercises with page references to the text, a chapter review where you can fill in the blanks to complete the summaries of each section, Internet and InfoTrac College Edition exercises, and practice tests consisting of multiple-choice, true/false, and short answer questions, as well as essay suggestions. Each chapter has an answer key in the back of the study guide, including answers to the key terms, key people, chapter review, and practice test sections.

**Practice Tests.** This collection of practice tests helps students adequately prepare for exams by presenting them with multiple-choice, true/false, short-answer, and essay questions that are similar in quality to the test bank questions. Multiple-choice and true/false answers are included, and page references are provided for all questions.

**Researching Society with MicroCase® Online Booklet.** This supplement contains MicroCase exercises for each chapter. Students can see the results of actual research by using the Wadsworth MicroCase Online feature available from the Wadsworth website. This feature allows students to look at some of the results from national surveys, census data, and other data sources. They can either explore this easy-to-use feature on their own or use the examples provided. Previously in the textbook, these MicroCase exercises are now in their own supplement.

## Internet-Based Supplements

**InfoTrac® College Edition.** Available as an option with newly purchased texts, InfoTrac College Edition gives instructors and students four months of free access to an extensive online database of reliable, full-length articles (not just abstracts) from thousands of scholarly and popular publications, going back as much as twenty-two years. Among the journals available are *American Journal of Sociology, Social Forces, Social Research,* and *Sociology.*

**WebTutor™ on WebCT® and Blackboard®.** This web-based software for students and instructors takes a course beyond the classroom to an anywhere, anytime environment. Students gain access to a full array of study tools, including chapter outlines, chapter-specific quizzing material, interactive games and maps, and videos. With WebTutor Advantage, instructors can provide virtual office hours, post syllabi, track student progress with the quizzing material, and even customize the content to suit their needs.

**Wadsworth's Sociology Home Page at www.cengage.com/sociology.** Combine this text with the exciting range of web resources on Wadsworth's Sociology Home Page and you will have truly integrated technology into your learning system. Wadsworth's Sociology Home Page provides instructors and students with a wealth of information and resources, such as *Sociology in Action, Census 2000: A Student Guide for Sociology,* Research Online, Sociology Timeline, a Spanish glossary of key sociological terms and concepts, and more.

**Companion Website for *Sociology: The Essentials.*** The book's companion website includes chapter-specific resources for instructors and students. For instructors, the site offers a password-protected instructor's manual, PowerPoint presentation slides, and more. For students, there is a multitude of text-specific study aids, including the following:

- Tutorial practice quizzes that can be scored and emailed to the instructor
- Web links
- Glossary
- Flash cards
- MicroCase Online data exercises
- Crossword puzzles
- Virtual explorations
- And much more!

You can visit the companion site for *Sociology: The Essentials* at **www.cengage.com/sociology/andersen.**

# Acknowledgments

We relied on the comments of many reviewers to improve the book, and we thank them for the time they gave in developing very thoughtful commentaries on the different chapters. Thanks to Megan L. Duesterhaus, University of Central Florida; Catherine M. Felton, Central Piedmont Community College; Jennifer Holz, University of Akorn–Wayne College; Dana Hysock, Macon State College; Gina Luby, DePaul University, Joanna Maatta, The Pennsylvania University; Aurea Osgood, Winona State University; and KC Williams, Coastal Carolina Community College.

We would also like to extend our thanks to those who reviewed the first five editions of *Sociology: The Essentials*. Brenda N. Bauch, Jefferson College; E. M. Beck, University of Georgia; Alessandro Bonanno, Sam Houston State University; G. M. Britten, Lenoir Community College (North Carolina); James E. Coverdill, University of Georgia; Susan Crafts, Niagara Community College; Jean E. Daniels, California State University; Angela D. Danzi, Farmingdale State University, Northridge; Ione Y. DeOllos, Ball State University; Marlese Durr, Wright State University; Lois Easterday, Onondaga Community College; Cynthia K. Epperson, St. Louis Community College at Meramec; Lynda Ann Ewen, Marshall University; Grant Farr, Portland State University; Irene Fiala, Kent State University–Ashtabula; James Fillman, Bucks County Community College; Lorna Forster, Clinton Community College; Darlaine Gardetto, St. Louis Community College–Meramec; Patricia Gibbs, Foothill College; Bethany Gizzi, Monroe Community College; Jennifer Hamer, Wayne State University; Sara E. Hanna, Oakland Community College, Highland Lakes Campus; Shannon Houvouras, University of West Georgia; James R. Hunter, Indiana University Purdue University Indianapolis; Jon Iannitti, SUNY College of Agriculture and Technology at Morrisville; Carol A. Jenkins, Glendale Community College; Diane E. Johnson, Kutztown University of Pennsylvania; Katherine Johnson, Niagara Community College; Anna Karpathakis, Kingsborough Community College, CUNY; Alice Abel Kemp, University of New Orleans; Keith Kirkpatrick, Victoria College (Texas); Tim Kubal, California State University, Fresno; Elizabeth D. Leonard, Vanguard University; James Lindberg, Montgomery College, Rockville Campus, Maryland; Martha O. Loustaunau, New Mexico State University; Brad Lyman, Baltimore City Community College; Susan A. Mann, University of New Orleans; Brian L. Maze, Franklin University; Leland C. McCormick, Minnesota State University–Mankato; Christine Monnier, College of DuPage; Brian Moss, Oakland Community College–Waterford Campus (MI); Timothy Owens, Purdue University; Tara Perrello, Fordham University; Linda L. Petroff, Central Community College; David L. Phillips, Arkansas State University; Billie Joyce Pool, Homes Community College; Ralph Pyle, Michigan State University; David

Redburn, Furman University; Lesley Williams Reid, Georgia State University; Lisa Riley, Creighton University; Fernando Rivera, University of Central Florida; Michael C. Smith, Milwaukee Area Technical College; Beverly Stiles, Midwestern State University; Tracey Steele, Wright State University; Melvin Thomas, North Carolina State University; Richard Sullivan, Illinois State University; Judith Warner, Texas A&M International University; Stephanie Williams, Arizona State University; Sheryline A. Zebroski, St. Louis Community College, Florissant; Carl W. Zeigler, Elgin Community College; and Brenda S. Zicha, Mott Community College.

We also thank the following people, each of whom provided critical support in different, but important ways: Alison Bianchi, Cindy Gibson, Linda Keen, Nancy Quillen, and Judy Watson.

We are fortunate to be working with a publishing team with great enthusiasm for this project. We thank all of the people at Wadsworth who have worked with us on this and other projects, but especially we thank Chris Caldeira, Dan Moneypenny, and Cheri Palmer for their efforts on behalf of our book and the guidance and advice, not to mention the hard work, they have given to this project. We especially thank Dusty Friedman of TBC Project Management for her extraordinary attention to detail; we appreciate enormously her talent and perseverance. We thank Jane Loftus for her very careful copyediting of the manuscript and Kelly Franz for her work on the photo research. Finally, our special thanks also go to our spouses Richard Morris Rosenfeld and Patricia Epps Taylor for their ongoing support of this project.

# About the Authors

**Margaret L. Andersen,** raised in Oakland, California; Rome, Georgia; and Boston, is Edward F. and Elizabeth Goodman Rosenberg Professor of Sociology at the University of Delaware. She received her Ph.D. from the University of Massachusetts, Amherst, and her B.A. from Georgia State University. She is the author of *Thinking about Women: Sociological Perspectives on Sex and Gender* (Allyn and Bacon) and the best-selling Wadsworth text, *Race, Class, and Gender: An Anthology* (with Patricia Hill Collins). She is also the author of *On Land and On Sea: A Century of Women in the Rosenfeld Collection* and *Living Art: The Life of Paul R. Jones, African American Art Collector.* She has recently served as Vice President of the American Sociological Association from which she has also received the prestigious Jessie Bernard Award. She has also been awarded the SWS Feminist Lecturer Award, given annually by SWS (Sociologists for Women in Society) to a social scientist whose work has contributed to improving the status of women in society. She currently serves as Chair of the National Advisory Board of the Center for Comparative Studies in Race and Ethnicity at Stanford University. She has served as the Interim Dean of the College of Arts and Science and Vice Provost for Academic Affairs at the University of Delaware, where she has also won the University's Excellence in Teaching Award. She lives on the Elk River in Maryland with her husband Richard Rosenfeld.

**Howard F. Taylor** was raised in Cleveland, Ohio. He graduated Phi Beta Kappa from Hiram College and has a Ph.D. in sociology from Yale University. He has taught at the Illinois Institute of Technology, Syracuse University, and Princeton University, where he is presently professor of sociology and former Director of the African American Studies Center. He has published over fifty articles in sociology, education, social psychology, and race relations. His books include *The IQ Game* (Rutgers University Press), a critique of hereditarian accounts of intelligence; *Balance in Small Groups* (Van Nostrand Reinhold), translated into Japanese; and the forthcoming *Race and Class and the Bell Curve in America.* He has appeared widely before college, radio, and TV audiences, including ABC's *Nightline.* He is past President of the Eastern Sociological Society, and a member of the American Sociological Association and the Sociological Research Association, an honorary society for distinguished research. He is a winner of the DuBois-Johnson-Frazier Award, given by the American Sociological Association for distinguished research in race and ethnic relations, and the President's Award for Distinguished Teaching at Princeton University. He lives in Pennington, New Jersey, with his wife, a corporate lawyer.

Chapter one
CHAPTER ONE

# The Sociological Perspective

[ ***Imagine that you*** had been switched with another infant at birth. How different would your life be? What if your accidental family was very poor … or very rich? How might this have affected the schools you attended, the health care you received, the possibilities for your future career? If you had been raised in a different religion, would this have affected your beliefs, values, and attitudes? Taking a greater leap, what if you had been born another sex or a different race? What would you be like now?

We are talking about changing the basic facts of your life—your family, social class, education, religion, sex, and race. Each has major consequences for who you are and how you will fare in life. These factors play a major part in writing your life script. Social location (meaning a person's place in society) establishes the limits and possibilities of a life.

Consider this:

- The pay gap between women and men, which had been declining since the 1980s, has recently *increased* between college-educated women and men (Blau and Kahn 2004; Leonhardt 2006).

*continued*

Jeff Greenberg/The Image Works

- Black Americans who kill Whites are much more likely to face the death penalty than Blacks who kill other Black people, and given the death penalty, Black Americans are more likely than Whites to actually be executed (Paternoster et al. 2003).

These conclusions, drawn from current sociological research, describe some consequences of particular social locations in society. Although we may take our place in society for granted, our social location has a profound effect on our chances in life. The power of sociology is that it teaches us to see how society influences our lives and the lives of others, and it helps us explain the consequences of different social arrangements.

*Sociology is the study of human behavior, including the significance of diversity.*

Sociology also has the power to help us understand the influence of major changes on people. Currently, rapidly developing technologies, increasing globalization, a more diverse population in the United States, and changes in women's roles are affecting everyone in society, although in different ways. How are these changes affecting your life? Perhaps you rely on a cell phone to keep in touch with friends, or maybe your community is witnessing an increase in immigrants from other places, or maybe you see women and men trying hard to balance the needs of both work and family life. All of these are issues that guide sociological questions. Sociology explains some of the causes and consequences of these changes.

Although society is always changing, it is also remarkably stable. People generally follow established patterns of human behavior, and you can generally anticipate how people will behave in certain situations. You can even anticipate how different social conditions will affect different groups of people in society. This is what sociologists find so interesting: *Society is marked by both change and stability.* Societies continually evolve, creating the need for people to adapt to change while still following generally established patterns of behavior.

## What Is Sociology?

**Sociology** is the study of human behavior in society. Sociologists are interested in the study of people and have learned a fundamental lesson: *All human*

*behavior occurs in a societal context*. That context—the institutions and culture that surround us—shapes what people do and think. In this book, we will examine the dimensions of society and analyze the elements of social context that influence human behavior.

Sociology is a scientific way of thinking about society and its influence on human groups. Observation, reasoning, and logical analysis are the tools of the sociologist, coupled with knowledge of the large body of theoretical and analytical work done by previous sociologists and others. Sociology is inspired by the fascination people have for the thoughts and actions of other people, but it goes far beyond casual observations. It attempts to build on observations that are objective and accurate to create analyses that are reliable and that can be validated by others.

Every day, the media in their various forms (television, film, video, digital, and print) bombard us with social commentary. Whether it is Oprah Winfrey or Ellen DeGeneres, media commentators provide endless opinion about the various and sometimes bizarre forms of behavior in our society. Sociology is different. Sociologists may appear in the media, and they often study the same subjects that the media examine, such as domestic violence or crime, but sociologists use specific research techniques and well-tested theories to explain social issues. Indeed, sociology can provide the tools for testing whether the things we hear about society are actually true. Much of what we hear in the media and elsewhere about society, although delivered with perfect earnestness, is misstated and sometimes completely wrong, as you will see in some of the "Debunking Society's Myths" examples featured throughout this book.

**Question:**

What do the following people have in common?

Michelle Obama

Robin Williams (actor, comedian)

Ronald Reagan

Rev. Martin Luther King, Jr.

Debra Winger (actress)

Regis Philbin (TV personality)

Rev. Jesse Jackson

Dr. Ruth Westheimer (the "sex doctor")

Saul Bellow (novelist; Nobel Prize recipient)

Joe Theismann (former football player)

Congresswoman Maxine Waters (from California)

Senator Barbara Mikulski (from Maryland)

**Answer:**

They were all sociology majors!

*Source:* Compiled by Peter Dreier, Occidental College. Full list available on the home page of the American Sociological Association (**www.asanet.org/page.ww?section=Students&name= Famous+Sociology+Majors**).

The subject matter of sociology is everywhere. This is why people sometimes wrongly believe that sociology just explains the obvious. But sociologists bring a unique perspective to understanding social behavior and social change. Even though sociologists often do research on familiar topics, such as youth cultures or relations between women and men—they do so using particular research tools and specific frames of analysis (known as sociological theory). Psychologists, anthropologists, political scientists, economists, social workers, and others also study social behavior, though each has a different perspective or "angle" on people in society. Together, these fields of study (also called disciplines) make up what are called the social sciences.

# The Sociological Perspective

Think back to the opening of this chapter where you were asked to imagine yourself growing up under completely different circumstances. Our goal in that passage was to make you feel the stirring of the *sociological perspective*—the ability to see the societal patterns that influence individual and group life. The beginnings of the sociological perspective can be as simple as the pleasures of watching people or wondering how society influences people's lives. Indeed, many students begin their study of sociology because they are "interested in people." Sociologists convert this curiosity into the systematic study of how society influences different people's experiences within it.

**C. Wright Mills** (1916–1962) was one of the first to write about the sociological perspective in his classic book, *The Sociological Imagination* (1959). He wrote that the task of sociology was to understand the relationship between individuals and the society in which they live. He defined the **sociological imagination** as the ability to see the societal patterns that influence the individual as well as groups of individuals. Sociology should be used, Mills argued, to reveal how the context of society shapes our lives. He thought that to understand the experience of a given person or group of people, one had to have knowledge of the social and historical context in which people lived.

Think, for example, about the time and effort that many people put into their appearance. You might ordinarily think of this merely as personal grooming or an individual attempt to "look good," but there are significant social origins of this behavior. When you stand in front of the mirror, you are probably not thinking about how society is present in your reflection. But as you look in the mirror, you are seeing how others see you and are very likely adjusting your appearance with that in mind, even if not consciously. Therefore, this seemingly individual behavior is actually a very social act. If you are trying to achieve a particular look, you are likely doing so because of social forces that establish particular ideals, which are produced by industries that profit enormously from the products and services that people buy, even when they do so believing this is an individual choice.

Some industries suggest that you should be thinner or curvier, your pants should be baggy or straight, your breasts should be minimized or maximized—either way you need more products. Maybe you should have a complete makeover! Many people go to great lengths to try to achieve a constantly changing beauty ideal, one that is probably not even attainable (such as flawless skin, hair never out of place, perfectly proportioned body parts). Sometimes trying to meet these ideals can even be hazardous to your physical and mental health.

The point is that the alleged standards of beauty are produced by social factors that extend far beyond an individual's concerns with personal appearance. Beauty ideals, like other socially established beliefs and practices, are produced in particular social and historical contexts. People may come up with all kinds of personal strategies for achieving these ideals: they may buy more products, try to lose more weight, get a Botox treatment, or even become extremely depressed and anxious if they think their efforts are failing. These personal behaviors may seem to be only individual issues, but they have basic social causes. That is, the origins of these behaviors exist beyond personal lives. The sociological imagination permits us to see that something as seemingly personal as how you look arises from a social context, not just individual behavior.

Sociologists are certainly concerned about individuals, but they are attuned to the social and historical context that shapes the experiences of individuals and groups. A distinction made by the sociological imagination is that between *troubles* and *issues*. **Troubles** are privately felt problems that spring from events or feelings in a person's life. **Issues** affect large numbers of people and have their origins in the institutional arrangements and history of a society (Mills 1959). This distinction is the crux of the difference between individual experience and **social structure,** defined as the organized pattern of social relationships and social institutions that together constitute society. Issues shape the context within which troubles arise. Sociologists employ the sociological perspective to understand how issues are shaped by social structures.

*Personal troubles are felt by individuals who are experiencing problems; social issues arise when large numbers of people experience problems that are rooted in the social structure of society.*

## SEE *FOR YOURSELF*
### *TROUBLES AND ISSUES*

Personal troubles are everywhere around us: alcohol abuse or worries about money or even being upset about how you look. At the individual level, these things can be deeply troubling, and people sometimes need personal help to deal with them. But most personal troubles, as C. Wright Mills would say, also have their origins in societal arrangements. Take the example of alcohol abuse or money problems—or, perhaps, another personal trouble with which you are familiar.

What are some of the things about society—not just individuals—that might influence this personal trouble? Make a list of things in society that might affect this personal trouble. How does this help you understand the distinction that Mills makes between *personal troubles* and *social issues*. Then explain what Mills means by saying that personal biographies are linked to the structure of society.

Mills used the example of unemployment to explain the meaning of troubles versus issues. When a person becomes unemployed, he or she has a personal trouble. In addition to financial problems, the person may feel a loss of identity, may become depressed, may lose touch with former work associates, or may have to uproot a family and move. The problem of unemployment, however, is deeper than the experience of one person. Unemployment is rooted in the structure of society; this is what interests sociologists. What societal forces cause unemployment? Who is most likely to become unemployed at different times? How does unemployment affect an entire community (for instance, when a large plant shuts down) or an entire nation (such as during the economic downturn of recent years)? Sociologists know that unemployment causes personal troubles, but understanding unemployment is more than understanding one person's experience. It requires understanding the social structural conditions that influence people's lives.

The specific task of sociology, according to Mills, is to comprehend the whole of human society—its personal and public dimensions, historical and contemporary—and its influence on the lives of human beings. Mills had an important point: People often feel that things are beyond their control, meaning that they are being shaped by social forces larger than their own individual life. Social forces influence our lives in profound ways, even though we may not always know how. Consider this. Most likely you remember what you were doing on September 11, 2001, when you first heard that terrorists had flown planes into the World Trade Center in New York City. Obviously, this affected people's personal lives, but its impact and its causes go beyond the personal troubles it produced. The sociological perspective explains many dimensions of this event and its aftermath, including, as one example, the significance of cultural symbols that have emerged in the aftermath of 9/11. Think of the T-shirts that many people now wear honoring New York's firefighters. Of course, the social forces that influence people's lives are not always that drastic and include the ordinary events of everyday life.

Sociology is an **empirical** discipline. This means that sociological conclusions are based on careful and systematic observations, as we will see in Chapter 3 on sociological research methods. In this way, sociology is very different from ordinary common sense. For empirical observations to be useful to other observers, they must be gathered and recorded rigorously. Sociologists are also obliged to reexamine their assumptions and conclusions constantly. Although the specific methods that sociologists use to examine different problems vary, as we will see, the empirical basis of sociology is what distinguishes it from mere opinion or other forms of social commentary.

## Discovering Unsettling Facts

In studying sociology, it is crucial to examine the most controversial topics and to do so with an open mind, even when you see the most disquieting facts. The facts we learn through sociological research can be "inconvenient" because the data can challenge familiar ways of thinking. Consider the following:

- Despite the widespread idea promoted in the media that well-educated women are opting out of professional careers to stay home and raise children, the proportion of college-educated White women who stay home with children has actually declined; those who do opt out do so more typically because of their frustrations with workplaces (Stone 2007).

- Same-sex couples are more likely to be interracial than are heterosexual couples (Rosenfeld and Kim 2005).
- The number of women prisoners has increased at almost twice the rate of increase for men; two-thirds of women and half of men in prison are parents (Sabol and Couture 2008; Glaze and Maruschak 2008).

These facts provide unsettling evidence of persistent problems in the United States, *problems that are embedded in society, not just in individual behavior.* Sociologists try to reveal the social factors that shape society and determine the chances of success for different groups. Some never get the chance to go to college; others are unlikely to ever go to jail. These divisions persist because of people's placement within society.

Sociologists study not just the disquieting side of society. Sociologists may study questions that affect everyday life, such as how young boys and men are affected by changing gender roles (Kimmel 2008), how children of immigrants fare (Park 2005), or how racism has changed in recent years (Zuberi 2001; Bonilla-Silva 2001). There are also many intriguing studies of unusual groups, such as cyberspace users (Kendall 2002), strip club dancers (Barton 2006), or heavily tattooed people, known as collectors (Irwin 2001). The subject matter of sociology is vast. Some research illuminates odd corners of society; other studies address urgent problems of society that may affect the lives of millions.

## Debunking in Sociology

The power of sociological thinking is that it helps us see everyday life in new ways. Sociologists question actions and ideas that are usually taken for granted. Peter Berger (1963) calls this process debunking. **Debunking** refers to looking behind the facades of

*Cultural practices that seem bizarre to outsiders may be taken for granted or defined as appropriate by insiders.*

everyday life—what Berger called the "unmasking tendency" of sociology (1963: 38). In other words, sociologists look at the behind-the-scenes patterns and processes that shape the behavior they observe in the social world.

Take schooling, for example: We can see how the sociological perspective debunks common assumptions about education. Most people think that education is primarily a way to learn and get ahead. Although this is true, a sociological perspective on education reveals something more. Sociologists have concluded that more than learning takes place in schools; other social processes are at work. Social cliques are formed where some students are "insiders" and others are excluded "outsiders." Young schoolchildren acquire not just formal knowledge but also the expectations of society and people's place within it. Race and class conflicts are often played out in schools (Lewis 2003). Relative to boys, girls are often shortchanged by the school system—receiving less attention and encouragement, less interaction with teachers, less instruction in the sciences, and many other deficits disproportionately forced upon them (American Association of University Women 1998; Sadker and Sadker 1994). Poor children seldom have the same resources in schools as middle-class or elite children, and they are often assumed to be incapable of doing schoolwork and are treated accordingly. The somber reality is that schools may actually stifle the opportunities of some children rather than launch all children toward success.

Debunking is sometimes easier to do when looking at a culture or society different from one's own. Consider how behaviors that are unquestioned in one society may seem positively bizarre to an outsider. For a thousand years in China, it was usual for the elite classes to bind the feet of young girls to keep the feet from growing bigger—a practice allegedly derived from a mistress of the emperor. Bound feet were a sign of delicacy and vulnerability. A woman with large feet (defined as more than 4 inches long !) was thought to bring shame to her husband's household. The practice was supported by the belief that men were highly aroused by small feet, even though men never actually saw the naked foot. If they had, they might have been repulsed, because a woman's actual foot was U-shaped and often rotten and covered with dead skin (Blake 1994). Outside the social, cultural, and historical context in which it was practiced, foot binding seems bizarre, even dangerous. Feminists have pointed out that Chinese women were crippled by this practice, making them unable to move about freely and more dependent on men (Chang 1991).

> ## doing sociological research

## Debunking the Myths of Black Teenage Motherhood

**Research Question:** Sociologist Elaine Bell Kaplan knew that there was a stereotypical view of Black teen mothers, that they had grown up in fatherless households where their mothers had no moral values and no control over their children. The myth of Black teenage motherhood also depicts teen mothers as unable to control their sexuality, as having children to collect welfare checks, and as having families who condone their behavior. Is this true?

**Research Method:** Kaplan did extensive research in two communities in the San Francisco Bay Area—East Oakland and Richmond—both communities with a large African American population and typical of many inner-city, poor neighborhoods. Once thriving Black communities, East Oakland and Richmond are now characterized by high rates of unemployment, poverty, inadequate schools, crime, drug-related violence, and high numbers of single-parent households. Having grown up herself in Harlem, Kaplan knew that communities like those she studied have not always had these problems, nor have they condoned teen pregnancy. She spent several months in these communities, working as a volunteer in a community teen center that provided educational programs, day care, and counseling to teen parents, and "hanging out" with a core group of teen mothers. She did extensive interviews with thirty-two teen mothers, supplementing them when she could with interviews with their mothers and, sometimes, the fathers of their children.

**Research Results:** Kaplan found that teen mothers adopt strategies for survival that help them cope with their environment, even though these same strategies do not help them overcome the problems they face. Unlike what the popular stereotype suggests, she did not find that the Black community condones teen pregnancy; quite the contrary, the teens felt embarrassed and stigmatized by being pregnant and experienced tension and conflict with their mothers, who saw their pregnancy as disrupting the hopes they had for their daughters' success. When the women

This is an example of outsiders debunking a practice that was taken for granted by those within the culture. Debunking can also call into question practices in one's own culture that may normally go unexamined. Strange as the practice of Chinese foot binding may seem to you, how might someone from another culture view wearing shoes that make it difficult to walk? Or piercing one's tongue or eyebrow? These practices of contemporary U.S. culture are taken for granted by many, just as was Chinese foot binding. Until these cultural processes are debunked, seen as if for the first time, they might seem normal.

## Debunking Society's Myths

**Myth:** Violence is at an all-time high.

**Sociological research:** Although rates of violence are high in the United States, at least twice before (in 1930 and 1980) the murder rate was at a comparable level. It is also true, however, that rates of violence in the United States are higher than in any other industrialized nation (Levine and Rosich 1996; Best 1999).

## Establishing Critical Distance

Debunking requires critical distance—that is, being able to detach from the situation at hand and view things with a critical mind. The role of critical distance in developing a sociological imagination is well explained by the early sociologist **Georg Simmel** (1858–1918). Simmel was especially interested in the role of *strangers* in social groups. Strangers have a position both inside and outside social groups; they are part of a group without necessarily sharing the group's assumptions and points of view. Because of this, the stranger can sometimes see the social structure of a group more readily than people who are thoroughly imbued with the group's worldview. Simmel suggests that the sociological perspective requires a combination of nearness and distance. One must have enough critical distance to avoid being taken in by the group's definition of the situation, but be near enough to understand the group's experience.

Sociologists are not typically strangers to the society they study. You can acquire critical distance through a willingness to question the forces that shape social behavior. Often, sociologists become interested in things because of their own experiences. The biographies of sociologists are rich with examples of how their personal lives informed the questions

had to go on welfare, they also felt embarrassed, often developing strategies to hide the fact that they were dependent on welfare to make ends meet. These conclusions run directly counter to the public image that such women do not value success and live in a culture that promotes welfare dependency.

*Conclusions and Implications:* Instead of simply stereotyping these teens as young and tough, Kaplan sees them as struggling to develop their own gender and sexual identity. Like other teens, they are highly vulnerable, searching for love and aspiring to create a meaningful and positive identity for themselves. But failed by the educational system and locked out of the job market, the young women's struggle to develop an identity is compounded by the disruptive social and economic conditions in which they live.

Kaplan's research is a fine example of how sociologists debunk some of the commonly shared myths that surround contemporary issues. Carefully placing her analysis in the context of the social structural changes

that affect these young women's lives, Kaplan provides an excellent example of how sociological research can shed new light on some of our most pressing social problems.

### Questions to Consider

1. Suppose that Kaplan had studied middle-class teen mothers. What similarities and differences would you predict in the experiences of middle-class and poor teen mothers? Does race matter? In what ways does your answer *debunk* myths about teen pregnancy?

2. Make a list of the challenges you would face were you to be a teen parent. Having done so, indicate those that would be considered personal troubles and those that are social issues. How are the two related?

*Source:* Kaplan, Elaine Bell. 1996. *Not Our Kind of Girl: Unraveling the Myths of Black Teenage Motherhood.* Berkeley, CA: University of California Press.

*understanding*
*diversity*

### Become a Sociologist

Individual biographies often have a great influence on the subjects sociologists choose to study. The authors of this book are no exception. Margaret Andersen, a White woman, now studies the sociology of race and women's studies. Howard Taylor, an African American man, studies race, social psychology, and especially race and intelligence testing. Here, each of them writes about the influence of their early experiences on becoming a sociologist.

Courtesy of Richard Rosenfeld

*Margaret Andersen*
As I was growing up in the 1950s and 1960s, my family moved from California to Georgia, then to Massachusetts, and then back to Georgia. Moving as we did from urban to small-town environments and in and out of regions of the country that were very different in their racial character, I probably could not help becoming fascinated by the sociology of race. Oakland, California, where I was born, was highly diverse; my neighborhood was mostly White and Asian American. When I moved to a small town in Georgia in the 1950s, I was ten years old, but I was shocked

by the racial norms I encountered. I had always loved riding in the back of the bus—our major mode of transportation in Oakland—and could not understand why this was no longer allowed. Labeled by my peers as an outsider because I was not southern, I painfully learned what it meant to feel excluded just because of "where you are from."

When I moved again to suburban Boston in the 1960s, I was defined by Bostonians as a southerner and ridiculed. Nicknamed "Dixie," I was teased for how I talked. Unlike in the South, where despite strict racial segregation Black people were part of White people's daily lives, Black people in Boston were even less visible. In my high school of 2500 or so students, Black students were rare. To me, the school seemed not much different from the strictly segregated schools I had attended in Georgia. My family soon returned to Georgia, where I was an outsider again; when I later returned to Massachusetts for graduate school in the 1970s, I worried about how a southerner would be accepted in this "Yankee" environment. Because I had acquired a southern accent, I think many of my teachers stereotyped me and thought I was not as smart as the students from other places.

These early lessons, which I may have been unaware of at the time, must have kindled my interest in the sociology of race relations. As I explored sociology, I wondered how the concepts and theories of race relations applied to women's lives. So much of

they asked. Among sociologists are former ministers and nuns now studying the sociology of religion, women who have encountered sexism who now study the significance of gender in society, rock-and-roll fans studying music in popular culture, and sons and daughters of immigrants now analyzing race and ethnic relations (see the box "Understanding Diversity: Becoming a Sociologist").

## The Significance of Diversity

The analysis of diversity is one central theme of sociology. Differences among groups, especially differences in the treatment of groups, are significant in any

society, but they are particularly compelling in a society as diverse as that in the United States.

### Defining Diversity

Today, the United States includes people from all nations and races. In 1900, one in eight Americans was not White; today, racial and ethnic minority groups, including African Americans, Latinos, American Indians, Native Hawaiians, Asian Americans, and people of more than one race represent 35 percent of Americans, and that proportion is growing (U.S. Census Bureau 2009; see Figure 1.1; see also Table 1.1). These broad categories themselves are internally diverse, including, for example, those with long-term roots in the United States, as well as Cuban Americans, Salvadorans, Cape Verdeans, Filipinos, and many others.

what I had experienced growing up as a woman in this society was completely unexamined in what I studied in school. As the women's movement developed in the 1970s, I found sociology to be the framework that helped me understand the significance of gender and race in people's lives. To this day, I write and teach about race and gender, using sociology to help students understand their significance in society.

Courtesy of Howard Taylor

### Howard Taylor

I grew up in Cleveland, Ohio, the son of African American professional parents. My mother, Murtis Taylor, was a social worker and the founder and then president of a social work agency called the Murtis H. Taylor Multi-Service Center in Cleveland, Ohio. She is well known for her contributions to the city of Cleveland and was an early "superwoman," working days and nights, cooking, caring for her two sons, and being active in many professional and civic activities. I think this gave me an early appreciation for the roles of women and the place of gender in society, although I surely would not have articulated it as such at the time. My father was a businessman in a then all-Black life insurance company. He was also a "closet scientist," always doing experiments and talking about scientific studies. He encouraged my brother and me to engage in science, so we were always experimenting with scientific studies in the basement of our house. In the summers, I worked for my mother in the social service agency where she worked, as a camp counselor, and in other jobs. Early on, I contemplated becoming a social worker, but I was also excited by science. As a young child, I acquired my father's love of science and my mother's interest in society. In college, the one field that would gratify both sides of me, science and social work, was sociology. I wanted to study human interaction, but I also wanted to be a scientist, so the appeal of sociology was clear.

At the same time, growing up African American meant that I faced the consequences of race every day. It was always there, and like other young African American children, I spent much of my childhood confronting racism and prejudice. When I discovered sociology, in addition to bridging the scientific and humanistic parts of my interests, I found a field that provided a framework for studying race and ethnic relations. The merging of two ways of thinking, coupled with the analysis of race that sociology has long provided, made sociology fascinating to me.

Today, my research on race, class, gender, and intelligence testing seems rooted in these early experiences. I do quantitative research in sociology and see sociology as a science that reveals the workings of race, class, and gender in society.

Perhaps the most basic lesson of sociology is that people are shaped by the social context around them. In the United States, with so much cultural diversity, people will share some experiences, but not all. Experiences not held in common can include some of the most important influences on social development, such as language, religion, and the traditions of family and community. Understanding diversity means recognizing this diversity and making it central to sociological analyses.

In this book, we use the term *diversity* to refer to the variety of group experiences that result from the social structure of society. **Diversity** is a broad concept that includes studying group differences in society's opportunities, the shaping of social institutions by different social factors, the formation of group and individual identity, and the process of social change. Diversity includes the study of different cultural orientations, although diversity is not exclusively about culture.

Understanding diversity is crucial to understanding society because fundamental patterns of social change and social structure are increasingly patterned by diverse group experiences. There are numerous sources of diversity, including race, class, gender, and others as well. Age, nationality, sexual orientation, and region of residence, among other factors, also differentiate the experience of diverse groups in the United States. And as the world is increasingly interconnected through global communication and a global economy, the study of diversity also encompasses a global perspective—that is, an understanding of the international connections existing across national borders and the impact of such connections on life throughout the world.

*Understanding diversity is important in a society comprising so many different groups, each with unique, but interconnected, experiences.*

## thinkingsociologically

**What are some of the sources of *diversity* on your campus? What questions might a sociologist pose about the significance of diversity in this environment?**

## Society in Global Perspective

No society can be understood apart from the global context that now influences the development of all societies. The social and economic system of any one society is increasingly intertwined with those of other nations. Coupled with the increasing ease of travel and telecom-

munication, this means that a global perspective is necessary to understand change both in the United States and in other parts of the world.

To understand globalization, you must look beyond the boundaries of your own society to see how patterns in any given society are increasingly being shaped by the connections between societies. Comparing and contrasting societies across different cultures is valuable. It helps you see patterns in your own society that you might otherwise take for granted, and it enriches your appreciation of the diverse patterns of culture that mark human society and human history. A global perspective, however, goes beyond just comparing different cultures; it also helps you see how events in one society or community may be linked to events occurring on the other side of the globe.

For instance, return to the example of unemployment that C. Wright Mills used to distinguish troubles and issues. One man may lose his job in Peoria, Illinois, and a woman in Los Angeles may employ a Latina domestic worker to take care of her child while

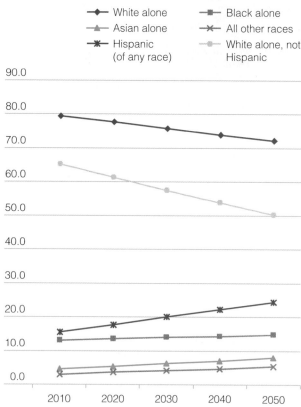

**FIGURE 1.1** *Percent of U.S. Population by Race and Ethnicity*

*It is a social fact that by 2050 White, non-Hispanics will make up half the U.S. population. Using the information above, what will the population percentages for different racial–ethnic groups be when you are thirty? Fifty? How do you think this will affect your life? How does this illustrate how social facts influence the lives of individual people and diverse groups in society?*

*Source:* U.S. Census Bureau. 2004. "U.S. Interim Projections by Age, Sex, Race, and Hispanic Origin." **www.census.gov/pc/www/usinterimproj/**

*"Actually, Lou, I think it was more than just my being in the right place at the right time. I think it was my being the right race, the right religion, the right sex, the right socioeconomic group, having the right accent, the right clothes, going to the right schools . . ."*

| table1.1 Minorities in the U.S. Population | | | | | |
|---|---|---|---|---|---|
| Percent of Total Population | 2010 | 2020 | 2030 | 2040 | 2050 |
| White alone[1] | 79.3% | 77.6% | 75.8% | 73.9% | 72.1% |
| Black alone | 13.1 | 13.5 | 13.9 | 14.3 | 14.6 |
| Asian alone | 4.6 | 5.4 | 6.2 | 7.1 | 8.0 |
| All other races[2] | 3.0 | 3.5 | 4.1 | 4.7 | 5.3 |
| Hispanic (may be of any race)[3] | 15.5 | 17.5 | 20.1 | 22.3 | 24.4 |
| White alone, not Hispanic | 65.1 | 61.3 | 57.5 | 53.7 | 50.1 |

*Note: The U.S. census counts race and Hispanic ethnicity separately. Thus Hispanics may fall into any of the race categories. As a result, only the percentages for White alone, Black alone, Asian alone, and all other races add to 100%.*

[1]The U.S. Census Bureau uses this designation to refer to those who indicated on the census form that they were only of one race.
[2]Includes American Indian and Alaska Natives alone, Native Hawaiian and other Pacific Islanders alone, and those of two or more races.
[3]See Note above.

*Source:* U.S. Census Bureau. 2004. "U.S. Interim Projections by Age, Sex, Race, and Hispanic Origin." **www.census.gov/pc/www/usinterimproj/**

she pursues a career. On the one hand, these are individual experiences for all three people, but they are linked in a pattern of globalization that shapes the lives of all three. The Latina domestic may have a family whom she has left in a different nation so that she can afford to support them. The corporation for which the Los Angeles woman works may have invested in a new plant overseas that employs cheap labor, resulting in the unemployment of the man in Peoria. The man in Peoria may have seen immigrant workers moving into his community, and one of his children may have made a friend at school who speaks a language other than English.

Such processes are increasingly shaping many of the subjects examined in this book—work, family, education, politics, just to name a few. Without a global perspective, you would not be able to fully understand the experience of any one of the people just mentioned much less how society is being shaped by these processes of change and global context. Throughout this book, we will use a global

*Globalization brings diverse cultures together, but it is also a process by which Western markets have penetrated much of the world.*

AP Images/Eugene Hoshiko

perspective to understand some of the developments shaping contemporary life in the United States.

# The Development of Sociological Theory

Like the subjects it studies, sociology is itself a social product. Sociology first emerged in western Europe during the eighteenth and nineteenth centuries. In this period, the political and economic systems of Europe were rapidly changing. Monarchy, the rule of society by kings and queens, was disappearing in western Europe. These changes generated new ways of thinking. Religion as the system of authority and law was giving way to scientific authority. At the same time, capitalism grew. Contact between different societies increased, and worldwide economic markets developed. The traditional ways of the past were giving way to a new social order. The time was ripe for a new understanding.

## The Influence of the Enlightenment

The **Enlightenment** in eighteenth- and nineteenth-century Europe had an enormous influence on the development of modern sociology. Also known as the Age of Reason, the Enlightenment was characterized by faith in the ability of human reason to solve society's problems. Intellectuals believed that there were natural laws and processes in society to be discovered and used for the general good. Modern science was gradually supplanting traditional and religious explanations for natural phenomena with theories confirmed by experiments.

The earliest sociologists promoted a vision of sociology grounded in careful observation. **Auguste Comte** (1798–1857), a French philosopher who coined the term

As one of the earliest observers of American culture, Harriet Martineau used the powers of social observation to record and analyze the social structure of American society. Long ignored for her contributions to sociology, she is now seen as one of the founders of early sociological thought.

© Culver Pictures

*sociology,* believed that just as science had discovered the laws of nature, sociology could discover the laws of human social behavior and thus help solve society's problems. This approach is called **positivism,** a system of thought, still prominent today, in which scientific observation and description is considered the highest form of knowledge, as opposed to, say, religious dogma or poetic inspiration. The modern scientific method, which guides sociological research, grew out of positivism.

**Alexis de Tocqueville** (1805–1859), a French citizen, traveled to the United States as an observer beginning in 1831. Tocqueville thought that democratic values and the belief in human equality positively influenced American social institutions and transformed personal relationships. Less admiringly, he felt that in the United States the tyranny of kings had been replaced by the "tyranny of the majority." He was referring to the ability of a majority to impose its will on everyone else in a democracy. Tocqueville also felt that despite the emphasis on individualism in American culture, Americans had little independence of mind, making them self-centered and anxious about their social class position (Collins and Makowsky 1972).

Another early sociologist is **Harriet Martineau** (1802–1876). Like Tocqueville, Martineau, a British citizen, embarked on a long tour of the United States in 1834. She was fascinated by the newly emerging culture in America. Her book *Society in America* (1837) is an analysis of the social customs that she observed. This important work was overlooked for many years, probably because the author was a woman. It is now recognized as a classic. Martineau also wrote the first sociological methods book, *How to Observe Morals and Manners* (1838), in which she discussed how to observe behavior when one is a participant in the situation being studied.

## Classical Sociological Theory

Of all the contributors to the development of sociology, the giants of the European tradition were Emile Durkheim, Karl Marx, and Max Weber. They are classical thinkers because the analyses they offered more than 150 years ago continue to enlighten our understanding of society, not just in sociology but in other fields as well (such as political science and history).

**Emile Durkheim.** During the early academic career of the Frenchman **Emile Durkheim** (1858–1917), France was in the throes of great political and religious upheaval. Anti-Semitism (hatred of Jews) was being expressed, along with ill feeling among other religions, as well. Durkheim, himself Jewish, was fascinated by how the public degradation of Jews by non-Jews seemed to calm and unify a large segment of the divided French public. Durkheim later wrote that public rituals have a special purpose in society, creating social solidarity, referring to the bonds that link the members of a group. Some of Durkheim's most significant works explore the question of what forces hold society together and make it stable.

According to Durkheim, people in society are glued together by belief systems (Durkheim 1947/1912). The rituals of religion and other institutions symbolize and reinforce the sense of belonging. Public ceremonies create a bond between people in a social unit. Durkheim thought that by publicly punishing people, such rituals sustain moral cohesion in society. Durkheim's views on this are further examined in Chapter 7, which discusses deviant behavior.

Durkheim also viewed society as an entity larger than the sum of its parts. He described this as society *sui generis* (which translates as "thing in itself"), meaning that society is a subject to be studied separately from the sum of the individuals who compose it. Society is external to individuals, yet its existence is internalized in people's minds—that is, people come to believe what society expects them to believe. Durkheim conceived of society as an integrated whole—each part contributing to the overall stability of the system. His work is the basis for *functionalism,* an important theoretical perspective that we will return to later in this chapter.

One contribution from Durkheim was his conceptualization of the *social.* Durkheim created the term **social facts** to indicate those social patterns that are *external* to individuals. Things such as customs and social values exist outside individuals, whereas psychological drives and motivation exist inside people. Social facts, therefore, are not to be explained by

*Emile Durkheim established the significance of society as something larger than the sum of its parts. Social facts stem from society and have profound influence on the lives of people within society.*

© Bettmann/Corbis

## what would they say now?

## Classical Theorists Reflect on the War in Iraq

Suppose some of the classical theorists of sociology were suddenly brought back to life. What might they say about the contemporary war in Iraq?

**Emile Durkheim:** War, though involving human tragedy, also promotes a sense of group and national identity. Patriotic symbols, such as bumper stickers saying Support Our Troops, promote a collective sense of national identity.

**Max Weber:** War involves multiple dimensions of society. Wars are often fought for political reasons, but also involve economic forces (such as the need for oil in Western societies). Cultural forces, such as the conflict between western values and Islamic value systems, are also a major social force.

**Karl Marx:** Wars must be understood as the result of the dynamics of capitalism. Not only do they involve economic greed (such as the profits garnered from the pursuit of oil), but private, economic interests are paramount in understanding war, such as the businesses that profit from them.

**Jane Addams:** As a sociologist who won the Nobel Peace Prize, I must advocate for peaceful resolutions to world conflicts. Were the more pacifist values of women to guide international affairs, we would not experience as many conflicts as we do in a more masculine-based political culture.

**W.E.B. Du Bois:** War has a disproportionate impact on people of color. Africans Americans (and, he would now note, Latinos) are most likely to be recruited to fight wars, and thus there is a disproportionate impact of tragedy on these as well as low-income, working-class families.

**Ida B. Wells:** War has a profound influence on the lives of women and people of color, often resulting in rape and other atrocious human rights violations by occupying armies.

biology or psychology but are the proper subject of sociology; they are its reason for being.

A striking illustration of this principle was Durkheim's study of suicide (Durkheim 1951/1897). He analyzed rates of suicide in a society, as opposed to looking at individual (psychological) causes of suicide. He showed that suicide rates varied according to how clear the norms and customs of the society were, whether the norms and customs were consistent with each other and noncontradictory. Anomie (normlessness) existed where norms were either grossly unclear or contradictory; the suicide rates were higher in such societies or such parts of a society. It is important to note that this condition was external, thus outside of each individual taken singly. In this sense such a condition is truly societal.

Durkheim held that social facts, though they exist outside individuals, nonetheless pose constraints on individual behavior. Durkheim's major contribution was the discovery of the social basis of human behavior. He proposed that society could be known through the discovery and analysis of social facts. This is the central task of sociology (Bellah 1973; Coser 1977; Durkheim 1950/1938).

**Karl Marx.** It is hard to imagine another scholar who has had as much influence on intellectual history as **Karl Marx** (1818–1883). Along with his collaborator, Friedrich Engels, Marx not only changed intellectual history but world history too.

Marx's work was devoted to explaining how capitalism shaped society. He argued that capitalism is an economic system based on the pursuit of profit and the sanctity of private property. Marx used a class analysis to explain capitalism, describing capitalism as a system of relationships among different classes, including capitalists (also known as the bourgeois class), the proletariat (or working class), the petty bourgeoisie (small business owners and managers), and the *lumpenproletariat* (those "discarded" by the capitalist system, such as the homeless). In Marx's view, profit, the goal of capitalist endeavors, is produced through the exploitation of the working class. Workers sell their labor in exchange for wages, and capitalists make certain that wages are worth less than the goods the workers produce. The difference in value is the profit of the capitalist. In the Marxist view, the capitalist class system is inherently unfair because the entire system rests on workers getting less than they give.

Marx thought that the economic organization of society was the most important influence on what humans think and how they behave. He found that the beliefs of the common people tended to support the interests of the capitalist system, not the interests of the workers themselves. Why? Because the capitalist class controls not only the production of goods but also the production of ideas. It owns the publishing companies, endows the universities where knowledge is produced, and controls information industries.

*Karl Marx analyzed capitalism as an economic system with enormous implications for how society is organized, in particular how inequality between groups stems from the economic organization of society.*

© Bettmann/Corbis

Marx considered all of society to be shaped by economic forces. Laws, family structures, schools, and other institutions all develop, according to Marx, to suit economic needs under capitalism. Like other early sociologists, Marx took social structure as his subject rather than the actions of individuals. It was the *system* of capitalism that dictated people's behavior. Marx saw social change as arising from tensions inherent in a capitalist system—the conflict between the capitalist and working classes. Marx's ideas are often misperceived by U.S. students because communist revolutionaries throughout the world have claimed Marx as their guiding spirit. It would be naive to reject his ideas solely on political grounds. Much that Marx predicted has not occurred—for instance, he claimed that the "laws" of history made a worldwide revolution of workers inevitable, and this has not happened. Still, he left us an important body of sociological thought springing from his insight that society is systematic and structural and that class is a fundamental dimension of society that shapes social behavior.

**Max Weber.** Max Weber (1864–1920; pronounced "Vay-ber") was greatly influenced by Marx's work and built upon it. But, whereas Marx saw economics as the basic organizing element of society, Weber theorized that society had three basic dimensions: political, economic, and cultural. According to Weber, a complete sociological analysis must recognize the interplay between economic, political, and cultural

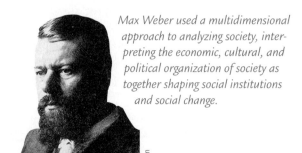

*Max Weber used a multidimensional approach to analyzing society, interpreting the economic, cultural, and political organization of society as together shaping social institutions and social change.*

© AKG/London

institutions (Parsons 1947). Weber is credited with developing a *multidimensional* analysis of society that goes beyond Marx's more one-dimensional focus on economics.

Weber also theorized extensively about the relationship of sociology to social and political values. He did not believe there could be a value-free sociology, because values would always influence what sociologists considered worthy of study. Weber thought sociologists should acknowledge the influence of values so that ingrained beliefs might not interfere with objectivity. Weber professed that the task of sociologists is to teach students the uncomfortable truth about the world. Faculty should not use their positions to promote their political opinions, he felt; rather, they have a responsibility to examine all opinions, including unpopular ones, and use the tools of rigorous sociological inquiry to understand why people believe and behave as they do.

An important concept in Weber's sociology is *verstehen* (pronounced "ver-shtay-en"). **Verstehen,** a German word, refers to understanding social behavior from the point of view of those engaged in it. Weber believed that to understand social behavior, one had to understand the meaning that a behavior had for people. He did not believe sociologists had to be born into a group to understand it (in other words, he didn't believe "it takes one to know one"), but he did think sociologists had to develop some subjective understanding of how other people experience their world. One major contribution from Weber was the definition of *social action* as a behavior to which people give meaning (Gerth and Mills 1946; Parsons 1951b; Weber 1962), such as placing a bumper sticker on your car that states pride in U.S. military troops.

## Sociology in America

American sociology was built on the earlier work of Europeans, but unique features of U.S. culture contribute to its distinctive flavor. Less theoretical and more practical than their European counterparts, early American sociologists believed that if they exposed the causes of social problems, they could alleviate some of the consequences, which are measured in human suffering.

Early sociologists in both Europe and the United States conceived of society as an organism, a system of interrelated functions and parts that work together to create the whole. This perspective is called the **organic metaphor.** Sociologists saw society as constantly evolving, like an organism. The question many early sociologists asked was to what extent humans could shape the evolution of society.

Many were influenced in this question by the work of British scholar **Charles Darwin** (1809–1882), who revolutionized biology when he identified the process termed *evolution,* a process by which new species are created through the survival of the fittest. **Social Darwinism** was the application of Darwinian thought to society. According to the social Darwinists, the "survival of the fittest" is the driving force of social evolution as well. They conceived of society as an organism that evolved from simple to complex in a process of adaptation to the environment. They theorized that society was best left alone to follow its natural evolutionary course. Because social Darwinists believed that evolution always took a course toward perfection, they advocated a *laissez-faire* (that is, "hands-off") approach to social change. Social Darwinism was thus a conservative mode of thought; it assumed that the current arrangements in society were natural and inevitable (Hofstadter 1944).

Most other early sociologists in the United States took a more reform-based approach. Nowhere was the emphasis on application more evident than at the University of Chicago, where a style of sociological thinking known as the Chicago School developed. The Chicago School is characterized by thinkers who were interested in how society shaped the mind and identity of people. We study some of these thinkers, such as George Herbert Mead and Charles Horton Cooley, in Chapter 4. They thought of society as a human laboratory where they could observe and understand human behavior in order to be better able to address human needs, and they used the city in which they lived as a living laboratory.

**Robert Park** (1864–1944), from the University of Chicago, was a key founder of sociology. Originally a journalist who worked in several midwestern cities, Park was interested in urban problems and how different racial groups interacted with each other. He was also fascinated by the sociological design of cities, noting that cities were typically sets of concentric circles. At the time, the very rich and the very poor lived in the middle, ringed by slums and low-income neighborhoods (Collins and Makowsky 1972; Coser 1977; Park and Burgess 1921). Park would still be intrigued by how boundaries are defined and maintained in urban neighborhoods. You might notice this yourself. A single street crossing might delineate a Vietnamese neighborhood from an Italian one, an affluent White neighborhood from a barrio. The social

*Jane Addams, the only sociologist to win the Nobel Peace Prize, used her sociological skills to try to improve people's lives. The settlement house movement provided social services to groups in need, while also providing a social laboratory in which to observe the sociological dimensions of problems such as poverty.*

© Bettmann/Corbis

*Ida B. Wells-Barnett is now well-known for her brave campaign against the lynching of African American people. Less known are her early contributions to sociological thought.*

Schomburg, New York Public Library

structure of cities continues to be a subject of sociological research.

Many early sociologists of the Chicago School were women whose work is only now being rediscovered. **Jane Addams** (1860–1935) was one of the most renowned sociologists of her day. She was a leader in the settlement house movement, which provided community services and did systematic research designed to improve the lives of slum dwellers, immigrants, and other dispossessed groups. Addams, the only practicing sociologist ever to win a Nobel Peace Prize (in 1931), never had a regular teaching job. Instead, she used her skills as a research sociologist to develop community projects that assisted people in need (Deegan 1988).

Another early sociologist, widely noted for her work in the anti-lynching movement, was **Ida B. Wells-Barnett** (1862–1931). Born a slave, Ida B. Wells learned to read and write at Rust College, a school established for freed slaves, later receiving her teaching credentials at Fisk University. She wrote numerous essays on the status of African Americans in the United States and was an active crusader against lynching and for women's rights, including the right to vote. Because she was so violently attacked—in writing and in actual threats—because of her passionate work, she often had to write under an assumed name. Until recently, her contributions to the field of sociology have been largely unexamined. Interestingly, her grandson, Troy Duster (b. 1936), now a faculty member at New York University and the University of California, Berkeley, became the president of the American Sociological Association

*An insightful observer of race and culture, W.E.B. Du Bois was one of the first sociologists to use community studies as the basis for sociological work. His work, long excluded from the "great works" of sociological theory, is now seen as a brilliant and lasting analysis of the significance of race in the United States.*

Courtesy of University of Massachusetts at Amherst

in 2004 (Lengermann and Niebrugge-Brantley 1998; Henry 2008; Giddings 2008).

**W.E.B. Du Bois** (1868–1963; pronounced "due boys") was one of the most important early sociological thinkers in America. Du Bois was a prominent Black scholar, a cofounder in 1909 of the NAACP (National Association for the Advancement of Colored People), a prolific writer, and one of America's best minds. He received the first Ph.D. ever awarded to a Black person in any field (from Harvard University), and he studied for a time in Germany, hearing several lectures by Max Weber. Du Bois was deeply troubled by the racial divisiveness in society, writing in a classic essay published in 1901 that "the problem of the twentieth century is the problem of the color line" (Du Bois 1901: 354). Like many of his women colleagues, he envisioned a community-based, activist profession committed to social justice (Deegan 1988); he was a friend and collaborator with Jane Addams. He believed in the importance of a scientific approach to sociological questions, but also thought that convictions always directed one's studies.

# Theoretical Frameworks in Sociology

The founders of sociology have established theoretical traditions that ask basic questions about society and inform sociological research. The idea of theory may seem dry to you because it connotes something that is only hypothetical and divorced from "real life"; however, sociological theory is one of the tools that sociologists use to interpret real life. Sociologists use theory to organize their observations and apply them to the broad questions sociologists ask, such as: How are individuals related to society? How is social order maintained? Why is there inequality in society? How does social change occur?

Different theoretical frameworks within sociology make different assumptions and provide different insights about the nature of society. In the realm of *macrosociology* are theories that strive to understand society as a whole. Durkheim, Marx, and Weber were macrosociological theorists. Theoretical frameworks that center on face-to-face social interaction are known as *microsociology*. Some of the work derived from the Chicago School—research that studies individuals and group processes in society—is microsociological. Although sociologists draw from diverse theoretical perspectives to understand society, three broad traditions form the major theoretical perspectives that they use: functionalism, conflict theory, and symbolic interaction.

## Functionalism

Functionalism has its origins in the work of Durkheim, who you will recall was especially interested in how social order is possible or how society remains

# Key Sociological Concepts

As you build your sociological perspective, you must learn certain key concepts in order to begin understanding how sociologists view human behavior. *Social structure*, *social institutions*, *social change*, and *social interaction* are not the only sociological concepts, but they are fundamental to grasping the sociological perspective.

**Social Structure.** Earlier, we defined social structure as the organized pattern of social relationships and social institutions that together constitute society. Social structure is not a "thing," but refers to the fact that social forces not always visible to the human eye guide and shape human behavior. Acknowledging that social structure exists does not mean that humans have no choice in how they behave, only that those choices are largely conditioned by one's location in society.

**Social Institutions.** In this book, you will also learn about the significance of **social institutions,** defined as established and organized systems of social behavior with a particular and recognized purpose. The family, religion, marriage, government,

and the economy are examples of major social institutions. Social institutions confront individuals at birth and they transcend individual experience, but they still influence individual behavior.

**Social Change.** As you can tell, sociologists are also interested in the process of **social change,** the alteration of society over time. As much as sociologists see society as producing certain outcomes, they do not see society as fixed, nor do they see humans as passive recipients of social expectations. Sociologists view society as stable but constantly changing.

**Social Interaction.** Sociologists see **social interaction** as behavior between two or more people that is given meaning. Through social interaction, people react and change, depending on the actions and reactions of others. Since society changes as new forms of human behavior emerge, change is always in the works. As you read this book, you will see that these key concepts—social structure, social institutions, social change, and social interaction—are central to the sociological imagination.

---

relatively stable. **Functionalism** interprets each part of society in terms of how it contributes to the stability of the whole. As Durkheim suggested, functionalism conceptualizes society as more than the sum of its component parts. Each part is "functional" for society—that is, contributes to the stability of the whole. The different parts are primarily the institutions of society, each of which is organized to fill different needs and each of which has particular consequences for the form and shape of society. The parts each then depend on one another.

The family as an institution, for example, serves multiple functions. At its most basic level, the family has a reproductive role. Within the family, infants receive protection and sustenance. As they grow older, they are exposed to the patterns and expectations of their culture. Across generations, the family supplies a broad unit of support and enriches individual experience with a sense of continuity with the past and future. All these aspects of family can be assessed by how they contribute to the stability and prosperity of society. The same is true for other institutions.

The functionalist framework emphasizes the consensus and order that exist in society, focusing on social stability and shared public values. From a functionalist perspective, disorganization in the system, such as deviant behavior and so forth, leads to change because societal components must adjust to achieve stability. This is a key part of functionalist theory—that when

one part of society is not working (or is *dysfunctional*, as they would say), it affects all the other parts and creates social problems. Change may be for better or worse; changes for the worse stem from instability in the social system, such as a breakdown in shared values or a social institution no longer meeting people's needs (Collins 1994; Eitzen and Baca Zinn 2006; Turner 1974).

## thinking sociologically

What are the *manifest functions* of grades in college? What are the *latent functions*?

Functionalism was a dominant theoretical perspective in sociology for many years, and one of its major theorists was **Talcott Parsons** (1902–1979). In Parsons's view, all parts of a social system are interrelated, with different parts of society having different basic functions. Functionalism was further developed by **Robert Merton** (1910–2003). Merton saw that social practices often have consequences for society that are not immediately apparent, not necessarily the same as the stated purpose. He suggested that human behavior has both manifest and latent functions. *Manifest functions* are the stated and intended goals of social behavior.

Critics of functionalism argue that its emphasis on social stability is inherently conservative and that it understates the roles of power and conflict in society. Critics also disagree with the explanation of inequality offered by functionalism—that it persists because social inequality creates a system for the fair and equitable distribution of societal resources. Functionalists would, for example, argue that it is fair and equitable that the higher social classes earn more money since they, so it is argued, are more important (functional) to society. Critics of functionalism argue that functionalism is too accepting of the status quo. Functionalists would counter this argument by saying that, regardless of the injustices that inequality produces, inequality serves a purpose in society: It provides an incentive system for people to work and promotes solidarity among groups linked by common social standing.

## Conflict Theory

**Conflict theory** emphasizes the role of coercion and power, a person's or group's ability to exercise influence and control over others, in producing social order. Whereas functionalism emphasizes cohesion within society, conflict theory emphasizes strife and friction. Derived from the work of Karl Marx, conflict theory pictures society as fragmented into groups that compete for social and economic resources. Social order is maintained not by consensus but by domination, with power in the hands of those with the greatest political, economic, and social resources. When consensus exists, according to conflict theorists, it is attributable to people being united around common interests, often in opposition to other groups (Dahrendorf 1959; Mills 1956).

According to conflict theory, inequality exists because those in control of a disproportionate share of society's resources actively defend their advantages. The masses are not bound to society by their shared values but by coercion at the hands of the powerful. In conflict theory, the emphasis is on social control, not consensus and conformity. Groups and individuals advance their own interests, struggling over control of societal resources. Those with the most resources exercise power over others; inequality and power struggles are the result. Conflict theory gives great attention to class, race, and gender in society because these are seen as the grounds of the most pertinent and enduring struggles in society.

Whereas functionalists find some benefit to society in the unequal distribution of resources, conflict theorists see inequality as inherently unfair, persisting only because groups who are economically advantaged use their social position to their own betterment. Their dominance even extends to the point of shaping the beliefs of other members of the society by controlling public information and having major influence over institutions such as education and religion. From the conflict perspective, power struggles between conflicting groups are the source of social change. Typically, those with the greatest power are able to maintain their advantage at the expense of other groups.

Conflict theory has been criticized for neglecting the importance of shared values and public consensus in society while overemphasizing inequality. Like functionalist theory, conflict theory finds the origins of social behavior in the structure of society, but it differs from functionalism in emphasizing the importance of power.

## Symbolic Interaction

The third major framework of sociological theory is **symbolic interaction theory.** Instead of thinking of society in terms of abstract institutions, symbolic interactionists consider immediate social interaction to be the place where "society" exists. Because of the human capacity for reflection, people give meaning to their behavior, and this is how they interpret the different behaviors, events, or things that are significant for sociological study.

Because of this, symbolic interaction, as its name implies, relies extensively on the symbolic meaning that people develop and rely upon in the process of social interaction. Symbolic interaction theory emphasizes face-to-face interaction and thus is a form of microsociology, whereas functionalism and conflict theory are more macrosociological.

Derived from the work of the Chicago School, symbolic interaction theory analyzes society by addressing the subjective meanings that people impose on objects, events, and behaviors. Subjective meanings are given primacy because, according to symbolic interactionists and according to Thomas's dictum mentioned earlier, people behave based on what they *believe,* not just on what is objectively true. Thus, society is considered to be socially constructed through human interpretation (Berger and Luckmann 1967; Blumer 1969; Shibutani 1961). Symbolic interactionists see meaning as constantly modified through social interaction. People interpret one another's behavior, and it is these interpretations that form the social bond. These interpretations are called the "definition of the situation." For example, why would young people smoke cigarettes even though all objective medical evidence points to the danger of doing so? The answer is in the definition of the situation that people create. Studies find that teenagers are well informed about the risks of tobacco, but they also think that "smoking is cool," that they themselves will be safe from harm, and that smoking projects an image—a positive identity for boys as a "tough guy" and for girls as fun-loving, mature, and glamorous. Smoking is also defined by young women as keeping you thin—an ideal constructed through dominant images of beauty. In other words, the symbolic meaning of smoking overrides the actual facts regarding smoking and risk (Stjerna et al. 2004).

## *thinkingsociologically*

Think about the example given about smoking, and using a *symbolic interaction* framework, how would you explain other risky behaviors, such as steroid use among athletes or eating disorders among young women?

Symbolic interaction interprets social order as constantly negotiated and created through the interpretations people give to their behavior. In observing society, symbolic interactionists see not simply facts but "social constructions," the meanings attached to things, whether those are concrete symbols (like a certain way of dress or a tattoo) or nonverbal behaviors. To a symbolic interactionist, society is highly subjective—existing in the minds of people, even though its effects are very real.

Functionalism, conflict theory, and symbolic interaction theory are by no means the only theoretical frameworks in sociology. For some time, however, they have provided the most prominent general explanations of society. Each has a unique view of the social realm. None is a perfect explanation of society, yet each has something to contribute. Functionalism gives special weight to the order and cohesion that usually characterizes society. Conflict theory emphasizes the inequalities and power imbalances in society. Symbolic interaction emphasizes the meanings that humans give to their behavior. Together, these frameworks provide a rich, comprehensive perspective on society, individuals within society, and social change (see Table 1.2).

## Diverse Theoretical Perspectives

Sociological theory is in transition. In addition to the three frameworks just discussed, other theories are also used within sociology. Contemporary sociological theory has been greatly influenced by the development of **feminist theory,** which analyzes the status of women and men in society with the purpose of using that knowledge to better women's lives. Feminist theory has created vital new knowledge about women and transformed what is understood about men. Feminist scholarship in sociology, by focusing on the experiences of women, provides new ways of seeing the world and contributes to a more complete view of society. We examine feminist theory throughout this book in the context of particular topics, such as family (see Chapter 13) and politics (see Chapter 15).

Many contemporary theorists are increasingly influenced by postmodernism—a strand of thinking now influencing many disciplines. **Postmodernism** is based on the idea that society is not an objective thing. Instead, it is found in the words and images that people use to represent behavior and ideas. Postmodernists think that images and texts reveal the underlying ways that people think and act. Postmodernist studies typically involve detailed analyses of images, words, film, music, and other forms of popular culture. In a civilization such as that in the United States, saturated by the imagery of the mass media, postmodernist analysis illuminates much about society. Postmodernist thinkers see contemporary life as involving multiple experiences and interpretations, but they avoid categorizing human experience into broad and abstract concepts such as institutions or society (Rosenau 1992).

Whatever the theoretical framework used, theory is evaluated in terms of its ability to explain observed social facts. The sociological imagination is not a single-minded way of looking at the world. It is the ability to observe social behavior and interpret that behavior in light of societal influences.

## table1.2    *Three Sociological Frameworks*

| Basic Questions | Functionalism | Conflict Theory | Symbolic Interaction |
|---|---|---|---|
| *What is the relationship of individuals to society?* | Individuals occupy fixed social roles. | Individuals are subordinated to society. | Individuals and society are interdependent. |
| *Why is there inequality?* | Inequality is inevitable and functional for society. | Inequality results from a struggle over scarce resources. | Inequality is demonstrated through the importance of symbols. |
| *How is social order possible?* | Social order stems from consensus on public values. | Social order is maintained through power and coercion. | Social order is sustained through social interaction and adherence to social norms. |
| *What is the source of social change?* | Society seeks equilibrium when there is social disorganization. | Change comes through the mobilization of people struggling for resources. | Change evolves from an ever-evolving set of social relationships and the creation of new meaning systems. |
| **Major Criticisms** | This is a conservative view of society that underplays power differences among and between groups. | The theory understates the degree of cohesion and stability in society. | There is little analysis of inequality, and it overstates the subjective basis of society. |

# Careers in Sociology

**Now that you understand a bit more what sociology is about, you may ask, What can I do with a degree in sociology?** This is a question we often hear from students. There is no single job called "sociologist" like there is "engineer" or "nurse" or "teacher," but sociology prepares you well for many different kinds of jobs, whether with a bachelor's degree or a postgraduate education. The skills you acquire from your sociological education are useful for jobs in business, health care, criminal justice, government agencies, various nonprofit organizations, and other job venues.

For example, the research skills one gains through sociology can be important in analyzing business data or organizing information for a food bank or homeless shelter. Students in sociology also gain experience working with and understanding those with different cultural and social backgrounds; this is an important and valued skill that employers seek. Also, the ability to dissect the different causes of a social problem can be an asset for jobs in various social service organizations.

Some sociologists have worked in their communities to deliver more effective social services. Some are employed in business organizations and social services where they use their sociological training to address issues such as poverty, crime and delinquency, population studies, substance abuse, violence against women, family social services, immigration policy, and any number of other important issues. Sociologists also work in the offices of U.S. representatives and senators, doing background research on the various issues addressed in the political process.

These are just a few examples of how sociology can prepare you for various careers. A good way to learn more about how sociology prepares you for work is to consider doing an internship while you are still in college.

For more information about careers in sociology, see the booklet, *Careers in Sociology,* available through the American Sociological Association. You can find it online at either **www.asanet.org/student/career/homepage .html** or **http://sociology.wadsworth.com**

**Critical Thinking Exercise**

1.  Read a national newspaper over a period of one week and identify any experts who use a sociological perspective in their commentary. What does this suggest to you as a possible career in sociology? What are some of the different subjects about which sociologists provide expert information?

2.  Identify some of the students from your college who have finished degrees in sociology. What different ways have they used their sociological knowledge?

# Chapter Summary

- **What is sociology?**

  Sociology is the study of human behavior in society. The *sociological imagination* is the ability to see societal patterns that influence individuals. Sociology is an *empirical* discipline, relying on careful observations as the basis for its knowledge.

- **What is debunking?**

  *Debunking* in sociology refers to the ability to look behind things taken for granted, looking instead to the origins of social behavior.

- *Why is diversity central to the study of sociology?*

  One of the central insights of sociology is its analysis of social diversity and inequality. Understanding *diversity* is critical to sociology because it is necessary to analyze *social institutions* and because diversity shapes most of our social and cultural institutions.

- *When and how did sociology emerge as a field of study?*

  Sociology emerged in western Europe during the *Enlightenment* and was influenced by the values of critical reason, humanitarianism, and positivism. *Auguste Comte,* one of the earliest sociologists, emphasized sociology as a positivist discipline. *Alexis de Tocqueville* and *Harriet Martineau* developed early and insightful analyses of American culture.

- *What are some of the basic insights of classical sociological theory?*

  *Emile Durkheim* is credited with conceptualizing society as a social system and with identifying *social facts* as patterns of behavior that are external to the individual. *Karl Marx* showed how capitalism shaped the development of society. *Max Weber* sought to explain society through cultural, political, and economic factors.

- *What are the major theoretical frameworks in sociology?*

  *Functionalism* emphasizes the stability and integration in society. *Conflict theory* sees society as organized around the unequal distribution of resources and held together through power and coercion. *Symbolic interaction* theory emphasizes the role of individuals in giving meaning to social behavior, thereby creating society. *Feminist theory* is the analysis of women and men in society and is intended to improve women's lives. *Postmodernism* argues that constructed cultural products are the realities of our postindustrial society.

# Key Terms

conflict theory   20
debunking   07
diversity   11
empirical   07
Enlightenment   13
feminist theory   21
functionalism   19
issues   06

organic metaphor   17
positivism   14
postmodernism   21
social change   19
social Darwinism   17
social facts   14
social institution   19
social interaction   19

social structure   06
sociological imagination   05
sociology   04
symbolic interaction theory   20
troubles   06
verstehen   17

# Online Resources

## *Sociology: The Essentials* Companion Website

**www.cengage.com/sociology/andersen**
Visit your book companion website where you will find more resources to help you study and write your research papers. Resources include web links, learning objectives, Internet exercises, quizzing, and flash cards.

 **is an easy-to-use online resource that helps you study in less time to get the grade you want NOW.**

**www.cengage.com/login**
Need help studying? This site is your one-stop study shop. Take a Pre-Test and CengageNOW will generate a Personalized Study Plan based on your test results. The Study Plan will identify the topics you need to review and direct you to online resources to help you master those topics. You can then take a Post-Test to determine the concepts you have mastered and what you still need to work on.

2

# Culture and the Media

*In one contemporary* society known for its technological sophistication, people—especially the young—walk around with plugs in their ears. The plugs are connected to small wires that are themselves coated with a plastic film. These little plastic-covered wires are then connected to small devices made of metal, plastic, silicon, and other modern components, although most of the people who use them have no idea how they are made. When turned on, the device puts music into people's ears or, in some cases, shows pictures and movies on a screen about the size of a postage stamp. Some of the people who use these devices wouldn't even consider walking around without them; it is as if the device shields them from some of the other elements of their culture.

The same people who carry these devices around have other habits that, when seen from the perspective of someone unfamiliar with this culture, might seem peculiar and certainly highly ritualized. Apparently, when the young people in this society go away to school, most take a large number of various technological devices along with them. According to recent reports from these young people, many of them sleep with one of these devices turned on all night. It looks like a large box—some square, others relatively flat—and it projects pictures and sound when the user clicks buttons on another small device that, though detached from the bigger box, can be placed anywhere in the room. If you click the buttons on this portable device, the pictures and sound coming forth from the larger box will change possibly hundreds of times, revealing a huge

*continued*

*David Young-Wolff/Photographer's Choice/Getty Images*

two Chapter

*The Tchikrin people of the Brazilian rain forest paint elaborate and beautiful designs on their bodies that define the relationship of people to social groups. Are there ways that cultural practices in the United States also define social relationships?*

© Joan Bamburger/Anthro Photos

assortment of images that seem to influence what people in this culture believe and, in many cases, how they behave. They say that in over 40 percent of the households in this culture, this device is turned on 24 hours a day (Gitlin 2002)!

The young people in this culture seem to get up every day and immediately go to another device where they do things with unusual names, such as to "IM" their friends (who, by the way, may be nowhere near them), pushing buttons with their thumbs on a small device with a tiny screen. Indeed, it seems that everything these young people do involves looking at some kind of screen, enough so that one of the authors of this book has labeled their generation "Screenagers."

Not everyone in this culture has access to all of these devices, although many want them. Indeed, having more of the devices seems to be a mark of one's social status, that is, how you are regarded in this culture. But very few people know where the devices are made, what they are made of, or how they work, even though the young often ridicule older people for not understanding how the devices work or why they are so important to them.[1]

From outside the culture, these practices seem strange, yet few within the culture think the behaviors associated with these devices are anything but perfectly ordinary. Most of the time, people do not spend much time thinking about the meaning of the behaviors associated with these devices unless, for some reason, they suddenly do not work.

You have surely guessed that the practices described here are taken from U.S. culture: iPods, MP3 players, text messaging, television/video viewing. These are such daily practices that they practically define modern American culture. Unless they are somehow interrupted, most people do not think much about their influence on society, on people's relationships, or on people's definitions of themselves.

When viewed from the outside, cultural habits that seem perfectly normal often seem strange. Take an example from a different culture. The Tchikrin people—a remote culture of the central Brazilian rain forest—paint their bodies in elaborate designs. Painted bodies communicate to others the relationship of the person to his or her body, to society, and to the spiritual world. The designs and colors symbolize the balance the Tchikrin people think exists between biological powers and the integration of people into the social group. The Tchikrin also associate hair with sexual powers; lovers get a special thrill from using their teeth to pluck an eyebrow or eyelash from their partner's face (Turner 1969). To the Tchikrin people, these practices are no more unusual or exotic than the daily habits we practice in the United States.

To study culture, to analyze it and measure its significance in society, we must separate ourselves from judgments such as "strange" or "normal." We must see a culture as it is seen by insiders, but we cannot be completely taken in by that view. We should know the culture as insiders and understand it as outsiders.

---

[1]This introduction is inspired by a classic article on the "Naci-rema"—*American*, backwards—by Horace Miner (1956). But it is also written based on the essays students at the University of Delaware have written based on the media blackout exercise described on page 44. Students have written that, without access to their usual media devices, they felt they "had no personality!" and that the period of the blackout was "the worst forty-eight hours of my life!"

# Defining Culture

**Culture** is the complex system of meaning and behavior that defines the way of life for a given group or society. It includes beliefs, values, knowledge, art, morals, laws, customs, habits, language, and dress, among other things. Culture includes ways of thinking as well as patterns of behavior. Observing culture involves studying what people think, how they interact, and the objects they use.

In any society, culture defines what is perceived as beautiful and ugly, right and wrong, good and bad. Culture helps hold society together, giving people a sense of belonging, instructing them on how to behave, and telling them what to think in particular situations. Culture gives meaning to society.

Culture is both material and nonmaterial. **Material culture** consists of the objects created in a given society its buildings, art, tools, toys, print and broadcast media, and other tangible objects, such as those discussed in the chapter opener. In the popular mind, material artifacts constitute culture because they can be collected in museums or archives and analyzed for what they represent. These objects are significant because of the meaning they are given. A temple, for example, is not merely a building, nor is it only a place of worship. Its form and presentation signify the religious meaning system of the faithful.

**Nonmaterial culture** includes the norms, laws, customs, ideas, and beliefs of a group of people. Nonmaterial culture is less tangible than material culture, but it has a strong presence in social behavior. Examples of nonmaterial culture are numerous and found in the patterns of everyday life. In some cultures, people eat with utensils, in others, people do not. The eating utensils are part of material culture, but the belief about whether to use them is nonmaterial culture.

It is cultural patterns that make humans so interesting. Is it culture that distinguishes human beings from animals? Some animal species develop what we might call culture. Chimpanzees, for example, learn behavior through observing and imitating others, a point proved by observing the different eating practices among chimpanzees in the same species but raised in different groups (Whiten et al. 1999). Others have observed elephants picking up the dead bones of other elephants and fondling them, perhaps evidence of grieving behavior (Meredith 2003). Dolphins are known to have a complex auditory language. And most people think that their pets communicate with them. Apparently, humans are not unique in their ability to develop systems of communication. But some scientists generally conclude that animals lack the elaborate symbol-based cultures common in human societies. Perhaps, as even Charles Darwin wrote, "The difference in mind between man and the higher animals, great as it is, certainly is one of degree and not of kind" (Darwin, cited in Gould 1999).

Studying animal groups reminds us of the interplay between biology and culture. Human biology sets limits and provides certain capacities for human life

Zave Smith/Photolibrary

and the development of culture. Similarly, the environment in which humans live establishes the possibilities and limitations for human society. Nutrition, for instance, is greatly influenced by environment, thereby affecting human body height and weight. Not everyone can swim like Michael Phelps or lob a tennis ball like Venus and Serena Williams, but with training and conditioning, people can enhance their physical abilities. Biological limits exist, but cultural factors have an enormous influence on the development of human life.

## Characteristics of Culture

Across societies, there are common characteristics of culture, even when the particulars vary. These different characteristics are as follows.

1.  ***Culture is shared.*** Culture would have no significance if people did not hold it in common. Culture is collectively experienced and collectively agreed upon. The shared nature of culture is what makes human society possible. The shared basis of culture may be difficult to see in complex societies where groups have different traditions, perspectives, and ways of thinking and behaving. In the United States, for example, different racial and ethnic groups have unique histories, languages, and beliefs—that is, different cultures. Even within these groups, there are diverse cultural traditions. Latinos, for example, comprise many groups with distinct origins and cultures. Still, there are features of Latino culture, such as the Spanish language and some values and traditions, that are shared. Latinos also share a culture that is shaped

*Different culture traditions create rituals that mark the passage from one phase of life to another. Here, a young boy undertakes the Bar Mitzvah ceremony marking his passage to adulthood (upper left); a young Apache girl experiences four-day-long puberty rites following the first onset of menstruation, celebrating her newfound womanhood (top right); a Navjote ceremony, the most important event in a young child's life, noting acceptance into the Parsi community in India (bottom left); a young girl awaits her quinceañera ceremony in Chiapas, Mexico (bottom right).*

© David Reed/Corbis

© Paul Chesley/Stone/Getty Images

© Lindsay Hebberd/Corbis

© Jack Kurtz/The Image Works

by their common experiences as minorities in the United States. Similarly, African Americans have created a rich and distinct culture that is the result of their unique experience within the United States. What identifies African American culture are the practices and traditions that have evolved from both the U.S. experience and African and Caribbean traditions. Placed in another country, such as an African nation, African Americans would likely recognize elements of their culture, but they would also feel culturally distinct as Americans.

Within the United States, culture varies by age, race, region, gender, ethnicity, religion, class, and other social factors. A person growing up in the South is likely to develop different tastes, modes of speech, and cultural interests than a person raised in the West. Despite these differences, there is a common cultural basis to life in the United States. Certain symbols, language patterns, belief systems, and ways of thinking are distinctively American and form a common culture, even though great cultural diversity exists.

2. ***Culture is learned.*** Cultural beliefs and practices are usually so well learned that they seem perfectly natural, but they are learned none the less. How do people come to prefer some foods to others? How is musical taste acquired? Culture may be taught through direct instruction, such as a parent teaching a child how to use silverware or teachers instructing children in songs, myths, and other traditions in school.

Culture is also learned indirectly through observation and imitation. Think of how a person learns what it means to be a man or a woman. Although the "proper" roles for men and women may never be explicitly taught, one learns what is expected from observing others. A person becomes a member of a culture through both formal and informal transmission of culture. Until the culture is learned, the person will feel like an outsider. The process of learning culture is referred to by sociologists as socialization, discussed in Chapter 4.

3. ***Culture is taken for granted.*** Because culture is learned, members of a given society seldom question the culture of which they are a part, unless for some reason they become outsiders or establish some critical distance from the usual cultural expectations. People engage unthinkingly in hundreds of specifically cultural practices every day; culture makes these practices seem "normal." If you suddenly stopped participating in your culture and questioned each belief and every behavior, you would soon find yourself feeling detached and perhaps a little disoriented; you would also become increasingly ineffective at functioning within your group. Little wonder that tourists stand out so much in a foreign culture. They rarely have much knowledge of the culture they are visiting and, even when they are well informed, typically approach the society from their own cultural orientation.

Think, for example, of how you might feel if you were a Native American student in a predominantly White classroom. Many, though not all, Native American people are raised to be quiet and not outspoken. If students in a classroom are expected to assert themselves and state what is on their minds, a Native American student may feel awkward, as will others for whom these expectations are contrary to their cultural upbringing. If the professor is not aware of these cultural differences, he or she may penalize students who are quiet, resulting perhaps in a lower grade for the student from a different cultural background. Culture binds us together, but lack of communication across cultures can have negative consequences, as this example shows.

4. ***Culture is symbolic.*** The significance of culture lies in the meaning it holds for people. **Symbols** are things or behaviors to which people give meaning; the meaning is not inherent in a symbol but is bestowed by the meaning people give it. The U.S. flag, for example, is literally a decorated piece of cloth. Its cultural significance derives not from the cloth of which it is made but from its meaning as a symbol of freedom and democracy, as was witnessed by the widespread flying of the flags after the terrorist attacks on the United States on September 11, 2001.

That something has symbolic meaning does not make it any less important or influential than objective facts. Symbols are powerful expressions of human culture. Think of the Confederate flag. Those who object to the Confederate flag being displayed on public buildings see it as a symbol of racism and the legacy of slavery. Those who defend it see it as representing southern heritage, a symbol of group pride and regional loyalty. Similarly, the use of Native American mascots to name and represent sports teams is symbolic of the exploitation of Native Americans. Native American activists and their supporters see the use of Native American mascots as derogatory and extremely insulting, representing gross caricatures of Native American traditions. (Think of the Washington Redskins, the Cleveland Indians, or the Atlanta Braves' "tomahawk chop.") The protests that have developed over controversial symbols are indicative of the enormous influence of cultural symbols.

## Debunking Society's Myths

**Myth:** The use of Native American names for school mascots is just for fun and is no big deal.

**Sociological perspective:** Language carries with it great meaning that reflects the perceived social value of diverse groups. Research finds that exposure to the trivial or degrading use of Native American images for such things as school mascots and sports teams actually lowers Native American children's sense of self-worth (Fryberg 2003).

# > doing sociological research

## Tattoos: Status Risk or Status Symbol?

***Research Question:*** Not so long ago tattoos were considered a mark of social outcasts. They were associated with gang members, sailors, and juvenile delinquents. But now tattoos are in vogue—a symbol of who's trendy and hip. How did this happen that a once stigmatized activity associated with the working class became a statement of middle-class fashion?

***Research Method:*** This is what sociologist Katherine Irwin wanted to know when she first noticed the increase in tattooing among the middle class. Irwin first encountered the culture of tattooing when she accompanied a friend getting a tattoo in a shop she calls Blue Mosque. She started hanging out in the shop and began a four-year study using participant observation in the shop along with interviews of people getting their first tattoos. Irwin also interviewed some of the parents of tattooees and potential tattooees.

***Research Results:*** Irwin found that middle-class tattoo patrons were initially fearful that their desire for a tattoo would associate them with low-status groups, but they reconciled this by adopting attitudes that associated tattooing with middle-class values and norms. Thus, they defined tattooing as symbolic of independence, liberation, and freedom from social constraints. Many of the women defined tattooing as symbolizing toughness and strength—values they thought rejected more conventional ideals of femininity.

Some saw tattoos as a way of increasing their attachment to alternative social groups or to gain entrée into "fringe" social worlds. Although tattoos held different cultural meanings to different groups, people getting tattooed used various techniques (what Irwin calls "legitimation techniques") to counter the negative stereotypes associated with tattooing.

***Conclusions and Implications:*** Irwin concludes that people try to align their behavior with legitimate cultural values and norms even when that behavior seemingly falls outside of prevailing standards.

### Questions to Consider

1. Do you think of tattoos as fashionable or deviant? What do you think influences your judgment about this, and how might your judgment be different were you in a different culture, age group, or historical moment?

2. Are there fashion adornments that you associate with different social classes? What are they, and what kinds of judgment (positive and negative) do people make about them? Where do these judgments come from, and why are they associated with social class?

*Source:* Irwin, Katherine. 2001. "Legitimating the First Tattoo: Moral Passage through Informal Interaction." *Symbolic Interaction* 24 (March): 49–73.

*Tattooing, once considered a working class symbol, has now become a middle-class fashion statement. Some, known as collectors, use extensive tattooing as a symbol of identity.*

Symbolic attachments can guide human behavior. For example, people stand when the national anthem is sung and may feel emotional from displays of the cross or the Star of David. Under some conditions, people organize mass movements to protest what they see as the defamation of important symbols, such as the burning of a flag or the burning of a cross. The significance of the symbolic value of culture can hardly be overestimated. Learning a culture means not just engaging in particular behaviors but also learning their symbolic meanings within the culture.

5. ***Culture varies across time and place.*** Culture develops as humans adapt to the physical and social environment around them. Culture is not fixed from one place to another. In the United States, for example, there is a strong cultural belief in scientific solutions to human problems; consequently,

Mark Duncan/AP Photo

*The use of American Indian stereotypes icons for school mascots is highly offensive to many and has been shown to lower the self-esteem of Native American children exposed to these negative images. Should similar stereotypes appear on team names that negatively stereotyped your ethnic group, how would you react?*

Culture also varies over time. As people encounter new situations, the culture that emerges is a mix of the past and present. Second generation immigrants to the United States are raised in the traditions of their culture of origin, and children of immigrants typically grow up with both the traditional cultural expectations of their parents' homeland and the cultural expectations of a new society. Adapting to the new society can create conflict between generations, especially if the older generation is intent on passing along their cultural traditions. The children may be more influenced by their peers and may choose to dress, speak, and behave in ways that are characteristic of their new society but unacceptable to their parents.

To sum up, culture is concrete because we can observe the cultural objects and practices that define human experience. Culture is abstract because it is a way of thinking, feeling, believing, and behaving. Culture links the past and the present because it is the knowledge that makes us part of human groups. Culture gives shape to human experience.

# The Elements of Culture

Culture is multifaceted, consisting of both material and nonmaterial things, some parts of culture being abstract, others more concrete. The different elements of culture include language, norms, beliefs, and values (see Table 2.1).

## Language

**Language** is a set of symbols and rules that, combined in a meaningful way, provides a complex communication system. The formation of culture among humans is made possible by language. Learning the language of a culture is essential to becoming part of a society, and it is one of the first things children learn. Indeed,

many think that problems of food supply and environmental deterioration can be addressed by scientific breakthroughs, such as genetic engineering to create high-yield tomatoes or cloning cows to eliminate mad cow disease. In other cultural settings, different solutions may seem preferable. Indeed, some religions think of genetic engineering as trespassing on divine territory.

| **table2.1** | **Elements of Culture** | |
|---|---|---|
| | **Definition** | **Examples** |
| **Language** | A set of symbols and rules that, put together in a meaningful way, provides a complex communication system | English; Spanish; hieroglyphics |
| **Norms** | The specific cultural expectations for how to behave in a given situation | Behavior involving use of personal space; manners |
| **Folkways** | General standards of behavior adhered to by a group | Cultural forms of dress; food habits |
| **Mores** | Strict norms that control moral and ethical behavior | Religious doctrines; formal law |
| **Values** | Abstract standards in a society or group that define ideal principles | Liberty; freedom |
| **Beliefs** | Shared ideas about what is true held collectively by people within a given culture | Belief in a higher being |

*Living in a multicultural society often juxtaposes diverse cultures, even in public places.*

Think about the experience of becoming part of a social group. When you enter a new society or a different social group, you have to learn its language to become a member of the group. This includes any special terms of reference used by the group. Lawyers, for example, have their own vocabulary and their own way of constructing sentences called, not always kindly, "legalese." Becoming a part of any social group—a friendship circle, fraternity or sorority, or any other group—involves learning the language they use. Those who do not share the language of a group cannot participate fully in its culture.

Language is fluid and dynamic and evolves in response to social change. Think, for example, of how the introduction of computers has affected the English language. People now talk about needing "downtime" and providing "input." Only a few years ago, had you said you were going to "text message" your friends, no one would have known what you were talking about. Text messaging has also introduced its own language: BFN (bye for now), LOL (laughing out loud), and GTG (got to go)—a new language shared among those in the text-messaging culture. There are now even online dictionaries listing and defining such "words" (see Table 2.2).

**Does Language Shape Culture?** Language is clearly a big part of culture. Edward Sapir (writing in the 1920s) and his student Benjamin Whorf (writing in the 1950s) thought that language was central in determining social thought. Their theory, the **Sapir–Whorf hypothesis,** asserts that language determines other aspects of culture because language provides the categories through which social reality is defined. Sapir and Whorf thought that language determines what people think because language forces people to perceive the world in certain terms (Sapir 1921; Whorf 1956).

If the Sapir–Whorf hypothesis is correct, then speakers of different languages have different perceptions of reality. Whorf used the example of the social meaning of time to illustrate cultural differences in how language shapes perceptions of reality. He noted that the Hopi Indians conceptualize time as a slowly turning cylinder, whereas English-speaking people conceive of time as running forward in one direction at a uniform pace. Linguistic constructions of time shape how the two different cultures think

until children acquire at least a rudimentary command of language, they seem unable to acquire other social skills. Language is so important to human interaction that it is difficult to think of life without it; indeed, as one commentator on language has said, "Life is lived as a series of conversations" (Tannen 1990: 13).

| table2.2 | The Language of the Internet |
| --- | --- |

Language often changes as society and culture change. One example is messaging, some samples of which are provided below.

| AAS | alive and smiling | MTFBWU | May the force be with you. |
| --- | --- | --- | --- |
| B/F | boyfriend | OP | on phone |
| BM&Y | between me and you | POS | parent over shoulder |
| BTDT | been there, done that | SLAP | sounds like a plan |
| CRBT | crying really big tears | SNAG | sensitive New Age guy |
| FYEO | for your eyes only | SUP | what's up |
| GFI | go for it | TMB | text me back |
| HAGO | have a good one | UCMU | you crack me up |
| KIR | keeping it real | WDYK | what do you know |
| KOTL | kiss on the lips | WOMBAT | waste of money, brains, and time |
| KWIM | know what I mean? | WWJD | What would Jesus do? |
| LD | later dude | YRYOCC | You're running your own cuckoo clock. |
| | | ZZ | bored |

*Source:* "Text Messaging Abbreviations" 2007. **www.webopedea.com; www.netlingo.com**

about time and therefore how they think about reality. In Hopi culture, events are located not in specific moments of time but in "categories of being," as if everything is in a state of becoming, not fixed in a particular time and place (Carroll 1956). In contrast, the English language locates things in a definite time and place, placing great importance on verb tense, with things located precisely in the past, present, or future.

Recent critics do not think that language determines culture to the extent that Sapir and Whorf proposed. Language does not single-handedly dictate the perception of reality—but, no doubt, language has a strong influence on culture. Most scholars now see two-way causality between language and culture. Asking whether language determines culture or vice versa is like asking which came first, the chicken or the egg. Language and culture are inextricable, each shaping the other.

Consider again the example of time. Contemporary Americans think of the week as divided into two parts: *weekdays* and *weekends*, words that reflect how we think about time. When does a week end? Having language that defines the weekend encourages us to think about the weekend in specific ways. It is a time for rest, play, chores, and family. In this sense, language shapes how we think about the passage of time—we look forward to the weekend, we prepare ourselves for the workweek—but the language itself (the very concept of the weekend) stems from patterns in the culture—specifically, the work patterns of advanced capitalism. The capitalist work ethic makes it morally offensive to merely "pass the time"; instead, time is to be managed. Concepts of time in preindustrial, agricultural societies follow a different pattern. In agricultural societies, time and calendars are based on agricultural and seasonal patterns; the year proceeds according to this rhythm, not the arbitrary units of time of weeks and months. This shows how language and culture shape each other.

**Social Inequality in Language.** The language of any culture reflects the nature of that society. Thus, in a society where there is group inequality, language is likely to communicate assumptions and stereotypes about different social groups. What people say—including what people are called—reinforces patterns of inequality in society (Moore 1992). We see this in what different groups in the United States are called (see also the box on page 34, "Understanding Diversity: The Social Meaning of Language"). What someone is called can be significant because it imposes an identity on that person. This is why the names for various racial and ethnic groups have been so heavily debated. Thus, for years, many Native Americans objected to being called "Indian," because it was a term created about them by White conquerors. To emphasize their native roots in the Americas,

the term *Native American* was adopted. Now, though many prefer to be called by their actual origin, *Native American* and *American Indian* are also used interchangeably. Likewise, Asian Americans tend to be offended by being called "Oriental," an expression that stemmed from Western (that is, European and American) views of Asian nations.

Language reflects the social value placed on different groups, and it reflects power relationships, depending on who gets to name whom. Derogatory terms such as *redneck, white trash*, or *trailer park trash* stigmatize people based on regional identity and social class. This is also why it is so demeaning when derogatory terms are used to describe racial–ethnic groups. For example, throughout the period of Jim Crow segregation in the American South, Black men, regardless of their age, were routinely called "boy" by Whites. Calling a grown man a "boy" is an insult; it diminishes his status by defining him as childlike. Referring to a woman as a "girl" has the same effect. Why are young women, even well into their twenties, routinely referred to as "girls"? Just as does calling a man "boy," this diminishes women's status.

## Debunking Society's Myths

**Myth:** Bilingual education discourages immigrant children from learning English and thus blocks their assimilation into American culture and reduces their chances for a good education.

**Sociological perspective:** Studies of students who are fluent bilinguals show that they outperform both English only students and students with limited bilingualism. Moreover, preserving the use of native languages can better meet the need for skilled bilingual workers in the labor market (Portes 2002).

Note, however, that terms such as *girl* and *boy* are pejorative only in the context of dominant and subordinate group relationships. African American women, as an example, often refer to each other as "girl" in informal conversation. The term *girl* used between those of similar status is not perceived as derogatory, but when used by someone in a position of dominance, such as when a male boss calls his secretary a "girl," it is demeaning. Likewise, terms such as *dyke, fag,* and *queer* are terms lesbians and gay men sometimes use without offense in referring to each other, even though the same terms are offensive to lesbians and gays when used about them by others. By reclaiming these terms as positive within their own culture, lesbians and gays build cohesiveness and solidarity (Due 1995). These examples show that power relationships between groups supply the social context for the connotations of language.

In sum, language can reproduce the inequalities that exist in society. At the same time, changing the

## The Social Meaning of Language

Language reflects the assumptions of a culture. This can be seen and exemplified in several ways:

- Language affects people's perception of reality.
  *Example:* Researchers have found that using male pronouns, even when intended to be gender-neutral, produces male-centered imagery and ideas. Studies also find that when college students look at job descriptions written using masculine pronouns, they assume that women are not qualified for the job (Gastil 1990; Hamilton 1988; Switzer 1990).

- Language reflects the social and political status of different groups in society.
  *Example:* A term such as *woman doctor* suggests that men are the standard and women the exception. The term *working woman* (used to refer to women who are employed) also suggests that women who do not work for wages are not working. Ask yourself what the term *working man* connotes and how this differs from working woman.

- Groups may advocate changing language referring to them as a way of asserting a positive group identity.
  *Example:* Some advocates for the disabled challenge the term *handicapped*, arguing that it stigmatizes people who may have many abilities, even if they are physically distinctive. Also, though someone may have one disabling condition, she or he may otherwise be perfectly able.

- The implications of language emerge from specific historical and cultural contexts.
  *Example:* The naming of so-called races comes from the social and historical processes that define different groups as inferior or superior. Racial labels do not come just from physical, national, or cultural differences. The term *Caucasian,* for example, was coined in the seventeenth century when racist thinkers developed alleged scientific classification systems to rank different societal groups. Alfred Blumenbach used the label Caucasian to refer to people from the Caucasus of Russia whom he thought were more beautiful and intelligent than any group in the world.

- Language can distort actual group experience.
  *Example:* Terms used to describe different racial and ethnic groups homogenize experiences that may be unique. Thus, the terms *Hispanic* and *Latino* lump together Mexican Americans, island Puerto Ricans, U.S.-born Puerto Ricans, as well as people from Honduras, Panama, El Salvador, and other Central and South American countries. *Hispanic* and *Latino* point to the shared experience of those from

language that people use can, to some extent, alter social stereotypes and thereby change the way people think.

## Norms

Social norms are another component of culture. **Norms** are the specific cultural expectations for how to behave in a given situation. Society without norms would be chaos; with norms in place, people know how to act, and social interactions are consistent, predictable, and learnable. There are norms governing every situation. Sometimes they are implicit; that is, they need not be spelled out for people to understand them. For example, when joining a line, there is an implicit norm that you should stand behind the last person, not barge in front of those ahead of you. Implicit norms may not be formal rules, but violation of these norms may nonetheless produce a harsh response. Implicit norms may be learned through specific instruction or by observation of the culture; they are part of a society's or group's customs. Norms are explicit when the rules governing behavior are written down or formally communicated. Typically, specific sanctions are imposed for violating explicit norms.

*thinkingsociologically*

Identify a *norm* that you commonly observe. Construct an experiment in which you, perhaps with the assistance of others, violate the norm. Record how others react and note the sanctions engaged through this norm violation exercise. *Note:* Be careful not to do anything that puts you in danger or causes serious problems for others.

In the early years of sociology, **William Graham Sumner** (1906) identified two types of norms: folkways and mores. **Folkways** are the general standards of

Latin cultures, but like the terms *Native American* and *American Indian*, they obscure the experiences of unique groups, such as the Sioux, Nanticoke, Cherokee, Yavapai, or Navajo.

- Language shapes people's perceptions of groups and events in society.
  *Example:* Following Hurricane Katrina in New Orleans, African American people taking food from abandoned stores were described as "looting" and White people as "finding food." Also, Native American victories during the nineteenth century are typically described as "massacres"; comparable victories by White settlers are described in heroic terms (Moore 1992).
- Terms used to define different groups change over time and can originate in movements to assert a positive identity.
  *Example:* In the 1960s, *Black American* replaced the term *Negro* because the civil rights and Black Power movements inspired Black pride and the importance of self-naming (Smith 1992). Earlier, *Negro* and *colored* were used to define African Americans. Currently, it is popular to refer to all so-called racial groups as "people of color." This phrase was derived from the phrase "women of color," created by feminist African American, Latina,[1] Asian American, and Native American women to emphasize their common experiences. Some people find the use of "color" in this label offensive since it harkens back to the phrase "colored people," a phrase generally seen as paternalistic and racist because it was a label used by dominant groups to refer to African Americans prior to the civil rights movement. The phrase "women of color" now has a more positive meaning than the earlier term *colored women* because it is meant to recognize common experiences, not just label people because of their presumed skin color.

In this book, we have tried to be sensitive to the language used to describe different groups. We recognize that the language we use is fraught with cultural and political assumptions and that what seems acceptable now may be offensive later. Perhaps the best way to solve this problem is for different groups to learn as much as they can about one another, becoming more aware of the meaning and nuances of naming and language and more conscious of the racial assumptions embedded in the language. Greater sensitivity to the language used in describing different group experiences is an important step in promoting better intergroup relationships.

[1] *Latina* is the feminine form in Spanish and refers to women; *Latino*, to men.

behavior adhered to by a group. You might think of folkways as the ordinary customs of different group cultures. Men wearing pants and not skirts is an example of a cultural folkway. Other examples are the ways that people greet each other, decorate their homes, and prepare their food. Folkways may be loosely defined and loosely adhered to, but they nevertheless structure group customs and implicitly govern much social behavior.

**Mores** (pronounced "more-ays") are strict norms that control moral and ethical behavior. Mores provide strict codes of behavior, such as the injunctions, legal and religious, against killing others and committing adultery. Mores are often upheld through rules or **laws,** the written set of guidelines that define right and wrong in society. Basically, laws are formalized mores. Violating mores can bring serious repercussions. When any social norm is violated, the violator is typically punished. **Social sanctions** are mechanisms of social control that enforce norms. The seriousness of a social sanction depends on how strictly the norm is held. The strictest norms in society are **taboos**—those behaviors that bring the most serious sanctions. Dressing in an unusual way that violates the folkways of dress may bring ridicule but is usually not seriously punished. In some cultures, the rules of dress are strictly interpreted, such as the requirement by Islamic fundamentalists that women who appear in public have their bodies cloaked and faces veiled. It would be considered a taboo for a woman in this culture to appear in public without being veiled. The sanctions for doing so can be as severe as whipping, branding, banishment, even death.

Sanctions can be positive or negative, that is, based on rewards or punishment. When children learn social norms, for example, correct behavior may elicit positive sanctions; the behavior is reinforced through praise, approval, or an explicit reward. Early on, for example, parents might praise children for learning to put on their own clothes; later, children might get an allowance if they keep their rooms clean. Bad behavior earns negative sanctions, such as getting spanked or grounded. In society, negative sanctions may be mild or severe, ranging from subtle mechanisms of control, such as ridicule, to overt forms of punishment, such as imprisonment, physical coercion, or death.

One way to study social norms is to observe what happens when they are violated. Once you become aware of how social situations are controlled by norms, you can see how easy it is to disrupt situations where adherence to the norms produces social order. **Ethnomethodology** is a theoretical approach in sociology based on the idea that you can discover the normal social order through disrupting it. As a technique of study, ethnomethodologists often deliberately disrupt social norms to see how people respond and try to reinstate social order (Garfinkel 1967).

In a famous series of ethnomethodological experiments, college students were asked to pretend they were boarders in their own homes for a period of fifteen minutes to one hour. They did not tell their families what they were doing. The students were instructed to be polite, circumspect, and impersonal; to use terms of formal address; and to speak only when spoken to. After the experiment, two of the participating students reported that their families treated the experiment as a joke; another's family thought the daughter was being extra nice because she wanted something. One family believed that the student was hiding some serious problem. In all the other cases, parents reacted with shock, bewilderment, and anger. Students were accused of being mean, nasty, impolite, and inconsiderate; the parents demanded explanations for their sons' and daughters' behavior (Garfinkel 1967). Through this experiment, the student researchers were able to see that even the informal norms governing behavior in one's home are carefully structured. By violating the norms of the household, the norms were revealed.

Ethnomethodological research teaches us that society proceeds on an "as if " basis. That is, society exists because people behave as if there were no other way to do so. Usually, people go along with what is expected of them. Culture is actually "enforced" through the social sanctions applied to those who violate social norms. Usually, specific sanctions are unnecessary because people have learned the normative expectations. When the norms are violated, their existence becomes apparent (see also Chapter 5).

## Beliefs

As important as social norms are the beliefs of people in society. **Beliefs** are shared ideas held collectively by people within a given culture about what is true. Shared beliefs are part of what binds people together in society. Beliefs are also the basis for many norms and values of a given culture. In the United States, beliefs that are widely held and cherished are the belief in God and the belief in democracy.

Some beliefs are so strongly held that people find it difficult to cope with ideas or experiences that contradict them. Someone who devoutly believes in God may find atheism intolerable; those who believe in reincarnation may seem irrational to those who think life ends at death. Similarly, those who believe in magic may seem merely superstitious to those with a more scientific and rational view of the world.

Whatever beliefs people hold, they orient us to the world. They provide answers to otherwise imponderable questions about the meaning of life. Beliefs provide a meaning system around which culture is organized. Whether belief stems from religion, myth, folklore, or science, it shapes what people take to be possible and true. Although a given belief may be logically impossible, it nonetheless guides people through their lives.

## Values

Deeply intertwined with beliefs are the values of a culture. **Values** are the abstract standards in a society or group that define ideal principles. Values define what is desirable and morally correct; thus, values determine what is considered right and wrong, beautiful and ugly, good and bad. Although values are abstract, they provide a general outline for behavior. Freedom, for example, is a value held to be important in U.S. culture, as is equality. Values are ideals forming the abstract standards for group behavior, but they are also ideals that may not be realized in every situation.

Values can be a basis for cultural cohesion, but they can also be a source of conflict. You may remember the conflicts that developed over the case of Terri Schiavo—a woman who collapsed from a chemical imbalance brought on by an eating disorder. She was left severely brain-damaged in a "permanent vegetative state" for over fifteen years. Her husband, Michael Schiavo, wanted to remove her feeding tube, thereby ending her life, something he argued she would have wanted. But her parents objected on religious grounds and took the case through numerous court decisions over several years and ultimately to the U.S. Supreme Court. By the time Terri Schiavo died in 2005 (after her feeding tube had been removed), the public had become embroiled in a huge national debate about differing values. There were those who believed she had the right to die in peace and with dignity, those who defined her death as murder, and others (in fact, the majority of Americans) who thought that the government simply had no business interfering in the private affairs of this family. The intensity of this issue, even the language by which people described Terri Schiavo, reflected different positions in a national conflict over competing values.

*Cultural values can clash when groups have strongly held, but clashing, value systems. Values can be a source of cultural cohesion, but also of cultural conflict. What are some of the different values that are being debated in society?*

Values guide the behavior of people in society; they also shape the social norms in a given culture. An example of the impact that values have on people's behavior comes from an American Indian society known as the Kwakiutl (pronounced "kwa-kee-YOO-tal"), a group from the coastal region of southern Alaska, Washington State, and British Columbia. The Kwakiutl developed a practice known as *potlatch,* in which wealthy chiefs would periodically pile up their possessions and give them away to their followers and rivals (Benedict 1934; Harris 1974; Wolcott 1996). The object of potlatch was to give away or destroy more of one's goods than did one's rivals. The potlatch reflected Kwakiutl values of reciprocity, the full use of food and goods, and the social status of the wealthiest chiefs in Kwakiutl society. (By the way, chiefs did not lose their status by giving away their goods because the goods were eventually returned in the course of other potlatches. They would even burn large piles of goods, knowing that others would soon replace their wealth through other potlatches.)

Compare this practice with the patterns of consumption in the United States. Imagine the CEOs of major corporations regularly gathering up their wealth and giving it away to their workers and rival CEOs! In the contemporary United States, *conspicuous consumption* (consuming for the sake of displaying one's wealth) celebrates values similar to those of the potlatch: High-status people demonstrate their position by accumulating more material possessions than those around them (Veblen 1899).

Together, norms, beliefs, and values guide the behavior of people in society. It is necessary to understand how they operate in a situation in order to understand why people behave as they do.

# Cultural Diversity

It is rare for a society to be culturally uniform. As societies develop and become more complex, different cultural traditions appear. The more complex the society, the more likely its culture will be internally varied and diverse. The United States, for example, hosts enormous cultural diversity stemming from religious, ethnic, and racial differences, as well as regional, age, gender, and class differences. Currently, more than 12.5 percent of people in the United States are foreign born. In a single year, immigrants from more than 100 countries come to the United States (U.S. Census Bureau 2009a). Whereas earlier immigrants were predominantly from Europe, now Latin America and Asia are the greatest sources of new immigrants. One result is a large increase in the number of U.S. residents for whom English is the second language. Cultural diversity is clearly a characteristic of contemporary American society.

The richness of American culture stems from the many traditions that different groups have brought with them to this society, as well as from the cultural forms that have emerged through their experience within the United States. Jazz, for example, is one of the few musical forms indigenous to the United States. An indigenous art form refers to something that originated in a particular region or culture. However, jazz also has roots in the musical traditions of slave communities and African cultures. Since the birth of jazz, cultural greats such as Ella Fitzgerald, Count Basie, Duke Ellington, Billie Holiday, and numerous others have not only enriched the jazz tradition but have also influenced other forms of music, including rock and roll.

map2.1 *MAPPING AMERICA'S DIVERSITY*

## Language as Evidence of Cultural Diversity

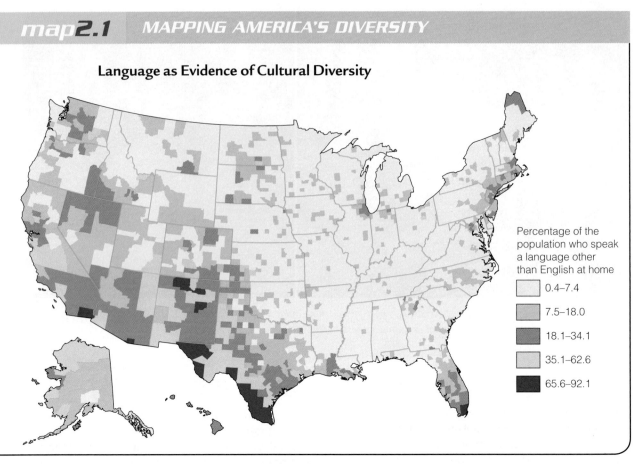

Percentage of the population who speak a language other than English at home

- 0.4–7.4
- 7.5–18.0
- 18.1–34.1
- 35.1–62.6
- 65.6–92.1

*With increased immigration and greater diversity in the U.S. population, evidence of cultural diversity can be seen in many homes—language being one type of evidence. This map shows the regional differences in the percentage of the population over age five who speak a language other than English at home. For the United States as a whole, 17.9 percent of the population—almost one-fifth—fit into this category. Eight percent of the population say they speak English less than very well. What implications does this have for the regions most affected? How might it influence relations between different generations within households?*

*Source:* U.S. Census Bureau. 2009b. "American FactFinder." **www.census.gov**

Native American cultures have likewise enriched the culture of our society, as have the cultures that various immigrant groups have brought with them to the United States. With such great variety, how can the United States be called one culture? The culture of the United States, including its language, arts, food customs, religious practices, and dress, can be seen as the sum of the diverse cultures that constitute this society.

## Dominant Culture

Two concepts from sociology help us understand the complexity of culture in a given society: dominant culture and subculture. The **dominant culture** is the culture of the most powerful group in a society. It is the cultural form that receives the most support from major institutions and that constitutes the major belief system. Although the dominant culture is not the only culture in a society, it is commonly believed to be "the" culture of a society despite the other cultures

present. Social institutions in the society perpetuate the dominant culture and give it a degree of legitimacy that is not shared by other cultures. Quite often, the dominant culture is the standard by which other cultures in the society are judged.

A dominant culture need not be the culture of the majority of people; rather, it is simply the culture of that group in society with enough power to define the cultural framework. As an example, think of a college or university that has a strong system of fraternities and sororities. On campus, the number of students belonging to fraternities and sororities is probably a numerical minority of the total student body, but the cultural system established by the Greeks may dominate campus life nonetheless. In a society as complex as the United States, it is hard to isolate a single dominant culture, although there is a widely acknowledged "American" culture that is considered to be the dominant one. Stemming from middle-class values, habits, and economic resources, this culture is strongly influenced by instruments of culture such as television, the fashion industry, and Anglo-European traditions and includes diverse elements such as fast food, Christmas shopping, and professional sports. It is also a culture that emphasizes achievement and individual effort—a cultural tradition that we will later see has a tremendous impact on how many in the United States view inequality (see Chapter 8).

## Subcultures

**Subcultures** are the cultures of groups whose values and norms of behavior differ to some degree from those of the dominant culture. Members of subcultures tend to interact frequently with one another and share a common worldview. They may be identifiable by their appearance (style of clothing or adornments) or perhaps by language, dialect, or other cultural markers. You can view subcultures along a continuum of how well they are integrated into the dominant culture. Subcultures typically share some elements of the dominant culture and coexist within it, although some subcultures may be quite separated from the dominant one. This separation occurs because they are either unwilling or unable to assimilate into the dominant culture, that is, share its values, norms, and beliefs (Dowd and Dowd 2003).

Rap and hip-hop music first emerged as a subculture where young African Americans developed their own style of dress and music to articulate their resistance to the dominant White culture. Now, rap and hip-hop have been incorporated into mainstream youth culture.

Indeed, they are now global phenomena, as cultural industries have turned hip-hop and rap into a profitable commodity. Even so, rap still expresses an oppositional identity for Black and White youth and other groups who feel marginalized by the dominant culture (Rose 1994).

Some subcultures retreat from the dominant culture, as do the Amish, some religious cults, and some communal groups. In these cases, the subculture is actually a separate community that lives as independently from the dominant culture as possible. Other subcultures may coexist with the dominant society, and members of the subculture may participate in both the subculture and the dominant culture.

Subcultures also develop when new groups enter a society. Puerto Rican immigration to the U.S. mainland, for example, has generated distinct Puerto Rican subcultures within many urban areas. Although Puerto Ricans also partake in the dominant culture, their unique heritage is part of their subcultural experience. Parts of this culture are now entering the dominant culture. Salsa music, now heard on mainstream radio stations, was created in the late 1960s by Puerto Rican musicians who were expressing the contours of their working-class culture (Sanchez 1999; Boggs 1992). The themes in salsa reflect the experience of barrio people and mix the musical traditions of other Latin music, including rumba, mambo, and cha-cha. As with other subcultures, the boundaries between the dominant culture and the subculture are permeable, resulting in cultural change as new groups enter society.

*The Amish people form a subculture in the United States, although preserving their traditional way of life can be a challenge in the context of contemporary society.*

## Countercultures

**Countercultures** are subcultures created as a reaction against the values of the dominant culture. Members of the counterculture reject the dominant cultural values, often for political or moral reasons, and develop cultural practices that explicitly defy the norms and values of the dominant group. Nonconformity to the dominant culture is often the hallmark of a counterculture. Youth groups often form countercultures. Why? In part, they do so to resist the culture of older generations, thereby asserting their independence and identity. Some also argue that young people establish countercultures because they have so little power in society that they have to construct their own cultures to have some sort of status, or social standing, at least among their peers (Milner 2004). Thus, countercultures among youth, like other countercultures, usually have a unique way of dress, their own special language, perhaps even different values and rituals.

Some countercultures directly challenge the dominant society. The white supremacist movement is an example. People affiliated with this movement have an extreme worldview, one that is in direct opposition to dominant values. White supremacist groups have developed a shared worldview, one based on extreme hostility to racial minorities, gays, lesbians, and feminists. Because of their self-contained culture—one focused on hate—they can be very dangerous (Ferber 1998; Stern 1996).

Countercultures may also develop in situations where there is political repression and some groups are forced "underground." Under a dictatorship, for example, some groups may be forbidden to practice their religion or speak their own language. In Spain under the dictator Francisco Franco, people were forbidden to speak Catalan—the language of the region around Barcelona. When Franco died in 1975 and Spain became more democratic, the Catalan language flourished—both in public speaking and in the press.

*The styles and practices of subcultures can be a source of innovation in society. Hip-hop, for example, once a subculture associated only with Black urban youth, has now influenced so-called mainstream style.*

## Ethnocentrism and Cultural Relativism

Because culture tends to be taken for granted, it can be difficult for people within a culture to see their culture as anything but "the way things are." It can thus be difficult to view other cultures without making judgments based on one's own cultural views. **Ethnocentrism** is the habit of seeing things only from the point of view of one's own group. Judging one culture by the standards of another culture is ethnocentric. An ethnocentric perspective prevents you from understanding the world as it is experienced by others, and it can lead to narrow-minded conclusions about the worth of diverse cultures.

Any group can be ethnocentric. Also, ethnocentrism can be extreme or subtle—as in the example of social groups who think their way of life is better than that of any other group. Is there such a ranking among groups in your community? Fraternities and sororities often build group rituals around such claims, youth groups see their way of life as superior to adults, and urbanites may think their cultural habits are more sophisticated than those of groups labeled "country hicks." Ethnocentrism is a powerful force because it combines a strong sense of group solidarity with the idea of group superiority.

Ethnocentrism can build group solidarity, but it also discourages intergroup understanding. Understanding ethnocentrism is critical to understanding some of the major conflicts that are shaping current history. Taken to extremes, ethnocentrism can lead to overt political conflict, war, terrorism, even *genocide,* which is the mass killing of people based on their membership in a particular group. Understanding ethnocentrism can help explain the belief of groups such as al Qaeda that terrorism is justified as a religious *jihad* (defined as a religious struggle to defend Islamic faith). You might wonder how someone could believe so much in the righteousness of their religious faith that they would murder people. Ethnocentrism is a key part of the answer. Understanding ethnocentrism does not excuse such behavior, but it helps you understand how such murderous behavior can occur, though it would be overly simple to explain current political conflicts only in terms of ethnocentrism.

Ethnocentrism can also help you to understand the view that many nations now have of the United States (see Figure 2.1)—a fact that people within the United States have difficulty understanding because we hold ethnocentric views of our own culture, as if it is superior to all others. Many other nations do not see U.S. culture in the positive light that U.S. citizens might expect. As this figure shows, cultural values in the Islamic world can clash with those of the West and are part of the complexity of U.S. relations with those cultures.

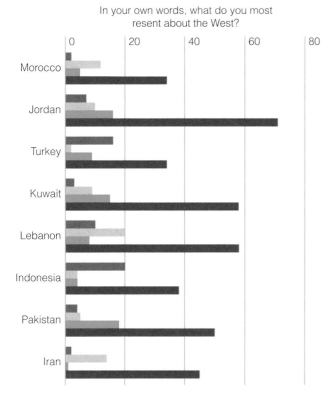

In your own words, what do you most resent about the West?

- ■ Arrogance, think they are the best/most powerful, advanced, civilized
- ▦ High crime rate, drugs, violence, alcoholism, corruption
- ▧ Negative attitude toward Arabs/Muslims
- ■ Social aspects (too free, low morals, free sex, impolite to elders, dislocation of family relations)

**FIGURE 2.1** *Islamic Views of the West*

*Data:* Burkholder, Richard. 2003. "Iraq and the West: How Wide Is the Morality Gap?" *The Gallup Poll*, Princeton, NJ. **www.gallup.com**

Contrasting with ethnocentrism is cultural relativism. **Cultural relativism** is the idea that something can be understood and judged only in relation to the cultural context in which it appears. This does not make every cultural practice morally acceptable, but it suggests that without knowing the cultural context, it is impossible to understand why people behave as they do. For example, in the United States, burying or cremating the dead is the cultural practice. It may be difficult for someone from this culture to understand that in parts of Tibet, with a ruggedly cold climate and the inability to dig the soil, the dead are cut into pieces and left for vultures to eat. Although this would be repulsive (and illegal) in the United States, within Tibetan culture, this practice is understandable.

Understanding cultural relativism gives insight into some controversies, such as the international debate about the practice of clitoridectomy—a form of genital mutilation. In a clitoridectomy (sometimes called female circumcision), all or part of a young woman's clitoris is removed, usually not by medical personnel, often in very unsanitary conditions, and without any pain killers. Sometimes, the lips of the vagina may be sewn together. Human rights and feminist organizations have documented this practice in some countries on the African continent, in some Middle Eastern nations, and in some parts of Southeast Asia; estimates are that around two million girls per year, worldwide, are at risk. This practice is most frequent in cultures where women's virginity is highly prized and where marriage dowries depend on some accepted proof of virginity (Toubia and Izett 1998).

From the point of view of Western cultures, clitoridectomy is genital mutilation and an example of violence against women. Many have called for international intervention to eliminate the practice, but there is also a debate about whether disgust at this practice should be balanced by a reluctance to impose Western cultural values on other societies. Should cultures have the right of self-determination or should cultural practices that maim people be treated as violations of human rights? This controversy is unresolved. The point is to see that understanding a cultural practice requires knowing the cultural values on which it is based.

## The Globalization of Culture

The infusion of Western culture throughout the world seems to be accelerating as the commercialized culture of the United States is marketed worldwide. One can go to quite distant places in the world and see familiar elements of U.S. culture, whether it is McDonald's in Hong Kong, The Gap in South Africa, or Disney products in western Europe. From films to fast food, the United States dominates international mass culture, largely through the influence of capitalist markets, as conflict theorists would argue. The diffusion of a single culture throughout the world is referred to as **global culture.** Despite the enormous diversity of cultures worldwide, fashion, food, entertainment, and other cultural values are increasingly dominated by U.S. markets, thereby creating a more homogenous world culture. Global culture is increasingly marked by capitalist interests, squeezing out the more diverse folk cultures that have been common throughout the world (Rieff 1993).

Does increasing globalization of culture change traditional cultural values? Some worry that globalization imposes Western values on non-Western cultures, thus eroding long-held cultural traditions. But global economic change can also introduce more tolerant values to cultures that might have had a narrower worldview previously. As globalization occurs, *both* economic changes *and* traditional cultural values shape the emerging national culture of different societies (Inglehart and Baker 2000).

The conflict between traditional and more commercial values is now being played out in world affairs, with some arguing that the conflicts we see in international relations are partially rooted in a struggle between the values of a consumer-based, capitalist Western culture and the traditional values of local communities. Benjamin Barber (1995) expresses this as the struggle between "McWorld" and "Jihad"—a struggle he interprets as the tension between global commerce and parochial values. As some people resist the influence of market-driven values, movements to reclaim or maintain ethnic and cultural identity can intensify. Thus, you can witness a proliferation of culturally based movements, including strong feelings of nationalism, such as among extremist groups in the Middle East.

# The Mass Media and Popular Culture

Increasingly, culture in the United States—as well as in many parts of the world—is dominated and shaped by the media. Indeed, the culture of the United States is so infused by the media that, when people think of U.S. culture, they are likely thinking of something connected to the media—television, film, and so forth. The term **mass media** refers to the channels of communication that are available to wide segments of the population—the print, film, and electronic media (radio and television), as well as the Internet.

The mass media have extraordinary power to shape culture, including what people believe and the information available to them. If you doubt this, observe how much the mass media affect your everyday life. Friends may talk about last night's episode of a particular show or laugh about the antics of their favorite sitcom character. Your way of dressing, talking, and even thinking has likely been shaped by the media. Now, even relationships are found and maintained via electronic networks such as Facebook—networks that are part of the mass media.

You can find the mass media everywhere—in airports, elevators, classrooms, bars and restaurants, and hospital waiting rooms. Enter an elevator in a major hotel and you might find CNN or The Weather Channel on twenty-four hours a day. You may even be born to the sounds and images of television, since they are turned on in many hospital delivery rooms. Television is now so ever-present in our lives that 42 percent of all U.S. households are now called "constant television households"—that is, those households where television is on most of the time (Gitlin 2002). For many families, TV is the "babysitter." Ninety-eight percent of all homes in the United States have at least one television. The average person consumes some form of media sixty-nine hours per week—more time than they likely spend in school or at work; thirty-three of these hours are spent watching television. On average, people spend only about two hours per week reading books (U.S. Census Bureau 2009a). In fact, television dominates leisure time for most Americans; one-quarter of all Americans say watching TV is their favorite way to spend an evening, compared to 9 percent who would rather read and 1 percent whose favorite evening activity is listening to music (Saad 2002).

Television is a powerful transmitter of culture, but it also portrays a very homogeneous view of culture because in seeking the widest possible audience, networks and sponsors find the most common ground and take few risks. The mass media (and television, in particular) also play a huge role in shaping people's perception and awareness of social issues. For example, even though crime has actually decreased, the amount of time spent reporting crime in the media has increased. Sociologists have found that people's fear of crime is directly related to the time they spend watching television or listening to the radio (Angotti 1997; Chiricos et al. 1997). The media shape our definition of social problems by determining the range of opinion or information that is defined as legitimate and by deciding which experts will be called on to elaborate an issue (Gitlin 2002).

Perhaps you think that, despite this information, the mass media have little effect on you—no matter how much you might enjoy it. But try to do without it—even for a brief period of time—by trying the experiment in the "See for Yourself" feature on page 44. Simply getting away from all of the forms of media that permeate daily life may be extremely difficult to do!

## The Organization of Mass Media

Mass media are not only a pervasive part of daily life, they are big business. On average, consumers spend $1000 per year on media consumption, half of that for television. That may not seem like much until you realize that the motion picture and video industry is a $73 billion industry; TV, $38 billion; telecommunications (including cell phones, Internet access, cable, and so forth), over $550 billion!

Thus, mass media are organized via powerful economic interests. And, increasingly, the media are owned by a small number of companies—companies that form huge media monopolies. This means that a few very powerful groups—media conglomerates—are the major producers and distributors of culture. A single corporation can control a huge share of television, radio, newspapers, music, publishing, film, and the Internet, as shown in Figure 2.2. As the production of popular culture becomes concentrated in the hands of just a few, there may be less diversity in the content.

The organization of the mass media as a system of economic interests means that there is enormous power in the hands of a few to shape the culture of the whole society. Sociologists refer to the concentration of cultural power as **cultural hegemony** (pronounced "heh-JEM-o-nee"), defined as the pervasive and excessive influence of one culture throughout society. Cultural hegemony means that people may conform to

**Hearst Corporation owns:**

17 magazines: including *Cosmo, Cosmo Girl, Marie Claire, O* (The Oprah Magazine), *Good Housekeeping, Redbook, Seventeen, Popular Mechanics,* and others), 12 newspapers, 27 local TV stations, several cable networks, including The History Channel, part of ESPN, Lifetime, A&E, Hearst Books, King Features TV syndicate; holds investments in Netscape, XM Satellite radio, drugstore.com, and more . . .

**News Corporation owns:**

World's largest newspaper publisher; Fox News; myspace.com (purchased in 2005 for $580 million); William Morrow and Avon Books; 35 local radio stations; 25 international newspapers; New York Post; Broadcasting rights for NFL in Asia; Harper Collins Publishing; TV Guide; 20th Century Fox Film; Los Angeles Dodgers (sold in 2004); Los Angeles Lakers; Los Angeles Kings; Staples Center (LA); and more . . .

**Time Warner owns:**

HBO; CNN; AOL Instant Messenger; Warner Brothers; Warner Brothers Studios; WB Television Network; Hanna-Barbera Cartoons; Castle Rock Entertainment; Warner Home Video; Turner Network Television; TBS Superstation; Netscape; Amazon.com (partial owner); Warner Brothers International Theaters (owns/operates multiplex theatres in over 12 countries); over 50 magazines (including *Time; Fortune; People; Life; Sports Illustrated; Money; In Style; Cooking Light; This Old House; Field and Stream; Popular Science; Snowboard Life; Yachting Magazine; Travel and Leisure;* and others); Atlanta Braves; and more . . .

**Viacom owns:**

MTV; BET (Black Entertainment Television); Nickelodeon; Paramount Pictures; Dreamworks; CBS (split in 2006); Simon and Schuster Publishers; College TV Network; Blockbuster Video; 39 television stations; 185 local radio stations; VH1; Comedy Central; Outdoor Systems billboards; Madison Square Garden (sold in 1995 for $1 billion); TV Land; Pearson Publishing (publisher of elementary, high school, and college textbooks); Rumored to be considering purchasing facebook.com for $2 billion; and more . . .

**Disney owns:**

Disney Pictures; Miramax Films; Touchstone Pictures; Buena Vista Home Entertainment; Pixar; ABC television network; 10 local television stations; ESPN network; ABC Family Television; Disney Channel; 68 local radio stations; 15 magazines; Buena Vista Music Group; 5 Disneylands; Disney stores; Disney Cruise Line; Disney Shopping Inc.; and more . . .

***FIGURE 2.2*** *Cultural Monopolies*

*Note:* Because corporate mergers are so common, these data were current as of 2007.

cultural patterns and interests that benefit powerful elites, even without those elites overtly forcing people into conformity. Thus, on the one hand, while there seems to be enormous choice in what media forms people consume, the cultural messages are largely homogenous (meaning "sameness"). Cultural hegemony produces a homogeneous mass culture, even when it appears that there is vast choice. Thus, cultural monopolies are a means through which powerful groups gain the assent of those they rule. The concept of cultural hegemony implies that culture is highly politicized, even if it does not appear so. Through cultural hegemony, those who control cultural institutions can also control people's political awareness because they create cultural beliefs that make the rule of those in power seem inevitable and right. As a result, political resistance to the dominant culture is blunted (Gramsci 1971). We explore this idea further in the section below on sociological theories of culture.

## The Media and Popular Culture

Because the mass media pervade the whole society, the media influence such things as popular styles, language, and value systems. Together, these create **popular culture,** meaning the beliefs, practices, and objects that are part of everyday traditions. In a society so dominated by the mass media, popular culture, including such things as music and films, mass-marketed books and magazines, large-circulation newspapers, and Internet websites, are mass-produced. Popular culture is distinct from elite culture, which

*The power of the mass media can be staggering, as evidenced by the popularity of* American Idol.

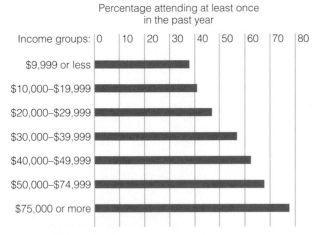

Percentage attending at least once
in the past year

Income groups:

- $9,999 or less
- $10,000–$19,999
- $20,000–$29,999
- $30,000–$39,999
- $40,000–$49,999
- $50,000–$74,999
- $75,000 or more

**FIGURE 2.3** *Who Goes to the Movies?*

*Source:* U.S. Census Bureau. 2009a. *Statistical Abstract of the United States 2009.* Washington, DC: U.S. Department of Commerce, p. 747.

is shared by only a select few but is highly valued. Unlike elite culture (sometimes referred to as "high culture"), popular culture is mass-consumed and has enormous significance in the formation of public attitudes and values. Popular culture is also supported by patterns of mass consumption, as the many objects associated with popular culture are promoted and sold to a consuming public.

The distinction between popular and elite culture means that culture is consumed in different ways by various segments of the population. This, too, is affected by patterns of social class, race, and gender in the society. While popular culture may be widely available and be relatively cheap for the consumer, some groups derive their cultural experiences from expensive theater shows or opera performances where tickets may cost hundreds of dollars. Meanwhile, millions of "ordinary" citizens get their primary cultural

experience from television, movie rentals, and increasingly, the Internet. Even something as seemingly common as Internet usage reflects patterns of social class differences in society, as you can see in Figure 2.4. This inequality has led many to advocate for free wireless service in some cities, as a way of trying to make Internet access more democratic.

## Race, Gender, and Class in the Media

Many sociologists argue that the mass media can promote narrow definitions of who people are and what they can be. What is considered beautiful, for example? Is there a universal idea of beauty, or do the media promote different ideals for different groups? The mass media have a huge impact on how we see beauty and who or what is defined as beautiful; moreover, these beauty ideals change over time. Aging is defined as not beautiful, youth is. Light skin is promoted as more beautiful than dark skin, regardless of race, although being tan is seen as more beautiful than being pale. In African American women's magazines, the models typified as most beautiful are generally those with the clearly Anglo features of light skin, blue eyes, and straight or wavy hair. European facial features are also pervasive in the images of Asian and Latino women appearing in U.S. magazines. The point is that the media communicate that only certain forms of beauty are culturally valued. These ideals are not somehow "natural." They are constructed by those who control cultural and economic institutions (Craig 2002; Gimlin 2002).

You can learn a lot about how the media shape popular culture by looking carefully and systematically at the images produced and disseminated via the media. Content analyses of the media (a research

## SEE FOR YOURSELF

### TWO DAYS WITHOUT THE MEDIA

Suppose that you lived for a few days without use of the mass media that permeate our lives. How would this affect you? In an intriguing experiment, Charles Gallagher (a sociologist at La University) has developed a research project for students in which he asks them to stage a media blackout in their lives for just forty-eight hours. You can try this LaSalle yourself.

Begin by keeping a written log for forty-eight hours of exactly how much time you spend with some form of media. Include all time spent watching television, on the Internet, reading books and magazines, listening to music, viewing films, even using cell phones—any

activity that can be construed as part of the media monopoly on people's time.

Next, eliminate all use of the media, except for that required for work, school, and emergencies for a forty-eight-hour period, keeping a journal as you go of what happens, what you are thinking, what others say, and how people interact with you. *Warning: If you try the media blackout, be sure to have some plan in place for having your family and/or friends contact you in case of an emergency!* When one of the authors of this book (Andersen) had her students do this experiment, they complained even before starting that they wouldn't be able to do it! But they had to try. What happened?

First, Andersen's students had help: the week of the assignment came during a hurricane on the East Coast when many were without power for several

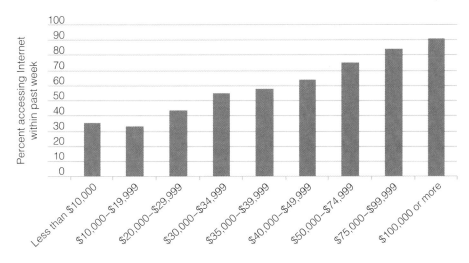

**FIGURE 2.4** *Social Class and the Internet*

*Source:* Mediamark Research and Intelligence. 2007. New York.

method discussed in the following chapter) show distinct patterns of how race and gender and class are depicted in various media forms. On prime-time television, men are still a large majority of the characters shown. Over the years, there has been an increase in the extent to which women are depicted in professional jobs, but such images usually depict professional women as young (suggesting that career success comes early), thin, and beautiful women (Signorielli and Bacue 1999). In music videos, women are more present, but typically wearing sexy and skimpy clothing and more often the object of another's gaze than is true for their male counterparts; Black women especially are represented in sexualized ways (Emerson 2002; Signorielli et al. 1994; Collins 2004).

Even though African Americans and Hispanics watch more television than White people do, they are a smaller proportion of TV characters, generally confined to a narrow variety of character types, depicted in stereotypical ways. Latinos are often stereotyped

as criminals, passionate lovers, or comic figures. African American men are most often seen as athletes and sports commentators, criminals, or entertainers. Women who work as football sports commentators are typically on the sidelines, reporting not so much on the play of the game, as the human interest or injury reports—suggesting that women's role in sports is limited to that of the nurturer. It is difficult to find a single show where Asians are the principal characters—usually they are depicted in silent roles as domestics or behind-the-scenes characters. Native Americans make occasional appearances, where they usually are depicted as mystics or warriors. Jewish women are generally invisible on popular TV programming, except when they are ridiculed in stereotypical roles. Arab Americans are likewise stereotyped, depicted as terrorists, rich oil magnates, or in the case of women, as perpetually veiled and secluded (Read 2003; Mandel 2001).

In a good example of how race and gender stereotypes merge in the mass media, one analyst carefully

days. This did not deter the students from thinking they just *had to have* their DVD players, music, TV, and cell phones! Many of the students said they could not stand being without access to the media—even for a few hours. Most could not go the full two days without using the media.

Most reported that they felt isolated during the media exercise, not just from information, but mostly from other people. They were excluded from conversations with friends about what happened on a given television episode or about film characters or movie stars profiled in magazines and from playing computer games. One even wrote that without the media she felt that she had no personality! Without their connection to the media, students were alienated, isolated, and detached, although most also reported that they studied more without the distrac-

tion of the media. A most interesting finding was that several reported that they were much more reflective during this time and had more meaningful conversations with friends.

After trying this experiment, think about the enormous influence that the mass media have in shaping everyday life, including your self-concept and your relationship with other people. What does this exercise teach you about *cultural hegemony?* The role of the mass media in shaping society? How would each of the following theoretical frameworks explain what happened during your media blackout: functionalism, conflict theory, feminist theory, symbolic interaction?

*Source*: Personal correspondence, Charles Gallagher, LaSalle University.

analyzed multiple episodes of the popular show, *The Bachelor* (Dubrofsky 2006). Supposedly, the women all have an equal chance at being selected as the bachelor's mate, the basic concept of the show asserting heterosexual relationships as the most appropriate romance. But, as Dubrofsky shows, women of color are never chosen as the bachelor's mate; they are, in fact, eliminated early from the competition. Equally revealing, Dubrofsky shows how the show's set suggests a harem-like quality—multiple women available to one man, women lounging around on plush furniture, assembled to resemble a stereotypical harem—with plush, overstuffed cushions, lush gardens, and often Middle-Eastern tapestries on the walls, thereby producing stereotypes about the supposed sexual excess and availability of Middle Eastern women. Research documents numerous examples of stereotyped portrayals in the media—stereotypes you will see for yourself if you step outside of the taken-for-granted views with which you ordinarily observe the media.

*thinkingsociologically*

Watch a particular kind of television show (situation comedy, sports broadcast, children's cartoon, or news program, for example) and make careful written notes on the depiction of different groups in this show. How often are women and men or boys and girls shown?

How are they depicted? You could also observe the portrayal of Asian Americans, Native Americans, African Americans, or Latinos. What do your observations tell you about the cultural ideals that are communicated through *popular culture*?

Class stereotypes abound in the media and popular culture as well, with working-class men typically portrayed as being ineffectual, even buffoonish (Butsch 1992; Dines and Humez 2002). A recent study of TV talk shows also demonstrates how such shows exploit working-class people. The researcher, Laura Grindstaff, spent six months working on two popular talk shows, carefully doing participant observation and interviewing staff and guests. She found that guests had to enact stereotypes of their groups to get airtime. She argues that, although these shows give ordinary people a place to air their problems and be heard, they exploit the working class, making a spectacle of their troubles (Grindstaff 2002; Press 2002).

Recently, there has been increased representation of gays and lesbians in the media, after years of being virtually invisible or only the subject of ridicule. As advertisers have sought to expand their commercial markets, they are showing more gay and lesbian characters on television. This makes gays and lesbians more visible, although critics point out that they are still cast in narrow and stereotypical terms, showing little about real life for gays and lesbians.

Nonetheless, cultural visibility for any group is important because it validates people and can influence the public's acceptance of and generate support for equal rights protection (Gamson 1998a).

Television is not the only form of popular culture that influences public consciousness, class, gender, and race. Music, film, books, and other industries play a significant role in molding public consciousness. What images are produced by these cultural forms? You can look for yourself. Try to buy a birthday card that contains neither an age or gender stereotype, or watch TV or a movie and see how different gender and race groups are portrayed. You will likely find that women are depicted as trying to get the attention of men; African Americans are more likely than Whites to be seen singing and dancing.

Do these images matter? Studies find that exposure to traditional sexualized imagery in music videos has a negative effect on college students' attitudes, for example, holding more adversarial attitudes about sexual relationships (Kalof 1999). Other studies find that even when viewers see media images as unrealistic, they think that others find the images important and will evaluate them accordingly; this has been found especially true for young White girls who think boys will judge them by how well they match the media ideal (Milkie 1999). Although people do not just passively internalize media images and do distinguish between fantasy and reality (Hollander 2002; Currie 1997), such images form cultural ideals that have a huge impact on people's behavior, values, and self-image.

# Theoretical Perspectives on Culture and the Media

Sociologists study culture and the media in a variety of ways, asking a variety of questions about the relationship of culture to other social institutions and the role of culture in modern life. One important question for sociologists studying the mass media is whether these images have any effect on those who see them. Do the media create popular values or reflect them? The **reflection hypothesis** contends that the mass media reflect the values of the general population (Tuchman 1979). The media try to appeal to the most broad-based audience, so they aim for the middle ground in depicting images and ideas. Maximizing popular appeal is central to television program development; media organizations spend huge amounts on market research to uncover what people think and believe and what they will like. Characters are then created with whom people will identify. Interestingly, the images in the media with which we identify are distorted versions of reality. Real people seldom live like the characters on television, although part of the appeal of these shows is how they build upon, but then mystify, the actual experiences of people.

The reflection hypothesis assumes that images and values portrayed in the media reflect the values existing in the public, but the reverse can also be true—that is, the ideals portrayed in the media also influence the values of those who see them. As an example, social scientists have studied the stereotyped images commonly found in children's programming. Among their findings, they have shown that the children who watch the most TV hold the most stereotypic gender attitudes (Signorielli 1991). Although there is not a simple and direct relationship between the content of mass media images and what people think of themselves, clearly these mass-produced images can have a significant impact on who we are and what we think.

## Culture and Group Solidarity

Many sociologists have studied particular forms of culture and have provided detailed analyses of the content of cultural artifacts, such as images in certain television programs or genres of popular music. Other sociologists take a broader view by analyzing the relationship of culture to other forms of social organization. Beginning with some of the classical sociological theorists (see Chapter 1), sociologists have studied the relationship of culture to other social institutions. Max Weber looked at the impact of culture on the formation of social and economic institutions. In his classic analysis of the Protestant work ethic and capitalism, Weber argued that the Protestant faith rested on cultural beliefs that were highly compatible with the development of modern capitalism. By promoting a strong work ethic and a need to display material success as a sign of religious salvation, the Protestant work ethic indirectly but effectively promoted the interests of an emerging capitalist economy. (We revisit this issue in Chapter 13.) In other words, culture influences other social institutions.

Many sociologists have also examined how culture integrates members into society and social groups. Functionalist theorists, for example, believe that norms and values create social bonds that attach people to society. Culture therefore provides coherence and stability in society. Robert Putnam examines this idea in his book *Bowling Alone* (2000), in which he argues that there has been a decline in *civic engagement*—defined as participation in voluntary organizations, religious activities, and other forms of public life—in recent years. As people become less engaged in such activities, there is a decline in the shared values and norms of the society so that social disorder results. Sociologists are debating the extent to which there has been such a decline in public life, but from a functionalist perspective, the point is that participation in a common culture is an important social bond—one that unites society (Etzioni et al. 2001).

Classical theoretical analyses of culture have placed special emphasis on nonmaterial culture—the values, norms, and belief systems of society. Sociologists who use this perspective emphasize the integrative function of culture, that is, its ability to give people a sense of belonging in an otherwise complex social system (Smelser 1992a). In the broadest sense, they see culture as a major integrative force in society, providing societies with a sense of collective identity and commonly shared worldviews.

## Culture, Power, and Social Conflict

Whereas the emphasis on shared values and group solidarity drives one sociological analysis of culture, conflicting values drives another. Conflict theorists (see Chapter 1) have analyzed culture as a source of power in society. You can find numerous examples throughout human history where conflict between different cultures has actually shaped the course of world affairs. One such example comes from the Middle East

## table 2.3    *Theoretical Perspectives on Culture*

| | According to: | | |
|---|---|---|---|
| **Functionalism** | **Conflict Theory** | **Symbolic Interaction** | **New Cultural Studies** |
| Culture . . . | | | |
| Integrates people into groups | Serves the interests of powerful groups | Creates group identity from diverse cultural meanings | Is ephemeral, unpredictable, and constantly changing |
| Provides coherence and stability in society | Can be a source of political resistance | Changes as people produce new cultural meanings | Is a material manifestation of a consumer-oriented society |
| Creates norms and values that integrate people in society | Is increasingly controlled by economic monopolies | Is socially constructed through the activities of social groups | Is best understood by analyzing its artifacts—books, films, television images |

and the situation for the Kurdish people. The Kurds are an ethnic group (see Chapter 10) who speak their own language and inhabit an area in the Middle East that includes parts of Iraq, Iran, Turkey, and Syria, though they mostly live in northern Iraq. Most are Sunni Muslims, and they have experienced years of political and economic repression and, under Saddam Hussein, mass murder. Attempting to eliminate Kurds altogether, Saddam Hussein ordered the execution of over 180,000 people in Kurdish villages, often using chemical and biological weapons (O'Leary 2002). This and other examples of so-called ethnic cleansing show how cultural conflict can be driven by intense group hatred and powerful forms of domination.

Conflict theorists see contemporary culture as produced within institutions that are based on inequality and capitalist principles. As a result, the cultural values and products that are produced and sold promote the economic and political interests of the few—those who own or benefit from these cultural industries. As we have seen, this is especially evident in the study of the mass media and popular culture, marketed to the masses by entities with a vast economic stake in distributing their products. Conflict theorists conclude that the cultural products most likely to be produced are consistent with the values, needs, and interests of the most powerful groups in society. The evening news, for example, typically is sponsored by major financial institutions, and oil companies. Conflict theorists then ask how this commercial sponsorship influences the content of the news. If the news were sponsored by labor unions, would conflicts between management and workers always be defined as "labor troubles," or might newscasters refer instead to "capitalist troubles"?

Conflict theorists see culture as increasingly controlled by economic monopolies. Whether it is books, music, films, news, or other cultural forms, monopolies in the communications industry (where culture is increasingly located) have a strong interest in protecting the status quo. As media conglomerates swallow up smaller companies and drive out smaller, less-efficient competitors, the control that economic monopolies have over the production and distribution of culture becomes enormous. Mega-communications companies then influence everything—from the movies and television shows you see to the books you read in school.

However, culture can also be a source of political resistance and social change. Reclaiming an indigenous culture that had been denied or repressed is one way that groups mobilize to assert their independence. An example from within the United States is the *repatriation movement* among American Indians who have argued for the return of both cultural artifacts and human remains held in museum collections. Many American Indians believe that, despite the public good that is derived from studying such remains and objects, cultural independence and spiritual respect outweigh such scientific arguments (Thornton 2001). Other social movements, such as the gay and lesbian movement, have also used cultural performance as a means of political and social protest. Cross-dressing, drag shows, and other forms of "gender play" can be seen as cultural performances that challenge homophobia and traditional sexual and gender roles (Rupp and Taylor 2003).

A final point of focus for sociologists studying culture from a conflict perspective lies in the concept of cultural capital. **Cultural capital** refers to the cultural resources that are deemed worthy (such as knowledge of elite culture) and that give advantages to groups possessing such capital. This idea has been most developed by the French sociologist Pierre Bourdieu (1984), who sees the appropriation of culture as one way that groups maintain their social status.

Bourdieu argues that members of the dominant class have distinctive lifestyles that mark their status in society. Their ability to display this cultural lifestyle signals their importance to others; that is, they possess cultural capital. From this point of view, culture has a role in reproducing inequality among groups. Those with cultural capital use it to improve their social and economic position in society. Sociologists have found a significant relationship, for example, between cultural capital and grades in school; that is, those from the more well-to-do classes (those with more cultural capital) are able to parlay their knowledge into higher grades, thereby reproducing their social position by being more competitive in school admissions and, eventually, in the labor market (Hill 2001; Treiman 2001).

## Symbolic Interaction and the Study of Culture

Especially productive when applied to the study of culture has been *symbolic interaction theory*—a perspective that analyzes behavior in terms of the meaning people give it. (See Chapter 1.) The concept of culture is central to this orientation. Symbolic interaction emphasizes the interpretive basis of social behavior, and culture provides the interpretive framework through which behavior is understood.

Symbolic interaction also emphasizes that culture, like all other forms of social behavior, is socially constructed; that is, culture is produced through social relationships and in social groups, such as the media organizations that produce and distribute culture. People do not just passively submit to cultural norms. Rather, they actively make, interpret, and respond to the culture around them. Culture is not one-dimensional; it contains diverse elements and provides people with a wide range of choices from which to select how they will behave (Swidler 1986). Culture, in fact, represents the creative dimension of human life.

In recent years, a new interdisciplinary field known as *cultural studies* has emerged that builds on the insights of the symbolic interaction perspective in sociology. Sociologists who work in cultural studies are often critical of classical sociological approaches to studying culture, arguing that the classical approach has overemphasized nonmaterial

### Classical Theorists on Hip-Hop!

Suppose some of the classical theorists of sociology were asked to comment on the popularity of hip-hop? What might they say?

**Emile Durkheim:** I notice that young people can name hip-hop musicians whom others in the society do not recognize. This commonly happens as different generations tend to grow up within a shared music culture. Whether it's hip-hop, country, or pop, music cultures bind groups together by creating a sense of shared and collective identity. For young people, this makes them feel like part of a generation instead of being completely alienated from an otherwise adult-dominated culture.

**Karl Marx:** It is interesting that White youth are now the major consumers of hip-hop. Hip-hop originated from young, Black youth who are disadvantaged by the economic system of society. Now capitalism has appropriated this creative work and turned it into a highly profitable commodity that benefits dominant groups who control the music industry. As this has happened, the critical perspective originated by young, Black urban men has been supplanted by race and gender stereotypes that support the interests of the powerful.

**Max Weber:** Emile and Karl, you just see it one way. It's not that you are wrong, but you have to take a multi-dimensional view. Yes, hip-hop is an economic and a cultural phenomenon, but it is also linked to power in society. Haven't you noticed how political candidates try to use popular music to appeal to different political constituencies? Don't be surprised to find hip-hop artists performing at political conventions! That's what I find so intriguing: Hip-hop is an economic, cultural, and political phenomenon.

**W.E.B. Du Bois:** I've said that Black people have a "double consciousness"—one where they always have to see themselves through the eyes of a world that devalues them—American and "Black" at the same time. But, concurrently, the "twoness" that Black people experience generates wonderful cultural forms such as hip-hop that reflect the unique spirit of African Americans. I once wrote that "there is no true American music but the wild sweet melodies of the Negro slave" (DuBois 1903: 14), but I wish I had lived to see this new spirited and soulful form of musical expression!

culture, that is, ideas, beliefs, values, and norms. The new scholars of cultural studies find that material culture has increasing importance in modern society (Crane 1994; Walters 1999). This includes cultural forms that are recorded through print, film, artifacts, or the electronic media. Postmodernist theory has greatly influenced new cultural studies (see Chapter 1). *Postmodernism* is based on the idea that society is not an objective thing; rather, it is found in the words and images that people use to represent behavior and ideas. Given this orientation, postmodernism often analyzes common images and cultural products found in everyday life.

Classical theorists have tended to study the unifying features of culture; cultural studies researchers tend to see culture as more fragmented and unpredictable. To them, culture is a series of images—images that can be interpreted in multiple ways, depending on the viewpoint of the observer. From the perspective of new cultural studies theorists, the ephemeral and rapidly changing quality of contemporary cultural forms is reflective of the highly technological and consumer-based culture on which the modern economy rests.

Modern culture, for example, is increasingly dominated by the ever-changing, but ever-present, images that the media bombard us with in everyday life. The fascination that cultural studies theorists have for these images is partially founded in illusions that such a dynamic and rapidly changing culture produces.

## Cultural Change

In one sense, culture is a conservative force in society; it tends to be based on tradition and is passed on through generations, conserving and regenerating the values and beliefs of society. Culture is also increasingly based on institutions that have an economic interest in maintaining the status quo. People are also often resistant to cultural change because familiar ways and established patterns of doing things are hard to give up. But in other ways, culture is completely taken for granted, and it may be hard to imagine a society different from that which is familiar.

Imagine, for example, the United States without fast food. Can you do so? Probably not. Fast food is so much a part of contemporary culture that it is hard to imagine life without it. Consider these facts about fast-food culture:

- The average person in the United States consumes three hamburgers and four orders of French fries per week.
- People in the United States spend more money on fast food than on movies, books, magazines, newspapers, videos, music, computers, and higher education combined.
- One in eight workers has at some point been employed by McDonald's.
- McDonald's is the largest private operator of playgrounds in the United States and the single largest purchaser of beef, pork, and potatoes.
- Ninety-six percent of American schoolchildren can identify Ronald McDonald—only exceeded by the number who can identify Santa Claus (Schlosser 2001).

Eric Schlosser, who has written about the permeation of society by fast-food culture, has written that "a nation's diet can be more revealing than its art or literature" (2001: 3). He relates the growth of the fast-food industry to other fundamental changes in American society, including the vast numbers of women entering the paid labor market, the development of an automobile culture, the increased reliance on low-wage service jobs, the decline of family farming, and the growth of agribusiness. One result is a cultural emphasis on uniformity, not to mention increased fat and calories in people's diets.

This example shows how cultures can change over time, sometimes in ways that are hardly visible to us unless we take a longer-range view or, as sociologists would do, question that which surrounds us. Culture is a dynamic, not static, force in society, and it develops as people respond to various changes in their physical and social environments.

## Culture Lag

Sometimes cultures adjust slowly to changing cultural conditions, and the result can be **culture lag** (Ogburn 1922). Some parts of culture may change more rapidly than others; thus, one aspect of culture may "lag" behind another. Rapid technological change is often attended by culture lag because some elements of the culture do not keep pace with technological innovation. In today's world, we have the technological ability to develop efficient, less-polluting rapid transit, but changing people's transportation habits is difficult.

When culture changes rapidly or someone is suddenly thrust into a new cultural situation, the result can be **culture shock,** the feeling of disorientation when one encounters a new or rapidly changed cultural situation. Even moving from one cultural environment to another within one's own society can make a person feel out of place. The greater the difference between cultural settings, the greater the culture shock. Some people displaced from New Orleans following Hurricane Katrina experienced culture shock in the host communities where they relocated. Accustomed to the food, customs, and environment in their New Orleans homes, many evacuees were relocated to remote, mostly White, rural parts of the country. On top of their disorientation from the trauma of the storm itself, living in these new environments could be very disorienting (Wilkerson 2005).

## Sources of Cultural Change

There are several causes of cultural change, including (1) a change in the societal conditions, (2) cultural diffusion, (3) innovation, and (4) the imposition of cultural change by an outside agency. Let us examine each.

1. *Cultures change in response to changed conditions in the society.* Economic changes, population changes, and other social transformations all influence the development of culture. A change in the makeup of a society's population may be enough by itself to cause a cultural transformation. The high rate of immigration in recent years has brought many cultural changes to the United States. Some cities, such as Miami and Los Angeles, have a Latin feel because of the large Hispanic population. But even outside urban areas, cultural change from immigration is apparent. Markets selling Asian, Mexican, and Middle Eastern foods are increasingly common; school districts include students who speak a huge variety of languages; popular music bears the imprint of different world cultures. This is not the first time U.S. culture has changed because of immigration. Many national traditions stem from the patterns of immigration that marked the earlier part of the twentieth century—think of St. Patrick's Day parades, Italian markets, and Chinatowns.

2. *Cultures change through cultural diffusion.* **Cultural diffusion** is the transmission of cultural elements from one society or cultural group to another. In our world of instantaneous communication, cultural diffusion is swift and widespread. This is evident in the degree to which worldwide cultures have been Westernized. Cultural diffusion also occurs when subcultural influences enter the dominant group. Dominant cultures are regularly enriched by minority cultures. An example is the influence of Black and Latino music on other musical forms. Rap music, for example, emerged within inner-city African American neighborhoods, describing and analyzing in its own form the economic and political

conditions of the urban ghetto. Now, rap music is listened to by White as well as Black audiences and is part of youth culture in general. Cultural diffusion is one thing that drives cultural evolution, especially in a society such as ours that is lush with diversity.

3. *Cultures change as the result of innovation, including inventions and technological developments.* Cultural innovations can create dramatic changes in society. Think, for example, of how the invention of trolleys, subways, and automobiles changed the character of cities. People no longer walked to work; instead, cities expanded outward to include suburbs. Furthermore, the invention of the elevator let cities expand not just out, but up.

Now the development of computer technology infiltrates every dimension of life. It is hard to overestimate the effect of innovation on contemporary cultural change. Technological innovation is so rapid and dynamic that one generation can barely maintain competence with the hardware of the next. The smallest laptop or handheld computer today weighs hardly more than a few ounces, and its capabilities rival that of computers that filled entire buildings only twenty years ago. Downloading music was not even imaginable just a few years ago; now it is a common practice.

What are some of the social changes that technology change is creating? People can now work and be miles—even nations—away from their places of employment. Families can communicate from multiple sites; children can be paged; grandparents can receive live photos of a family event; criminals are tracked via cellular technology; music can be stolen without even going in to a music store. Conveniences multiply with the growth of such technology, but so do the invasions of privacy and, perhaps, identity theft.

## a sociological eye on the media

### The Blogging Culture

With the widespread use of the Internet, a new form of culture has emerged: the blog. A *blog* (short for "web log") is a chronological display of entries that people make on the Internet on topics that can be about anything, but most often involve politics or popular culture. A blog is an active diary of sorts in which multiple people participate, either as those who make the entries ("bloggers") or those who simply read them.

This new cultural phenomenon raises interesting questions for sociological research. Studies of blogs to date find, for example, that women are a small proportion of bloggers—only 10 percent of the bloggers on the most widely used political sites. Some use blogs as support systems—for example, a gay person in a very traditional and isolated community may participate in a blog that provides a national community of support. One study in China found that many women are using blogs to subvert traditional concepts of womanhood.

Blogs are also increasingly important in political organizing—not just in mainstream campaigns but in grassroots movements. The presidential campaign of President Barack Obama is a case in point. The extensive and innovative use of blogs and the Internet in the Obama campaign has been widely heralded as contributing to his support—especially among young, Internet-savvy voters.

The use of blogs is a good example of how technological innovation can create new forms of culture. Unlike traditional communities, blogging communities can cross vast geographic distances that connect people who might not ever meet face to face. Just as town meetings might have created a sense of community in the past, cyberspace communities can now create new "imagined communities." Some suggest that blogs can actually create a more democratic society by directly engaging more people in political discussion and activity.

*Sources:* Dolan, Jill. 2006. "Blogging on Queer Connections in the Arts and the Five Lesbian Brothers." *GLQ* 12: 491–506; Harp, Dustin, and Mark Tremayne. 2006. "The Gendered Blogosphere: Examining Inequality Using Network and Feminist Theory." *Journalism & Mass Communication Quarterly* 83: 247-264; Lawson-Borders, Gracie, and Rita Kirk. 2005. "Blogs in Campaign Communication." *American Behavioral Scientist* 49: 548-559; Macdougall, Robert. 2005. "Identity, Electronic Ethos, and Blogs: A Technologic Analysis of Symbolic Exchange on the New News Medium." *American Behavioral Scientist* 49: 575-599; Schaffer, Kay, and Song Xianlin. 2007. "Unruly Spaces: Gender, Women's Writing and Indigenous Feminism in China." *Journal of Gender Studies* 16 (1): 17-30; Perlmutter, David. 2008. *Blogwars: The New Political Battleground.* New York: Oxford University Press.

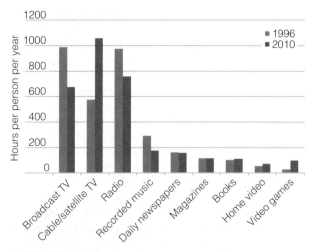

**FIGURE 2.5** *The Changing Use of the Media*

*Data:* U.S. Census Bureau. 2009a. *The 2009 Statistical Abstract*. Washington, DC: U.S. Department of Commerce, p. 695.

*Notes:* Does not include Internet-related use of traditional media.

Examples include music downloaded from a computer, reading downloaded to e-books, listening to radio via the Internet, reading web-based newspapers, and so forth.

In such a rapidly changing technological world, it is hard to imagine what will be common in just a few years.

4. *Cultural change can be imposed.* Change can occur when a powerful group takes over a society and imposes a new culture. The dominating group may arise internally, as in a political revolution, or it may appear from outside, perhaps as an invasion. When an external group takes over the society of a "native," or indigenous, group—as White settlers did with Native American societies—they typically impose their own culture while prohibiting the indigenous group from expressing its original cultural ways. Manipulating the culture of a group is a way of exerting social control. Many have argued that public education in the United States, which developed during a period of mass immigration, was designed to force White, northern European, middle-class values onto a diverse immigrant population that was perceived to be potentially unruly and politically disruptive. Likewise, the schools run by the Bureau of Indian Affairs have been used to impose dominant group values on Native American children (Snipp 1996).

Resistance to political oppression often takes the form of a cultural movement that asserts or revives the culture of an oppressed group; thus, cultural expression can be a form of political protest. Identification with a common culture can be the basis for group solidarity, as found in the example of the "Black is beautiful" movement in the 1970s that encouraged Black Americans to celebrate their African heritage with Afro hairstyles, African dress, and African awareness. Cultural solidarity has also been encouraged among Latinos through La Raza Unida (meaning "the race," or "the people, united"). Cultural change can promote social change, just as social change can transform culture.

## Chapter Summary

- **What is culture?**

*Culture* is the complex and elaborate system of meaning and behavior that defines the way of life for a group or society. It is shared, learned, taken for granted, symbolic, and emergent and varies from one society to another.

- **How do sociologists define norms, beliefs, and values?**

*Norms* are rules of social behavior that guide every situation and may be formal or informal. When norms are violated, *social sanctions* are applied. *Beliefs* are strongly shared ideas about the nature of social reality. *Values* are the abstract concepts in a society that define the worth of different things and ideas.

- **What is the significance of diversity in human cultures?**

As societies develop and become more complex, cultural diversity can appear. The United States is highly diverse culturally, with many of its traditions influenced by immigrant cultures and the cultures of African Americans, Latinos, and Native Americans. The *dominant culture* is the culture of the most powerful group in society. *Subcultures* are groups whose *values* and cultural patterns depart significantly from the *dominant culture*.

- *What is the sociological significance of the mass media and popular culture?*

  Elements of popular culture, such as the *mass media,* have an enormous influence on groups' beliefs and values, including images associated with racism and sexism. *Popular culture* includes the beliefs, practices, and objects of everyday traditions.

- *What do different sociological theories reveal about culture?*

  Sociological theory provides different perspectives on the significance of culture. *Functionalist theory* emphasizes the influence of values, norms, and beliefs on the whole society. *Conflict theorists* see culture as influenced by economic interests and power relations in society. *Symbolic interactionists* emphasize that culture is socially constructed. This has influenced new cultural studies, which interpret culture as a series of images that can be analyzed from the viewpoint of different observers.

- *How do cultures change?*

  There are several sources of cultural change, including change in societal conditions, *cultural diffusion,* innovation, and the imposition of change by dominant groups. As cultures change, *culture lag* can result, meaning that sometimes cultural adjustments are out of synchrony with each other. Persons who experience new cultural situations may experience *culture shock.*

# Key Terms

| | | |
|---|---|---|
| beliefs 36 | ethnocentrism 40 | norms 34 |
| counterculture 40 | ethnomethodology 36 | popular culture 43 |
| cultural capital 48 | folkways 34 | reflection hypothesis 46 |
| cultural diffusion 50 | global culture 41 | Sapir–Whorf hypothesis 32 |
| cultural hegemony 42 | language 31 | social sanctions 35 |
| cultural relativism 41 | laws 35 | subculture 39 |
| culture 27 | mass media 42 | symbols 29 |
| culture lag 50 | material culture 27 | taboo 35 |
| culture shock 50 | mores 35 | values 36 |
| dominant culture 38 | nonmaterial culture 27 | |

# Online Resources

## *Sociology: The Essentials* Companion Website

**www.cengage.com/sociology/andersen**
Visit your book companion website where you will find more resources to help you study and write your research papers. Resources include web links, learning objectives, Internet exercises, quizzing, and flash cards.

 **is an easy-to-use online resource that helps you study in less time to get the grade you want NOW.**

**www.cengage.com/login**
Need help studying? This site is your one-stop study shop. Take a Pre-Test and Cengage NOW will generate a Personalized Study Plan based on your test results. The Study Plan will identify the topics you need to review and direct you to online resources to help you master those topics. You can then take a Post-Test to determine the concepts you have mastered and what you still need to work on.

Chapter three
CHAPTER THREE

# Doing Sociological Research

**The Research Process**

**The Tools of Sociological Research**

**Research Ethics: Is Sociology Value Free?**

**Chapter Summary**

[

*You have now* seen some of the interesting things sociologists study through a glimpse into the sociology of culture. You also have a basic foundation in sociological perspective and the major concepts in the field. We turn now to the tools sociologists use to study social phenomena: the tools of sociological research methods. These tools are varied, and the best tool to use depends on the sociological question that is being asked. Let us start with this example.

Suppose you wanted to do some sociological research on how homeless people lived. What is life like for them? How dangerous is it? Where are the homeless to be found? Do they interact and associate with each other? Do they work at all, and if so, doing what? Do they feel rejected by society? Do they really sleep on park benches at night?

Sociologist Mitch Duneier (1999) in his study entitled "Sidewalk" wanted to know all these things, plus more. So he decided to study a group of homeless people by living with them. And that is exactly what he did. He lived with them on their park benches and in doorways on New York City's lower East Side. He spent four years with them. He interacted with them. He worked with them—a group consisting largely of African American men who sold books and magazines on the street. Duneier himself is White: He tells how becoming accepted into this society of African American men was itself an interesting process. Contrary to popular belief, he discovered that these men make up a rather well-organized mini-society, with a social status structure, rules, norms, and a culture. He discovered many unknown elements of this "sidewalk society."

*continued*

Richard G. Bingham II/Alamy

Duneier used a method of sociological research called *participant observation*. In this chapter we examine this method plus other methods of sociological research. Each method is different from the others, but they all share a common goal: a deeper understanding of how society operates.

# The Research Process

Sociological research is the tool sociologists use to answer questions. There are various methods that sociologists use to do research, all of which involve rigorous observation and careful analysis.

As we saw in the chapter opener, sociologist Mitch Duneier (1999) examined several questions about a group of homeless people by living with them. Duneier was engaged in what is called **participant observation**—a sociological research technique in which the researcher actually becomes simultaneously both participant in and observer of that which she or he studies. In another example of participant observation, sociologist Peter Moskos (2008), as research for his doctoral dissertation, actually went through a police academy and spent two years as a beat policeman in a major American city, thus subjecting himself to both the rigid discipline of the police force as well as the dangers of the street in this role.

There are other kinds of sociological research that sociologists do as well. Some approaches are more structured and focused than participant observation, such as survey research. Other methods may involve the use of official records or interviews. The different approaches used reflect the different questions asked in the first place. Other methods may require statistical analysis of a large set of quantitative information. Either way, the chosen research method must be appropriate to the sociological question being asked. (In the Doing Sociological Research boxes throughout this book, we explore different research projects that sociologists have done, showing what question they started with, how they did their research, and what they found.)

However it is done, research is an engaging and demanding process. It requires skill, careful observation, and the ability to think logically about the things that spark your sociological curiosity.

## Sociology and the Scientific Method

Sociological research derives from what is called the *scientific method,* originally defined and elaborated by the British philosopher **Sir Francis Bacon** (1561–1626). The **scientific method** involves several steps in a research process, including observation, hypothesis testing, analysis of data, and generalization. Since its beginnings, sociology has attempted to adhere to the scientific method. To the

degree that it has succeeded, sociology is a science; yet, there is also an art to developing sociological knowledge. Sociology aspires to be both scientific and humanistic, but sociological research varies in how strictly it adheres to the scientific method. Some sociologists test hypotheses (discussed later); others use more open-ended methods, such as in Duneier's study of homeless men or in Moskos's study of police officers on the beat.

Science is empirical, meaning it is based on careful and systematic observation, not just on conjecture. Although some sociological studies are highly *quantitative* and statistically sophisticated, others are *qualitatively* based, that is, based on more interpretive observations, not statistical analysis. Both quantitative and qualitative studies are empirical. Sociological studies may be based on surveys, observations, and many other forms of analysis, but they always depend on an empirical underpinning.

Sociological knowledge is not the same as philosophy or personal belief. Philosophy, theology, and personal experience can deliver insights into human behavior, but at the heart of the scientific method is the notion that a theory must be testable. This requirement distinguishes science from purely humanistic pursuits such as theology and literature.

One wellspring of sociological insight is **deductive reasoning.** When a sociologist uses deductive reasoning, he or she creates a specific research question about a focused point that is based on a more general or universal principle (see Figure 3.1). Here is an example of deductive reasoning: One might reason that because Catholic doctrine forbids abortion, Catholics would then

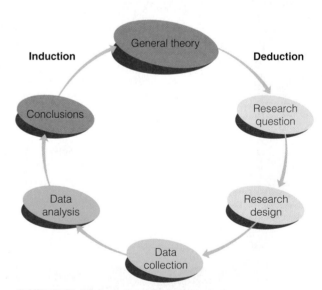

**FIGURE 3.1** *The Research Process*

*Research can begin by asking a research question derived from general theory or earlier studies, but it can also begin with an observation or even from the conclusion of prior research. One's research question is the basis for a research design and the subsequent collection of data. As this figure shows, the steps in the research process flow logically from what is being asked.*

be less likely than other religious groups to support abortion rights. This notion is "deduced" from a general principle (Catholic doctrine). You could test this notion (the research question) via a survey. As it turns out, the testing of this hypothesis shows that it is incorrect: Surveys show that Catholics are more likely to support abortion rights than are other religious groups.

**Inductive reasoning**—another source of sociological insight—reverses this logic: that is, it arrives at general conclusions from specific observations. For example, if you observe that most of the demonstrators protesting abortion in front of a family planning clinic are evangelical Christians, you might infer that strongly held religious beliefs are important in determining human behavior. Again, referring to Figure 3.1, inductive reasoning would begin with one's observations. Either way—deductively or inductively—you are engaged in research.

## Research Design

When sociologists do research, they engage in a process of discovery. They organize their research questions and procedures systematically—their research site being the social world. Through research, sociologists organize their observations and interpret them.

**Developing a Research Question.** Sociological research is an organized practice that can be described in a series of steps (see Figure 3.1). The first step in sociological research is to develop a research question. One source of research questions is past research. For any number of reasons, the sociologist might disagree with a research finding and decide to carry out further research or develop a detailed criticism of previous research. A research question can also begin from an observation that you make in everyday life, such as wondering about the lives of homeless people.

Developing a sociological research question typically involves reviewing existing studies on the subject, such as past research reports or articles. This process is often called a *literature review*. Digital technology has vastly simplified the task of reviewing past studies, that is, the "literature." Researchers who once had to burrow through paper indexes and card catalogs to find material relevant to their studies can now scan much larger swaths of material in far less time using online databases. The catalogs of most major libraries in the world are accessible on the Internet, as are specialized indexes, discussion groups, and other research tools developed to assist sociological researchers.

Increasingly, many journals that report new sociological research are now available online in full-text format. You must be careful using the Internet for research, however. How do you know when something found on the Web is valid or true? Much of what is found on the Web is invalid, that is, unsubstantiated by accurate research or empirical study. Pay attention, for example, to what person or group has

*The research process involves several operations that can be performed on the computer, such as entering data in numerical form and writing the findings in a research report.*

posted the website. Is it a political organization? An organization promoting a cause? A person expressing an opinion? See the box "A Sociological Eye on the Media: Research and the Media" on page 60 for some guidelines about interpreting what you see on the Web and in the media.

When you review prior research, you may wonder if the same results would be found if the study were repeated, perhaps examining a different group or studying the phenomenon at a different time. Research that is repeated exactly, but on a different group of people or in a different time or place, is called a **replication study.** Suppose earlier research found that women managers have fewer opportunities for promotion than do men. You might want to know if this still holds true. You would then replicate the original study, probably using a different group of women and men managers, but asking the same questions that were asked earlier. A replication study can tell you what changes have occurred since the original study and may also refine the results of the earlier work. Research findings should be reproducible; if research is sound, other researchers who repeat a study should get the same results unless, of course, some change has occurred in the interim.

Sociological research questions can also come from casual observation of human behavior. Perhaps you have observed the seating patterns in your college dining hall at lunch and wondered why people sit with the same group day after day. Does the answer point to similarity on the basis of race, gender, age, or perhaps political views? Answering this question would be an example of inductive reasoning: going from a specific observation (such as seating patterns at lunch) to a generalization (a theory about the effects of race and gender).

**Creating a Research Design.** A research **design** is the overall logic and strategy underlying a research project. Sociologists engaged in research may distribute questionnaires, interview people, or make direct observations in a social setting or laboratory. They might analyze cultural artifacts, such as magazines, newspapers, television shows, or other media. Some do research using historical records. Others base their work on the analysis of social policy. All these are forms of sociological observation. Research design consists of choosing the observational technique best suited to a particular research question.

## thinkingsociologically

If you wanted to conduct research that would examine the relationship between student alcohol use and family background, what measures, or *indicators*, would you use to get at the two variables: alcohol use and family background? How might you *design* your study?

Suppose you wanted to study the career goals of student athletes. In reviewing earlier studies, perhaps you found research discussing how athletics is related to academic achievement (Messner 1992; Schacht 1996). You might also have read an article in your student newspaper reporting that the rate of graduation for women college athletes is much higher than the rate for men athletes and wondered if women athletes are better students than men athletes. In other words, are athletic participation, academic achievement, and gender interrelated, and if so, how?

Your research design would lay out a plan for investigating these questions. Which athletes would

Some research is done by analyzing the content of various cultural artifacts. Content analysis is one tool of sociological research.

you study? How will you study them? To begin, you will need to get sound data on the graduation rates of the groups you are studying to verify that your assumption of better graduation rates among women athletes is actually true. Perhaps, you think, the differences between men and women are not so great when the men and women play the same sports. Or perhaps the differences depend on other factors, such as what kind of financial support they get or whether coaches encourage academic success. To observe the influence of coaches, you might observe interactions between coaches and student athletes, recording what coaches say about class work. As you proceed, you would probably refine your research design and even your research question. Do coaches encourage different traits in men and women athletes? To answer this question, you have to build into your research design a comparison of coaches interacting with men and with women. Perhaps you even want to compare female and male coaches and how they interact with women and men. *The details of your research design flow from the specific questions you ask.*

### Quantitative Versus Qualitative Research.

The research design often involves deciding whether the research will be qualitative or quantitative or perhaps some combination of both. **Quantitative research** is that which uses numerical analysis. In essence, this approach reduces the data into numbers, for example, the percentage of teenage mothers in California. **Qualitative research** is somewhat less structured than quantitative research, yet still focuses on a central research question. Qualitative

Surveys and polls are a tool for sociological research. Here, presidential candidate Barack Obama is the winner of an election-night "exit poll" in the state of South Carolina. Exit polls gather the information from respondents as soon as they leave the polling place.

research allows for more interpretation and nuance in what people say and do and thus can provide an in-depth look at a particular social behavior. Both forms of research are useful, and both are used extensively in sociology.

Some research designs involve the testing of **hypotheses.** A hypothesis (pronounced "hy-POTH-i-sis") is a prediction or a hunch, a tentative assumption that one intends to test. If you have a research design that calls for the investigation of a very specific hunch, you might formulate a hypothesis. Hypotheses are often formulated as if–then statements. For example:

> *Hypothesis:* If a person's parents are racially prejudiced, then that person will, on average, be more prejudiced than a person whose parents are relatively free of prejudice.

This is merely a hypothesis or expectation, not a demonstration of fact. Having phrased a hypothesis, the sociologist must then determine if it is true or false. To test the preceding example, one might take a large sample of people and determine their prejudice level by interviews or some other mechanism. One would then determine the prejudice level of their parents. According to the hypothesis, one would expect to find more prejudiced children among prejudiced parents and more nonprejudiced children among nonprejudiced parents. If this association is found, the hypothesis is supported. If it is not found, then the hypothesis would be rejected.

Not all sociological research follows the model of hypothesis testing, but all research does include a plan for how **data** will be gathered. (Note that *data* is the plural form; one says, "data are used ...," not "data is used ....") Data can be qualitative or quantitative; either way, they are still data. Sociologists often try to convert their observations into a quantitative form (see the "Statistics in Sociology" box on page 64).

Sociologists frequently design research to test the influence of one variable on another. A **variable** is a characteristic that can have more than one value or score. A variable can be relatively straightforward, such as age or income, or a variable may be more abstract, such as social class or degree of prejudice. In much sociological research, variables are analyzed to understand how they influence each other. With proper measurement techniques and a good research design, the relationships between different variables can be discerned. In the example of student athletes given above, the variables you use would likely be student graduation rates, gender, and perhaps the sport played. In the hypothesis about race prejudice, parental prejudice and their child's prejudice would be the two variables you would study.

An **independent variable** (see Figure 3.2) is one that the researcher wants to test as the presumed cause of something else. The **dependent variable** is one on which there is a presumed effect. That is, if $X$ is the independent variable, then $X$ leads to $Y$, the dependent variable. In the previous example of the hypothesis, the amount of prejudice of the parent is the independent variable, and the amount of prejudice of the child is the dependent variable. In some sociological research, *intervening variables* are also studied—variables that fall between the independent and dependent variables.

Sociological research proceeds through the study of concepts. A **concept** is any abstract characteristic or attribute that can potentially be measured. Social class and social power are concepts. These are not things that can be seen directly, although they are key concepts in the field of sociology. When sociologists want to study concepts, they must develop ways of "seeing" them.

Variables are sometimes used to show more abstract concepts that cannot be directly measured, such as the concept of social class. In such cases the variables are **indicators**—something that points to or reflects an abstract concept. An indicator is a way of "seeing" a concept. An example is shown in Map 3.1 (page 62) on the United Nations' human development index. Here, the human development index is composed of several *indicators,* including life expectancy and educational attainment, combined to show levels of well-being. "Level of well-being" is the *concept.*

The **validity** of a measurement (an indicator) is the degree to which it accurately measures or reflects a concept. To ensure the validity of their findings, researchers usually use more than one indicator for a particular concept. If two or more chosen measures of a concept give similar results, it is likely that the measurements are giving an accurate—that is, valid—depiction of the concept. For example, using a person's occupation, years of formal education, and annual earnings—namely, using three indicators of her or his social class—would likely be more valid than using only one indicator.

Sociologists also must be concerned with the **reliability** of their research results. A measurement is reliable if repeating the measurement under the same circumstances gives the same result. If a person is given a test daily and every day the test gives different results, then the reliability of the test is poor. One way to ensure that sociological measurements are reliable is to use measures that have proved sound in past studies. Another technique is to have

**FIGURE 3.2** *The Analysis of Variables*

*Sociological research seeks to find out whether some independent variable (X) affects an intervening variable (Z), which in turn affects a dependent variable (Y).*

a variety of people gather the data to make certain the results are not skewed by the tester's appearance, personality, and so forth. The researcher must be sensitive to all factors that affect the reliability of a study.

Sometimes sociologists want to gather data that would almost certainly be unreliable if the subjects (the people in the study) knew they were being stud-ied. Knowing that they are being studied might cause people to change their behavior, a phenomenon in research known as the *Hawthorne effect*—an effect first discovered while observing work groups at a Western Electric plant in Hawthorne, Illinois. The work groups increased their productivity right after they were observed by the researchers—an effect not noticed at first by the researchers themselves.

# a sociological eye
# on the media

## Research and the Media

On any given day, if you watch the news, read a newspaper, or search the Web, you are likely to learn about various new research studies purporting some new finding. How do you know if the research results reported in the media are accurate?

Most people are not likely to check the details of the study or have the research skills to verify the study's claims. But one benefit of learning the basic concepts and tools of sociological research is to be able to critically assess the research frequently reported in the media. The following questions will help.

1. **What are the major variables in the study? Are the researchers claiming a causal connection between two or more variables?** For example, the press reported that one way parents can reduce the chances of their children becoming sexually active at an early age is to quit smoking (O'Neil 2002). The researcher who conducted this study actually claimed there was no direct link between parental smoking and teen sex, although she did find a correlation between parents' risky behaviors—smoking, heavy drinking, and not using seat belts—and children's sexual activity. She argued that parents who engage in unsafe activities provide a model for their children's own risky behavior (Wilder and Watt 2002).

   Just because there is a link, or "correlation," between two variables does not necessarily mean one caused the other. Seeing parental behavior as a model for what children do is hardly the same thing as seeing parents' smoking as the cause of early sexual activity!

2. **How have researchers defined and measured the major topics of their study?** For example, if someone claims that 10 percent of all people are gay, how is "being gay" defined? Does it mean having had only one such experience over one's entire lifetime or does it mean actually having a gay identity? The difference matters because one definition will likely inflate the number reported. Sometimes you must look up the original study, which may be online, to learn how things are defined or how they are measured. Ask yourself if the same conclusions would be reached had the researchers used different definitions and measurements.

3. **Is the research based on a truly random scientific sample, or is it biased?** You might have to go to the original source of the study to learn this, but often the sample will be reported in the press (even if in nonscientific language). For example, a study widely reported in the media had headlines exclaiming: "Study Links Working Mothers to Slower Learning" (Lewin 2002). But, if you read even the news report closely, you will learn that this study included only White, non-Hispanic families. Black and Hispanic children were dropped from some of the published results because there were too few cases in the sample to make meaningful statistical comparisons (Brooks-Gunn et al. 2002). Another study by the same research team found that there were no significant effects of mother's employment on children's intellectual development among African American or Hispanic children (Waldfogel et al. 2002). The point is not that the study is invalid, but that its results have more limited implications than the headlines suggest.

4. **Is there false generalization in the media report?** Often a study has more limited claims in the scientific version than what is reported in the media. Using the example just given about the connection between maternal employment and children's learning, it would be a big mistake to generalize from the study's results to all children and families. Remember that some groups were

An example of this effect would be a professor who wants to measure student attentiveness by observing how many notes are taken during class. Students who know they are being scrutinized will magically become more diligent!

**Gathering Data.** After research design comes data collection. During this stage of the research process, the researcher interviews people, observes behaviors, or collects facts that throw light on the research question. When sociologists gather original material, the product is known as *primary data*. Examples include the answers to questionnaires or notes made while observing group behavior. Sociologists often rely on *secondary data,* namely data that have already been gathered and organized by some other party. This can include national opinion polls, census data, national crime statistics, or data from an earlier study made available by the original researcher. Secondary data may also come from official sources, such as university records, city or county records, national health statistics, or historical records.

not included. Even within the study, the researchers found less effect due to mothers' employment in female-headed households than among married couples. You cannot generalize the findings reported in the media to all families.

5. **Can the study be replicated?** Unless there is full disclosure of the research methodology (that is, how the study was conducted), this will not be possible. But you can ask yourself how the study was conducted, whether the procedures used were reasonable and logical, and whether the researchers made good decisions in constructing their research question and research design.

6. **Who sponsored the study and do they have a vested interest in the study's results?** Find out if a group or organization with a particular vested interest in the outcome sponsors the research. For example, would you give as much validity to a study of environmental pollution that was funded and secretly conducted by a chemical company as you would a study on the same topic conducted by independent scientists who openly report their research methods and results? Research sponsored by interested parties does not necessarily negate research findings, but it can raise questions about the researchers' objectivity and the standards of inquiry they used.

7. **Who benefits from the study's conclusions?** Although this question does not necessarily challenge the study's findings, it can help you think about whom the findings are likely to help.

8. **What assumptions did the researchers have to make to ask the question they did?** For example, if you started from the assumption that poverty is not the individual's fault, but is the result of how society is structured, would you study the values of the poor or perhaps the values of policymakers? When research

studies explore matters where social values influence people's opinions, it is especially important to identify the assumptions made by certain questions.

9. **What are the implications of the study's claims?** Thinking through the policy implications of a given result can often help you see things in a new light, particularly given how the media tend to sensationalize much of what is reported.

    Consider the study of maternal employment and children's intellectual development examined in question 3 above. If you take the media headlines at face value, you might leap to the conclusion that working mothers hurt their children's intellectual development, and you might then think it would be best if mothers quit their jobs and stayed at home. But is this a reasonable implication of this study? Does the study not have just as many implications for day-care policies as it does for encouraging stay-at-home mothers? Especially when reported research studies involve politically charged topics (such as issues of "family values"), it is important to ask questions that explore various implications of social policies.

10. **Do these questions mean you should never believe anything you hear in the media?** Of course not. Thinking critically about research does not mean being negative or cynical about everything you hear or read. The point is not to reject all media claims out of hand, but instead to be able to evaluate good versus bad research. All research has limitations. Learning the basic tools of research, even if you never conduct research yourself or pursue a career where you would use such skills, can make you a better-informed citizen and prevent you from being duped by claims that are neither scientifically nor sociologically valid.

## map3.1 | VIEWING SOCIETY IN GLOBAL PERSPECTIVE

### The Human Development Index

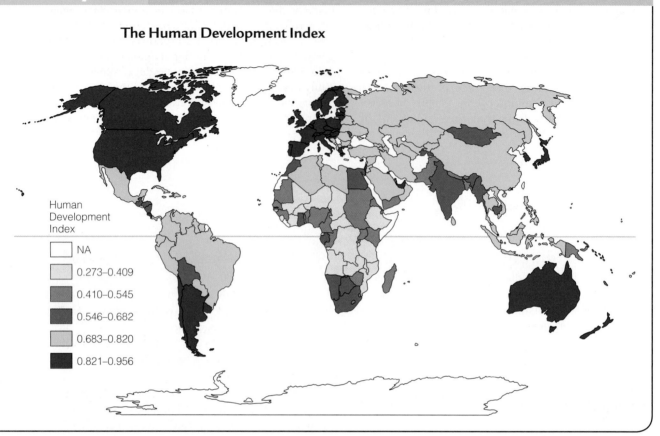

Human
Development
Index

| | |
|---|---|
| ☐ | NA |
| ☐ | 0.273–0.409 |
| ☐ | 0.410–0.545 |
| ☐ | 0.546–0.682 |
| ☐ | 0.683–0.820 |
| ☐ | 0.821–0.956 |

*The human development index is a series of indicators developed by the United Nations and used to show the differing levels of well-being in nations around the world. The index is calculated using a number of indicators, including life expectancy, educational attainment, and standard of living. (Are these reasonable indicators of well-being? What else might you use?)*

*Data:* United Nations. 2007. *Human Development Annual Report 2007.* **www.undp.org**

*Rhoda Sidney/PhotoEdit*

*A census taker interviews a man in his home.*

When gathering data, often the groups that sociologists want to study are so large or so dispersed that research on the whole group is impossible. To construct a picture of the entire group, sociologists take data from a subset of the group and extrapolate to get a picture of the whole. A **sample** is any subset of people (or groups or categories) of a population. A **population** is a relatively large collection of people (or groups or categories) that a researcher studies and about which generalizations are made. Suppose a sociologist wants to study the students at your school. All the students together constitute the population being studied. A survey could be done that reached every student, but conducting a detailed interview with every student would be highly impractical. If the sociologist wants the sort of information that can be gathered only during a personal interview, she would study only a portion, or sample, of all the students at your school.

How is it possible to draw accurate conclusions about a population by studying only part of it?

The secret lies in making sure that the sample is *representative* of the population as a whole. The sample should have the same mix of people as the larger population and in the same proportions. If the sample is representative, then the researcher can *generalize* what she finds from the sample to the entire population. For example, if she interviews a sample of 100 students and finds that 10 percent of them are in favor of a tuition increase, and if the sample is representative of the population, then she can conclude that about 10 percent of *all* the students at your school are in favor of a tuition increase. Note that a sample of 5 or 6 students would probably result in generalizations of poor quality, because the sample is not large enough to be representative. A *biased* (nonrepresentative) sample can lead to grossly inaccurate conclusions.

The best way to ensure a representative sample is to make certain that the sample population is selected randomly. A scientific **random sample** gives everyone in the population an equal chance of being selected. Quite often, striking and controversial research findings prove to be distorted by inadequate sampling. The man-on-the-street survey, much favored by radio and TV news reports, and certain other media as well, is the least-scientific type of sample and the least representative.

**Analyzing the Data.** After the data have been collected, whether primary or secondary data, they must be analyzed. **Data analysis** is the process by which sociologists organize collected data to discover the patterns and uniformities that the data reveal. The analysis may be statistical or qualitative. When the data analysis is completed, conclusions and generalizations can be made.

Data analysis is labor intensive, but it is also an exciting phase of research. Here is where research discoveries are made. Sometimes while pursuing one question, a researcher will stumble across an unexpected finding, referred to by researchers as **serendipity.** A serendipitous finding is something that emerges from a study that was not anticipated, perhaps the discovery of an association between two variables that the researcher was not looking for or some pattern of behavior that was outside the scope of the research design. Such findings can be minor sidelines to the researcher's major conclusions or, in some cases, lead to major new discoveries. They are part of the excitement of doing sociological research.

**Reaching Conclusions and Reporting Results.** The final stage in research is developing conclusions, relating findings to sociological theory and past research, and reporting the findings. An important question researchers will ask at this stage is whether their findings can be generalized. **Generalization** is the ability to draw conclusions from specific data and to apply them to a broader population.

Researchers ask, do my results apply only to those people who were studied, or do they also apply to the world beyond? Assuming that the results have wide application, the researcher can then ask if the findings refine or refute existing theories and whether the research has direct application to social issues. Using the earlier example of the relationship between parent and offspring prejudice, if you found that racially prejudiced people did tend to have racially prejudiced parents (thus supporting your hypothesis), then you might report these results in a paper or research report. You might also ask, what kinds of programs for reducing prejudice do the results of your study suggest?

# The Tools of Sociological Research

There are several tools or techniques sociologists use to gather data. Among the most widely used are survey research, participant observation, controlled experiments, content analysis, historical research, and evaluation research.

## The Survey: Polls, Questionnaires, and Interviews

Whether in the form of a questionnaire, interview, or telephone poll, surveys are among the most commonly used tools of sociological research. Questionnaires are typically distributed to large groups of people. The *return rate* is the percentage of questionnaires returned out of all those distributed. A low return rate introduces possible bias because the small number of responses may not be representative of the whole group.

Like questionnaires, interviews provide a structured way to ask people questions. They may be conducted face to face, by phone, even by electronic mail (email). Interview questions may be open-ended or closed-ended, though the open-ended form is particularly accommodating if respondents wish to elaborate.

Typically, a survey questionnaire will solicit data about the respondent, such as income, occupation or employment status (employed or unemployed), years of formal education, yearly income, age, race, and gender, coupled with additional questions that throw light upon a particular research question. For *closed-ended* questions, people must reply from a list of possible answers, like a multiple choice test. For *open-ended* questions, the respondent is allowed to elaborate on her or his answer. Closed-ended questions are generally analyzed quantitatively, and open-ended questions are generally analyzed qualitatively.

# Statistics in Sociology

### Certain fundamental statistical concepts are basic to sociological research

Although not all sociologists do quantitative research, basic statistics are important to interpreting sociological studies.

A **percentage** is the same as parts per hundred. To say that 22 percent of U.S. children are poor tells you that for every 100 children randomly selected from the whole population, approximately 22 will be poor. A **rate** is the same as parts per some number, such as per 10,000 or 100,000. The homicide rate in 2007 was about 6.0, meaning that for every 100,000 people in the population, approximately 6 were murdered (Federal Bureau of Investigation 2008). A rate is meaningless without knowing the numeric base on which it is founded; it is always the number per some other number.

A **mean** is the same as an average. Adding a list of fifteen numbers and dividing by fifteen gives the mean. The **median** is often confused with the mean but is actually quite different. The median is the midpoint in a series of values arranged in numeric order. In a list of fifteen numbers arrayed in numeric order, the eighth number (the middle number) is the median. In some cases, the median is a better measure than the mean because the mean can be skewed ("pulled" up or down) by extremes at either end. Another often-used measure is the **mode,** which is simply the value (or score) that appears most frequently in a set of data.

Let's illustrate the difference between mean and median using national income distribution as an example. Suppose that you have a group of ten people. Two make $10,000 per year, seven make $40,000 per year, and one makes $1 million per year. If you calculate the mean (the average), it comes to $130,000. The median, on the other hand, is $40,000—a figure that more accurately suggests the income profile of the group. That single million-a-year earner dramatically distorts, or skews, the picture of the group's income. If we want information about how the group in general lives, we are wiser to use the median income figure as a rough guide, not the mean. Note also that in this example the mode is the same as the median: $40,000.

Sociologists frequently examine the relationship between two variables. **Correlation** is a widely used technique for analyzing the patterns of association, or correlation, between pairs of variables such as income and education. We might begin with a questionnaire that asks for annual earnings (which we designate as the dependent variable, $Y$) and level of education (the independent variable, $X$). Correlation analysis delivers two dimensions of information: It tells us the "direction" of the relationship between $X$ and $Y$ and also the strength of that relationship. The direction of a relationship is *positive* (that is, a positive correlation exists) if $X$ is low when $Y$ is low *and* if $X$ is high when $Y$ is high. But there is also a correlation if $Y$ is low when $X$ is high (or vice versa); this is a *negative*, or inverse, correlation. The strength of a correlation is simply how closely or tightly the variables are associated, regardless of the direction of correlation.

A correlation does not necessarily imply cause and effect. A correlation is simply an association, one whose cause must be explained by means other than simple correlation analysis. A **spurious correlation** exists when there is no meaningful causal connection between apparently associated variables.

Another widely used method of analyzing sociological data is **cross-tabulation,** a way of seeing if two variables are related by breaking them down into categories for comparison. Take the following example. In a Gallup Poll (2006), the following question was asked: "Do you feel that the laws covering the sale of firearms should be

Thus a survey can involve both qualitative as well as quantitative research.

As a research tool, surveys make it possible to ask specific questions about a large number of topics and then to perform sophisticated analyses to find patterns and relationships among variables. The disadvantages of surveys arise from their rigidity (see Table 3.1, page 68). Responses may not accurately capture the opinions of the respondent or may fail to capture nuances in people's behavior and attitudes. Also, what people say and what they do are not always the same. Survey researchers must be persistent in order to get answers that are truthful, one reason for allowing respondents to be anonymous.

made more strict, or less strict? "The following results, a cross-tabulation of answers to the question (the dependent variable) by gender (the independent variable) were obtained:

|          | More strict: | Less strict: |
|----------|:------------:|:------------:|
| *Women:* | 70%          | 30%          |
| *Men:*   | 54%          | 46%          |

*Source:* **www.gallup.com/poll/indicators**

As you can see from this cross-tabulation, women and men differed on the question. In general, men wanted less strict laws than did women. This means that the two variables—gender and the answer to the question—are related.

Statistical information is notoriously easy to misinterpret, willfully or accidentally. Examples of some statistical mistakes include the following:

- **Citing a correlation as a cause.** A correlation reveals an association between things (variables). Correlations do not necessarily indicate that one causes the other. Sociologists often say "Correlation is not proof of causation."

- **Overgeneralizing.** Statistical findings are limited by the extent to which the sample group actually reflects or represents the population from which the sample was obtained. Generalizing beyond the population is a misuse of statistics. Studying only men and then generalizing conclusions to both men and women would be an example of overgeneralizing. This kind of mistake is not uncommon in the media and also in some sociological research.

- **Interpreting probability as certainty.** Probability is a statement about chance or likelihood only. For example, in the cross-tabulation given above, women are more *likely* than men to favor strict gun control. This means that women have a higher probability (a greater chance) of favoring strict gun control than men; it does *not* mean that all women favor strict gun control, or that all men do not.

- **Building in bias.** In a famous advertising campaign, public taste tests were offered between two soft drinks. A wily journalist verified that in at least one site, the brand sold by the sponsor of the test was a few degrees colder than its competitor when it was given to the people being tested, which biased the results. Bias can also be built into studies by careless wording on questionnaires.

- **Faking data.** Perhaps one of the worse misuses of statistics is actually making up, or faking, data. A famous instance of this occurred in a study of identical twins who were separated early in life and raised apart (Burt 1966). The researcher wished to show that despite their separation, the twins remained highly similar in certain traits, such as measured intelligence (IQ), thus suggesting that their (identical) genes caused their striking similarity in intelligence. It was later shown that the data were fabricated (Kamin 1974; Hearnshaw 1979; Taylor 1980; Mackintosh 1995).

- **Using data selectively.** Sometimes a survey includes many questions, but the researcher reports on only a few of the answers. Doing so makes it quite easy to misstate the findings. Researchers often do not report findings that show no association between variables, but these can be just as telling as associations that do exist. For example, researchers on gender differences typically report the differences they find between men and women, but seldom publish their findings when the results for men and women are identical. This tends to exaggerate the differences between women and men and falsely confirms certain social stereotypes about gender differences.

Survey researchers sometimes get at this problem by asking essentially the same question in different ways. In this way, *validity* is increased.

## Participant Observation

A unique and interesting way for sociologists to collect data and study society is to actually become part of the group they are studying. This is the method of *participant observation*. Two roles are played at the same time: subjective participant and objective observer. Usually, the group is aware that the sociologist is studying them, but not always. Participant observation is sometimes called *field research,* a term borrowed from anthropology.

Participant observation combines subjective knowledge gained through personal involvement and objective knowledge acquired by disciplined recording of what one has seen. The subjective component supplies a dimension of information that is lacking in survey data.

## Debunking Society's Myths

**Myth:** People who are just hanging out together and relaxing don't care much about social differences between them.

**Sociological research:** Even casual groups have organized social hierarchies. That is, they make distinctions within the group that give some people higher status than others. This has been shown in participant observation studies such as Duneier's (1999) study of the homeless on New York City's lower East Side; in Anderson's (1976) study of the people just hanging out in "Jelly's Bar"; in Anderson's (1999) "Code of the Street" study, which showed a rigid hierarchy among those engaged in street crime; and in the study of "Pam's Place" (Gimlin 1996, 2002), which showed the classlike distinctions hair dressers and their customers made between each other.

The men in this bar, as shown by participant observation as in Anderson's (1976) classic study of "Jelly's Bar" in A Place on the Corner, *reveal status differences among themselves that they create, such as (in descending status order) "regulars," "hoodlums," and "winos."*

*Street Corner Society* (1943), a classic work by sociologist William Foote Whyte, documents one of the first qualitative participant observation studies ever done. Whyte studied the Cornerville Gang, a group of Italian American men whose territory was a street corner in Boston in the late 1930s and early 1940s. Although not Italian, Whyte learned to speak the language, lived with an Italian family, and then infiltrated the gang by befriending the gang's leader, whose pseudonym was "Doc." Doc was the *informant* for Whyte, a person with whom the participant observer works closely in order to learn about the group. For the duration of the study, Doc was the only gang member who knew that Whyte was doing research on his gang. This represents what is called *covert participant observation*—in which the members of the group being studied do not know that they are being researched. (If the group is told that they are being studied and that they are the research subjects, then it is called *overt participant observation.*)

Most social scientists of the 1940s and 1950s thought gangs were socially disorganized, random deviant groups, but Whyte's study showed otherwise—as have participant observation studies since then, notably those of Anderson (1976, 1990, 1999). He found that the Cornerville Gang, and by implication other urban street corner gangs as well, was a highly organized mini-society with its own social hierarchy (social stratification), morals, practices, and punishments (sanctions) for deviating from the norms of the gang.

There are a few built-in weaknesses to participant observation as a research technique. We already

mentioned that it is very time-consuming. Participant observers have to cull data from vast amounts of notes. Such studies usually focus on fairly small groups, posing problems of generalization. Participant observation can also pose real physical dangers to the researcher, such as being "found out" or "outed" if one is studying a street gang (Sanchez-Jankowski 1991). Observers may also lose their objectivity by becoming too much a part of what they study. If this happens—the observer becomes so much a part of the group that she or he is no longer observer but participant—it is called "going native" and is seen as one of the disadvantages of participant observation research. These limitations aside, participant observation has been the source of some of the most arresting and valuable studies in sociology (see "A Cop in the Hood" on page 70.).

## Controlled Experiments

**Controlled experiments** are highly focused ways of collecting data and are especially useful for determining a pattern of cause and effect. To conduct a controlled experiment, two groups are created, an *experimental group,* which is exposed to the factor or variable one is examining, and the *control group,* which is not. In a controlled experiment, external influences are either eliminated or equalized, that is, held constant, between the experimental and the control group. This is necessary in order to establish cause and effect.

Suppose you wanted to study whether violent television programming causes aggressive behavior in children. You could conduct a controlled experiment to investigate this question. The behavior of children would be the dependent variable; the independent variable is whether or not the children are exposed to violent programming. To investigate your question, you would expose an experimental group of children (under monitored conditions) to a movie containing lots of violence (ultimate fighting, for example, or gunfighting). The control group would watch a movie that is free of violence. Aggressiveness in the children (the dependent variable) would be measured twice: a *pretest* measurement made before the movies are shown and a *posttest* measurement made afterward. You would take pretest and posttest measures on both the control and the experimental groups. Studies of this sort actually find that the children who watched the violent movie are indeed more violent and aggressive afterward than those who watched a movie containing no violence (Taylor et al. 2009; Worchel et al. 2000; Bushman 1998).

Among its advantages, a controlled experiment can establish causation, and it can zero in on a single independent variable. On the downside, controlled experiments can be artificial. They are for the most part done in a contrived laboratory setting (unless it is a *field experiment*), and they tend to eliminate many real-life effects. Analysis of controlled experiments includes making judgments about how much the artificial setting has affected the results (see Table 3.1).

## Content Analysis

Researchers can learn a vast amount about a society by analyzing *cultural artifacts* such as newspapers, magazines, TV programs, or popular music. **Content analysis** is a way of measuring by examining the cultural artifacts of what people write, say, see, and hear. The researcher studies not people but the

*Media violence tends to desensitize children to the effects of violence, including engendering less sympathy for victims of violence (Baumeister and Bushman 2008; Huesmann et al. 2003; Cantor 2000). Many also think that violent video games (another form of media) may be a cause of school shootings. Perhaps there is some link here; it is too simplistic to see a direct causal connection between viewing violence and actually engaging in it. For one thing, such an argument ignores the broader social context of violent behavior (including such things as the availability of guns, family characteristics, youth alienation from school, to name a few [Steinhamer 2007]).*

© Dwayne Newton/PhotoEdit

communications the people produce as a way of creating a picture of their society.

Content analysis is frequently used to measure cultural change and to study different aspects of culture (Lamont 1992). Sociologists also use content analysis as an indirect way to determine how social groups are perceived—they might examine, for example, how Asian Americans are depicted in television dramas or how women are depicted in advertisements.

Children's books have been the subject of many content analyses. In acknowledgment of their impact on the development of youngsters, a team of sociologists compared images of Black Americans in children's books from the 1930s to the present (Pescosolido et al. 1997). They obtained three important findings: First, they found a declining representation of African Americans from the 1930s through the 1950s, with practically no representation from 1950 through 1964. Beginning in 1964, an increase in representation lasted until the mid-1970s, when the appearance of African American characters leveled off. Second, they found that the symbolic images of African Americans did change significantly over time. In the 1960s—a period of much racial unrest—African Americans were mostly portrayed in "safe," distant images, such as in secondary and nearly invisible occupational roles. Third, they found few portrayals of Black adults in intimate, egalitarian, or interracial relationships. Recent research on stereotyping generally confirms these three findings (Baumeister and Bushman 2008: 419–421).

Content analysis has the advantage of being *unobtrusive,* or "nonreactive." The research has no effect on the person being studied because the cultural artifact has already been produced. Content analysis is limited in what it can study, however, because it is based on mass communication—either visual, oral, or written. It cannot tell us what people really think about these images or whether they affect people's behavior. Other methods of research, such as interviewing or participant observation, would be used to answer these questions.

## Historical Research

Historical research examines sociological themes over time. It is commonly done in historical archives, such as official records, church records, town archives, private diaries, or oral histories. The sources of this sort of material are critical to its quality and applicability. Oral histories have been especially illuminating, most dramatically in revealing the unknown histories of groups that have been ignored or misrepresented in other historical accounts. For example, when developing an account of the spirituality of Native Americans, one would be misguided to rely solely on the records left by Christian missionaries or U.S. Army officials. These records would give a useful picture of how Whites perceived Native American religion, but they would be a very poor source for discovering how Native Americans understood their own spirituality.

In a similar vein, the writings of a slave owner can deliver fascinating insights into slavery, but a slave owner's diary will certainly present a different picture of slavery as a social institution than will the written or oral histories of former slaves themselves.

Handled properly, comparative and historical research is rich with the ability to capture long-term social changes and is the perfect tool for sociologists who want to ground their studies in historical or comparative perspectives.

## Evaluation Research

**Evaluation research** assesses the effect of policies and programs on people in society. If the research is intended to produce policy recommendations, then it is called *policy research*.

Suppose you want to know if an educational program is actually improving student performance. You could design a study that measured the academic performance of two groups of students, one that participates in the program and one that does not (a "control" group). If the academic performance of students in the program is better than that of those not

in the program, and if the groups are alike in other ways (they are often matched to accomplish this), you would conclude that the program was effective. If the academic performance of the students in the program ended up being the same (or even worse) as those not in the program, then you would conclude that the program was not effective. If you use this research to recommend social policy, you would be doing policy research.

# Research Ethics: Is Sociology Value Free?

The topics dealt with by sociology are often controversial. People have strong opinions about social questions, and in some cases, the settings for sociological work are highly politicized. Imagine spending time in an urban precinct house to do research on police brutality or doing research on acquired immune deficiency syndrome (AIDS) and sex education in a

## table3.1 Comparison of Six Research Techniques

| Technique (Tool) | Qualitative Analysis or Quantitative Analysis | Advantages | Disadvantages |
|---|---|---|---|
| The survey (polls, questionnaires, interviews) | Usually quantitative, often qualitative | Permits the study of a large number of variables; results can be generalized to a larger population if sampling is accurate | Difficult to focus in great depth on a few variables; difficult to measure subtle nuances in people's attitudes |
| Participant observation | Usually qualitative | Studies actual behavior in its home setting; affords great depth of inquiry | Is very time-consuming; difficult to generalize beyond the research setting |
| Controlled experiment | Usually quantitative | Focuses on only two or three variables; able to study cause and effect | Difficult or impossible to measure large number of variables; may have an artificial quality |
| Content analysis | Can be either qualitative or quantitative | A way of measuring culture | Limited by studying only cultural products or artifacts (music, TV programs, stories, other), rather than people's actual attitudes |
| Historical research | Usually qualitative | Saves time and expense in data collection; takes differences over time into account | Data often reflect biases of the original researcher and reflect cultural norms that were in effect when the data were collected |
| Evaluation research | Can be either qualitative or quantitative | Evaluates the actual outcomes of a program or strategy; often direct policy application | Limited in the number of variables that can be measured; maintaining objectivity is problematic if research is done or commissioned by administrators of the program being evaluated |

conservative public school system. Under these conditions, can sociology be scientifically objective? How do researchers balance their own political and moral commitments against the need to be objective and open-minded? Sociological knowledge has an intimate connection to political values and social views. Often the very purpose of sociological research is to gather data as a step in creating social policy. Can sociology be value free? Should it be?

This is an important question without a simple answer. Most sociologists do not claim to be value free, but they do try as best they can to produce objective research. It must be acknowledged that researchers make choices throughout their research that can influence their results. The problems sociologists choose to study, the people they decide to observe, the research design they select, and the type of media they use to distribute their research can all be influenced by the personal values of the researcher.

Sociological research often raises ethical questions. In fact, ethical considerations of one sort or another exist with any type of research. In a survey, the person being questioned is often not told the purpose of the survey or who is funding the study. Is it ethical to conceal this type of information?

In controlled experiments, *deception* is often employed, as in the now-famous studies by Stanley Milgram, to be reviewed later in Chapter 6, where people were led to believe that they were causing harm to another, when in fact they were not. Researchers often reveal the true purpose of an experiment only after it is completed. This is called **debriefing.** The deception is therefore temporary. But does that lessen the potential ethical violation? Does it lessen any potential damage to the self-concept of the subject or respondent?

One of the clearest ethical violations in all of the history of science has come to be known as the *Tuskegee Syphilis Study*. The study was conducted at the Tuskegee Institute in Macon County, Alabama, a historically Black college. For this study, begun in 1932 by the government's United States Health Service, a sample of about 400 Black males who were infected with the sexually transmitted disease syphilis (this was the "experimental" group) were allowed to go untreated medically for over forty years. Another 200 Black males who had not contracted syphilis were used as a control group. The purpose of the study was to examine the effects of "untreated syphilis in the male negro." The study was not unlike similar "studies" carried out against Jews by Hitler's Nazi regime in Germany at the same time—just before and during World War II in the 1930s and early 1940s. Untreated syphilis causes blindness, mental retardation, and death, and this is how many of the untreated men fared over the forty-plus-year period. In the 1950s, penicillin was discovered as an effective treatment for infectious diseases, including syphilis, and was widely available. Nonetheless, the scientists conducting the study decided *not* to give penicillin to the

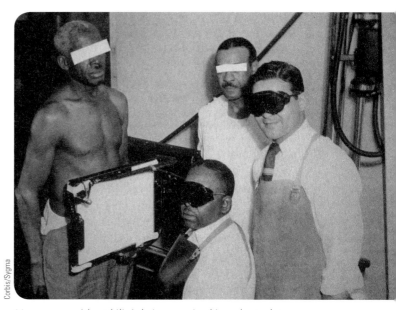

Corbis/Sygma

*Here a man with syphilis is being examined in order to determine the "progress" of syphilis in his case. This unfortunate man was an experimental subject in the U.S. government's infamous* Tuskegee Syphilis Study, *one of the clearest ethical violations in all the history of science.*

infected men in the study on the grounds that it would "interfere" with the study of the physical and mental harm caused by untreated syphilis. The U.S. government itself authorized the study to be continued until the early 1970s—that is, until quite recently. By the mid-1970s pressure from the public and the press caused the federal government to terminate the study, but by then it was too late to save approximately 100 men who had already died of the ravages of untreated syphilis, plus many others who were forced to live with major mental and physical damage.

Following the ethical horrors of studies such as the Tuskegee study, the American Sociological Association (ASA) has since developed a professional code of ethics (see the ASA website for the full code of ethics). The federal government also has many regulations about the protection of human subjects. Ethical researchers adhere to these guidelines and must ensure that research subjects are not subjected to physical, mental, or legal harm. Research subjects must also be informed of the rights and responsibilities of both researcher and subject. Sociologists, like other scientists, also should not involve people in research without what is called **informed consent**—that is, getting agreement beforehand to participate from the respondents or subjects after the purposes of the study are explained to them. There may be exceptions to the need for informed consent, such as when observing people in public places. Sociologists also take measures to avoid identifying their respondents and to assure confidentiality through the use of pseudonyms or by not using names at all and by assigning random ID (code) numbers to all respondents during data analysis.

# > doing sociological research

## A Cop in the Hood: Participant Observation

An excellent example of participant observation research of the overt type is sociologist Peter Moskos's eighteen months as a bone fide police officer in Baltimore, Maryland. For his doctoral dissertation research, Moskos, who is White, underwent the standard six months of training in the police academy and was then assigned to Baltimore's Eastern District, a heavily African American and depressed ghetto with a heavy drug trade. He got to know and trust the other officers with whom he worked, and he became familiar with the social life of the homeless individuals, drug dealers, and neighborhood residents in East Baltimore. He lived minute by minute and day by day with the ever-present extreme dangers of police work, carried a Glock semi-automatic pistol with a seventeen-shot clip (which he never had to fire but had to "show" on occasion), and discovered that "danger creates a bond" among police officers. He wrote his field notes each day after work—numbering overall 350 typed, single-spaced pages. His study ranks with other classic participant observation studies in sociology, such as Whyte's *Street Corner Society* (1943), Anderson's *A Place on the Corner* (1976) and *Streetwise* (1990), and Duneier's *Sidewalk* (1999).

Moskos's study is important because, among other things, it dispels a number of myths that the public has about police officers and police work. For example, many think that summoning the police by calling 911 will get a quick solution to the problem—whether it be a drug deal taking place, an incident of domestic violence, or gunfire on the street. While the police are indeed generally quick to respond, in reality the drug deal or the domestic violence reconvenes immediately after the police leave the scene. Moskos even concludes that, unfortunately, 911 is "a joke."

Many assume that if a suspected drug dealer is standing close to a vial of cocaine in the street, the observing police officer will report that he or she "saw" the dealer throw the vial into the street. Moskos found, however, that this was rarely the case: The vast majority of officers over the vast majority of such incidents only reported "seeing" the dealer toss the vial if they indeed *saw* the dealer do so and were able to verify this act by another officer witnessing it. A veteran officer warned Moskos that "if you don't see him drop it, then just kick it or crush it."

Also of importance is Moskos's discovery of certain elements of social structure characterizing street drug trade. For example, virtually each and every illicit drug transaction on the street corner involves five social roles in addition to the person who actually purchases a drug or drugs: lookouts (who watch for police cars, the lowest-status role in the street transaction); steerers (who "hawk" or advertise their drug to passersby); money-men (who collect the money paid for the drug); slingers (who actually give the drugs to the purchaser); and gunmen (who stand ready in the shadows in case they feel needed). Engaging in such roles serves the function of limiting the legal liability of each individual in the event of arrests.

Such insights into the social structure and culture of street activity (in this case, street drug trade) ranks Moskos's work with other participant observation studies that reveal the structures and cultures of, for example, those of Whyte, Anderson, and Duneier.

*Source:* Moskos, Peter. 2008. *Cop in the Hood: My Year Policing Baltimore's Eastern District.* Princeton, NJ: Princeton University Press.

# Chapter Summary

- ### What is sociological research?
  Sociological research is used by sociologists to answer questions and in many cases test hypotheses. The research method one uses depends upon the question that is asked.

- ### Is sociological research scientific?
  Sociological research is derived from the scientific method, meaning that it relies on empirical observation and, sometimes, the testing of *hypotheses*. The research process involves several steps: developing a

research question, designing the research, collecting data, analyzing data, and developing conclusions. Different research designs are appropriate to different research questions, but sociologists have to be concerned with the *validity,* the *reliability,* and the *generalization* of their results. Applying one's results obtained from a sample to a broader population is an example of generalization.

- ### What is the difference between qualitative research and quantitative research?
  *Qualitative research* is research that is relatively unstructured, does not rely heavily upon statistics, and is closely focused on a question being asked. *Quantitative research* is research that uses statistical methods. Both kinds of research are used in sociology.

- ### What are some of the statistical concepts in sociology?
  Through research, sociologists are able to make statements of *probability,* or likelihood. Sociologists use *percentages* and *rates.* The *mean* is the same as an average. The *median* represents the midpoint in an array of values or scores. The *mode* is the most common value or score. *Correlation* and *cross-tabulation* are statistical procedures that allow sociologists to see how two (or more) different variables are associated. There have been

instances of misuse of statistics in the behavioral and social sciences, including sociology, and these have resulted in incorrect conclusions.

- ### What different tools of research do sociologists use?
  The most common tools of sociological research are surveys and interviews, participant observation, controlled experiments, content analysis, comparative and historical research, and evaluation research. Each method has its own strengths and weaknesses. You can better generalize from surveys, for example, than participant observation, but participant observation is better for capturing subtle nuances and depth in social behavior. Table 3.1 gives a comparison of these six research techniques.

- ### Can sociology be value free?
  Although no research in any field can always be value free, sociological research nonetheless strives for objectivity while recognizing that the values of the researcher may have some influence on the work. One of the worst cases of ethical violation in scientific research was the Tuskegee Syphilis Study. There are ethical considerations in doing sociological research, such as whether one should collect data without letting research subjects (people) know they are being observed.

## Key Terms

| | | |
|---|---|---|
| concept 59 | hypothesis 59 | quantitative research 58 |
| content analysis 67 | independent variable 59 | random sample 63 |
| controlled experiment 66 | informed consent 69 | rate 64 |
| correlation 64 | indicator 59 | reliability 59 |
| cross-tabulation 64 | inductive reasoning 57 | replication study 57 |
| data 59 | mean 64 | research design 58 |
| data analysis 63 | median 64 | sample 62 |
| debriefing 69 | mode 64 | scientific method 56 |
| deductive reasoning 56 | participant observation 56 | serendipity 63 |
| dependent variable 59 | percentage 64 | spurious correlation 64 |
| evaluation research 68 | population 62 | validity 59 |
| generalization 63 | qualitative research 58 | variable 59 |

## Online Resources

### *Sociology: The Essentials* Companion Website

www.cengage.com/sociology/andersen

Visit your book companion website where you will find more resources to help you study and write your research papers. Resources include web links, learning objectives, Internet exercises, quizzing, and flash cards.

 **is an easy-to-use online resource that helps you study in less time to get the grade you want NOW.**

www.cengage.com/login

Need help studying? This site is your one-stop study shop. Take a Pre-Test and Cengage NOW will generate a Personalized Study Plan based on your test results. The Study Plan will identify the topics you need to review and direct you to online resources to help you master those topics. You can then take a Post-Test to determine the concepts you have mastered and what you still need to work on.

# 4

Chapter four
CHAPTER FOUR
Chapter

# Socialization and the Life Course

©Jim Erickson/Corbis

*During the summer* of 2000, scientists working on the human genome project announced that they had deciphered the human genetic code. By mapping the complex structure of DNA (deoxyribonucleic acid) on high-speed computers, scientists identified the 3.12 billion chemical base pairs in human DNA and put them in proper sequence, unlocking the genetic code of human life. Scientists likened this to assembling "the book of life," that is, having the knowledge to make and maintain human beings. The stated purpose of the human genome project is to see how genetics influences the development of disease, but it raises numerous ethical questions about human cloning and the possibility of creating human life in the laboratory. Is our genetic constitution what makes us human? Suppose you created a human being in the laboratory but left that creature without social contact. Would the "person" be human?

*continued*

Rare cases of **feral children,** who have been raised in the absence of human contact, provide some clues as to what happens during human development when a person has little or no social contact. One such case, discovered in 1970, involved a young girl given the pseudonym of Genie. When her blind mother appeared in the Los Angeles County welfare office seeking assistance for herself, case workers first thought the girl was six years old. In fact, she was thirteen, although she weighed only 59 pounds and was 4 feet, 6 inches tall. She was small and withered, unable to stand up straight, incontinent, and severely malnourished. Her eyes did not focus, and she had two nearly complete sets of teeth. A strange ring of calluses circled her buttocks. She could not talk.

As the case unfolded, it was discovered that the girl had been kept in nearly total isolation for most of her life. The first scientific report about Genie stated:

> In the house Genie was confined to a small bedroom, harnessed to an infant's potty seat. Genie's father sewed the harness himself; unclad except for the harness, Genie was left to sit on that chair. Unable to move anything except her fingers and hands, feet and toes, Genie was left to sit, tied-up, hour after hour, often into the night, day after day, month after month, year after year (Curtiss 1977: 5).

At night, she was restrained in a handmade sleeping bag that held her arms stationary and placed in a crib. If she made a sound, her father beat her. She was given no toys and was allowed to play only with two old raincoats and her father's censored version of *TV Guide*. (He had deleted everything "suggestive," such as pictures of women in bathing suits.) Genie's mother, timid and blind, was also victimized by her husband. Shortly after the mother sought help after years of abuse, the father committed suicide.

Genie was studied intensively by scientists interested in language acquisition and the social effects of extreme confinement. They hoped that her development would throw some light on the question of nature versus nurture; that is, are people relatively more the product of their genes, or of their social training? After intense language instruction and psychological treatment, Genie developed some verbal ability and, after a year, showed progress in her mental and physical development. Yet the years of isolation and severe abuse had taken their toll, and she was never able to catch up to her age peers. Genie was placed in a home for mentally disabled adults (Rymer 1993).

This rare case of a feral child sheds some light on the consequences of life without social contact. Knowing the sequence of the human genome may raise the specter of making human beings in the laboratory, but without society, what would humans be like? Genes may confer skin and bone and brain, but only by learning the values, norms, and roles that culture bestows on people do we become social beings—literally, *human* beings. Sociologists refer to this process as *socialization*—the subject of this chapter.

# The Socialization Process

**Socialization** is the process through which people learn the expectations of society. **Roles** are the expected behavior associated with a given status in society. When you occupy a given social role, you tend to take on the expectations of others. For example, when you enter a new group of friends, you probably observe their behavior, their language, their dress, perhaps even their opinions of others, and often modify your own behavior accordingly. Before you know it, you are a member of the group, perhaps socializing others into the same set of expectations. We explore roles further

*Formal and informal learning, through schools and other socialization agents, are important elements of the socialization process. Here hearing impaired children are learning sign language.*

# [understanding diversity]

## My Childhood (Bong Hwan Kim)

Childhood is a time when children learn their gender, as well as their racial and ethnic identity. This excerpt from an interview with Bong Hwan Kim, a Korean American man, is a reflection on growing up and learning both Korean and American culture.

*I came to the United States in 1962, when I was three or four years old. My father had come before us to get a Ph.D. in chemistry. He had planned to return to Korea afterward, but it was hard for him to support three children in Korea while he was studying in the United States, and he wasn't happy alone, so he brought the family over. . . . The Bergenfeld, New Jersey, community where I grew up was a blue-collar town of about 40,000 people, mostly Irish and Italian Americans. I lived a schizophrenic existence. I had one life in the family, where I felt warmth, closeness, love, and protection, and another life outside—school, friends, television, the feeling that I was on my own. I accepted that my parents would not be able to help me much.*

*I can remember clearly my first childhood memory about difference. I had been in this country for maybe a year. It was the first day of kindergarten, and I was very excited about having lunch at school. All morning I could think only of the lunch that was waiting for me in my desk. My mother had made kimpahp [rice balls rolled up in dried seaweed] and wrapped it all up in aluminum foil. I was eagerly looking forward to that special treat. I could hardly wait. When the lunch bell rang I happily took out my foil-wrapped kimpahp. But all the other kids pointed and gawked. "What is that? How could you eat that?" they shrieked. I don't remember whether I ate my lunch or not, but I told my mother I would only bring tuna or peanut butter sandwiches for lunch after that.*

*I have always liked Korean food, but I had to like it secretly, at home. There are things you don't show to your non-Korean friends. At various times when I was growing up, I felt ashamed of the food in the refrigerator, but only when friends would come over and wonder what it was. They'd see a jar of garlic and say, "You don't eat that stuff, do you?" I would say, "I don't eat it, but my parents do; they do a lot of weird stuff like that."*

*. . . As a child you are sensitive; you don't want to be different. You want to be like the other kids. They made fun of my face. They called me "flat face." When I got older, they called me "Chink" or "Jap" or said "Remember Pearl Harbor." In all cases, it made me feel terrible. I would get angry and get into fights. Even in high school, even the guys I hung around with on a regular basis, would say, "You're just a Chink" when they got angry. Later, they would say they didn't mean it, but that was not much consolation. When you are angry, your true perceptions and emotions come out. The rest is a facade.*

*They used to say, "We consider you to be just like us. You don't seem Korean." That would give rise to such mixed feelings in me. I wanted to believe that I was no different from my White classmates. It was painful to be reminded that I was different, which people did when they wanted to put me in my place, as if I should be grateful to them for allowing me to be their friend.*

*I wanted to be as American as possible—playing football, dating cheerleaders. I drank a lot and tried to be cool. I had convinced myself that I was "American," whatever that meant, all the while knowing underneath that I'd have to reconcile myself to try to figure out where I would fit in a society that never sanctioned that identity as a public possibility. Part of growing up in America meant denying my cultural and ethnic identity. . . . When I got to college, I experienced an identity crisis. . . . I decided to go to Korea, hoping to find something to make me feel more whole. Being in Korea somehow gave me a sense of freedom I had never really felt in America. It also made me love my parents even more. I could imagine where they came from and what they experienced. I began to understand and appreciate their sacrifice and love and what parental support means. Visiting Korea didn't provide answers about the meaning of life, but it gave me a sense of comfort and belonging, the feeling that there was somewhere in this world that validated that part of me that I knew was real but few others outside my immediate family ever recognized.*

Source: Edited by Karin Aguilar-San Juan. Copyright © 1994. *The State of Asian America.* Boston, MA: South End Press. Reprinted with permission of South End Press.

in Chapter 5, but it is important to know here that roles are learned through the socialization process.

Through socialization, people absorb their culture—customs, habits, laws, practices, and means of expression. Socialization is the basis for **identity:** how one defines oneself. Identity is both personal and social. To a great extent, it is bestowed by others, because we come to see ourselves as others see us. Socialization also establishes **personality,** defined as a person's relatively consistent pattern of behavior, feelings, predispositions, and beliefs.

The socialization experience differs for individuals, depending on factors such as age, race, gender, and class, as well as more subtle factors such as introversion-extroversion and other such aspects of personality. Women and men encounter different socialization patterns as they grow up because each gender brings with it different social expectations (see Chapter 11). Likewise, growing up Jewish, Asian, Latino, or African American involves different socialization experiences, as the box "Understanding Diversity: My Childhood (Bong Hwan Kim)" shows. In the example, a Korean American man reflects on the cultural habits he learned growing up in two cultures, Korean and American. His comments reveal the strain felt when socialization involves competing expectations—as when his schoolmates comment, "We consider you to be just like us—you don't seem Korean." Such strain can be particularly acute when a person grows up within different, even overlapping, cultures.

Through socialization, people internalize cultural expectations, then pass these expectations on to others. **Internalization** occurs when behaviors and assumptions are learned so thoroughly that people no longer question them, but simply accept them as correct. Through socialization, one internalizes the expectations of society. The lessons that are internalized can have a powerful influence on attitudes and behavior. For example, someone socialized to believe that homosexuality is morally repugnant is unlikely to be tolerant of gays and lesbians. If such a person, say a man, experiences erotic feelings about another man, he is likely to have deep inner conflicts about his identity. Similarly, someone socialized to believe that racism is morally repugnant is likely to be more accepting of different races. However, people can change the cultural expectations they learn. New experiences can undermine narrow cultural expectations. Attending college often has a liberalizing effect, supplanting old expectations with new ones generated by exposure to the diversity of college life.

## The Nature–Nurture Controversy

Examining the socialization process helps reveal the degree to which our lives are *socially constructed,* meaning that the organization of society and the life outcomes of people within it are the result of social definitions and processes. Is it "nature" (what is natural) or is it "nurture" (what is social)—or both—that makes us human? This question has been the basis for debate for many years.

From a sociological perspective, what a person becomes results more from social experiences than from *innate* (inborn or natural) traits, although innate traits have some influence, as we saw in Chapter 2 on culture. For example, a person may be born with a great capacity for knowledge, but without a good education that person is unlikely to achieve his or her full potential and may not be recognized as intellectually gifted.

From a sociological perspective, nature provides a certain stage for what is possible, but society provides the full drama of what we become. The expression *tabula rasa*, for example, means a human is born as a "blank

slate." But our values and social attitudes are not inborn; they emerge through the interactions we have with others and our social position in society. Such factors as your family environment, how people of your social group are treated, and the historic influences of the time all shape how we are nurtured by society or not.

Perhaps the best way to understand the nature–nurture controversy is not that one or the other fully controls who we become, but that life involves a complex interplay, or *interaction*, between natural and social influences on human beings. The emphasis in sociology, however, is to see the social realities of our lives as far more important in shaping human experience (Freese 2008; Freese et al. 2003; Ridley 2003; Guo and Stearns 2002).

## Socialization as Social Control

Sociologist Peter Berger pointed out that not only do people live in society but society also lives in people (Berger 1963). Socialization is, therefore, a mode of social control. **Social control** is the process by which groups and individuals within those groups are brought into conformity with dominant social expectations. Sometimes the individual rebels and attempts to resist this conformity, but because people generally conform to cultural expectations, socialization gives society a certain degree of predictability. Patterns are established that become the basis for social order.

To understand how socialization is a form of social control, imagine the individual in society as surrounded by a series of concentric circles (see Figure 4.1). Each circle is a layer of social controls, ranging from the most subtle, such as the expectations of others, to the most overt, such as physical coercion and violence. Coercion and violence are usually not necessary to extract conformity because learned beliefs and the expectations of others are enough to keep people in line. These socializing forces can be subtle, because even when a person disagrees with others, he or she can feel pressure to conform and may experience stress and discomfort in choosing not to conform. People

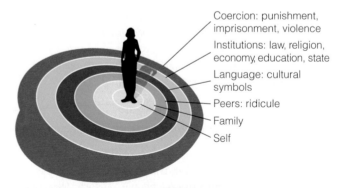

**FIGURE 4.1** *Socialization as Social Control*

*Though we are all individuals, the process of socialization also keeps us in line with society's expectations. This may occur subtly through peer pressure or, in some circumstances, through coercion and/or violence.*

learn through a lifetime of experience that deviating from the expectations of others invites peer pressure, ridicule, and other social judgments that remind one of what is expected.

## Conformity and Individuality

Saying that people conform to social expectations does not eliminate individuality. We are all unique to some degree. Our uniqueness arises from different experiences, different patterns of socialization, the choices we make, and the imperfect ways we learn our roles; furthermore, people resist some of society's expectations. Sociologists warn against seeing human beings as totally passive creatures because people interact with their environment in creative ways. Yet, most people conform, although to differing degrees. Socialization is profoundly significant, but this does not mean that people are robots. Instead, socialization emphasizes the adaptations people make as they learn to live in society.

Some people conform too much, for which they pay a price. Socialization into men's roles can encourage aggression and a zeal for risk-taking. Men have a lower life expectancy and higher rate of accidental death than do women, probably because of the risky behaviors associated with men's roles, that is, simply "being a man" (National Center for Health Statistics 2007; Kimmel and Messner 2004). Women's gender roles carry their own risks. Striving excessively to meet the beauty ideals of the dominant culture can result in feelings of low self-worth and may encourage harmful behaviors, such as smoking or severely restricting eating to keep one's weight down. It is not that being a man or woman is inherently bad for your health, but conforming to gender roles to an extreme can compromise your physical and mental health. (A convincing case in point is the affliction called *anorexia*, a pathological condition resulting from overly severe dieting, discussed more fully in Chapter 14.)

## The Consequences of Socialization

Socialization is a lifelong process with consequences that affect how we behave toward others and what we think of ourselves. First, socialization *establishes self-concepts*. **Self-concept** is how we think of ourselves as the result of the socialization experiences we have over a lifetime. Socialization is also influenced by various social factors, as shown in Figure 4.2, which describes how students' self-concepts are shaped by gender.

Second, *socialization creates the capacity for role-taking*, or, put another way, for the ability to see oneself through the perspective of another. Socialization

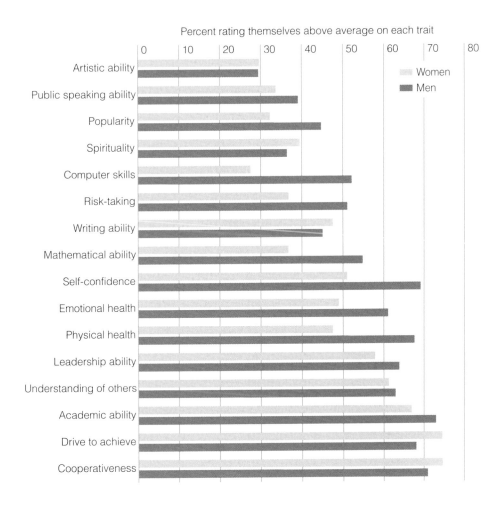

Percent rating themselves above average on each trait

**FIGURE 4.2** *Student Self-Concepts: The Difference Gender Makes*

*Based on national sample of first-year college students, Fall 2003.

*Source:* Sax, L. J., et al. 2003. *The American Freshman: National Norms for Fall 2003.* Higher Education Research Institute. Los Angeles, CA: University of California, Los Angeles. Used by permission.

is fundamentally reflective; that is, it involves self-conscious human beings seeing and reacting to the expectations of others. The capacity for reflection and the development of identity are ongoing. As we encounter new situations in life, such as going away to college or getting a new job, we are able to see what is expected and to adapt to the situation accordingly. Of course, not all people do so successfully. This can become the basis for social deviance (explored in Chapter 7) or for many common problems in social and psychological adjustment.

Third, *socialization creates the tendency for people to act in socially acceptable ways.* Through socialization, people learn the normative expectations attached to social situations and the expectations of society in general. As a result, socialization creates some predictability in human behavior and brings some order to what might otherwise be social chaos.

Finally, *socialization makes people bearers of culture.* Socialization is the process by which people learn and internalize the attitudes, beliefs, and behaviors of their culture. At the same time, socialization is a two-way process—that is, a person is not only the recipient of culture but also is the creator of culture, passing cultural expectations on to others. The main product of socialization, then, is society itself.

# Agents of Socialization

**Socialization agents** are people, or sources, or structures that pass on social expectations. Everyone is a socializing agent because social expectations are communicated in countless ways and in every interaction people have, whether intentionally or not. When people are simply doing what they consider "normal,"

*Dress at work is a form of socialization.*

Thinkstock/Jupiter Images

they are communicating social expectations to others. When you dress a particular way, you may not feel you are telling others they must dress that way. Yet, when everyone in the same environment dresses similarly, some expectation about appropriate dress is clearly being conveyed. People feel pressure to become what society expects of them even though the pressure may be subtle and unrecognized.

## thinkingsociologically

Think about the first week that you were attending college. What expectations were communicated to you and by whom? Who were the most significant *socialization agents* during this period? Which expectations were communicated formally and which informally? If you were analyzing this experience sociologically, what would be some of the most important concepts to help you understand how one "becomes a college student"?

Socialization does not occur simply between individual persons; it occurs in the context of social institutions. Recall from Chapter 1 that institutions are established patterns of social behavior that persist over time. Institutions are a level of society above individuals. Many social institutions shape the process of socialization, including, as we will see, the family, the media, peers, religion, sports, and schools.

## The Family

For most people, the family is the first source of socialization. Through families, children are introduced to the expectations of society. Children learn to see themselves through their parents' eyes. Thus, how parents define and treat a child is crucial to the development of the child's sense of self.

An interesting example of the subtlety in familial socialization comes from a study comparing how U.S. and Japanese mothers talk to their children (Fernald and Morikawa 1993). Observers watched mothers from both cultures speak to their infant children, ranging in age from six to nineteen months. Both Japanese and U.S. mothers simplified and repeated words for their children, but strong cultural differences were evident in their context. U.S. mothers focused on naming objects for their babies: "Is that a *car*?" "Kiss the *doggy*." Japanese mothers were more likely to use their verbal interactions with children as an opportunity to practice social routines such as "give me" and "thank you." The behavior of the Japanese mothers implied that the name of the object was less important than the polite exchange. Japanese mothers also were more likely to use sounds to represent the objects, such as "oink-oink" for a pig, or "vroom-vroom" for a vehicle. U.S. mothers were more likely to use the actual names for objects. The researchers interpreted these interactions as reflecting the beliefs and practices of each culture. Japanese mothers used objects as part of a ritual of social exchange, emphasizing polite routines, whereas U.S. mothers focused on labeling things. In each case, the child receives a message about what is most significant in the culture.

What children learn in families is certainly not uniform. Even though families pass on the expectations of a given culture, within that culture families may be highly diverse, as we will see in Chapter 13. Some families may emphasize educational achievement; some may be more permissive, whereas others emphasize strict obedience and discipline. Even within families, children may experience different expectations based on gender or birth order (being first, second, or third born). Researchers have found, for example, that fathers' and mothers' support for gender equity increases when they have only daughters (Warner and Steel 1999). Living in a family experiencing the strain of social problems such as alcoholism, unemployment, domestic violence, or teen pregnancy also affects how children are socialized. The specific effects of different family structures and processes are the basis for ongoing and extensive sociological research.

As important as the family is in socializing the young, it is not the only socialization agent. As children grow up, they encounter other socializing influences, sometimes in ways that might contradict family expectations. Parents who want to socialize their children in less gender-stereotyped ways might be frustrated by the influence of the media, which promotes highly gender-typed toys and activities to boys and girls. These multiple influences on the socialization process create a reflection of society in us.

## The Media

As we saw in Chapter 2, the mass media increasingly are important agents of socialization. Television alone has a huge impact on what we are socialized to believe and become. Add to that the print messages received in books, comics, newspapers, and now blogs and the Internet, plus images from film, music, video games, and radio, and you begin to see the enormous influence the media have on the values we form, our images of society, our desires for ourselves, and our relationships with others. These images are powerful throughout our lifetimes, but many worry that their effect during childhood may be particularly deleterious.

The high degree of violence in the media has led to the development of a rating system for televised programming. There is no doubt that violence is extensive in the media. Analysts estimate that by age eighteen, the average child will have witnessed at least 18,000 simulated murders on television (Wilson et al. 2002). Moreover, violence in children's programming is frequently shown as humorous, or with no serious consequences (National Television Violence Study 1997).

Media violence also tends to desensitize children to the effects of violence, including engendering less sympathy for victims of violence (Baumeister and Bushman 2008; Huesmann et al. 2003; Cantor 2000). Many also think that violent video games (another form of media) may be a cause of school shootings. Perhaps there is some link here, but; it is too simplistic to see a direct causal connection between viewing violence and actually engaging in it. For one thing, such an argument ignores the broader social context of violent behavior (including such things as the availability of guns, family characteristics, youth alienation from school, to name a few (Steinhamer 2007).

Still, children tend to imitate the aggressive behavior they see in the media. Violence in the media is not solely to blame for violent behavior in society, however. Children do not watch television in a vacuum; they live in families where they learn different values and attitudes about violent behavior, and they observe the society around them, not just the images they see in fictional representations. Most likely, children are influenced not only by the images of televised and filmed violence but also by the social context in which they live. The images of violence in the media in some ways only reflect the violence in society.

The media expose us to numerous images that shape our definitions of ourselves and the world around us. What we think of as beautiful, sexy, politically acceptable, and materially necessary is strongly influenced by the media. If every week, as you read a newsmagazine, someone shows you the new car that will give you status and distinction, or if every weekend, as we watch televised sports, someone tells us that to have fun we should drink the right beer, it is little wonder that we begin to think that our self-worth can be measured by the car we drive and that parties are perceived as better when everyone is drunk. The values represented in the media, whether they are about violence, racist and sexist stereotypes, or any number of other social images, have a great effect on what we think and who we come to be.

## Peers

**Peers** are those with whom you interact on equal terms, such as friends, fellow students, and coworkers. Among peers, there are no formally defined superior and subordinate roles, although status distinctions commonly arise in peer group interactions. Without peer approval, most people find it hard to feel socially accepted.

*The media have the power to transform people into superstars so that they are recognizable to people worldwide.*

Dima Gavrysh/AP Photo

Peers are an important agent of socialization. Young girls and boys learn society's images of what they are supposed to be through the socialization process.

Support from peers and family is an important source of strong self-esteem. Organized peer groups such as the Special Olympics can also foster a desire for achievement and enhance one's sense of self-worth.

Peers are enormously important in the socialization process. Peer cultures for young people often take the form of *cliques*—friendship circles where members identify with each other and hold a sense of common identity. You probably had cliques in your high school and may even be able to name them. Did your school have "jocks," "preps," "goths," "nerds," "freaks," "stoners," and so forth? Sociologists studying cliques have found that they are formed based on a sense of exclusive membership, like the in-groups and out-groups we will examine in Chapter 6. Cliques are cohesive but also have an internal hierarchy, with certain group leaders having more power and status than other members. Interaction techniques, like making fun of people, produce group boundaries, defining who's in and who's out. The influence of peers is strong in childhood and adolescence, but it also persists into adulthood.

As agents of socialization, peers are important sources of social approval, disapproval, and support. This is one reason groups without peers of similar status are often at a disadvantage in various settings, such as women in male-dominated professions or minority students on predominantly White campuses. Being a "token" or an "only," as it has come to be called, places unique stresses on those in settings with relatively few peers from whom to draw support (Thoits 2009). This is one reason those who are minorities in a dominant group context often form same-sex or same-race groups for support, social activities, and the sharing of information about how to succeed in their environment (Tatum 1997).

## Religion

Religion is another powerful agent of socialization, and religious instruction contributes greatly to the identities children construct for themselves. Children tend to develop the same religious beliefs as their parents; switching to a religious faith different from the one in which a person is raised is rare (Hadaway and Marler 1993). Even those who renounce the religion of their youth are deeply affected by the attitudes, images, and beliefs instilled by early religious training. Very often those who disavow religion return to their original faith at some point in their life, especially if they have strong ties to their family of origin and if they form families of their own (Wuthnow 1998; Wilson 1994).

Religious socialization shapes the beliefs that people develop. An example comes from studies of people who believe in creationism. **Creationism** is a set of beliefs that largely reject the theory of human biological evolution and instead argue that human beings as now exist were created by a central force or God. Those who believe this have generally been taught to believe so over a long period; that is, they have been specifically socialized to believe in the creationist view of the world's origin and to reject scientific explanations, such as the theory of evolution. Sociological research further finds that socialization into creationist beliefs is more likely to be effective among people who grow up in small-town environments where they are less exposed to other influences. Those who believe in creationism are also likely to have mothers who have filled the traditional homemaker's role (Eckberg 1992). This shows the influence that social context has on the religious socialization people experience.

Religious socialization influences a large number of beliefs that guide adults in how they organize their lives, including beliefs about moral development and behavior, the roles of men and women, and sexuality, to name a few. One's religious beliefs strongly influence belief about gender roles within the family, including men's engagement in housework and the odds that wives will be employed outside the home (Ellison and Bartkowski 2002; Becker and Hofmeister 2001; Scott 2000). Religious socialization also influences beliefs about sexuality, including the likelihood of tolerance for gay and lesbian sexuality (Reynolds 2003; Sherkat 2002). Religion can even influence child-rearing practices. Thus, sociologists have found that conservative Protestants are more likely to use strict discipline in raising children, but they are also more likely to hug and praise their children than are parents with less conservative religious views.

## Sports

Most people perhaps think of sports as something that is just for fun and relaxation—or perhaps to provide opportunities for college scholarships and athletic careers—but sports are also an agent of socialization. Through sports, men and women learn concepts of self that stay with them in their later lives.

Sports are also where many ideas about gender differences are formed and reinforced (Messner 2002; Dworkin and Messner 1999). For men, success or failure as an athlete can be a major part of a man's identity. Even for men who have not been athletes, knowing about and participating in sports is an important source of men's gender socialization. Men learn that being competitive in sports is considered a part of manhood. Indeed, the attitude that "sports builds character" runs deep in the culture. Sports are supposed to pass on values such as competitiveness, the work ethic, fair play, and a winning attitude. Sports are considered to be where one learns to be a man.

## Debunking Society's Myths

**Myth:** Many people feel that sports are for the most part played just for the fun of it.

**Sociological perspective:** Although sports are a form of entertainment, playing sports is also a source for socialization into roles, such as gender roles.

Michael Messner's research on men and sports reveals the extent to which sports shape masculine identity. Messner interviewed thirty former athletes: Latino, Black, and White men from poor, working-class, and middle-class backgrounds. All of them spoke of the extraordinary influence of sports on them as they grew up. Not only are sports a major source of gender socialization, but many working-class, African American, and Latino men often see sports as their only possibility for a good career, even though the number of men who succeed in athletic careers is a minuscule percentage of those who hold such hopes.

Messner's research shows that, for most men, playing or watching sports is often the context for developing relationships with fathers, even when the father is absent or emotionally distant in other areas of life. Older brothers and other male relatives also socialize young men into sports. For many of the men in Messner's study, the athletic accomplishments of other family members created uncomfortable pressure to perform and compete, although on the whole, they recalled their early sporting years with positive emotions. It was through sports relationships with male peers, more than anyone else, however, that the men's identity was shaped. As boys, the men could form "safe" bonds with other men; still, through sports activity, men learned homophobic attitudes (that is, fear and hatred of homosexuals) and rarely developed intimate, emotional relationships with each other (Messner 2002, 1992).

Sports historically have been less significant in the formation of women's identity, although this has changed, largely as the result of Title IX. Title IX opened more opportunities in athletics to girls and women by legally defining the exclusion of women from school sports as sex discrimination. Women who participate in sports typically develop a strong sense of bodily competence—something usually denied to them by the prevailing, unattainable cultural images of women's bodies. Sports also give women a strong sense of self-confidence and encourage them to seek challenges, take risks, and set goals (Blinde et al. 1994, 1993).

Still, athletic prowess, highly esteemed in men, is not tied to cultural images of womanliness. Quite the contrary, women who excel at sports are sometimes stereotyped as lesbians, or "butches," and may be ridiculed for not being womanly enough. These stereotypes reinforce traditional gender roles for women, as do media images of women athletes that emphasize family images and the personality of women athletes (Cavalier 2003; Blinde and Taub 1992a, 1992b). Research in the sociology of sports shows how activities as ordinary as shooting baskets on a city lot, playing on the soccer team for one's high school, or playing touch football on a Saturday afternoon can convey powerful cultural messages about our identity and our place in the world. Sports are a good example of the power of socialization in our everyday lives.

## Schools

Once young people enter kindergarten (or, even earlier, day care), another process of socialization begins. At home, parents are the overwhelmingly dominant source of socialization cues. In school, teachers and other students are the source of expectations that encourage children to think and behave in particular ways. The expectations encountered in schools vary for different groups of students. These differences are shaped by a number of factors, including teachers' expectations for different groups and the resources that different parents can bring to bear on the educational process. The parents of children attending elite, private schools, for example, often have more influence on school policies and classroom activities than do parents in low-income communities. In any context, studying socialization in the schools is an excellent way to see the influence of gender, class, and race in shaping the socialization process.

## Debunking Society's Myths

**Myth:** Schools are primarily places where young people learn skills and other knowledge.

**Sociological perspective:** There is a hidden curriculum in schools where students learn expectations associated with race, class, and gender relations in society as influenced by the socialization process.

For example, research finds that teachers respond differently to boys and girls in school. Boys receive more attention from teachers than do girls. Even when teachers respond negatively to boys who are misbehaving, they are paying more attention to the boys (American Association of University Women 1998; Sadker and Sadker 1994). Social class stereotypes also affect teachers' interactions with students. Teachers are likely to perceive working-class children and poor children as less bright and less motivated than middle-class children; teachers are also more likely to define working-class students as troublemakers (Oakes et al. 2000; Bowditch 1993). These negative appraisals are *self-fulfilling prophecies,* meaning that the expectations they create often become the cause of actual behavior in the children; thus, they affect the odds of success for children. (We will return to a discussion of self-fulfilling prophecies in Chapter 14.)

Boys also receive more attention in the curriculum than girls. The characters in texts are more frequently boys; the accomplishments of boys are more likely portrayed in classroom materials; and boys and men are more typically depicted as active players in history, society, and culture (American Association of University Women 1998; Sadker and Sadker 1994). This is called the *hidden curriculum* in the schools—the informal and often subtle messages about social roles that are conveyed through classroom interaction and classroom materials—roles that are clearly linked to gender, race, and class.

In schools, boys and girls are quite often segregated into different groups, with significant sociological consequences. Differences between boys and girls become exaggerated when they are defined as distinct groups (Thorne 1993). Seating boys and girls in separate groups or sorting them into separate play groups heightens gender differences and greatly increases the significance of gender in the children's interactions with each other. Equally important is that gender becomes less relevant in the interactions between boys and girls when they are grouped together in common working groups, although gender does not disappear altogether as an influence. Barrie Thorne, who has observed gender interaction in schools, concludes from her observations that gender has a "fluid" character and that gender relations between boys and girls can be improved through conscious changes that discourage gender separation.

While in school, young people acquire identities and learn patterns of behavior that are congruent with the needs of other social institutions. Sociologists using conflict theory to understand schools would say that U.S. schools reflect the needs of a capitalist society. School is typically the place where children are first exposed to a hierarchical, bureaucratic environment. Not only does school teach them the skills of reading, writing, and other subject areas, but it is also where children are trained to respect authority, be punctual, and follow rules—thereby preparing them for their future lives as workers in organizations that value these traits. Schools emphasize conformity to societal needs, although not everyone internalizes these lessons to the same degree (Bowles and Gintis 1976; Lever 1978). Research has found, for example, that working-class schoolchildren form subcultures in school that resist the dominant culture.

## *thinkingsociologically*

Visit a local day-care center, preschool, or elementary school and observe children at play. Record the activities they are involved in, and note what both girls and boys are doing. Do you observe any differences between boys' and girls' play? What do your observations tell you about *socialization* patterns for boys and girls?

# Theories of Socialization

Knowing that people become socialized does not explain how it happens. Different theoretical perspectives explain socialization, including psychoanalytic theory, social learning theory, and symbolic interaction theory. Each perspective, including functionalism as well as conflict theory, carries a unique set of assumptions about socialization and its effect on the development of the self (see Table 4.1).

## Psychoanalytic Theory

Psychoanalytic theory originates in the work of **Sigmund Freud** (1856–1939). Perhaps Freud's greatest contribution was the idea that the unconscious mind shapes human behavior. Freud is also known for developing the technique of *psychoanalysis* to help discover the causes of psychological problems in the recesses of troubled patients' minds.

**Psychoanalytic theory** depicts the human psyche in three parts: the id, the superego, and the ego. The **id** consists of deep drives and impulses. Freud was particularly absorbed by the sexual component of the id, which he considered an especially forceful denizen of the unconscious mind. The **superego** is the dimension of the self that represents the standards of society. The superego incorporates or internalizes acquired values and norms—in short, culture. According to Freud, an ordered society requires that people repress the wild impulses generated by the id.

| | Psychoanalytic Theory | Social Learning Theories | Functional Theory | Conflict Theory | Symbolic Interaction Theory |
|---|---|---|---|---|---|
| **table4.1** | Theories of Socialization | | | | |
| *How each theory views:* | | | | | |
| *Individual learning process* | The unconscious mind shapes behavior. | People respond to social stimuli in their environment. | People internalize the role expectations that are present in society. | Individual and group aspirations are shaped by the opportunities available to different groups. | Children learn through taking the role of significant others. |
| *Formation of self* | The self (ego) emerges from tension between the id and the superego. | Identity is created through the interaction of mental and social worlds. | Internalizing the values of society reinforces social consensus. | Group consciousness is formed in the context of a system of inequality. | Identity emerges as the creative self interacts with the social expectations of others. |
| *Influence of society* | Societal expectations are represented by the superego. | Young children learn the principles that shape the external world. | Society relies upon conformity to maintain stability and social equilibrium. | Social control agents exert pressure to conform. | Expectations of others form the social context for learning social roles. |

Consequently, the id is in permanent conflict with the superego. The superego represents what Freud saw as the inherent repressiveness of society. People cope with the tension between social expectations (the superego) and their impulses (the id) by developing defense mechanisms, typically repression, avoidance, or denial (Freud 1960/1923, 1961/1930, 1965/1901). Suppose someone has a great desire for the wrong person or even for another person's property. This person might refuse to admit this (repression); or, acknowledging the impulse, might avoid the opportunity for temptation (avoidance); or might indulge in misconduct, believing it was not misconduct (denial).

The third component of the self in Freud's theory, the **ego,** is the seat of reason and common sense. The ego plays a balancing act between the id and the superego, adapting the desires of the id to the social expectations of the superego. In psychoanalytic theory, the conflict between the id and the superego occurs in the subconscious mind, yet it shapes human behavior. We get a glimpse of the unconscious mind in dreams and in occasional slips of the tongue—the famous "Freudian slip" that is believed to reveal an underlying state of mind. For example, someone might intend to say, "There were six people at the party," but instead says, "There were sex people at the party"!

Some sociologists have criticized Freud's work for not being generalizable because he worked with only a small and unrepresentative group of clients. Still, psychoanalytic theory is an influential analysis of human personality. We often speak of what motivates people, as if motives were internal, unconscious states of mind that direct human behavior.

The psychoanalytic perspective interprets human identity as relatively fixed at an early age in a process greatly influenced by one's family. Nancy Chodorow, a sociologist, uses psychoanalytic theory to explain how gendered personalities develop. She argues that infants are strongly attached to their primary caregiver in our society, typically the mother. As they grow older, they try to separate themselves from their parents, both physically and emotionally, becoming freestanding individuals. However, early attachments to the primary caregiver persist. At the same time, children identify with their same-sex parent, meaning that boys and girls separate themselves from their parents differently. Because girls identify with the mother, they are less able to detach themselves from their primary caregiver. This is the basis, according to Chodorow, for why—even in adulthood—women tend to have personalities based on attachment and an orientation toward others and men have personalities based on greater detachment (Chodorow 1978).

## Social Learning Theory

Whereas psychoanalytic theory places great importance on the *internal* unconscious processes of the human mind, **social learning theory** considers the formation of identity to be a learned response to *external* social stimuli (Bandura and Walters 1963). Social learning theory emphasizes the societal context of socialization. Identity is regarded not as the product of the unconscious but as the result of modeling oneself in response to the expectations of others. According to social learning theory, behaviors and attitudes develop in response to reinforcement and encouragement from those around us.

Early models of social learning theory regarded learning rather simplistically in terms of stimulus and response. People were seen as passive creatures who merely responded to stimuli in their environment. This mechanistic view of social learning was transformed by the work of the Swiss psychologist **Jean Piaget** (1896–1980), who believed that learning was crucial to socialization but that imagination also had a critical role. He argued that the human mind organizes experience into mental categories, or configurations, which he called *schema.* Schema are then modified and developed as social experiences accumulate. Schema might be compared to a person's understanding of the rules of a game. Humans do not simply respond to stimulus but actively absorb experience and figure out what they are seeing to construct a picture (a schema) of the world.

Piaget proposed that children go through distinct stages of cognitive development as they learn the basic rules of reasoning. They must master the skills at each level before they go on to the next (Piaget 1926). In the initial *sensorimotor stage,* children experience the world only through their senses—touch, taste, sight, smell, and sound. Next comes the *preoperational stage,* in which children begin to use language and other symbols. Children in the preoperational stage cannot think in abstract terms, but they do gain an appreciation of meanings that go beyond their immediate senses. They also begin to see things as others might see them. Third, the *concrete operational stage* is when children learn logical principles regarding the concrete world. This stage prepares them for more abstract forms of reasoning. In the *formal operational stage,* children are able to think abstractly and imagine alternatives to the reality in which they live.

Building on Piaget's model of stages of development, psychologist Lawrence Kohlberg (1969) developed a theory of what he called moral development. Kohlberg interpreted the process of developing moral reasoning as occurring in several stages grouped into

three levels: the *preconventional stage,* the *conventional stage,* and the *postconventional stage.* In the first, young children judge right and wrong in simple terms of obedience and punishment, based on their own needs and feelings. In adolescence (the conventional stage), Kohlberg argued, young people develop moral judgment in terms of cultural norms, particularly social acceptance and following authority. In the final stage of moral development, the postconventional stage, people are able to consider abstract ethical questions, thereby showing maturity in their moral reasoning. In Kohlberg's original research, men, he argued, reached a "higher" level of moral development than women because women remained more concerned with feelings and social opinions (a lower phase), whereas men were concerned with authority.

Kohlberg's work was later criticized by social psychologist Carol Gilligan. Gilligan (1982) found that women conceptualize morality in different terms than men. Instead of judging women by a standard set by men's experience, Gilligan showed that women's moral judgments were more contextual than those of men. In other words, when faced with a moral dilemma, women were more likely to consider the different relationships in the social context that would be affected by any decision instead of making moral judgments according to abstract principles. Gilligan's research made an important point, not just about the importance of including women in studies of human development but also about being careful not to assume that social learning follows a universal course for all groups.

## Functionalism and Conflict Theory

Sociologists use a variety of theoretical perspectives to understand the socialization process, including those just described. They can also draw from the major theoretical frameworks we have introduced to understand socialization. From the vantage point of functionalist theory, socialization integrates people into society because it is the mechanism through which they internalize social roles and the values of society. This reinforces social consensus because it encourages at least some degree of conformity. Thus, socialization is one way that society maintains its stability.

Conflict theorists would see this differently. Because of the emphasis in conflict theory on the role of power and coercion in society, in thinking about socialization conflict theorists would be most interested in how group identity is shaped by patterns of inequality in society. A person's or group's identity always emerges in a context, and if that context is one marked by different opportunities for different groups, then one's identity will be shaped by that fact. This may help you understand why, for example, women are more likely to choose college majors in areas of study that have traditionally been associated with women's work opportunities (that is, in the so-called helping professions and in the arts and humanities and less frequently

*Social learning theory emphasizes how people model their behaviors and attitudes on those of others.*

in math and sciences). Furthermore, though social control agents pressure people to conform, people also resist oppression. Thus, the identities of people oppressed in society often include some form of resistance to oppression. This can help you understand why members of racial groups who identify with their own group, not the dominant White group, tend to have higher self-esteem (that is, a stronger valuing of self). In other words, resisting the expectations of a dominant group (such as being subservient or internalizing a feeling of inferiority) can actually heighten one's perceived self-worth.

## Symbolic Interaction Theory

Recall that *symbolic interaction* theory centers on the idea that human actions are based on the meanings people attribute to behavior; these meanings emerge through social interaction (Blumer 1969). Symbolic interaction has been especially important in developing an understanding of socialization. People learn identities and values through socialization. For example, learning to become a good student, then, means taking on the characteristics associated with that role. Because roles are socially defined, they are not real, like objects or things, but are real because of the meanings people give them.

For symbolic interactionists, meaning is constantly reconstructed as people act within their social environments. The **self** is what we imagine we are; it is not only an interior bundle of drives, instincts, and motives. Because of the importance attributed to reflection in symbolic interaction theory, symbolic interactionists use the term *self,* rather than the term *personality,* to refer to a person's identity. Symbolic interaction theory emphasizes that human beings make conscious and meaningful adaptations to their social environment. From a symbolic interactionist perspective, identity is not something that is unconscious and hidden from view, but is socially bestowed and socially sustained (Berger 1963).

Two theorists have greatly influenced the development of symbolic interactionist theory in sociology. **Charles Horton Cooley** (1864–1929) and **George Herbert Mead** (1863–1931) were both sociologists at the University of Chicago in the early 1900s (see Chapter 1). Cooley and Mead saw the self developing in response to the expectations and judgments of others in their social environment.

Charles Horton Cooley postulated the **looking glass self** to explain how a person's conception of self arises through considering our relationships to others (Cooley 1902, 1967/1909). The development of the looking glass self emerges from (1) how we think we appear to others; (2) how we think others judge us; and (3) how the first two make us feel—proud, embarrassed, or other feelings. The looking glass self involves perception and effect, the perception of how others see us and the effect of others' judgment on us (see Figure 4.3).

How others see us is fundamental to the idea of the looking glass self. In seeing ourselves as others do, we respond to the expectations others have of us. This means that the formation of the self is fundamentally a social process—one based in the interaction people have with each other, as well as the human capacity for self-examination. One unique feature of human life is the ability to see ourselves through others' eyes. People can imagine themselves in relationship to others and develop a definition of themselves accordingly. From a symbolic interactionist perspective, the

I'm an INDIVIDUAL

**FIGURE 4.3** *The Looking Glass Self*

*The looking glass self refers to the process by which we attempt to see ourselves as others see us.*

Drawing conceptualized by Norman Andersen.

reflective process is key to the development of the self. If you grow up with others who think you are smart and sharp-witted, chances are you will develop this definition of yourself. If others see you as dull-witted and withdrawn, chances are good that you will see yourself this way. George Herbert Mead agreed with Cooley that children are socialized by responding to others' attitudes toward them. According to Mead, social roles are the basis of all social interaction.

**Taking the role of the other** is the process of putting oneself into the point of view of another. To Mead, role-taking is a source of self-awareness. As people take on new roles, their awareness of self changes. According to Mead, identity emerges from the roles one plays. He explained this process in detail by examining childhood socialization, which he saw as occurring in three stages: the imitation stage, the play stage, and the game stage (Mead 1934). In each phase of development, the child becomes more proficient at taking the role of the other. In the first stage, the **imitation stage,** children merely copy the behavior of those around them. Role-taking in this phase is nonexistent because the child simply mimics the behavior of those in the surrounding environment without much understanding of the social meaning of the behavior. Although the child in the imitation stage has little understanding of the behavior being copied, he or she is learning to become a social being. For example, think of young children who simply mimic the behavior of people around them (such as pretending to read a book, but doing so with the book upside down).

In the second stage, the **play stage,** children begin to take on the roles of significant people in their environment, not just imitating but incorporating their relationship to the other. Especially meaningful is when children take on the role of **significant others,** those with whom they have a close affiliation. A child pretending to be his mother may talk to himself as the mother would. The child begins to develop self-awareness, seeing himself or herself as others do.

In the third stage of socialization, the **game stage,** the child becomes capable of taking on multiple roles at the same time. These roles are organized in a complex system that gives the child a more general or comprehensive view of the self. In this stage, the child begins to comprehend the system of social relationships in which he or she is located. The child not only sees himself or herself from the perspective of a significant other, but also understands how people are related to each other and how others are related to him or her. This is the phase where children internalize (incorporate into the self) an abstract understanding of how society sees them.

Mead compared the lessons of the game stage to a baseball game. In baseball, all roles together make the game. The pitcher does not just throw the ball past the batter as if they were the only two people on the field; rather, each player has a specific role, and each role intersects with the others. The network of social roles and the division of labor in the baseball game is a social system, like the social systems children must learn as they develop a concept of themselves in society.

---

## SEE *FOR YOURSELF*

### *CHILDHOOD PLAY AND SOCIALIZATION*

The purpose of this exercise is to explain how *childhood socialization* is a mechanism for passing on social *norms* and *values*. Begin by identifying a form of play that you engaged in as a young child. What did you play? Who did you play with? Was it structured or unstructured play? What were the rules? Were they formal or informal, and who controlled whether they were observed?

1. Now think about what *norms* and *values* were being taught to you by way of this play. Do they still affect you today? If so, how?

2. How does your experience compare to those of students in your class who differ from you in terms of gender, race, ethnicity, regional origin, and so forth. Are there differences in learned norms and values that can be attributed to these different social characteristics?

---

In the game stage, children learn more than just the roles of significant others in their environment. They also acquire a concept of the **generalized other**—the abstract composite of social roles and social expectations. In the generalized other, they have an example of community values and general social expectations that adds to their understanding of self; however, children do not all learn the same generalized other. Depending on one's social position (that is, race, class, gender, region, or religion), one learns a particular set of social and cultural expectations.

If the self is socially constructed through the expectations of others, how do people become individuals? Mead answered this by saying that the self has two dimensions: the "I" and the "me." The "I" is the unique part of individual personality, the active, creative, self-defining part. The "me" is the passive, conforming self, the part that reacts to others. In each person, there is a balance between the I and the me, similar to the tension Freud proposed between the id and the superego. Mead differed from Freud, however, in his judgment about when identity is formed. Freud felt that identity was fixed in childhood and henceforth driven by internal, not external, forces. In Mead's version, social identity is always in flux, constantly emerging (or "becoming") and dependent on social situations. Over time, identity stabilizes as one learns to respond consistently to common situations.

Social expectations associated with given roles change as people redefine situations and as social and historical conditions change; thus, the social expectations learned through the socialization process are not permanently fixed. For example, as more women enter the paid labor force and as men take on additional responsibilities in the home, the expectations associated with motherhood and fatherhood are changing. Men now experience some of the role conflicts that women have faced in balancing work and family. As the roles of mother and father are redefined, children are learning new socialization patterns; however, traditional gender expectations maintain a remarkable grip. Despite many changes in family life and organization, young girls are still socialized for motherhood and young boys are still socialized for greater independence and autonomy.

# Growing Up in a Diverse Society

Understanding the institutional context of socialization is important for understanding how socialization affects different groups in society. Socialization makes us members of our society. It instills in us the values of the culture and brings society into our self-definition, our perceptions of others, and our understanding of the world around us. Socialization is not, however, a uniform process, as the different examples developed in this chapter show. In a society as complex and diverse as the United States, no two people will have exactly the same experiences. We can find similarities between us, often across vast social and cultural differences, but variation in social contexts creates vastly different socialization experiences.

Furthermore, current changes in the U.S. population are creating new multiracial and multicultural environments in which young people grow up. Schools, as an example, are in many places being transformed by the large number of immigrant groups entering the school system. In such places, children come into contact with other children from a variety of different groups. This creates a new context in which children form their social values and learn their social identities (see the box "Doing Sociological Research: Children's Understanding of Race").

One task of the sociological imagination is to examine the influence of different contexts on socialization. Where you grow up; how your family is structured; what resources you have at your disposal; your racial–ethnic identity, gender, and nationality—all shape the socialization experience. Socialization experiences for all groups are shaped by many factors that intermingle and intersect to form the context for socialization.

One way that this has been demonstrated is in research by sociologist Annette Lareau (2003). Over an extended period of time, Lareau and her research assistants carefully observed White and Black families from middle-class, working-class, and poor back-

*The family serves as a major agent of socialization, especially of the young.*

grounds. The researchers spent many hours in the homes of the families studied, including following the children and parents as they went about their daily routines. Based on these detailed observations, they observed important class differences in how families— both Black and White—socialize their children.

The middle-class children were highly programmed in their activities, their lives filled with various organized activities—music lessons, sports, school groups, and so forth. In contrast, the working-class and poor children, regardless of race, were less structured in their activities, and economic constraints were a constant theme in their daily lives. But the pace of life for working-class and poor children was slower and more relaxed. These children had more unstructured play time, whereas middle-class children's lives were a constant barrage of highly structured activities with intense time demands. Lareau argues that middle-class families engaged in *concerted cultivation* of childhood, meaning they made "deliberate and sustained effort to stimulate children's development and to cultivate their cognitive and social skills" (Lareau 2003: 238). Working-class and poor children experienced more "natural growth," that is, childhood experiences that allow them to develop in a less-structured environment with more time for creative play.

As a result, middle-class children tend to learn a more individualized self-concept and a sense of entitlement, but the price is an overly programmed daily life. Working-class and poor children experience obvious costs in that they have more financial constraints, but even more fundamentally, Lareau argues, they are left unable to negotiate their way through various social institutions as effectively as the middle-class. In a sense, these childhood socialization patterns are also reshaping the class system in which children will likely find themselves as adults. Middle-class children are being prepared, even if inadvertently, for lives with a sense of privilege and entitlement; working-class children, for responding to the directives of others. In this way, patterns of socialization occurring because of social class origins are training children to take their place in the class system that will likely mark their adult lives. Thus, social class is an important—although often invisible—force shaping the socialization of young people.

# Aging and the Life Course

Socialization begins the moment a person is born. As soon as the sex of a child is known (which now can be even before birth), parents, grandparents, brothers, and sisters greet the infant with different expectations, depending on whether it is a boy or a girl. Socialization does not come to an end as we reach adulthood; rather, it continues through our lifetime. As we enter new situations, and even as we interact in familiar ones, we learn new roles and undergo changes in identity.

Sociologists use the term **life course** perspective to describe and analyze the connection between people's personal attributes, the roles they occupy, the life events they experience, and the social and historical aspects of these events (Stoller and Gibson 2000). The life course perspective underscores the point made by C. Wright Mills (introduced in Chapter 1) that personal biographies are linked to specific social–historical periods. Thus, different generations are strongly influenced by large-scale events (such as war, immigration, economic prosperity, or depression, for example).

The phases of the life course are familiar: childhood, youth and adolescence, adulthood, and old age. These phases of the life course bind different generations and define some of life's most significant events, such as birth, marriage, retirement, and death.

## Childhood

During childhood, socialization establishes one's initial identity and values. In this period, the family is an extremely influential source of socialization, but experiences in school, peer relationships, sports, religion, and the media also have a profound effect. Children acquire knowledge of their culture through countless subtle cues that provide them with an understanding of what it means to live in society.

Socializing cues begin as early as infancy, when parents and others begin to describe their children based on their perceptions. Frequently, these perceptions are derived from the cultural expectations parents have for children. Parents of girls may describe their babies as "sweet" and "cuddly," whereas boys are described as "strong" and "alert." Even though when they are tiny infants it is difficult to physically identify baby boys and girls, in this culture parents dress even their tiny infants in colors and styles that typically distinguish one gender from the other.

The lessons of childhood socialization come in myriad ways, some more subtle than others. In an example of how gender influences childhood socialization, researchers observed mothers and fathers who were walking young children through public places. Although the parents may not have been aware of it, both mothers and fathers were more protective toward girl toddlers than boy toddlers. Parents were more likely to let boy toddlers walk alone, but held girls' hands, carried them, or kept them in strollers (Mitchell et al. 1992).

Much socialization in early childhood takes place through play and games. Games that encourage competition help instill the value of competitiveness throughout someone's life. Likewise, play with other children and games that are challenging give children important intellectual, social, and interpersonal skills. Extensive research has been done on how children's play and games influence their identities as boys and girls (Campenni 1999). Generally, the research finds that boys' play tends to be rougher, more aggressive, and involve more specific rules. Boys are also more likely to be involved in group play, and girls engage in more conversational play (Moller et al. 1992). Sociologists have concluded that the games children play significantly influence their development into adults.

Another enormous influence on childhood socialization is what children observe of the adult world. Children are keen observers, and what they perceive will influence their self-concept and how they relate to others. This is vividly illustrated by research revealing how many adult child abusers were themselves victims of child abuse (Fattah 1994). Children become socialized by observing the roles of those around them and internalizing the values, beliefs, and expectations of their culture.

## Adolescence

Only recently has adolescence been thought of as a separate phase in the life cycle. Until the early twentieth century, children moved directly from childhood roles to adult roles. It was only when formal education was extended to all classes that adolescence emerged as a particular phase in life when young people are regarded as no longer children, but not yet adults. There are no clear boundaries to adolescence, although it generally lasts from junior high school until the time one takes on adult roles by getting a job, marrying, and so forth. Adolescence can include the period through high school and extend right up through college graduation.

**Erik Erikson** (1980), the noted psychologist, stated that the central task of adolescence is the

> ## doing sociological research

## Children's Understanding of Race

In a racially stratified society, people learn concepts about race that shape their interactions with others. Sociologists Debra Van Ausdale and Joe Feagin wanted to know how children understand racial and ethnic concepts and how this influences their interaction with other children.

**Research Questions:** How do children learn about race? Prior to Van Ausdale and Feagin's study, most knowledge about children's understandings of race came from experimental studies in a laboratory or from psychological tests and interviews with children. Van Ausdale and Feagin wanted to study children in a natural setting so they observed children in school, systematically observing children's interactions with one another.

**Research Method:** They observed three-, four-, and five-year-olds in an urban preschool. Twenty-four of the children were White; nineteen, Asian; four, Black; three, biracial; three, Middle Eastern; two, Latino; and three classified as "other." The children's racial designations were provided by their parents.

The researchers observed in the school five days a week for eleven months and saw one to three episodes involving significant racial or ethnic matters every day.

**Research Results:** The researchers found that young children use racial and ethnic concepts to exclude other children from play. Sometimes language is the ethnic marker; other times, skin color. The children showed an awareness of negative racial attitudes, even though they were attending a school that prided itself on limiting children's exposure to prejudice and discrimination and used a multicultural curriculum to teach students to value racial and ethnic diversity. At times, the children also used racial–ethnic understandings to include others—teaching other students about

racial–ethnic identities. Race and ethnicity were also the basis for children's concepts of themselves and others. As an example, one four-year-old White child insisted that her classmate was Indian because she wore her long, dark hair in a braid. When the classmate explained that she was not Indian, the young girl remarked that maybe her mother was Indian.

**Conclusions and Implications:** Throughout the research, the children showed how significant racial-ethnic concepts were in their interactions with others. Race and ethnicity are powerful identifiers of self and others. Despite the importance of race in the children's interactions, Van Ausdale and Feagin also noted a strong tendency for the adults they observed to *deny* that race and ethnicity were significant to the children. The implication is that *while adults tend to deny the reality of race in their everyday lives*, observing the interaction of children helps to instruct adults about the relevance of race and how racial awareness develops.

*Through the socialization process, young children learn the values of their culture. These values shape their relationships with other people.*

*Source:* Van Ausdale, Debra, and Joe R. Feagin. 2000. *The First R: How Children Learn Race and Racism.* Lanham, MD: Rowman and Littlefield.

formation of a consistent identity. Adolescents are trying to become independent of their families, but they have not yet moved into adult roles. Conflict and confusion can arise as the adolescent swings between childhood and adult maturity. Some argue that adolescence is a period of delayed maturity. Although society expects adolescents to behave like adults, they

are denied many privileges associated with adult life. Until age eighteen, they cannot vote or marry without permission, and sexual activity is condemned. In addition, until age twenty-one they cannot legally drink alcohol. The tensions of adolescence have been blamed for numerous social problems, such as drug and alcohol abuse, youth violence, and the school dropout rate.

The issues that young people face are a good barometer of social change across generations. Today's young people face an uncertain world where adult roles are less predictable than in the past. Marriage later in life, high divorce rates, frequent technological change, and economic recession all create a confusing environment for young people (Csikzentmihalyi and Schneider 2000). Studies of adolescents find that, in this context, young people understand the need for flexibility, specialization, and, likely, frequent job change. Although the media stereotype adolescents as slackers, most teens are willing to work hard, do not engage in criminal or violent activity, and have high expectations for an education that will lead to a good job. Many, however, find that their expectations are out of alignment with the opportunities that are actually available, particularly during periods of economic downturn, such as the recession of 2008–2009.

Patterns of adolescent socialization vary significantly by race and social class. National surveys find some intriguing class and race differences in how young people think about work and play in their lives.

In general, the most economically privileged young people see their activities as more like play than work, whereas those less well off are more likely to define their activities as work. Likewise, White youth (boys especially) are more likely than other groups to see their lives as playful. The researchers interpret these findings to mean that being economically privileged allows you to think of your work as if it were play. Being in a less advantaged position, on the other hand, makes you see the world as more "worklike." This is supported by further findings that young people from less advantaged backgrounds spend more time in activities they define as purposeless (Schneider and Stevenson 1999).

## Adulthood

Socialization does not end when one becomes an adult. Building on the identity formed in childhood and adolescence, adult socialization is the process of learning new roles and expectations in adult life. More so than at earlier stages in life, **adult socialization** involves learning behaviors and attitudes appropriate to specific situations and roles.

## map 4.1 VIEWING SOCIETY IN GLOBAL PERSPECTIVE

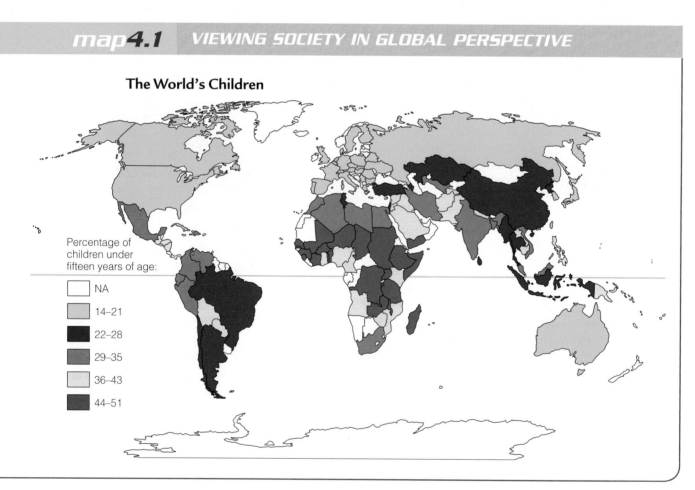

### The World's Children

Percentage of children under fifteen years of age:

- NA
- 14–21
- 22–28
- 29–35
- 36–43
- 44–51

*Throughout the world, the proportion of children as a percentage of the population of a given country tends to be higher in those countries that are most economically disadvantaged and most overpopulated. In such countries, children are also more likely to die young but are needed to contribute to the labor that families do. What consequences do you think the proportion of children in a given society has for the society as a whole?*

*Data:* From the U.S. Census Bureau. 2008. *Statistical Abstract of the United States 2007.* Washington, DC: U.S. Government Printing Office

Youths entering college, to take an example from young adulthood, are newly independent and have new responsibilities. In college, one acquires not just an education but also a new identity. Those who enter college directly from high school may encounter conflicts with their family over their newfound status. Older students who work and attend college may experience difficulties (defined as *role conflict*; see Chapter 5) trying to meet dual responsibilities, especially if their family is not supportive. Meeting multiple and conflicting demands may require the returning student to develop different expectations about how much she can accomplish or to establish different priorities about what she will attempt. These changes reflect a new stage in her socialization (Settersten and Lovegreen 1998).

Adult life is peppered with events that may require the adult to adapt to new roles. Marriage, a new career, starting a family, entering the military, getting a divorce, or dealing with a death in the family all transform an individual's previous social identity. In today's world, these transitions through the life course are not as orderly as they were in the past. Where there was once a sequential and predictable trajectory of schooling, work, and family roles through one's twenties and thirties, that is no longer the case. Younger generations now experience diverse patterns in the sequencing of work, schooling, and family formation—even returning home—than was true in the past. These changes complicate the life course, and people have to make different adaptations to these changing roles (Cooksey and Rindfuss 2001; Rindfuss et al. 1999).

Becoming an adult is also taking longer than before. People stay in school longer, are marrying later, and postponing childbearing (see Table 4.2). With these social changes, people have to be inventive in the roles they occupy because some of the old expectations no longer apply.

Another part of learning a new role is **anticipatory socialization,** the learning of expectations associated with a role a person expects to enter in the future. One might rehearse the expectations associated with being a professor by working as a teaching assistant, taking a class in preparation for becoming a father, or attending a summer program to prepare for entering college. Anticipatory socialization allows a person to foresee the expectations associated with a new role and to learn what is expected in that role in advance.

In the transition from an old role to a new one, individuals often vacillate between their old and new identities as they adjust to fresh settings and expectations. An interesting example is *coming out,* the process of identifying oneself as gay or lesbian. This can be either a public coming out or a private acknowledgment of sexual orientation. The process can take years, and generally means coming out to a few people, at first selective family members or friends who are likely to have the most positive reaction. Coming out is rarely a single event, but occurs in stages on the way to developing a new identity—one that is not only a new sexual identity but also a new sense of self (Due 1995).

## Age and Aging

Passage through adulthood involves many transitions. In our society, one of the most difficult transitions is the passage to old age. We are taught to fear aging in this society, and many people spend a lot of time and money trying to keep looking young. Unlike many other societies, ours does not revere the elderly, but instead devalues them, making the aging process even more difficult.

It is easy to think that aging is just a natural fact. Despite desperate attempts to hide gray hair, eliminate wrinkles, and reduce middle-aged bulge, aging is inevitable. The skin creases and sags, the hair thins, metabolism slows, and bones become less dense and more brittle by losing bone mass. Although aging is a physical process, the social dimensions of aging are just as important, if not more so, in determining the aging process. Just think about how some people appear to age much more rapidly than others. Some sixty-year-olds look only forty, and some forty-year-olds look sixty.

| table4.2 | *Showing the Transition to Adulthood* | |
|---|---|---|
| | **1980** | **2007** |
| Percentage aged 20–21 in school | 31.9% | 33.0% |
| Median age at first marriage | | |
| Women | 22.0 yrs | 25.8 yrs |
| Men | 24.7 yrs | 27.5 yrs |
| Fertility rate, women aged 15–19 | 68.4 (per 1000 women) | 60.0 (per 1000 women) |
| Percentage aged 16–19 in labor force | | |
| Women | 9.6% | 4.9% |
| Men | 8.1% | 4.3% |

*Source:* U.S. Census Bureau. 2008. *Statistical Abstract of the United States 2007.* Washington, DC: U.S. Government Printing Office.

Bob E. Daemmrich/Sygma/Corbis

BrooksKraft/Corbis

*The stresses of life that accompany age can change a person in many ways, as is evident in these "before" and "after" photographs of former President George W. Bush.*

These differences result from combinations of biological and social factors, such as genetics, eating and exercise habits, stress, smoking habits, pollution in the physical environment, and many other factors. The social dimensions of aging are what interest sociologists.

Although the physiology of aging proceeds according to biological processes, what it *means* to grow older is a social phenomenon. **Age stereotypes** are preconceived judgments about what different age groups are like. Stereotypes abound for both old and young people. Young people, especially teenagers, are stereotyped as irresponsible, addicted to loud music, lazy ("slackers"), sloppy, and so on; the elderly are stereotyped as forgetful, set in their ways, mentally dim, and unproductive. Though like any stereotype, these stereotypes are largely myths, they are widely believed. Age stereotypes also differ for different groups. Older women are stereotyped as having lost their sexual appeal, contrary to the stereotype of older men as handsome or "dashing" and desirable. Gender is, in fact, one of the most significant factors in age stereotypes. Women may even be viewed as becoming old sooner than men because people describe women as old a decade sooner than they do men (Stoller and Gibson 2000)!

Age stereotypes are also reinforced through popular culture. Advertisements depict women as needing creams and lotions to hide "the telltale signs of aging." Men are admonished to cover the patches of gray hair that appear or to use other products to prevent baldness. Entire industries are constructed on the fear

of aging that popular culture promotes. Facelifts, tummy tucks, and vitamin advertisements all claim to "reverse the process of aging," even though the aging process is a fact of life.

**Age Prejudice and Discrimination Age prejudice** refers to a negative attitude about an age group that is generalized to all people in that group. Prejudice against the elderly is prominent. The elderly are often thought of as childlike and thus incapable of adult responsibility. Prejudice relegates people to a perceived lower status in society and stems from the stereotypes associated with different age groups.

**Age discrimination** is the different and unequal treatment of people based solely on their age. Whereas age prejudice is an attitude, age discrimination involves actual behavior. As an example, people may talk "baby talk" to the elderly. This reinforces the stereotype of the elderly as childlike and incompetent. Some forms of age discrimination are illegal. The Age Discrimination Employment Act, first passed in 1967 but amended several times since, protects people from age discrimination in employment. It states that age discrimination is a violation of the individual's civil rights. An employer can neither hire nor fire someone based solely on age, nor segregate or classify workers based on age. Age discrimination cases have become one of the most frequently filed cases through the Equal Employment Opportunity Commission (EEOC), the federal agency set up to monitor violations of civil rights in employment.

**Ageism** is a term sociologists use to describe the institutionalized practice of age prejudice and discrimination. More than a single attitude or an explicit act of discrimination, ageism is structured into the institutional fabric of society. Like racism and sexism, ageism encompasses both prejudice and discrimination, but it is also manifested in the structure of institutions. As such, it does not have to be intentional or overt to affect how age groups are treated. Ageism in society means that, regardless of laws that prohibit age discrimination, a person's age is a significant predictor of his or her life chances. Resources are distributed in society in ways that advantage some age groups and disadvantage others; cultural belief systems devalue the elderly; society's systems of care are often inadequate to meet people's needs as they grow old—these are the manifestations of ageism, a persistent and institutionalized feature of society.

**Age Stratification.** Most societies produce age hierarchies—systems in which some age groups have more power and better life chances than others. **Age stratification** refers to the hierarchical ranking of different age groups in society. Age stratification exists because processes in society ensure that people of different ages differ in their access to society's rewards, power, and privileges. As we will see, in the United States and elsewhere, age is a major source of inequality (see Figure 4.4).

Age is an *ascribed status*; that is, age is determined by when you were born. Different from other ascribed statuses, which remain relatively constant over the duration of a person's life, age changes steadily throughout your life. Still, you remain part of a particular generation—something sociologists call an **age cohort**—an aggregate group of people born during the same period.

People in the same age cohort share the same historical experiences—wars, technological developments, and economic fluctuations—although they might do so in different ways, depending on other life factors. Living through the Great Depression, for example, shaped an entire generation's attitudes and behaviors, as did growing up in the 1960s, as will being a member of the contemporary youth generation. Depending on how the major economic recession of 2009 shakes out, it too may significantly shape the current youth generation. Recall from Chapter 1 that C. Wright Mills saw the task of the sociological imagination as analyzing the relationship between biography and history. Understanding the experiences of different age cohorts is one way you can do this. People who live through the same historic period experience a similar impact of that period in their personal lives. The troubles and triumphs they experience and the societal issues they face are rooted in the commonality established by their age cohort. The shared historical experiences of age cohorts result in discernible generational patterns in social attitudes and similarity of life chances (Stoller and Gibson 2000).

Different generations must grapple with and respond to different social contexts. Someone born just after World War II would, upon graduation from high school or college, enter a labor market where there was widespread availability of jobs and, for many, expanding opportunities. Now young people face a labor market where entry-level jobs in secure corporate environments are rare and where many are trapped in low-level jobs with little opportunity for advancement. Many young people worry, as a result, about whether they will be able to achieve even the same degree of economic status as their parents—the first time this has happened in U.S. history. Understanding how society shapes the experiences of different generations is what sociologists mean by saying that age is a structural feature of society (see Figure 4.5).

The age structure of society shapes people's opportunities and is the basis for cultural understandings of age itself. In the very poor regions of northeast Brazil, for example, mothers show little attachment to those who are born small and weak; if they die, there is little ceremony, and their graves remain unmarked. Because sick infants are believed to be angels who fly to heaven, mother's tears are believed to dampen their wings, risking their flight. Anthropologists interpret this as the mothers' reaction to their impoverishment: They cannot invest attention or emotion in the lives of children who are unlikely to live (Scheper-Hughes 1992; Peoples and Bailey 2003).

There is also great variation in how the old are treated. In many societies, older people are given enormous respect. There may be traditions to honor the elders, and they may be given authority over decisions in society, as they are perceived as most wise. On the other hand, among some cultures, adults who can no longer contribute to the society because of old

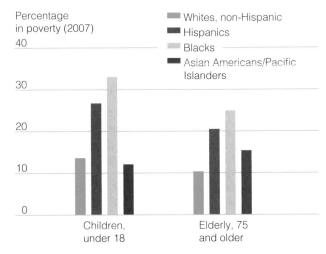

**FIGURE 4.4** *Poverty by Age and Race*

*Source:* DeNavas-Walt, Carmen, Bernadette D. Proctor, and Cheryl Hill Lee. *Income, Poverty, and Health Insurance Coverage in the United States: 2008.* Washington, DC: U.S. Census Bureau. **www.census.gov**

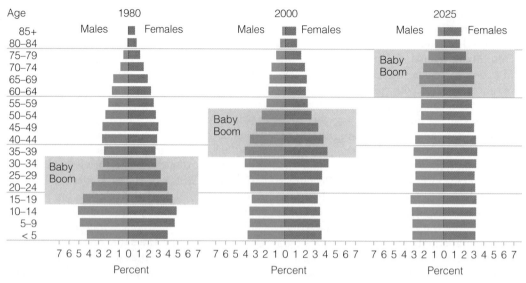

**FIGURE 4.5** *An Aging Society*

*This figure represents a* population pyramid *and shows the decreasing number of people in an age cohort as that cohort becomes older—as the cohort moves up the pyramid. This is illustrated by the Baby Boom cohort in this figure, and individuals in it share many experiences not shared by those not in the particular cohort. Shown here are the shapes of the pyramid for three different periods (projected for the year 2025).*

Source: U.S. Census Bureau. 2008. *Statistical Abstract of the United States 2007.* Washington, DC: U.S. Department of Commerce.

age or illness may be perceived as extreme burdens. You might ask yourself how cultural definitions in this society affect how people grieve for different age groups. Is the death of a young person perceived as somehow more tragic than the death of a very old person? How do people react in each circumstance? Your answer will likely reveal the cultural beliefs surrounding aging in this culture.

Why does society stratify people on the basis of age? Once again we find that the three main theoretical perspectives of sociological analysis—functionalism, conflict theory, and symbolic interaction—offer different explanations (see Table 4.3). Functionalist sociologists ask whether the grouping of individuals contributes in some way to the common good of society. From this perspective, adulthood is functional to society because adults are seen as the group contributing most fully to it; the elderly are not. Functionalists argue that older people are seen as less useful and are therefore granted lower status in society. Youth are in between. The constraints and expectations placed on youth—they are prohibited from engaging in a variety of "adult" activities, expected to go to school, not expected to support themselves—are seen to free them from the cares of adulthood and give them time and opportunity to learn an occupation and prepare to contribute to society.

According to the functionalist argument, the elderly voluntarily withdraw from society by retiring and lessening their participation in social activities such as church, civic affairs, and family. **Disengagement theory,** drawn from functionalism, predicts that as people age, they gradually withdraw from participation

in society and are simultaneously relieved of responsibilities. This withdrawal is functional to society because it provides for an orderly transition from one generation to the next. The young presumably infuse the roles they take over from the elderly with youthful energy and stamina. According to the functionalist argument, the diminished usefulness of the elderly justifies their depressed earning power and their relative neglect in social support networks.

Conflict theory focuses on the competition over scarce resources between age groups. Among the most important scarce resources are jobs. Unlike functionalist theory, conflict theory offers an explanation of why both youth and the elderly are assigned lower status in society and are most likely to be poor. Barring youth and the elderly from the labor market eliminates these groups from competition, improving the prospects for middle-aged workers. Removed from competition, both the young and the old have very little power, and like other minorities, they are denied access to the resources they need to change their situation. Conflict theory also helps explain that competition can emerge between age groups, such as deciding whether to limit Social Security payments to save for future generations.

Symbolic interaction theory analyzes the different meanings attributed to social entities. Symbolic interactionists ask what meanings become attached to different age groups and to what extent these meanings explain how society ranks such groups. Definitions of aging are socially constructed, as we saw in our discussion of age stereotypes. Moreover, in some societies, the elderly may be perceived as having higher status

| table 4.3 | Sociological Theories of Aging | | |
| --- | --- | --- | --- |
| | **Functional Theory** | **Conflict Theory** | **Symbolic Interaction** |
| *Age differentiation* | Contributes to the common good of society because each group has varying levels of utility in society | Results from the different economic status and power of age cohorts | Occurs in most societies, but the social value placed on different age groups varies across diverse cultures |
| *Age groups* | Are valued according to their usefulness in society | Compete for resources in society, resulting in generational inequities and thus potential conflict | Are stereotyped according to the perceived value of different groups |
| *Age stratification* | Results from the functional value of different age cohorts | Intertwines with inequalities of class, race, and gender | Promotes ageism, which is institutionalized prejudice and discrimination against old people |

© piluhin/Alamy

*For many, old age is a time for new accomplishments and achievements, such as for this marathon runner.*

than in other societies. Symbolic interaction considers the role of social perception in understanding the sociology of age. Age clearly takes on significant social meaning—meaning that varies from society to society for a given age group and that varies within a society for different age groups.

Growing old in a society such as the United States with such a strong emphasis on youth means encountering social stereotypes about the old, adjusting to diminished social and financial resources, and sometimes living in the absence of social supports, even when facing some of life's most difficult transitions, such as declining health and the loss of loved ones. Still, many people experience old age as a time of great satisfaction and enjoy a sense of accomplishment connected to work, family, and friends. The degree of satisfaction during old age depends to a great extent on the social support networks established earlier in life—evidence of the continuing influence of socialization.

## Rites of Passage

A **rite of passage** is a ceremony or ritual that marks the transition of an individual from one role to another. Rites of passage define and legitimize abrupt role changes that begin or end each stage of life. The ceremonies surrounding rites of passage are often dramatic and infused with awe and solemnity. Examples include graduation ceremonies; weddings; and religious affirmations, such as the Jewish ceremony of the bar mitzvah for boys or the bat mitzvah for girls, confirmation for Catholics, and adult baptism for many Christian denominations.

Formal promotions or entry into some new careers may also include rites of passage. Completing police academy training or being handed one's diploma are examples. Such rites usually include family and friends, who watch the ceremony with pride; people frequently keep mementos of these rites as markers of the transition through life's major stages. Bridal showers and baby showers have been analyzed as rites of passage. At a shower, the person who is being honored is about to assume a new role and identity—from young woman to wife or mother. Rites of passage entail public announcement of the new status for the benefit of both the individual and those with whom the newly anointed person will interact. In the absence of such rituals, the transformation of identity would not be formally recognized, perhaps leaving uncertainty in the youngster or the community about

*Every culture has important rites of passage that mark the transition from one phase in the life course to another. Here different cultural traditions distinguish the rites of passage associated with marriage: a traditional Nigerian wedding (upper left); a young American couple (upper right); a Shinto (Japanese) bride taking a marital pledge by drinking sake (lower left); and a newlywed orthodox Christian couple in Macedonia (lower right).*

the individual's worthiness, preparedness, or community acceptance.

Sociologists have noted that in the United States there is no standard and formalized rite of passage marking the transition from childhood to adulthood. As a consequence, the period of adolescence is attended by ambivalence and uncertainty. As adolescents hover between adult and child status, they may not have the clear sense of identity that a rite of passage can provide. However, although there is no universal ceremony in our culture by which young people are noted as moving from child to adult, some subcultures do mark the occasion. Among the wealthy, the debutante's coming out celebration is a traditional introduction of a young woman to adult society. Latinos may celebrate the *quinceañera* (fifteenth birthday) of young girls. A tradition of the Catholic Church, this rite recognizes the girl's coming of age, while also keeping faith with an ethnic heritage. Dressed in white, she is introduced by her parents to the larger community. Formerly associated mostly with working-class families and other Latinos, the quinceañera has also become popular among affluent Mexican Americans, who may

match New York debutante society by spending as much as $50,000–$100,000 on the event.

## Resocialization

Most transitions people experience in their lifetimes involve continuity with the former self as it undergoes gradual redefinition. Sometimes, however, adults are forced to undergo a radical shift of identity. **Resocialization** is the process by which existing social roles are radically altered or replaced (Fein 1988). Resocialization is especially likely when people enter institutional settings where the institution claims enormous control over the individual. Examples include the military, prisons, monastic orders, and some cults (see also Chapter 6 for a discussion of total institutions). When military recruits enter boot camp, they are stripped of personal belongings, their heads are shaved, and they are issued identical uniforms. Although military recruits do not discard their former identities, the changes brought about by becoming a soldier can be dramatic and are meant to make the military one's *primary group*, not one's family, friends, or personal history. The military represents an extreme form of resocialization in which individuals are expected to subordinate their identity to that of the group. In such organizations, individuals are interchangeable, and group consensus (meaning, in the military, unanimous, unquestioned subordination to higher ranks) is an essential component of group cohesion and effectiveness. Military personnel are expected to act as soldiers, not as individuals. Understanding the importance of resocialization on entry to the military helps us understand such practices as "the rat line" at VMI (Virginia Military Institute) where members of the senior class taunt and harass new recruits.

Resocialization often occurs when people enter hierarchical organizations that require them to respond to authority on principle, not out of individual loyalty. The resocialization process promotes group solidarity and generates a feeling of belonging. Participants in these settings are expected to honor the symbols and objectives of the organization; disloyalty is seen as a threat to the entire group. In a convent, for example, nuns are expected to subordinate their own identity to the calling they have taken on, a calling that requires obedience both to God and to an abbess.

Angela Hampton Picture Library/Alamy

*Hazings are good examples of rites of passage that often accompany induction into a group. The hazing scene here (hair pulling) is relatively mild compared to many high school hazing incidents.*

## thinkingsociologically

**Find a group of adults (young or old) who have just entered a new stage of life (getting a new or first job, getting married, becoming a grandparent, retiring, entering a nursing home, and so forth), and ask them to describe this new experience. Ask questions such as what others expect of them in this new role, how these expectations are communicated to them, what changes they see in their own behavior, and what expectations they have of their new situation. What do your observations tell you about *adult socialization*?**

Resocialization may involve degrading initiates physically and psychologically with the aim of breaking down or redefining their old identity. They may be given menial and humiliating tasks and be expected to act in a subservient manner. Social control in such a setting may be exerted by peer ridicule or actual punishment. Fraternities and sororities offer an interesting everyday example of this pattern of resocialization. Intense resocialization rituals, whether in jailhouses, barracks, convents, or sorority and fraternity houses, serve the same purpose: imposing some sort of ordeal to cement the seriousness and permanence of new roles and expectations.

### The Process of Conversion

Resocialization also occurs during what people popularly think of as conversion. A conversion is a far-reaching transformation of identity, often related to religious or political beliefs. People usually think of conversion in the context of cults, but it happens in other settings as well.

John Walker Lindh was a U.S. citizen when the United States entered the Iraq war. He joined the Taliban in Afghanistan and was later charged with conspiring to kill Americans abroad and supporting terrorist organizations. Lindh is an example of an *extreme conversion*. He was raised Catholic in an affluent family, but he converted to Islam as a teenager, changing not just his ideas, but also his dress. Neighbors described him as being transformed from "a boy who wore blue jeans and T-shirts to an imposing figure in flowing Muslim garb" (Robertson and Burke 2001). As a young man, he traveled to Yemen and Pakistan to study language and the Koran and was introduced there to the Taliban. News sources have since named him the "American Taliban."

As when people join religious cults, this is extreme conversion, but conversion happens in less extreme situations, too. People may convert to a different religion, thereby undergoing resocialization by changing beliefs and religious practices. Or someone may become strongly influenced by the beliefs of a social movement and abruptly or gradually change beliefs—even identity—as a result.

### The Brainwashing Debate

Extreme examples of resocialization are seen in the phenomenon popularly called "brainwashing." In the popular view of brainwashing, converts have their previous identities totally stripped; the transformation is seen as so complete that only deprogramming can restore the former self. Potential candidates of brainwashing include people who enter religious cults, prisoners of war, and hostages. Sociologists have examined brainwashing to illustrate the process of resocialization.

As the result of their research, sociologists have cautioned against using the word *brainwashing* when referring to this form of conversion. The term implies that humans are mere puppets or passive victims whose free will can be taken away during these conversions (Robbins 1988). In religious cults, however, converts do not necessarily drop their former identity.

Sociological research has found that the people most susceptible to cult influence are the most suggestible, primarily young adults who are socially isolated, drifting, and having difficulty performing in other areas (such as in their jobs or in school). Such people may choose to affiliate with cults voluntarily. Despite the widespread belief that people have to be deprogrammed to be freed from the influence of cults, many people are able to leave on their own (Robbins 1988). So-called brainwashing is simply a manifestation of the *social influence people experience through interaction with others*. Even in cult settings, socialization is an interactive process, not just a transfer of group expectations to passive victims.

Forcible confinement and physical torture can be instruments of extreme resocialization. Under severe captivity and deprivation, a captured person may come to identify with the captor; this is known as the **Stockholm Syndrome.** In such instances, the captured person has become dependent on the captor. On release, the captive frequently needs debriefing, or deprogramming. Prisoners of war and hostages may not lose free will altogether, but they do lose freedom of movement and association, which makes prisoners intensely dependent on their captors and therefore vulnerable to the captor's influence.

The Stockholm Syndrome can help explain why some battered women do not leave their abusing spouses or boyfriends. Dependent on their abuser both financially and emotionally, battered women often develop identities that keep them attached to men who abuse them. In these cases, outsiders often think the women should leave instantly, whereas the women themselves may find leaving difficult, even in the most abusive situations.

# Chapter Summary

- ### What is socialization, and why is it significant for society?

  *Socialization* is the process by which human beings learn the social expectations of society. Socialization creates the expectations that are the basis for people's attitudes and behaviors. Through socialization, people conform to social expectations, although people still express themselves as individuals.

- ### What are the agents of socialization?

  *Socialization agents* are those who pass on social expectations. They include the family, the media, peers, sports, religious institutions, and schools, among others. The family is usually the first source of socialization. The media also influence people's values and behaviors. Peers are an important source of individual identity; without peer approval, most people find it hard to be socially accepted. Schools also pass on expectations that are influenced by gender, race, and other social characteristics of people and groups.

- ### What theoretical perspectives do sociologists use to explain socialization?

  *Psychoanalytic theory* sees the self as driven by unconscious drives and forces that interact with the expectations of society. *Social learning theory* sees identity as a learned response to social stimuli such as role models. *Functionalism* interprets socialization as key to social stability because socialization establishes shared roles and values. *Conflict theory* interprets socialization in the context of inequality and power relations. *Symbolic interaction theory* sees people as constructing the self as they interact with the environment and give meaning to their experience. Charles Horton Cooley described this process as the *looking glass self*. Another sociologist, George Herbert Mead, described childhood socialization as occurring in three stages: imitation, play, and games.

- **Does socialization mean that everyone grows up the same?**

  *Socialization* is not a uniform process. Growing up in different environments and in such a diverse society means that different people and different groups are exposed to different expectations. Factors such as family structure, social class, regional differences, and many others influence how one is socialized.

- **Does socialization end during childhood?**

  Socialization continues through a lifetime, although childhood is an especially significant time for the formation of *identity*. Adolescence is also a period when peer cultures have an enormous influence on the formation of people's self-concepts. *Adult socialization* involves the learning of specific expectations associated with new roles.

- **What are the social dimensions of the aging process?**

  Although aging is a physiological process, its significance stems from social meanings attached to aging. *Age prejudice* and *age discrimination* result in the devaluation of older people. *Age stratification*—referring to the inequality that occurs among different age groups—is the result.

- **What does resocialization mean?**

  *Resocialization* is the process by which existing social roles are radically altered or replaced. It can take place in an organization that maintains strict social control and demands that the individual conform to the needs of the group or organization.

## Key Terms

## Online Resources

### *Sociology: The Essentials* Companion Website

**www.cengage.com/sociology/andersen**
Visit your book companion website where you will find more resources to help you study and write your research papers. Resources include web links, learning objectives, Internet exercises, quizzing, and flash cards.

 **is an easy-to-use online resource that helps you study in less time to get the grade you want NOW.**

**www.cengage.com/login**
Need help studying? This site is your one-stop study shop. Take a Pre-Test and Cengage NOW will generate a Personalized Study Plan based on your test results. The Study Plan will identify the topics you need to review and direct you to online resources to help you master those topics. You can then take a Post-Test to determine the concepts you have mastered and what you still need to work on.

5

Chapter five
CHAPTER FIVE
Chapter

# Social Interaction and Social Structure

[ *Picture a college* classroom on your campus. Students sit, and some are taking notes; others, listening; a few, perhaps, sleeping. The class period ends and students stand, gathering their books, backpacks, bags, and other gear. As they stand, many whip out their cell phones, place them to their ears, and quickly push buttons that connect them to a friend. As the students exit the room, many are engaged in *social interaction*—chatting with their friends: some by phone, others by text messaging, some by talking face-to-face. Few, if any, of them realize that their behavior is at that moment influenced by *society*—a society whose influence extends into their immediate social relationships, even when the contours of that society—its *social structure*—are likely invisible to them.

These same students might plug a music player into their ears as they move on to their next class, possibly tuning in to the latest sounds while tuning out the sounds of the environment around them. Some will return to their residences and perhaps text message friends, download some music, or connect with "friends" on Facebook or MySpace. Some might watch a video or podcast on a small, handheld device. Surrounding all of this behavior are social changes

*continued*

Darrin Klimek/Digital Vision/Getty Images

that are taking place in society, including changes in technology, in global communication, and in how people now interact with each other. How we make sense of these changes requires an understanding of the connection between society and social interaction. In this way, a sociological perspective can help you see the relationship between individuals and the larger society of which they are a part.

# What Is Society?

In Chapter 2, we studied culture as one force that holds society together. *Culture* is the general way of life, including norms, customs, beliefs, and language. Human **society** is a system of social interaction that includes both culture and social organization. Within a society, members have a common culture, even though there may also be great diversity within it. Members of a society think of themselves as distinct from other societies, maintain ties of social interaction, and have a high degree of interdependence. The interaction they have, whether based on harmony or conflict, is one element of society. Within society, **social interaction** is behavior between two or more people that is given meaning by them. Social interaction is how people relate to each other and form a social bond.

Social interaction is the foundation of society, but society is more than a collection of individual social actions. Emile Durkheim, the classical sociological theorist, described society as *sui generis*—a Latin phrase meaning "a thing in itself, of its own particular kind." To sociologists, seeing society *sui generis* means that society is more than just the sum of its parts. Durkheim saw society as an organism, something comprising different parts that work together to create a unique whole. Just as a human body is not just a collection of organs but is alive as a whole organism with relationships between its organs, society is not only a simple collection of individuals, groups, or institutions but is a whole entity that consists of all these elements and their interrelationships.

Durkheim's point—central to sociological analysis—is that society is much more than the sum of the individuals in it. Society takes on a life of its own. It is patterned on humans and their interactions, but it is something that

*The introduction of new technologies is transforming how people interact with each other.*

endures and takes on shape and structure beyond the immediacy of any given group of people. This is a basic idea that guides sociological thinking.

You can think of it this way: Imagine how a photographer views a landscape. The landscape is not just the sum of its individual parts—mountains, pastures, trees, or clouds—although each part contributes to the whole. The power and beauty of the landscape is that all its parts *relate* to each other, some in harmony and some in contrast, to create a panoramic view. The photographer who tries to capture this landscape will likely use a wide-angle lens. This method of photography captures the breadth and comprehensive scope of what the photographer sees. Similarly, sociologists try to picture society as a whole, not only by seeing its individual parts but also recognizing the relatedness of these parts and their vast complexity.

## Macro- and Microanalysis

Sociologists use different lenses to see the different parts of society. Some views are more macroscopic—that is, sociologists try to comprehend the whole of society, how it is organized, and how it changes. This is called **macroanalysis,** a sociological approach that takes the broadest view of society by studying large patterns of social interaction that are vast, complex, and highly differentiated. You might do this by looking at a whole society or comparing different total societies to each other. For example, as we opened this chapter, you saw that large-scale changes in technology influence even the most immediate social interaction that we have with other people. Thus, whereas only a few years ago it would not have been imaginable to create a network of friends in cyberspace, today it is a common practice, especially for young people.

Other views are more microscopic—that is, the focus is on the smallest, most immediately visible parts of social life, such as specific people interacting with each other. This is called **microanalysis.** In this approach, sociologists study patterns of social interactions that are relatively small, less complex, and less differentiated—the microlevel of society. Again, thinking of how this chapter opened, you might want to study how people engage in texting each other on a one-to-one basis. How are they similar or different, on the basis of age, or gender, or social class or race? For example, do people text (that is, interact) with each other within racial groups more than between racial groups? Observing this would be an example of microanalysis. Thus a sociologist who studies social interaction via texting or on the Internet would be engaging in microanalysis but might interpret what is found in the context of macrolevel processes (such as race relations in society). Just as a photographer might use a wide-angle lens to photograph a landscape or a telephoto lens for a closer view, sociologists use both macro- and microanalyses to reveal different dimensions of society.

In this chapter, we continue our study of sociology by starting with the macrolevel of social life (by studying total social structures), then continuing through the microlevel (by studying groups and face-to-face interaction). The idea is to help you see how large-scale dimensions of society shape even the most immediate forms of social interaction.

Sociologists use the term **social organization** to describe the order established in social groups at any level. Specifically, social organization brings regularity and predictability to human behavior; social organization is present at every level of interaction, from the whole society to the smallest groups.

## Social Institutions

Societies are identified by their cultural characteristics and the social institutions that compose each society. A **social institution** (or simply an institution) is an established and organized system of social behavior with a recognized purpose. The term refers to the broad systems that organize specific functions in society. Unlike individual behavior, social institutions cannot be directly observed, but their impact and structure can still be seen. For example, the family is an institution that provides for the care of the young and the transmission of culture. Religion is an institution that organizes sacred beliefs. Education is the institution through which people learn the skills needed to live in the society.

The concept of the social institution is important to sociological thinking. You can think of social institutions as the enduring consequences of social behavior, but what fascinates sociologists is how social institutions take on a life of their own. For example, you were likely born in a hospital, which itself is part of the health care institution. The simple act of birth, which you might think of as an individual experience, is shaped by the structure of this social institution. Thus, you were likely delivered by a doctor, accompanied by nurses and, perhaps, a midwife—each of whom exists in a specific social relationship to the health care institution. Each of these persons is in an *institutional* role. Moreover, the practices surrounding your birth were also shaped by this social institution. Thus, you might be initially removed from your mother and examined by a doctor, which is very different from the institutional practices in other societies.

The major institutions in society include the family, education, work and the economy, the political institution (or state), religion, and health care, as well as the mass media, organized sports, and the military. These are all complex structures that exist to meet certain needs that are necessary for society to exist. *Functionalist theorists* have traditionally identified these needs (functions) as follows (Aberle et al. 1950; Parsons 1951a; Levy 1949):

1. *The socialization of new members of the society.* This is primarily accomplished by the family, but involves others institutions as well, such as education.

2. *The production and distribution of goods and services.* The economy is generally the institution that performs this set of tasks, but this may also involve the family as an institution—especially in societies where production takes place within households.

3. *Replacement of society's members.* All societies must have a means of replacing members who die, move or migrate away, or otherwise leave the society. Families are typically organized to do this.

4. *The maintenance of stability and existence.* Certain institutions within a society (such as the government, the police force, and the military) contribute toward the stability and continuance of the society.

5. *Providing the members with an ultimate sense of purpose.* Societies accomplish this task by creating national anthems, for instance, and by encouraging patriotism in addition to providing basic values and moral codes through institutions such as religion, the family, and education.

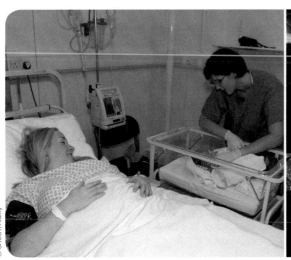

*Birth, though a natural process, occurs within social institutions—institutions that vary in different societies, depending on the social organization of society. Here you see how birth in the United States, which is mainly defined as a medical event, contrasts with a health assistant attending a birth in rural Mexico.*

In contrast to functional list theory, conflict theory further notes that because conflict is inherent in most societies, the social institutions of society do not provide for all its members equally. Some members are provided for better than others, thus demonstrating that institutions affect people by granting more power to some social groups than to others. Using the example of the health care institution given above, some groups have considerably less power within the institution than do others. Thus, nurses are generally subordinate to doctors and doctors to hospital administrators. And beyond these specific actors within the health care institutions, different social groups in society have more or less power within social institutions. Thus, racial and ethnic minorities in general have poorer access to health care than others; the poor have less access, as do those of lower social class status. (For more information, see Chapter 14 on health care.)

## Social Structure

Sociologists use the term **social structure** to refer to the organized pattern of social relationships and social institutions that together compose society. Social structures are not immediately visible to the untrained observer; nevertheless, they are present, and they affect all dimensions of human experience in society. Social structural analysis is a way of looking at society in which the sociologist analyzes the patterns in social life that reflect and produce social behavior.

Social class distinctions are an example of a social structure. Class shapes the access that different groups have to the resources of society, and it shapes many interactions people have with each other. People may form cliques with those who share similar class standing, or they may identify with certain values associated with a given class. Class then forms a social structure—one that shapes and guides human behavior at all levels, no matter how overtly visible or invisible this structure is to someone at a given time.

The philosopher Marilyn Frye aptly describes the concept of social structure in her writing. Using the metaphor of a birdcage, she writes that if you look closely at only one wire in a cage, you cannot see the other wires. You might then wonder why the bird within does not fly away. Only when you step back and see the whole cage instead of a single wire do you understand why the bird does not escape. Frye writes:

> It is perfectly obvious that the bird is surrounded by a network of systematically related barriers, no one of which would be the least hindrance to its flight, but all of which, by their relations to each other, are as confining as the solid walls of a dungeon.... One can study the elements of ... structure with great care and some good will without seeing or being able to understand that one is looking at a cage and that there are people there who are caged, whose motion and mobility are restricted, whose lives are shaped and reduced. (Frye 1983: 4–5)

Just as a birdcage is a network of wires, society is a network of social structures, both micro and macro.

*thinkingsociologically*

Using Marilyn Frye's analogy of the birdcage, think of a time when you believed your choices were constrained by *social structure*. When you applied to college, for example, could you go anywhere you wanted? What social structural conditions guided your ultimate selection of schools to attend?

# What Holds Society Together?

What holds societies together? We ask this question throughout this chapter. This central question in sociology was first addressed by Emile Durkheim, the French sociologist writing in the late 1800s and early 1900s. He argued that people in society had a **collective consciousness,** defined as the body of beliefs common to a community or society that give people a sense of belonging and a feeling of moral obligation to its demands and values. According to Durkheim, collective consciousness gives groups social solidarity because members of a group feel they are part of one society.

Where does the collective consciousness come from? Durkheim argued that it stems from people's participation in common activities, such as work, family, education, and religion—in short, society's institutions.

## Mechanical and Organic Solidarity

According to Durkheim, there are two types of social solidarity: mechanical and organic. **Mechanical solidarity** arises when individuals play similar—rather than different—roles within the society. Individuals in societies marked by mechanical solidarity share the same values and hold the same things sacred. This particular kind of cohesiveness is weakened when a society becomes more complex. Contemporary examples of mechanical solidarity are rare because most societies of the world have been absorbed in the global trend for greater complexity and interrelatedness. Native American groups before European conquest were bound together by mechanical solidarity; indeed, many Native American groups are now trying to regain the mechanical solidarity on which their cultural heritage rests, but they are finding that the superimposition of White institutions on Native American life interferes with the adoption of traditional ways of thinking and being, which prevents mechanical solidarity from gaining its original strength.

In contrast, **organic solidarity** occurs when people play a great variety of roles, and unity is based on role differentiation, not similarity. The United States and other industrial societies are built on organic solidarity, and each is cohesive because of the differentiation within each. Roles are no longer necessarily similar, but they are necessarily interlinked—the performance of multiple roles is necessary for the execution of society's complex and integrated functions.

Durkheim described this state as the **division of labor,** defined as the relatedness of *different* tasks that develop in complex societies. The labor force within the contemporary U.S. economy, for example, is divided according to the kinds of work people do. Within any division of labor, tasks become distinct from one another, but they are still woven into a whole.

The division of labor is a central concept in sociology because it represents how the different pieces of society fit together. The division of labor in most contemporary societies is often marked by distinctions such as age, gender, race, and class. In other words, if you look at who does what in society, you will see that women and men tend to do different things; this is the gender division of labor. Similarly, old and young to some extent do different things; this is a division of labor by age. This is crosscut by the racial division of labor, the pattern whereby those in different racial–ethnic groups tend to do different work—or are often forced to do different work—in society. At the same time, the division of labor is also marked by class distinctions, with some groups providing work that is highly valued and rewarded and others doing work that is devalued and poorly rewarded. As you will see throughout this book, gender, race, and class intersect and overlap in the division of labor in society.

Durkheim's thinking about the origins of social cohesion can bring light to contemporary discussions over "family values." Some want to promote traditional family values as the moral standards of society. Is such a thing necessarily good, or even possible? The United States is an increasingly diverse society, and family life differs among different groups. It is unlikely that a single set of family values can be the basis for social solidarity.

### Gemeinschaft and Gesellschaft

Different societies are held together by different forms of solidarity. Some societies are characterized by what sociologists call **gemeinschaft,** a German word that means "community"; others are characterized as **gesellschaft,** which literally means "society" (Tönnies 1963/1887). Each involves a type of solidarity or cohesiveness. Those societies that are *gemeinschafts* (communities) are characterized by a sense of "we" feeling, a moderate division of labor, strong personal ties, strong family relationships, and a sense of personal loyalty. The sense of solidarity between members of the gemeinschaft society arises from personal ties; small, relatively simple social institutions;

and a collective sense of loyalty to the whole society. People tend to be well integrated into the whole, and social cohesion comes from deeply shared values and beliefs (often, sacred values). Social control need not be imposed externally because control comes from the internal sense of belonging that members share. You might think of a small community church as an example.

In contrast, in societies marked by *gesellschaft,* an increasing importance is placed on the secondary relationships people have—that is, less intimate and more instrumental relationships such as work roles instead of family or community roles. Gesellschaft is characterized by less prominence of personal ties, a somewhat diminished role of the nuclear family, and a lessened sense of personal loyalty to the total society. The solidarity and cohesion remain, and it can be very cohesive, but the cohesion comes from an elaborated *division of labor* (thus, *organic* solidarity), greater flexibility in social roles, and the instrumental ties that people have to one another.

Social solidarity under gesellschaft is weaker than in the gemeinschaft society, however. Gesellschaft is more likely than gemeinschaft to be torn by class conflict because class distinctions are less prominent, though still present, in the gemeinschaft. Racial–ethnic conflict is more likely within gesellschaft societies because the gemeinschaft tends to be ethically and racially very homogeneous; often it is characterized by only one racial or ethnic group. This means that conflict between gemeinschaft societies, such as ethnically based wars, can be very high, because both groups have a strong internal sense of group identity that may be intolerant of others (for example, Palestinians versus Israelis, or Shiite Muslims versus Sunni Muslims in Iraq).

In sum, complexity and differentiation are what make the gesellschaft cohesive, whereas similarity and unity cohere the gemeinschaft society. In a single society, such as the United States, you can conceptualize the whole society as gesellschaft, with some internal groups marked by gemeinschaft. Our national motto seems to embody this idea: *E pluribus unum* (Unity within diversity), although clearly this idealistic motto has only been partly realized.

# Types of Societies

In addition to comparing how different societies are bound together, sociologists are interested in how social organization evolves in different societies. Simple things such as the size of a society can also shape its social organization, as do the different roles that men and women engage in as they produce goods, care for the old and young, and pass on societal traditions. Societies also differ according to their resource base—whether they are predominantly agricultural or industrial, for example, and whether they are sparsely or densely populated.

Thousands of years ago, societies were small, sparsely populated, and technologically limited. In the competition for scarce resources, larger and more technologically advanced societies dominated smaller ones. Today, we have arrived at a global society with highly evolved degrees of social differentiation and inequality, notably along class, gender, racial, and ethnic lines (Nolan and Lenski 2005).

Sociologists distinguish six types of societies based on the complexity of their social structure, the amount of overall cultural accumulation, and the level of their technology. They are *foraging, pastoral, horticultural, agricultural* (these four are called *preindustrial* societies), then *industrial* and *postindustrial* societies (see Table 5.1). Each type of society can still be found on Earth, though all but the most isolated societies are rapidly moving toward the industrial and postindustrial stages of development.

These different societies vary in the basis for their organization and the complexity of their division of labor. Some, such as foraging societies, are subsistence economies, where men and women hunt and gather food but accumulate very little. Others, such as pastoral societies and horticultural societies, develop a more elaborate division of labor as the social roles that are needed for raising livestock and farming become more numerous. With the development of agricultural societies, production becomes more large scale and strong patterns of social differentiation develop, sometimes taking the form of a caste system or even slavery.

The key driving force that distinguishes these different societies from each other is the development of technology. All societies use technology to help fill human needs, and the form of technology differs for the different types of society.

## Preindustrial Societies

A **preindustrial society** is one that directly uses, modifies, and/or tills the land as a major means of survival. There are four kinds of preindustrial societies, listed here by degree of technological development: foraging (or hunting–gathering) societies, pastoral societies, horticultural societies, and agricultural societies (see Table 5.1).

In *foraging (hunting–gathering) societies,* the technology enables the hunting of animals and gathering of vegetation. The technology does not permit the refrigeration or processing of food, hence these individuals must search continuously for plants and game. Because hunting and gathering are activities that require large amounts of land, most foraging societies are nomadic; that is, they constantly travel as they deplete the plant supply or follow the migrations of animals. The central institution is the family, which serves as the means of distributing food, training children, and protecting its members. There is usually role differentiation on the basis of gender, although the specific form of the gender division of labor varies in different societies. They occasionally wage war with other clans or similar societies, and spears and bows and arrows are the weapons used. An example of a foraging society are the Pygmies of Central Africa.

In *pastoral societies,* technology is based on the domestication of animals. Such societies tend to develop in desert areas that are too arid to provide rich vegetation. The pastoral society is nomadic,

*Different types of societies produce different kinds of social relationships. Some may involve more direct and personal relationships (called* gemeinschafts), *whereas others produce more fragmented and impersonal relationships (called* gesellschafts).

| table5.1 | | *Types of Societies* | | |
|---|---|---|---|---|
| | | **Economic Base** | **Social Organization** | **Examples** |
| **Preindustrial Societies** | *Foraging Societies* | Economic sustenance dependent on hunting and foraging | Gender is important basis for social organization, although division of labor is not rigid; little accumulation of wealth | Pygmies of Central Africa |
| | *Pastoral Societies* | Nomadic societies, with substantial dependence on domesticated animals for economic production | Complex social system with an elite upper class and greater gender role differentiation than in foraging societies | Bedouins of Africa and Middle East |
| | *Horticultural Societies* | Society marked by relatively permanent settlement and production of domesticated crops | Accumulation of wealth and elaboration of the division of labor, with different occupational roles (farmers, traders, craftspeople, and so on) | Aztecs of Mexico; Inca empire of Peru |
| | *Agricultural Societies* | Livelihood dependent on elaborate and large-scale patterns of agriculture and increased use of technology in agricultural production | Caste system develops that differentiates the elite and agricultural laborers; may include system of slavery | American South, pre–Civil War |
| **Industrial Societies** | | Economic system based on the development of elaborate machinery and a factory system; economy based on cash and wages | Highly differentiated labor force with a complex division of labor and large formal organizations | Nineteenth- and most of twentieth-century United States and Western Europe |
| **Postindustrial Societies** | | Information-based societies in which technology plays a vital role in social organization | Education increasingly important to the division of labor | Contemporary United States, Japan, and others |

necessitated by the endless search for fresh grazing grounds for the herds of their domesticated animals. The animals are used as sources of hard work that enable the creation of a material surplus. Unlike a foraging society, this surplus frees some individuals from the tasks of hunting and gathering and allows them to create crafts, make pottery, cut hair, build tents, and apply tattoos. The surplus generates a more complex and differentiated social system with an elite or upper class and more role differentiation on the basis of gender. The nomadic Bedouins of Africa and the Middle East are pastoral societies.

In *horticultural societies,* hand tools are used to cultivate the land, such as the hoe and the digging stick. The individuals in horticultural societies practice ancestor worship and conceive of a deity or deities (God or gods) as a creator. This distinguishes them from foraging societies that generally employ the notion of numerous spirits to explain the unknowable. Horticultural societies recultivate the land each year and tend to establish relatively permanent settlements and villages. Role differentiation is extensive, resulting in different and interdependent occupational roles such as farmer, trader, and craftsperson. The Aztecs of Mexico and the Incas of Peru represent examples of horticultural societies.

The *agricultural society* is exemplified by the pre–Civil War American South, a society of slavery. Such societies have a large and complex economic system that is based on large-scale farming. Such societies rely on technologies such as use of the wheel and use of metals. Farms tend to be considerably larger than the cultivated land in horticultural societies. Large and permanent settlements characterize agricultural societies, which also exhibit dramatic social inequalities. A rigid caste system develops, separating the peasants, or slaves, from the controlling elite caste, which is then freed from manual work allowing time for art, literature, and philosophy, activities of which they can then claim the lower castes are incapable.

## Industrial Societies

An *industrial society* is one that uses machines and other advanced technologies to produce and distribute goods and services. The Industrial Revolution began over 250 years ago when the steam engine was invented in England, delivering previously unattainable amounts of mechanical power for the performance of work. Steam engines powered locomotives, factories, and dynamos and transformed societies as the Industrial Revolution spread. The growth of science led to advances in farming techniques such as crop rotation, harvesting, and ginning cotton, as well as industrial-scale projects such as dams for generating hydroelectric power. Joining these advances were developments in medicine, new techniques to prolong and improve life, and the emergence of birth control to limit population growth.

Unlike agricultural societies, industrial societies rely on a highly differentiated labor force and the intensive use of capital and technology. Large formal organizations are common. The task of holding society together, falling on institutions such as religion in preindustrial societies, now falls more on the institutions that have a high division of labor, such as the economy and work, government, politics, and large bureaucracies.

Within industrial societies, the forms of gender inequality that we see in contemporary U.S. society tend to develop. With the advent of industrialization, societies move to a cash-based economy, with labor performed in factories and mills paid on a wage basis and household labor remaining unpaid. This introduced what is known as the *family-wage economy,* in which families become dependent on wages to support themselves, but work within the family (housework, child care, and other forms of household work) is unpaid and therefore increasingly devalued (Tilly and Scott 1978). In addition, even though women (and young children) worked in factories and mills from the first inception of industrialization, the family-wage economy is based on the idea that men are the primary breadwinners. A system of inequality in men's and women's wages was introduced—an economic system that even today continues to produce a wage gap between men and women.

Industrial societies tend to be highly productive economically, with a large working class of industrial laborers. People become increasingly urbanized as they move from farmlands to urban centers or other areas where factories are located. Immigration is common in industrial societies, particularly because industries are forming where there is a high demand for more, cheap labor.

Industrialization has brought many benefits to U.S. society—a highly productive and efficient economic system, expansion of international markets, extraordinary availability of consumer products, and for many, a good working wage. Industrialization has, at the same time, also produced some of the most serious social problems that our nation faces: industrial pollution, an overdependence on consumer goods, wage inequality and job dislocation for millions,

## map 5.1   *MAPPING AMERICA'S DIVERSITY*

### Population Density and Social Interaction

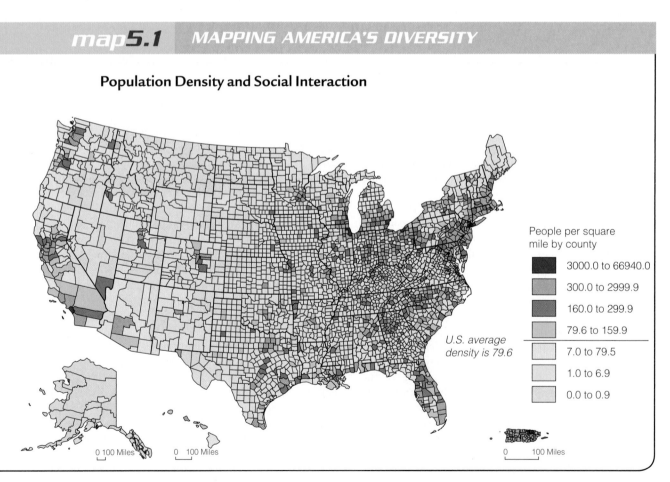

People per square mile by county

- 3000.0 to 66940.0
- 300.0 to 2999.9
- 160.0 to 299.9
- 79.6 to 159.9
- 7.0 to 79.5
- 1.0 to 6.9
- 0.0 to 0.9

*U.S. average density is 79.6*

*As this map shows, population density (measured as the number of people per square mile) varies enormously in different regions and areas of the country. In what ways do you think the density of a given area might affect people's social interaction?*

*Data:* U.S. Census Bureau. 2006. **www.census.gov/population**

and problems of crime and crowding in urban areas (see Map 5.1 on population density). The recent economic recession/depression that began in 2008 has been significantly responsible for many of these ills—including an exceptionally high rate of unemployment. Understanding the process of industrialization and its accompanying process of urbanization is a major avenue for sociological research and is explored further in Chapter 16.

### Postindustrial Societies

In the contemporary era, a new type of society is emerging. Whereas most twentieth-century societies can be characterized in terms of their generation of material goods, **postindustrial society** depends economically on the production and distribution of services, information, and knowledge. Postindustrial societies are information-based societies in which technology plays a vital role in the social organization. The United States is fast becoming a postindustrial society, and Japan may be even further along. Many of the workers provide services such as administration, education, legal services, scientific research, and banking, or they engage in the development, management, and distribution of information, particularly in the areas of computer use and design. Central to the economy of the postindustrial society are the highly advanced technologies of computers, robotics, genetic engineering, and laser technology. Multinational corporations globally link the economies of postindustrial societies.

The transition to a postindustrial society has a strong influence on the character of social institutions. Educational institutions acquire paramount importance in the postindustrial society, and science takes an especially prominent place. For some, the transition to a postindustrial society means more discretionary income for leisure activities—tourism, entertainment, and relaxation industries (spas, massage centers, and exercise) become more prominent—at least for people in certain classes and in the absence of severe economic recession, which has recently plagued not only the United States but Japan, Germany, and other technologically advanced countries as well. The transition to postindustrialism can mean permanent joblessness for many or the need to hold down more than one job simply to make ends meet. Workers without highly technical skills may not fit in such a society, and millions have already found themselves out of work.

# Social Interaction and Society

You can see by now that society is an entity that exists above and beyond individuals. Also, different societies are marked by different forms of *social organization*. Although societies differ, emerge, and change, they are also highly predictable. Your society shapes virtually every aspect of your life from the structure of its social institutions to the more immediate ways that you interact with people. It is to that level—the microlevel of society—that we now turn.

### Groups

At the microlevel, society is made up of many different social groups. At any given moment, each of us is a member of many groups simultaneously, and we are subject to their influence: family, friendship groups, athletic teams, work groups, racial and ethnic groups, and so on. Groups impinge on every aspect of our lives and are a major determinant of our attitudes and values regarding everything from personal issues such as sexual attitudes and family values to major social issues such as the death penalty and physician-assisted suicide.

To sociologists a **group** is a collection of individuals who

- interact and communicate with each other;
- share goals and norms; and,
- have a subjective awareness of themselves as "we," that is, as a distinct social unit.

To be a group, the social unit in question must possess all three of these characteristics. We will examine the nature and behavior of groups in greater detail in Chapter 6.

In sociological terms, not all collections of people are groups. People may be lumped together into *social categories* based on one or more shared characteristics, such as teenagers (an age category), truck drivers (an occupational category), and even those who have lost their life savings and pensions as a result of criminal Ponzi investment schemes, such as occurred in the fall of 2008 with those who unknowingly invested money with the now-infamous Bernard Madoff (more about him in Chapter 7).

Social categories can become social groups, depending on the amount of "we" feeling the group has. Only when there is this sense of common identity, as defined in the characteristics of groups above, is a collection of people an actual group. For example, all people nationwide watching TV programs at 8 o'clock Wednesday evening form a distinct social unit, an *audience*. But they are not a group because they do not interact with one another, nor do they possess an awareness of themselves as "we." However, if many of the same viewers were to come together for a large meeting, such as fans of the long-running TV series *Star Trek* (the fans call themselves "Trekkies") coming together for a convention where they could interact and develop a "we" feeling, then they would constitute a group.

We now know that people do not need to be face-to-face in order to constitute a group. Online communities, for example, are people who interact with each other regularly, share a common identity, and think of themselves as being a distinct social unit. On the Internet community Facebook, for example, you may have a group of "friends," some of whom you know personally and others whom you only know online. But these *friends*, as they are known on Facebook, make up a social group that might interact on a regular, indeed, daily basis—possibly even across great distances.

Groups also need not be small or "close-up" and personal. *Formal organizations* are highly structured social groupings that form to pursue a set of goals. Bureaucracies, such as business corporations or municipal governments or associations such as the Parent-Teacher Association (PTA), are examples of formal organizations. A deeper analysis of bureaucracies and formal organizations appears in Chapter 6.

## Status

Within groups, people occupy different statuses. **Status** is an established position in a social structure that carries with it a degree of prestige (that is, social value). A status is a rank in society. For example, the position "Vice President of the United States" is a status, one that carries relatively high prestige as well as a complex set of expectations. "High school teacher" is another status; it carries less prestige than "Vice President of the United States," but more prestige than, say, "cabdriver." Statuses occur within institutions. "High school teacher" is a status within the education institution. Other statuses in the same institution are "student," "principal," and "school superintendent."

Typically, a person occupies many statuses simultaneously. The combination of statuses composes a **status set,** which is the complete set of statuses occupied by a person at a given time (Merton 1968). A person may occupy different statuses in different institutions. Simultaneously, a person may be a bank president (in the economic institution), voter (in the political institution), church member (in the religious institution), and treasurer of the PTA (in the education institution). Each status may be associated with a different level of prestige.

Sometimes the multiple statuses of an individual conflict with one another. **Status inconsistency** exists where the statuses occupied by a person bring with them significantly different amounts of prestige and thus differing expectations. For example, someone trained as a lawyer, but working as a cabdriver, experiences status inconsistency. Some recent immigrants from Vietnam and Korea have experienced status inconsistency. Many refugees who had been in high-status occupations in their home country, such as teachers, doctors, and lawyers, could find work in the United States only as grocers or technicians—jobs of relatively lower status than the jobs they left behind. A relatively large body of research in sociology has demonstrated that status inconsistency can

Simon Jarratt/Corbis

*Social groups are organized around different kinds of relationships, but involve a "we" feeling.*

lead to stress and depression (Thoits 2009; Taylor et al. 2009; Blalock 1991; Taylor and Hornung 1979; Hornung 1977).

**Achieved statuses** are those attained by virtue of individual effort. Most occupational statuses—police officer, pharmacist, or boatbuilder—are achieved statuses. In contrast, **ascribed statuses** are those occupied from the moment a person is born. Your biological sex is an ascribed status. Yet, even ascribed statuses are not exempt from the process of social construction. For most individuals, race is an ascribed status fixed at birth, although an individual with one light-skinned African American parent and one White parent may appear to be White and may go through life as a White person. This is called *passing*, although this term is used considerably less often now than it was several years ago. Ascribed status may not be rigidly defined, as for individuals who are *biracial* or *multiracial* (see also Chapter 10.) Finally, ascribed statuses can arise through means beyond an individual's control, such as severe disability or chronic illness.

Some seemingly ascribed statuses, such as gender, can become achieved statuses. Gender, typically thought of as fixed at birth, is a social construct. You can be born female or male, but becoming a woman or a man is the result of social behaviors associated with your ascribed status. In other words, gender is also achieved. People who cross-dress, have a sex change, or develop some characteristics associated with the other sex are good examples of how gender is achieved, but you do not have to see these exceptional behaviors to observe that. People "do" gender in everyday life. They put on appearances and behaviors that are associated with their presumed gender (West and Zimmerman 1987; West and Fenstermaker 1995; Andersen 2009).

If you doubt this, ask yourself what you did today to "achieve" your gender status. Did you dress a certain way? Wear "manly" cologne or deodorant? Splash on a "feminine" fragrance? These behaviors—all performed at the microlevel—reflect the macrolevel of your gender status.

## Debunking Society's Myths

**Myth:** Gender is an *ascribed status* where one's gender identity is established at birth.

**Sociological perspective:** Although one's biological sex identity is an ascribed status, gender is a social construct and thus is also an *achieved status*—that is, accomplished through routine, everyday behavior, including patterns of dress, speech, touch, and other social behaviors. Sex is not the same as gender. (Andersen 2009).

The line between achieved and ascribed status can be hard to draw. Social class, for example, is determined by occupation, education, and annual income—all of which are achieved statuses—yet one's job, education, and income are known to correlate strongly with the social class of one's parents. Hence, one's social class status is at least partly—though not perfectly—determined at birth. It is an achieved status that includes an inseparable component of ascribed status as well.

Although people occupy many statuses at one time, it is usually the case that one status is dominant, called the **master status,** overriding all other features of the person's identity. The master status may be imposed by others, or a person may define his or her own master status. A woman judge, for example, may carry the master status "woman" in the eyes of many. She is seen not just as a judge, but as a woman judge, thus making gender a master status (Webster and Hysom 1998). A master status can completely supplant all other statuses in someone's status set. Being in a wheelchair is another example of a master status. People may see this, at least at first, as the most important, or salient, part of identity, ignoring other statuses that define someone as a person.

### *thinkingsociologically*

Make a list of terms that describe who you are. Which of these are *ascribed statuses* and which are *achieved statuses*? What do you think your *master status* is in the eyes of others? Does one's *master status* depend on who is defining you? What does this tell you about the significance of social judgments in determining who you are?

## Roles

A **role** is the behavior others expect from a person associated with a particular status. Statuses are occupied;

roles are acted or "played." The status of police officer carries with it many expectations; this is the role of police officer. Police officers are expected to uphold the law, pursue suspected criminals, assist victims of crimes, fill out forms for reports, and so on. Usually, people behave in their roles as others expect them to, but not always. When a police officer commits a crime, such as physically brutalizing someone, he or she has violated the role expectations. Role expectations may vary according to the role of the observer—whether the person observing the police officer is a member of a minority group, for example.

As we saw in Chapter 4, social learning theory predicts that we learn attitudes and behaviors in response to the positive reinforcement and encouragement received from those around us. This is important in the formation of our own identity in society. "I am Linda, the skater," or "I am John, the guitarist." These identities are often obtained through **role modeling,** a process by which we imitate the behavior of another person we admire who is in a particular role. A ten-year-old girl or boy who greatly admires the teenage expert skateboarder next door will attempt, through role modeling, to closely imitate the tricks that neighbor performs on the skateboard. As a result, the formation of the child's self-identity is significantly influenced.

A person may occupy several statuses and roles at one time. A person's **role set** includes all the roles occupied by the person at a given time. Thus, a person may be not only Linda the skater but also Linda the student, the daughter, and the lover. Roles may clash with each other, a situation called **role conflict,**

*In role modeling, a person imitates the behavior of an admired other.*

wherein two or more roles are associated with contradictory expectations. Notice that in Figure 5.1 some of the roles diagrammed for this college student may conflict with others. Can you speculate about which might and which might not?

In U.S. society, some of the most common forms of role conflict arise from the dual responsibilities of job and family. The parental role demands extensive time and commitment and so does the job role. Time given to one role is time taken away from the other. Although the norms pertaining to working women and men are rapidly changing, it is still true that women are more often expected to uphold traditional role expectations associated with their gender role and are more likely held responsible for minding the family when job and family conflict. The sociologist Arlie Hochschild captured the predicament of today's women when she described the "second shift": a working mother spends time and energy all day on the job, only to come home to the "second shift" of family and home responsibilities. These are sometimes delegated to a husband or boyfriend, who encounters less well-formed role expectations that he will take on those responsibilities and is therefore more likely to leave the jobs undone (Hochschild 1997).

Hochschild has found that some companies have instituted "family friendly" policies, designed to reduce the conflicts generated by the "second shift." Ironically, however, in her study she found that few workers take advantage of programs such as more flexible hours, paid maternity leave, and job sharing—except for the on-site child care that actually allowed parents to work more!

Hochschild's studies point to the conflict between two social roles: family roles and work roles. Her

*Changes in the roles for women who are mothers can create role strain.*

research is also illustrative of a different sociological concept: **role strain,** a condition wherein a single role brings conflicting expectations. Different from role conflict, which involves tensions *between* two roles, role strain involves conflicts within a single role. In Hochschild's study, the work role has not only the expectations traditionally associated with work, but also the expectation that one "love" one's work and be as devoted to it as to one's family. The result is role strain. The role of student often involves role strain. For example, students are expected to be independent thinkers, yet they feel—quite correctly—that they are often required to simply repeat on an exam what a professor tells them. The tension between the two competing expectations is an example of role strain.

## Everyday Social Interaction

You can also see the influence of society in everyday behavior, including such basics as how you talk, patterns of touch, and who you are attracted to. Although you might think of such things as "just coming naturally," they are deeply patterned by society. The cultural context of social interaction really matters in our understanding of what given behaviors mean. An action is defined as positive or negative by the cultural context because social behavior is that to which people give meaning. An action that is positive in one culture can be negative in another. For example, shaking the right hand in greeting is a positive action in the United States, but the same action in East India or certain Arab countries might be an insult. Social and cultural context matter. A kiss on the lips is a positive act in most cultures, yet if you were kissed on the lips

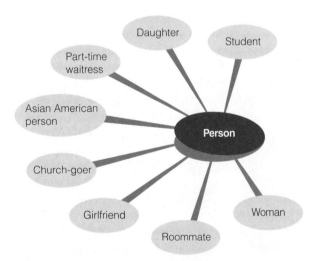

**FIGURE 5.1** *Roles in a College Student's Role Set*

*Identify the different roles that you occupy and draw a similar diagram of your own role set. Then identify which roles are consistent with each other and which might produce* role conflict *and* role strain. *Are there institutional reasons why these conflicts and strains occur in your case?*

by a stranger, you would probably consider it a negative act, perhaps even repulsive.

### Verbal and Nonverbal Communication.

We saw in the culture chapter (Chapter 2) how patterns of social interaction are embedded in the language we use, and language is deeply influenced by culture and society. Furthermore, communication is not just what you say, but also how you say it and to whom. You can see the influence of society on *how* people speak, especially in different contexts. Under some circumstances, a pause in speaking may communicate emphasis; for others, it may indicate uncertainty. Cultural differences across society make this obvious. Thus, during interactions between Japanese businessmen, long periods of silence often occur. Unlike U.S. citizens, who are experts in "small talk" and who try at all costs to avoid periods of silence in conversation, Japanese people do not need to talk all the time and regard periods of silence as desirable opportunities for collecting their thoughts (Worchel et al. 2000; Fukuda 1994). American businesspeople in their first meetings with Japanese executives often think, erroneously, that these silent interludes mean the Japanese are responding negatively to a presentation. Even though some find the Japanese mode of conversation highly uncomfortable, getting used to it is a key tool in successful negotiations. The fate of a deal may depend on a glance, an exhalation, or a smile.

**Nonverbal communication** is also a form of social interaction and can be seen in various social patterns. A surprisingly large portion of our everyday communication with others is nonverbal, although we are generally only conscious of a small fraction of the nonverbal "conversations" in which we take part. Consider all the nonverbal signals exchanged in a casual chat: body position, head nods, eye contact, facial expressions, touching, and so on. Studies of nonverbal communication, like those of verbal communication, show that it is much influenced by social forces, including the relationships between diverse groups of people. The meanings of nonverbal communications depend heavily on race, ethnicity, social class, and gender, as we shall see.

For example, patterns of touch (called **tactile communication**) are strongly influenced by gender. Parents vary their touching behavior depending on whether the child is a boy or a girl. Boys tend to be touched more roughly; girls, more tenderly and protectively. Such patterns continue into adulthood, where women touch each other more often in everyday conversation than do men. Women are on the average more likely to touch and hug as an expression of emotional support, whereas men touch and hug more often to assert power or to express sexual interest (Worchel et al. 2000; Wood 1994). Clearly, there are also instances where women touch to express sexual interest and/or dominance, but research shows that, in general, for women touch is a supportive activity. For men, touch is often a dominance-asserting activity, except in athletic contexts where hugging and patting among men is a supportive activity (Worchel et al. 2000; Wood 1994; Tannen 1990).

In observing patterns of touch, you can see where social status influences the meaning of nonverbal behaviors. Professors, male or female, may pat a man or woman student on the back as a gesture of approval; students will rarely do this to a professor. Male professors touch students more often than do female professors, showing the additional effect of gender. Because such patterns of touching reflect power relationships between women and men, they can also be offensive and may even involve sexual harassment (see Chapters 11 and 15).

You can also see the social meaning of interaction by observing how people use personal space. **Proxemic communication** refers to the amount of space between interacting individuals. Although people are generally unaware of how they use personal space, usually the more friendly people feel toward each other, the closer they will stand. In casual conversation, friends stand closer to each other than do strangers. People who are sexually attracted to each other stand especially close, whether the sexual attraction is gay, lesbian, or heterosexual. According to anthropologist E. T. Hall (1966; Hall and Hall 1987), we all carry around us a *proxemic bubble* that represents our personal, three-dimensional space. When people we do not know enter our proxemic bubble, we feel threatened and may take evasive action. Friends stand close; enemies tend to avoid interaction and keep far apart. According to Hall's theory, we attempt to exclude from our private space those whom we do not know or do not like, even though we may not be fully aware that we are doing so.

*Patterns of touch reflect differences in the power that is part of many social relationships.*

## SEE *FOR YOURSELF*

### *RIDING IN ELEVATORS*

1. Try a simple experiment. Ride in an elevator and closely observe the behavior of everyone in the elevator with you. Write down in a notebook such things as how far away people stand from each other. What do they look at? Do they tend to stand in the corners? Do they converse with strangers or the people they are with? If so, what do they talk about?

2. Now return to the same elevator and do something that breaks the usual norms of elevator behavior, such as standing too close to someone. How did people react? How did you feel?

How does this experiment show how social norms are maintained through informal norms of social control?

The proxemic bubbles of different ethnic groups on average have different sizes. Hispanic people tend to stand much closer to each other than do White, middle-class Americans; their proxemic bubble is, on average, smaller. Similarly, African Americans also tend to stand close to each other while conversing. Interaction distance is quite large between White, middle-class, British males—their average interaction distances can be as much as several feet.

Proxemic interactions also differ between men and women (Taylor et al. 2009; Romain 1999; Tannen 1990). Women of the same race and culture tend to stand closer to each other in casual conversation than do men of the same race and culture. When a Middle Eastern man (who has a relatively small proxemic bubble) engages in conversation with a White, middle-class, U.S. man (who has a larger proxemic bubble), the Middle Eastern man tends to move toward the White American, who tends to back away. You can observe the negotiations of proxemic space at cocktail parties or any other setting that involves casual social interaction.

In a society as diverse as the United States, understanding how diversity shapes social interaction is an essential part of understanding human behavior. Ignorance of the meanings that gestures have in a society can get you in trouble. For example, some Mexicans and Mexican Americans may display the right hand held up, palm inward, all fingers extended, as an obscene gesture meaning "screw you many times over." This provocative gesture has no meaning at all in Anglo (White) society. Likewise, people who grow up in urban environments learn to avoid eye contact on the streets. Staring at someone for only two or three seconds can be interpreted as a hostile act, if done man to man (Anderson 1999, 1990).

If a woman maintains mutual eye contact with a male stranger for more than two or three seconds, she may be assumed by the man to be sexually interested in him. In contrast, during sustained conversation with acquaintances, women maintain mutual eye contact longer than do men (Romain 1999; Wood 1994).

## Interpersonal Attraction

We have already asked, "What holds society together?" This was asked at the macroanalysis level—that is, the level of society. But what holds relationships together—or, for that matter, makes them fall apart? You will not be surprised to learn that formation of relationships has a strong social structural component—that is, it is patterned by social forces and can to a great extent be predicted.

Humans have a powerful desire to be with other human beings; in other words, they have a strong need for *affiliation*. We tend to spend about 75 percent of our time with other people when doing all sorts of activities—eating, watching television, studying, doing hobbies, working, and so on (Cassidy and Shaver 1999). People who lack all forms of human contact are very rare in the general population, and their isolation is usually rooted in psychotic or schizophrenic disorders. Extreme social isolation at an early age causes severe disruption of mental, emotional, and language development, as we saw in Chapter 4.

The affiliation tendency has been likened to **imprinting,** a phenomenon seen in newborn or newly hatched animals who attach themselves to the first living creature they encounter, even if it is of another species (Lorenz 1966). Studies of geese and squirrels show that once the young animal attaches itself to a human experimenter, the process is irreversible. The young animal prefers the company of the human to the company of its own species. A degree of imprinting may be discernible in human infant attachment, but researchers note that in infants the process is more complex, more changeable, and more influenced by social factors (Brown 1986).

Somewhat similar to affiliation is interpersonal attraction, a nonspecific positive response toward another person. Attraction occurs in ordinary day-to-day interaction and varies from mild attraction (such as thinking your grocer is a nice person) all the way to deep feelings of love. According to one view, attractions fall on a continuum ranging from hate to strong dislike to mild dislike to mild liking to strong liking to love. Another view is that attraction and love are two different continua, able to exist separately. In this view, you can actually like someone a whole lot, but not be in love. Conversely, you can feel passionate love for someone, including strong sexual feelings and intense emotion, yet not really "like" the person. Have you ever been in love with someone you did not particularly like?

Can attraction be scientifically predicted? Can you identify with whom you are most likely to fall in love?

Konrad Lorenz, the animal behaviorist, shows that adult Graylag geese *that have imprinted on him the moment they were hatched will follow him anywhere, as though he were their mother goose (Tweed Roosevelt, personal communication)!*

Romantic love is idealized in this society as something that "just happens," but research shows that interpersonal attraction follows predictable patterns.

The surprising answer to these questions is a loud, although somewhat qualified, yes. Most of us have been raised to believe that love is impossible to measure and certainly impossible to predict scientifically. We think of love, especially romantic love, as quick and mysterious—a lightning bolt. Couples report falling in love at first sight, thinking that they were "meant to be together" (McCollum 2002). Countless novels and stories support this view, but extensive research in sociology and social psychology suggests otherwise: In a probabilistic sense, love can be predicted beyond the level of pure chance. Let us take a look at some of these intriguing findings.

A strong determinant of your attraction to others is simply whether you live near them, work next to them, or have frequent contact with them. You are more likely to form friendships with people from your own city than with people from a thousand miles away. One classic study even showed that you are more likely to be attracted to someone on your floor, your residence hall, or your apartment building than to someone even two floors down or two streets over (Festinger et al. 1950). Such is the effect of proximity in the formation of human friendships.

Now, though the general principle still holds, many people form relationships without being in close proximity, such as in online dating. Studies of Internet dating show that, even in this cyberworld, social norms still apply. Studies of Internet dating find, for example, that unlike other dating behavior, on the Internet there is pressure to disclose more secrets about oneself in a shorter period of time (Lawson and Leck 2006).

Our attraction to another person is also greatly affected simply by how frequently we see that person or even his or her photograph. When watching a movie, have you ever noticed that the central character seems more attractive at the end of the movie than at the beginning? This is particularly true if you already find the person very attractive when the movie begins. Have you ever noticed that the fabulous-looking person sitting next to you in class looks better every day? You may be experiencing *mere exposure effect:* The more you see someone in person—or even in a photograph—the more you like him or her. In studies where people are repeatedly shown photographs of the same face, the more often a person sees a particular face, the more he or she likes that person (Moreland and Beach 1992; Zajonc 1968).

There are two qualifications to the effect. First, overexposure can result when a photograph is seen too often. The viewer becomes saturated and ceases to like the pictured person more with each exposure. Second, the initial response of the viewer can determine how much liking will increase. If someone starts out liking a particular person, seeing that person frequently will increase the liking for that person; however, if one starts out disliking the pictured person, the amount of dislike tends to remain about the same, regardless of how often one sees the person (Taylor et al. 2009).

We hear that "beauty is only skin deep." Apparently, that is deep enough. To a surprisingly large degree, the attractions we feel toward people of either gender are based on our perception of their physical attractiveness. A vast amount of research over the years has consistently shown the importance of attractiveness in human interactions: Adults react more leniently to the bad behavior of an attractive child than to the same behavior of an unattractive child (Berscheid and

Reis 1998; Dion 1972). Teachers evaluate cute children of either gender as "smarter" than unattractive children with identical academic records (Worchel et al. 2000; Clifford and Walster 1973). In studies of mock jury trials, attractive defendants, male or female, receive lighter jury-recommended sentences on average than unattractive defendants convicted of the same crime (Gilbert et al. 1998; Sigall and Ostrove 1975).

Of course, standards of attractiveness vary between cultures and between subcultures within the same society. What is highly attractive in one culture may be repulsive in another. In the United States, there is a maxim that you can never be too thin—a major cause of eating disorders such as *anorexia* and *bulimia*, especially among White women (Hesse-Biber 2007). The maxim is oppressive for women in U.S. society, yet it is clearly highly culturally relative, even within U.S. culture. Among certain African Americans, chubbiness in women is considered attractive. Such women are called "healthy" and "phatt" (not "fat"), which means the same as "stacked" or curvaceous. Similar cultural norms often apply in certain U.S. Hispanic populations. The skinny woman is not considered attractive. Nonetheless, studies show that anorexia and bulimia are now increasing among women of color, showing how cultural norms can change—even though Black women, in general, are more satisfied with their body image than White women (Lovejoy 2001; Fitzgibbon and Stolley 2000; see also Chapter 14).

Studies of dating patterns among college students show that the more attractive one is, the more likely one will be asked on a date. This applies to gay and lesbian dating as well as to heterosexual dating (Berscheid and Reiss 1998; Speed and Gangestad 1997). However, one very important exception can be added to this finding: Physical attractiveness predicts only the early stages of a relationship. When one measures relationships that last a while, other factors come into play, principally religion, political attitudes, social class background, educational aspirations, and race. Perceived physical attractiveness may predict who is attracted to whom initially, but other variables are better predictors of how long a relationship will last (Berscheid and Reis 1998).

So, do "opposites attract"? Not according to the research. We have all heard that people are attracted to their "opposite" in personality, social status, background, and other characteristics. Many of us grow up believing this to be true. However, if the research tells us one thing about interpersonal attraction, it is that with few exceptions we are attracted to people who are similar or even identical to us in socioeconomic status, race, ethnicity, religion, perceived personality traits, and general attitudes and opinions (Taylor et al. 2009; Brehm et al. 2002). "Dominant" people tend to be attracted to other dominant people, not to "submissive" people. Couples tend to have similar opinions about political issues of great importance to them, such as attitudes about abortion, crime, animal rights, and

urban violence. Overall, couples tend to exhibit strong cultural or subcultural similarity, not difference.

There are exceptions, of course. We sometimes fall in love with the *exotic*—the culturally or socially different. Novels and movies return endlessly to the story of the rich young woman who falls in love with a rough-and-ready biker, but such a pairing is by far the exception and not the rule. That rich young woman is far more likely to fall in love with a rich young man. When it comes to long-term relationships, including both friends and lovers (whether heterosexual, gay, or lesbian), humans vastly prefer a great degree of similarity, even though, if asked, they might deny it. In fact, the less similar a heterosexual relationship is with respect to race, social class, age, and educational aspirations (how far in school the person wants to go), the quicker the relationship is likely to break up (Silverthorne and Quinsey 2000; Worchel et al. 2000; Berscheid and Reis 1998; Stover and Hope 1993; Hill et al. 1976).

## Debunking Society's Myths

**Myth:** Love is purely an emotional experience that you cannot predict or control.

**Sociological perspective:** Whom you fall in love with can be predicted beyond chance by such factors as proximity, how often you see the person, how attractive you perceive the person to be, and whether you are similar (not different) to her or him in social class, race–ethnicity, religion, age, educational aspirations, and general attitudes, including political attitudes and beliefs.

Most young romantic relationships, regrettably, come to an end. On campus, relationships tend to break up most often during gaps in the school calendar, such as winter and spring break. Summers are especially brutal on relationships formed during the academic year. Breakups are seldom mutual. Almost always, only one member of the pair wants to break off the relationship, whereas the other wants to keep it going. The sad truth means that the next time someone tells you that their breakup last week was "mutual," you know they are probably lying or deceiving themselves (Taylor et al. 2009).

# Theories About Analyzing Social Interaction

Groups, statuses, and roles form a web of social interaction. The interaction people have with one another is a basic element of society. Sociologists have developed different ways of understanding social interaction. Functionalist theory, discussed in Chapter 1, is one such concept. Here we detail four others: the social construction of reality, ethnomethodology, impression management, and social exchange. The first three theories come directly from the symbolic interaction perspective.

## The Social Construction of Reality

What holds society together? This is a basic question for sociologists, one that, as we have seen, has long guided sociological thinking. Sociologists note that society cannot hold together without something that is shared—a shared social reality.

Some sociological theorists have argued convincingly that there is little actual reality beyond that produced by the process of social interaction itself. This is the principle of the *social construction of reality,* the idea that our perception of what is real is determined by the subjective meaning that we attribute to an experience, a principle central to symbolic interaction theory (Berger and Luckmann 1967; Blumer 1969). Hence, there is no objective "reality" in itself. Things do not have their own intrinsic meaning. We subjectively impose meaning on things.

Children do this routinely—impose inherent meaning on things. Upon seeing a marble roll off a table, the child attributes causation (meaning) to the marble: The marble rolled off the table "because it wanted to." Such perceptions carry into adulthood: The man walking down the street who accidentally walks smack into a telephone pole, at first thought glares at the pole, as though the pole somehow caused the accident! He inadvertently attributes causation and meaning to an inanimate object—the telephone pole (Heider 1958).

Considerable evidence exists that people do just that; they force meaning on something when doing so allows them to see or perceive what they want to perceive—even if that perception seems to someone else to be contrary to actual fact. They then come to believe that what they perceived is indeed "fact." A classic and convincing study of this is Hastorf and Cantril's (1954) study of Princeton and Dartmouth students who watched a film of a game of basketball between the two schools. Both sets of students watched the same film. The students were instructed to watch carefully for rule infractions by each team. The results were that the Princeton students reported twice as many rule infractions involving the Dartmouth team as the Dartmouth students saw. The Dartmouth students saw about twice as many rule infractions by Princeton as the Princeton students saw! Remember that they all saw exactly the same game—the same "facts." We see the "facts" we want to see, as a result of the social construction of reality. Subsequent research has strongly supported the Hastorf and Cantril findings (Taylor et al. 2009; Ross 1977; Jones and Nisbett 1972).

As we saw in Chapter 1, our perceptions of reality are determined by what is called the *definition of the situation:* We observe the context in which we find ourselves and then adjust our attitudes and perceptions accordingly. Sociological theorist W. I. Thomas embodies this idea in his well-known dictum that *situations defined as real are real in their consequences* (Thomas 1966/1931). The Princeton and Dartmouth students saw different "realities" depending on what college they were attending, and the consequences (the perceived rule infractions) were very real to them.

The definition of the situation is a principle that can also affect a "factual" event such as whether an emergency room patient is perceived to be dead by the doctors. In his research in the emergency room of a hospital, Sudnow (1967) found that patients who arrived at the emergency room with no discernible heartbeat or breathing were treated differently by the attending physician depending on the patient's age. A person in his or her early twenties or younger was not immediately pronounced "dead on arrival" (DOA). Instead, the physicians spent a lot of time listening for and testing for a heartbeat, stimulating the heart, examining the patient's eyes, giving oxygen, and administering other stimulation to revive the patient. If the doctor obtained no lifelike responses, the patient was pronounced dead. Older patients, however, were on the average less likely to receive such extensive procedures. The older person was examined less thoroughly and often was pronounced dead on the spot with only a stethoscopic examination of the heart. In such instances, how the physicians defined the situation—how they socially constructed reality—was indeed real in its consequence for the patient!

Understanding the social construction of reality helps one see many aspects of society in a new light. Race and gender are significant influences on social experience because people believe them to be so. Indeed, society is constructed based on certain assumptions about the significance of race and gender. These assumptions have guided the formation of social institutions, including what work people do, how families are organized, and how power is exercised.

## Ethnomethodology

Our interactions are guided by rules that we follow. Sometimes these rules are non-obvious and subtle. These rules are the *norms* of social interaction. Again, what holds society together? Society cannot hold together without norms, but what rules do we follow? How do we know what these rules or norms are? An approach in sociology called *ethnomethodology* is a clever technique for finding out.

**Ethnomethodology** (Garfinkel 1967), after *ethno* for "people" and *methodology* for "mode of study," is a clever technique for studying human interaction by deliberately disrupting social norms and observing how individuals attempt to restore normalcy. The idea is that to study such norms, one must first break them, because the subsequent behavior of the people involved will reveal just what the norms were in the first place.

Ethnomethodology is based on the premise that human interaction takes place within a consensus, and interaction is not possible without this consensus. The consensus is part of what holds society together. According to Garfinkel, this consensus will be revealed by people's *background expectancies,* namely, the norms for behavior that they carry with them into situations of interaction. It is presumed that these expectancies are to a great degree shared, and thus studying norms by deliberately violating them will reveal the norms that most people bring with them into interaction. The ethnomethodologist argues that you cannot simply walk up to someone and ask what norms the person has and uses, because most people will not be able to articulate them. We are not wholly conscious of what norms we use even though they are shared. Ethnomethodology is designed to "uncover" those norms.

Ethnomethodologists often use ingenious procedures for uncovering those norms by thinking up clever ways to interrupt "normal" interaction. William Gamson, a sociology professor, had one of his students go into a grocery store where jelly beans, normally priced at that time at 49 cents per pound, were on sale for 35 cents. The student engaged the saleswoman in conversation about the various candies and then asked for a pound of jelly beans. The saleswoman then wrapped them and asked for 35 cents. The rest of the conversation went like this:

> *Student:* Oh, only 35 cents for all those nice jelly beans? There are so many of them. I think I will pay $1 for them.

> *Saleswoman:* Yes, there are a lot, and today they are on sale for only 35 cents.

> *Student:* I know they are on sale, but I want to pay $1 for them. I just love jelly beans, and they are worth a lot to me.

> *Saleswoman:* Well, uh, no, you see, they are selling for 35 cents today, and you wanted a pound, and they are 35 cents a pound.

> *Student:* (voice rising) I am perfectly capable of seeing that they are on sale at 35 cents a pound. That has nothing to do with it. It is just that I personally feel that they are worth more, and I want to pay more for them.

> *Saleswoman:* (becoming quite angry) What is the matter with you? Are you crazy or something? Everything in this store is priced more than what it is worth. Those jelly beans probably cost the store only a nickel. Now do you want them or should I put them back?

At this point the student became quite embarrassed, paid the 35 cents, and hurriedly left (Gamson and Modigliani 1974).

The point here is that the saleswoman approached the situation with a presumed consensus, a consensus that becomes revealed by its deliberate violation by the student. The puzzled saleswoman took measures to attempt to normalize the interaction, even to *force* it to be normal.

## Impression Management and Dramaturgy

Another way of analyzing social interaction is to study impression management, a term coined by symbolic interaction theorist Erving Goffman (1959). **Impression management** is a process by which people control how others perceive them. A student handing in a term paper late may wish to give the instructor the impression that it was not the student's fault but was because of uncontrollable circumstances ("my computer hard drive crashed," "my dog ate the last hard copy," and so on). The impression that one wishes to "give off" (to use Goffman's phrase) is that "I am usually a very diligent person, but today—just today—I have been betrayed by circumstances."

## table 5.2    *Theories of Social Interaction*

| | The Social Construction of Reality | Ethnomethodology | Dramaturgy | Social Exchange Theory | Game Theory |
|---|---|---|---|---|---|
| *Interprets society as:* | Organized around the subjective meaning that people give to social behavior | Held together through the consensus that people share around social norms; you can discover these norms by violating them | A stage on which actors play their social roles and give impression to those in their "audience" | A series of interactions that are based on estimates of rewards and punishments | A system in which people strategize "winning" and "losing" in their interactions with each other |
| *Analyzes social interaction as:* | Based on the meaning people give to actions in society | A series of encounters in which people manage their impressions in front of others | Enactment of social roles played before a social audience | A rational balancing act involving perceived costs and benefits of a given behavior | Calculated risks to balance rewards and punishments |

Impression management can be seen as a type of con game. We willfully attempt to manipulate others' impression of us. Goffman regarded everyday interaction as a series of attempts to con the other. In fact, trying in various ways to con the other is, according to Goffman, at the very center of much social interaction and social organization in society: Social interaction is just a big con game!

Perhaps this cynical view is not true of all social interaction, but we do present different "selves" to others in different settings. The settings are, in effect, different stages on which we act as we relate to others. For this reason, Goffman's theory is sometimes called the *dramaturgy model* of social interaction, a way of analyzing interaction that assumes the participants are actors on a stage in the drama of everyday social life. People present different faces (give off different impressions) on different stages (in different situations or different roles) with different others. To your mother, you may present yourself as the dutiful, obedient daughter, which may not be how you present yourself to a friend. Perhaps you think acting like a diligent student makes you seem a jerk, so you hide from your friends that you are really interested in a class or enjoy your homework. Analyzing impression management reveals that we try to con the other into perceiving us as we want to be perceived. The box "Doing Sociological Research: Doing Hair, Doing Class" shows how impression management can be involved in many settings, including the everyday world of the hair salon.

A clever study by Albas and Albas (1988) demonstrates just how pervasive impression management is in social interaction. The Albases studied how college students interacted with one another when the instructor returned graded papers during class. Some students got good grades ("aces"), others got poor grades ("bombers"), but both employed a variety of devices (cons) to maintain or give off a favorable impression. For example, the aces wanted to show off their grades, but they did not want to appear to be braggarts, so they casually or "accidentally" let others see their papers. In contrast, the bombers hid or covered their papers to hide their poor grades, said they "didn't care" what they got, or simply lied about their grades.

One thing that Goffman's theory makes clear is that social interaction is a very perilous undertaking. Have you ever been embarrassed? Of course you have; we all have. Think of a really big embarrassment that you experienced. Goffman defines embarrassment as a spontaneous reaction to a sudden or transitory challenge to our identity: We attempt to restore a prior perception of our "self" by others. Perhaps you were giving a talk before a class and then suddenly forgot the rest of the talk. Or perhaps you recently bent over and split your pants. Or perhaps you are a man and barged accidentally into a women's bathroom. All these actions will result in embarrassment, causing you to "lose face."

*Rich Abrahamson/The Fort Collins Coloradoan/AP Photo*

*Impression management is the display of how you want others to define you. It can be especially obvious when you feel strong attachments to a particular group or identity.*

You will then attempt to *restore face* ("save face"), that is, eliminate the conditions causing the embarrassment. You thus will attempt to con others into perceiving you as they might have before the embarrassing incident. One way to do this is to shift blame from the self to some other, for example, claiming in the first example that the teacher did not give you time to adequately memorize the talk; or in the second example, claiming that you will never buy that particular, obviously inferior brand of pants again; or in the third example, claiming that the sign saying "Women's Room" was not clearly visible. All these represent deliberate manipulations (cons) to save face on your part—to restore the other's prior perception of you.

## Social Exchange and Game Theory

Another way of analyzing social interaction is through the social exchange model. The *social exchange model* of social interaction holds that our interactions are determined by the rewards or punishments that we receive from others (Homans 1974; Blau 1986; Cook and Gerbasi 2006). A fundamental principle of exchange theory is that an interaction that elicits approval from another (a type of reward) is more likely to be repeated than an interaction that incites disapproval (a type of punishment). According to the exchange principle, one can predict whether a given interaction is likely to be repeated or continued by calculating the degree of reward or punishment inspired by the interaction. If the reward for an interaction exceeds the punishment, then a potential for *social profit* exists and the interaction is likely to occur or continue.

Rewards can take many forms. They can include tangible gains such as gifts, recognition, and money, or subtle everyday rewards such as smiles, nods, and

# >doing sociological research

## Doing Hair, Doing Class

**Research Question:** Sociologist Debra Gimlin was curious about a common site for social interaction—hair salons. She noticed that the interaction that occurs in hair salons is often marked by differences in the social class status of clients and stylists. Her research question was, How do women attempt to cultivate the cultural ideals of beauty, and in particular, how is this achieved through the interaction between hair stylists and their clients?

**Research Method:** She did her research by spending more than 200 hours observing social interaction in a hair salon. She watched the interaction between clients and stylists and conducted interviews with the owner, the staff, and twenty women customers. During the course of her fieldwork, she recorded her observations of the conversations and interaction in the salon, frequently asking questions of patrons and staff. The patrons were mostly middle- and upper-middle class; the stylists, working

class. All the stylists were White, as were most of the clients.

**Research Results:** "Beauty work" as Gimlin calls it, involves the stylist bridging the gap between those who seek beauty and those who define it; her (or his) role is to be the expert in beauty culture, bringing the latest fashion and technique to clients. Beauticians are also expected to engage in some "emotion work"—that is, they are expected to nurture clients and be interested in their lives; often they are put in the position of sacrificing their professional expertise to meet clients' wishes.

According to Gimlin, since stylists typically have lower class status than their clients, this introduces an element into the relationship that stylists negotiate carefully in their routine social interaction. Hairdressers emphasize their special knowledge of beauty and taste as a way of reducing the status

pats on the back. Similarly, punishments come in many varieties, from extremes such as public humiliation, beating, banishment, or execution, to gestures as subtle as a raised eyebrow or a frown. For example, if you ask someone out for a date and the person says yes, you have gained a reward, and you are likely to repeat the interaction. You are likely to ask the person out again, or to ask someone else out. If you ask someone out, and he or she glares at you and says, "No way!", then you have elicited a punishment that will probably cause you to shy away from repeating this type of interaction with that person.

Social exchange theory has grown partly out of **game theory,** a mathematic and economic theory that predicts that human interaction has the characteristics of a "game," namely, strategies, winners and losers, rewards and punishments, and profits and costs (Nash 1951; Dixit and Sneath 1997; Kuhn and Nasar 2002). Simply asking someone out for a date indeed has a gamelike aspect to it, and you will probably use some kind of strategy to "win" (have the other agree to go out with you) and "get rewarded" (have a pleasant or fun time) at minimal "cost" to you (you don't want to spend a large amount of money on the date or you do not want to get into an unpleasant argument on the date). The interesting thing about game theory is

that it sees human interaction as just that: a game. Impression management theory also contains a game-like element in its hypothesis that human interaction is a big con game. The mathematician John Nash is one of the inventors of game theory and was featured in the movie, *A Beautiful Mind.*

# Interaction in Cyberspace

When people interact and communicate with one another by means of personal computers—through email, chat rooms, computer bulletin boards, virtual communities such as LinkedIn and the like, and other computer-to-computer interactions—they are engaging in **cyberspace interaction** (or virtual interaction).

The character of cyberspace interaction is changing as new technologies emerge. Not long ago, nonverbal interaction was absent in cyberspace as people could not "see" what others were like. But with the introduction of video-based cyberspace, such as YouTube and photos on Facebook and MySpace, people can now display still and moving images of themselves. These differences between themselves and their clients. They also try to nullify the existing class hierarchy by conceiving an alternative hierarchy, not one based on education, income, or occupation but only on the ability to style hair competently. Thus, stylists describe clients as perhaps "having a ton of money," but unable to do their hair or know what looks best on them. Stylists become confidantes with clients, who often tell them highly personal information about their lives. Appearing to create personal relationships with their clients, even though they never see them outside the salon, also reduces status differences.

*Conclusions and Implications:* Gimlin concludes that beauty ideals are shaped in this society by an awareness of social location and cultural distinctions. As she says, "Beauty is . . . one tool women use as they make claims to particular social statuses" (1996: 525).

**Questions to Consider**

The next time you get your hair cut, you might observe the social interaction around you and ask how class, gender, and race shape interaction in the salon or barbershop that you use. Try to get someone in class to collaborate with you so that you can compare observations in different salon settings. In doing so, you will be studying how gender, race, and class shape social interaction in everyday life.

1. Would you expect the same dynamic in a salon where men are the stylists?

2. Do Gimlin's findings hold in settings where the customers and stylists are not White or where they are all working class?

3. In your opinion, would Gimlin's findings hold in an African American *men's* barbershop?

*Source:* Gimlin, Debra. 1996. "Pamela's Place: Power and Negotiation in the Hair Salon." *Gender & Society* 10 (October): 505–526.

images provide new opportunities, as we noted above, for what sociologists would call the presentation of self and impression management. Sometimes this comes with embarrassing consequences. The young college student who displays a seminude photo of herself, projecting a sexual presentation of self, may be horrified if one of her parents or a potential employer visits her Facebook site!

Cyberspace interaction is becoming increasingly common among all age, gender, and race groups, although clear patterns are also present in who is engaged in this form of social interaction and how people use it (see Table 5.3 on page 124; Hargittai 2008). Women, for example, still lag behind men in use of the Internet, but young women and Black women use the Internet more than their male peers. Older women lag behind older men in their use. Men are also, in general, more intense users, meaning that they log on more often, spend more time online, and are more likely to use broadband.

Gender differences also prevail in how women and men use the Internet. Women are more likely to use email to write to friends and family, share news, plan events, and forward jokes. And women are more likely to report that email nurtures their relationships. Men, on the other hand, use the Internet more to transact business, and they look for a wider array of information than women do. Men are also more likely to use the Internet for hobbies, including such things as sports fantasy leagues, downloading music, and listening to radio (Pew Internet and American Life Project 2009).

More than 75 percent of those aged 18–24 now use online social networking sites, with women among the most frequent users of such sites. The popularity of these sites is also growing rapidly among youth. Again, gender patterns emerge in how young people interact online. Boys are more likely than girls to say they use these sites to make new friends and to flirt; girls use it more to stay in touch with friends they already have (Pew Internet and American Life Project 2009).

It is too early to know the implications of these cyberspace interactions. Some think it will make social life more alienating, with people developing weaker social skills and less ability for successful face-to-face interaction. Some studies have noted that people can develop extremely close and in-depth relationships as a result of their interaction in cyberspace (Hargittai 2008). The Internet also creates more opportunity for people to misrepresent themselves or even create completely false—or even stolen—identities.

## Social Interaction in an Age of Technology

Just as the invention of new technologies during the Industrial Revolution changed how people worked and lived, so is the Cyberspace Revolution transforming social interaction in society. Only a few years ago, forms of interaction and communication that are now common would have been seen as science fiction. What are some of the changes in social interaction—and, thus, in society—that have come as the result of technological changes?

© Bob Daemmrich/The Image Works

### How have new technologies affected the interaction in social groups?

If you look, you will frequently see groups of friends, often young people, gathered together, but with everyone talking to someone else on a cell phone. Although new technologies allow people to stay closely in touch, do they also intrude on the intimacy that one might otherwise share in face-to-face interaction?

Matt Sayles/AP Photo

### Is there a "digital divide" in new technologies—that is, inequalities of usage across different groups?

Many people have noted that, even with the increasing presence of computer technology, there is still a large racial and class divide in who has access to these various devices. White adults are far more likely, for example, to have Internet access than are Black adults, as are groups in higher income brackets. It remains to be seen whether this will hold up over time, since younger people under age 30 are far more likely to have Internet access than older adults.

Joanne Carole/AP Photo

### How do new technologies change parts of the culture?

New forms of technology also have introduced new language into society—a form of cultural innovation. If you were asked to "TMB," would you "KWIM"? (If not, see the table in Chapter 2 on page 32.)

Kevork Djansezian/AP Photo

### Can new technologies create new social problems?

The new forms of social interaction that computer technologies have created also raise new social issues. For example, what social issues arise from the intrusions on privacy that these new technologies can involve?

### Do new technologies have any negative effects on social interaction?

Using new technologies is commonplace. The ability to communicate instantly, including around the globe, is a tremendous convenience and can draw distant groups closer together, but do they also produce more alienating social relationships?

© Jeff Greenberg/PhotoEdit

© Syracuse Newspapers/Michele Gabel/The Image Works

### What new work skills do new technologies require and how do these affect different social groups?

The introduction of new technologies relies on new skills that people learn to be able to work (and play) effectively, but what new forms of inequality might be produced as the result?

| table 5.3 | Teens Online: Who is Most Likely to Create an Online Profile? | | | |
|---|---|---|---|---|
| | **Percentage in Each Group Who Create Online Profiles** | | | **Percentage in Each Group Who Create Online Profiles** |
| **Sex** | | | **Age by Sex** | |
| Boys | 51% | | Boys aged 15–17 | 57% |
| Girls | 58 | | Girls aged 15–17 | 70 |
| **Age** | | | **Household Income** | |
| 12–14 | 45 | | Less than $50,000 | 55 |
| 15–17 | 64 | | $50,000 or more | 56 |
| **Age by Sex** | | | **Race–Ethnicity** | |
| Boys aged 12–14 | 46 | | White non-Hispanic | 53 |
| Girls aged 12–14 | 44 | | Non-White | 58 |

*Source:* Pew Internet and American Life Project: *Teens and Parents Survey.* 2009. **www.pewinternet.org.** Reprinted by permission.

But studies find that computer-mediated interactions also follow some of the same patterns that are found in face-to-face interaction. People still "manage" identities in front of a presumed audience; they project images of self to others that are consistent with the identity they have created for themselves, and they form social networks that become the source for evolving identities, just as people do in traditional forms of social interaction (Brignall and Van Valey 2005).

In this respect, cyberspace interaction is the application of Goffman's principle of *impression management.* The person can put forward a totally different and wholly created self, or identity. One can "give off," in Goffman's terms, any impression one wishes and, at the same time, know that one's true self is protected by anonymity. This gives the individual quite a large

and free range of roles and identities from which to choose. As predicted by symbolic interaction theory, of which Goffman's is one variety, *the reality of the situation grows out of the interaction process itself.* This is a central point of symbolic interaction theory and is central to sociological analysis generally: Interaction creates reality.

Cyberspace interaction has thus resulted in new forms of social interaction in society—in fact, a new social order containing both deviants and conformists. These new forms of social interaction have their own rules and norms, their own language, their own sets of beliefs, and practices or rituals—in short, all the elements of culture, as defined in Chapter 2. For sociologists, cyberspace also provides an intriguing new venue in which to study the connection between society and social interaction.

# Chapter Summary

- **What is society?**

  *Society* is a system of social interaction that includes both culture and *social organization.* Society includes *social institutions,* or established organized social behavior, and exists for a recognized purpose; *social structure* is the patterned relationships within a society.

- **What holds society together?**

  According to theorist Emile Durkheim, society with all its complex social organization and culture, is held together, depending on overall type, by *mechanical solidarity* (based on individual similarity) and *organic solidarity* (based on a *division of labor* among dissimilar individuals).

Two other forms of social organization also contribute to the cohesion of a society: *gemeinschaft* ("community," characterized by cohesion based on friendships and loyalties) and *gesellschaft* ("society," characterized by cohesion based on complexity and differentiation).

- ### *What are the types of societies?*

  Societies across the globe vary in type, as determined mainly by the complexity of their social structures, their division of labor, and their technologies. From least to most complex, they are *foraging, pastoral, horticultural, agricultural* (these four constitute *preindustrial* societies), *industrial*, and *postindustrial* societies.

- ### *What are the forms of social interaction in society?*

  All forms of social interaction in society are shaped by the structure of its social institutions. A *group* is a collection of individuals who interact and communicate with each other, share goals and norms, and have a subjective awareness of themselves as a distinct social unit. *Status* is a hierarchical position in a structure; a *role* is the expected behavior associated with a particular status. A *role* is the behavior others expect from a person associated with a particular status. Patterns of social interaction influence nonverbal interaction as well as patterns of attraction and affiliation.

- ### *What theories are there about social interaction?*

  Social interaction takes place in society within the context of social structure and social institutions. Social interaction is analyzed in several ways, including the *social construction of reality* (we impose meaning and reality on our interactions with others); *ethnomethodology* (deliberate interruption of interaction to observe how a return to "normal" interaction is accomplished); *impression management* (a person "gives off" a particular impression to "con" the other and achieve certain goals, as in *cyberspace interaction*); and *social exchange* and *game theory* (one engages in gamelike reward and punishment interactions to achieve one's goals).

- ### *How is technology changing social interaction?*

  Increasingly, people engage with each other through *cyberspace interaction*. Social norms develop in cyberspace as they do in face-to-face interaction, but a person in cyberspace can also manipulate the impression that he or she gives off, thus creating a new "virtual" self.

## Key Terms

achieved status   110
ascribed status   110
collective consciousness   104
cyberspace interaction   120
division of labor   105
ethnomethodology   117
game theory   120
gemeinschaft   105
gesellschaft   105
group   109
impression management   118
imprinting   114

macroanalysis   102
master status   111
mechanical solidarity   104
microanalysis   102
nonverbal communication   113
organic solidarity   105
postindustrial society   109
preindustrial society   106
proxemic communication   113
role   111
role conflict   111
role modeling   111

role set   111
role strain   112
social institution   103
social interaction   102
social organization   103
social structure   104
society   102
status   110
status inconsistency   110
status set   110
tactile communication   113

## Online Resources

### *Sociology: The Essentials* Companion Website

**www.cengage.com/sociology/andersen**
Visit your book companion website where you will find more resources to help you study and write your research papers. Resources include web links, learning objectives, Internet exercises, quizzing, and flash cards.

**is an easy-to-use online resource that helps you study in less time to get the grade you want NOW.**

**www.cengage.com/login**
Need help studying? This site is your one-stop study shop. Take a Pre-Test and Cengage NOW will generate a Personalized Study Plan based on your test results. The Study Plan will identify the topics you need to review and direct you to online resources to help you master those topics. You can then take a Post-Test to determine the concepts you have mastered and what you still need to work on.

Chapter six
CHAPTER SIX Chapter

# Groups and Organizations

[ *Twelve citizens sit* together in an elevated enclosure, like a choir loft, and silently watch a drama unfold before them, day after day. They are respectfully addressed by highly paid professionals: lawyers, judges, expert witnesses. Their job, ruling on the innocence or guilt of a defendant or the settlement of a legal claim, was once the prerogative only of kings. Their decision may mean freedom or incarceration, fortune or penury, even life or death.

Juries have been the focus of much research, in part because they fill such a vital role in our society and in part because within this curiously artificial, yet intimate, group of random strangers can be found a wealth of interesting sociological phenomena. Jury verdicts and jury deliberations show the same inescapable influences of status, race, and gender that affect the rest of society (Vidmar and Hans 2007; Hans 2006). They also show the powerful effects of group pressure on the individual. Juries are, in some ways, society in miniature.

During jury selection, in a process called the *voir dire*, lawyers on both sides are entitled to eliminate any potential jurors and no explanation is required. Many lawyers who have great faith in their ability to judge jurors consider jury selection to be the most important part of a trial. By choosing jurors, they are choosing the verdict. Consider some of the folk wisdom clung to by trial lawyers in the past, with varying degrees of accuracy: Farmers believe in strict responsibility, whereas waiters

*continued*

and bartenders are forgiving; avoid the clergy; select married women. A guideline for Dallas, Texas, prosecutors advised against selecting "Yankees ... unless they appear to have common sense" (Guinther 1988: 54). High-powered legal teams now make room for a new breed of legal specialist—the *trial consultant,* trained in sociological and psychological techniques—who contributes nothing but juror analysis as part of the jury selection process.

These analyses go beyond simply identifying the bias of a given juror. Juries are *groups,* and groups behave differently from individuals. Understanding group behavior is critical to predicting the performance of a jury. For instance, it is possible to make an educated prediction about who in a jury will become the most influential. Researchers have found that people with high status in society do the most talking in jury deliberations, and other jurors consider them to be the most helpful in reaching a verdict (Hans 2006; Hans and Martinez 1994; Berger and Zelditch 1985).

Factions or subgroupings form during jury deliberations, and if jury analysts expect a difficult decision, they can attempt to influence how factionalized juries will resolve their disputes based on sociological and psychological data about small group decision making (Saks and Marti 1997). For instance, jurors are much less likely to defect from large factions than from small ones. The larger the faction, the less willing a juror will be to defy the weight of group opinion. As we shall see

below, this is a *group size effect*: an effect of sheer numbers in the group independent of the effects of their own personalities.

What does this say about the state of justice in our legal system, when guilt or innocence depends not only on the legal facts but also on sociological aspects of the jury? Like society as a whole, and like organizations and bureaucracies, groups are subject to social influences. Whether a relatively small group, such as a jury, or a large organization, such as a major corporation, people and groups are influenced by sociological forces.

# Types of Groups

Each of us is a member of many groups simultaneously. We have relationships in groups with family, friends, team members, and professional colleagues. Within these groups are gradations in relationships: We are generally closer to our siblings (our sisters and brothers) than to our cousins; we are intimate with some friends, merely sociable with others. If we count all our group associations, ranging from the powerful associations that define our daily lives to the thinnest connections with little feeling (other pet lovers, other company employees), we will uncover connections to literally hundreds of groups.

What is a group? Recall from Chapter 5, a **group** is two or more individuals who interact, share goals and norms, and have a subjective awareness as "we." To be considered a group, a social unit must have all three characteristics. The hazy boundaries of the definition are necessary. Consider two superficially similar examples: The individuals in a line waiting to board a train are unlikely to have a sense of themselves as one group. A line of prisoners chained together and waiting to board a bus to the penitentiary is more likely to have a stronger sense of common feeling.

As you remember from the previous chapter, certain gatherings are not groups in the strict sense, but may be *social categories* (for example, teenagers, truck drivers) or *audiences* (everyone watching a movie). The importance of defining a group is not to perfectly decide if a social unit is a group—an unnecessary endeavor—but to help us understand the behavior of people in society. As we inspect groups, we can identify characteristics that reliably predict trends in the behavior of the group and even the behavior of individuals in the group.

The study of groups has application at all levels of society, from the attraction between people who fall in love to the characteristics that make some corporations drastically outperform their competitors—or that lead them into bankruptcy. The aggregation of individuals into groups has a transforming power, and sociologists understand the social forces that make these transformations possible.

Michael Kelly/Getty Images

*This jury of twelve persons is voting on something, perhaps on whether to acquit a person accused of a serious crime. The social pressures in a jury are extremely strong, making the lone "holdout" person very unlikely.*

In this chapter, we move from the *microlevel* of analysis (the analysis of groups and face-to-face social influence) to the relatively more *macrolevel* of analysis (the analysis of formal organizations and bureaucracies).

## Dyads and Triads: Group Size Effects

Even the smallest groups are of acute sociological interest. A **dyad** is a group consisting of exactly two people. A **triad** consists of three people. This seemingly minor distinction, first scrutinized by the German sociologist **Georg Simmel** (1858–1918), can have critical consequences for group behavior (Simmel 1902). Simmel was interested in discovering the effects of size on groups, and he found that the mere difference between two and three people spawned entirely different group dynamics (the behavior of a group over time).

Imagine two people standing in line for lunch. First one talks, then the other, then the first again. The interaction proceeds in this way for several minutes. Now a third person enters the interaction. The character of the interaction suddenly changes: At any given moment, two people are interacting more with each other than either is with the third. When the third person wins the attention of the other two, a new dyad is formed, supplanting the previous pairing. The group, a triad, then consists of a dyad (the pair that is interacting) plus an *isolate.*

**Triadic segregation** is what Simmel called the tendency for triads to segregate into a pair and an isolate (a single person). A triad tends to segregate into a *coalition* of the dyad against the isolate. The isolate then has the option of initiating a coalition with either member of the dyad. This choice is a type of social advantage, leading Simmel to coin the principle of *tertius gaudens,* a Latin term meaning "the third one gains." Simmel's reasoning has led to numerous contemporary studies of coalition formation in groups (for example, Konishi and Ray 2003; Caplow 1968; and many others).

For example, interactions in a triad often end up as "two against one." You may have noticed this principle of coalition formation in your own conversations. Perhaps two friends want to go to a movie you do not want to see. You appeal to one of them to go instead to a minor league baseball game. She wavers and comes over to your point of view. Now you have formed a coalition of two against one. The friend who wants to go to the movies is now the isolate. He may recover lost social ground by trying to form a new coalition by suggesting a new alternative (going bowling or to a different movie). This flip-flop interaction may continue for some time, demonstrating another observation by Simmel: A triad is a decidedly unstable social grouping, whereas dyads are relatively stable. The minor distinction between dyads and triads is one person but has important consequences because it changes the character of the interaction within the group. Simmel is known as the discoverer of **group size effects**—the effects of group number on group behavior *independent of the personality characteristics of the members themselves.*

## Primary and Secondary Groups

**Charles Horton Cooley** (1864–1929), a famous sociologist of the Chicago School of sociology, introduced the concept of the **primary group,** defined as a group consisting of intimate, face-to-face interaction and relatively long-lasting relationships. Cooley had in mind the family and the early peer group. In his original formulation, *primary* was used in the sense of "first," the intimate group of the formative years (Cooley 1967/1909). The insight that there was an important distinction between intimate groups and other groups proved extremely fruitful. Cooley's somewhat narrow concept of family and childhood peers has been elaborated upon over the years to include a variety of intimate relations as examples of primary groups.

Primary groups have a powerful influence on an individual's personality or self-identity. The effect of family on an individual can hardly be overstated. The weight of peer pressure on schoolchildren is particularly notorious. Street gangs are a primary group, and their influence on the individual is significant; in fact, gang members frequently think of themselves as a family. Inmates in prison very frequently become members of a gang—primary groups based mainly upon race–ethnicity—as a matter of their own personal survival. The intense camaraderie formed among Marine Corps units in boot camp and in war, such as the war in Iraq, is another classic example of primary group formation and the resulting intense effect on the individual and upon her or his survival.

In contrast to primary groups are **secondary groups,** those that are larger in membership, less intimate, and less long-lasting. Secondary groups tend to be less significant in the emotional lives of people. Secondary groups include all the students at a college or university, all the people in your neighborhood, and all the people in a bureaucracy or corporation.

*One of the best examples of the primary group is that consisting of parent and child.*

# >*doing* sociological research

## Sharing the Journey

Modern society is often characterized as remote, alienating, and without much feeling of community or belonging to a group. This image of society has been carefully studied by sociologist Robert Wuthnow, who noticed that in the United States people are increasingly looking to small groups as a place where they can find emotional and spiritual support and where they find meaning and commitment, despite the image of society as an increasingly impersonal force.

*Research Question:* Wuthnow began his research by noting that, even with the individualistic culture of U.S. society, small groups play a major role in this society. He saw the increasing tendency of people to join recovery groups, reading groups, spiritual groups, and myriad other support groups. Wuthnow began his research by asking some specific questions, including, "What motivates people to join support groups?" "How do these groups function?" and "What do

members like most and least about such groups?" His broadest question, however, was to wonder how the wider society is influenced by the proliferation of small support groups.

*Research Methods:* To answer these questions, a large research team of fifteen scholars designed a study that included both a quantitative and a qualitative dimension. They distributed a survey to a representative sample of more than 1000 people in the United States. Supplementing the survey were interviews with more than 100 support group members, group leaders, and clergy. The researchers chose twelve groups for extensive study; researchers spent six months to three years tracing the history of these groups, meeting with members and attending group sessions.

*Research Results:* Based on this research, Wuthnow concludes that the small group movement is

## SEE *FOR YOURSELF*

### *ANALYZING GROUPS*

Identify a *group* of which you are a part. How does one become a member of this group? Who gets included and who gets excluded? Does the group share any unique language or other cultural characteristics (such as dress, jargon, or other group identifiers)? Does anyone ever leave the group, and if so, why?

1. Would you describe this group mainly as a *primary* or a *secondary group*? Why?

2. Now think about this group from the perspective of functionalist theory, conflict theory, and symbolic interaction theory. What are the *manifest* and *latent functions* of the group? Is there a hierarchy within the group? Is there competition between group members? What social meanings do members of the group share?

Secondary groups occasionally take on the characteristics of primary groups. The process can be accelerated in situations of high stress or crisis. For example, when a neighborhood meets with catastrophe, such as a flood, people who may be only acquaintances often come to depend on each other and in the process become more intimate. The secondary group of neighbors becomes, for a time, a primary group. This is precisely what happened in the otherwise highly impersonal neighborhoods in New York City near ground zero after the September 11, 2001, terrorist attack on the World Trade Center: Thousands of people pitched in to help, and as a result, many primary groups formed.

The same phenomenon occurred immediately after US Airways Flight 1549, on January 15, 2009—guided by the superior skills of pilot Chesley B. "Sully" Sullenberger—was forced to "land" in the cold waters of New York City's Hudson River, after both of the aircraft's jet engines had been blown out by a bird strike. Because of the tremendous skill of Sullenberger, the plane floated, and not a single death occurred. Immediately thereafter, the passengers, a secondary group before the landing, became intimately acquainted with each other—a quickly formed primary group. They even vowed to have annual reunions, further evidence of a secondary group's transformation into a primary group.

Primary and secondary groups serve different needs. Primary groups give people intimacy, companionship, and emotional support. These human fundamentally altering U.S. society. Forty percent of all Americans belong to some kind of small support group. As the result of people's participation in these groups, social values of community and spirituality are undergoing major transformation. People say they are seeking community when they join small groups whether the group is a recovery group, a religious group, a civic association, or some other small group. People turn to these small groups for emotional support more than for physical or monetary support.

***Conclusions and Implications:*** Wuthnow argues that large-scale participation in small groups has arisen in a social context in which the traditional support structures in U.S. society, such as the family, no longer provide the sense of belonging and social integration that they provided in the past. Geographic mobility, mass society, and the erosion of local ties all contribute to this trend.

People still seek a sense of community, but they create it in groups that also allow them to maintain their individuality. In voluntary small groups, you are free to leave the group if it no longer meets your needs.

Wuthnow also concludes that these groups represent a quest for spirituality in a society when, for many, traditional religious values have declined. As a consequence, support groups are redefining what is sacred. They also replace explicit religious tenets imposed from the outside with internal norms that are implicit and devised by individual groups. At the same time, these groups reflect the pluralism and diversity that characterize society. In the end, they buffer the trend toward disintegration and isolation that people often feel in mass societies.

*Source:* Wuthnow, Robert. 1994. *Sharing the Journey: Support Groups and America's New Quest for Community.* New York: Free Press.

---

desires are termed **expressive needs** (also called socioemotional needs). Family and friends share and amplify your good fortune, rescue you when you misbehave, and cheer you up when life looks grim. Primary groups are a major influence on social life and an important source of social control. They are also a dominant influence on your likes and dislikes, preferences in clothing, political views, religious attitudes, and other characteristics. Many studies have shown the overwhelming influence of family and friendship groups on religious and political affiliation, as shown in the box "Doing Sociological Research: Sharing the Journey" (Wuthnow 1994).

Secondary groups serve **instrumental needs** (also called task-oriented needs). Athletic teams form to have fun and win games. Political groups form to raise funds and influence the government. Corporations form to make profits, and employees join corporations to earn a living. Needless to say, intimacies can develop in the act of fulfilling instrumental needs, and primary groups may also devote themselves to meeting instrumental needs. The true distinction between primary and secondary groups is in how intimate the group members feel about one another and how dependent they are on the group for sustenance and identity. Both primary and secondary groups are indispensable elements of life in society.

## Reference Groups

Primary and secondary groups are groups to which members belong. Both are called *membership groups*.

*Identification with a reference group has a significant influence on one's identity.*

In contrast, **reference groups** are those to which you may or may not belong but use as a standard for evaluating your values, attitudes, and behaviors (Merton and Rossi 1950). Reference groups are generalized versions of role models. They are not "groups" in the sense that the individual interacts within (or in) them. Do you pattern your behavior on that of sports stars, musicians, military officers, or business executives? If so, those models are reference groups for you.

Imitation of reference groups can have both positive and negative effects. Members of a Little League baseball team may revere major league baseball players and attempt to imitate laudable behaviors such as tenacity and sportsmanship. But young baseball fans are also liable to be exposed to tantrums, fights, and tobacco chewing and spitting. This illustrates that the influence of a reference group can be both positive and negative.

Research has shown that identification with reference groups can strongly influence self-evaluation and self-esteem. Before the push for school desegregation began, it was thought that all-Black schools contributed to negative self-evaluation among Black students. Desegregation was expected to raise the self-esteem of Black children (Clark and Clark 1947). The original Clark and Clark study suggested that Black children in all-Black schools preferred playing with White dolls over Black dolls. This behavior was presumed to demonstrate a negative self-evaluation and self-rejection on the part of Black children.

In some cases desegregation did raise the self-esteem of Black children, but later research has also found that identification with a positive reference group was more important than desegregation. When racial or ethnic groups were consistently presented in a positive way, as in later multicultural educational programs designed to increase pride in Black culture, the self-esteem of the children was greater than that of Black children in integrated programs with no multicultural component. The same has been found for Latino children enrolled in Latino cultural awareness programs. Plainly, the representation of racial and ethnic groups in a society can have a striking positive effect on children acquiring their lifetime set of group affiliations (Harris 2006; Zhou and Bankston 2000; Baumeister and Bushman 2008; Steele 1996, 1992; Steele and Aronson 1995; Banks 1976).

## In-Groups and Out-Groups

When groups have a sense of themselves as "us," they will also have a complementary sense of other groups as "them." The distinction is commonly characterized as *in-groups* versus *out-groups*. The concept was originally elaborated by the early sociological theorist **W. I. Thomas** (Thomas 1931). College fraternities and sororities certainly exemplify "in" versus "out." So do families. So do gangs—especially so. The same can be true of the members of your high school class, your sports team, your racial group, your gender, and your social class. Members of the upper classes in the United States occasionally refer to one another as PLUs "people like us" (Graham 1999; Frazier 1957).

**Attribution theory** is the principle that we all make inferences about the personalities of others, such as concluding what the other is "really like." These attributions depend on whether you are in the in-group or the out-group. Thomas F. Pettigrew has summarized the research on attribution theory, showing that individuals commonly generate a significantly distorted perception of the motives and capabilities of other people's acts based on whether that person is an in-group or out-group member (Baumeister and Bushman 2008; Pettigrew 1992; Gilbert and Malone 1995). Pettigrew describes the misperception as **attribution error,** meaning errors made in attributing causes for people's behavior to their membership in a particular group, such as a racial group. Attribution error has several dimensions, all tending to favor the in-group over the out-group. *All else being assumed equal, we tend to perceive people in our in-group positively and those in out-groups negatively, regardless of their actual personal characteristics:*

1. When onlookers observe improper behavior by an out-group member, onlookers are likely to attribute the deviance to the disposition (the personality) of the wrongdoer. Disposition refers to the perceived "true nature" or "inherent nature" of the person, often considered to be genetically determined. *Example:* A White person sees a Hispanic person carrying a knife and, without further information, attributes this behavior to the presumed "inherent tendency" for Hispanics to be violent. The same would be true if a Hispanic person, without

*People often counteract the impersonality of society by forming informal friendship groups, as here, or joining a more formal small support group.*

Bebeto Matthews/AP Photo

additional information, assumed that all Whites have an "inherent tendency" to be racist.

2. When the *same* behavior is exhibited by an in-group member, the perception is commonly held that the act is due to the *situation* of the wrongdoer, not to the in-group member's inherent disposition or personality. *Example:* A White person sees another White person carrying a knife and concludes, without further information, that the weapon must be carried for protection in a dangerous area.

3. If an out-group member is seen to perform in some laudable way, the behavior is often attributed to a variety of special circumstances, and the out-group member is seen as "the exception."

4. An in-group member who performs in the same laudable way is given credit for a worthy personality disposition.

Typical attribution errors include misperceptions between racial groups and between men and women. If a White police officer shoots a Black or Latino, a White individual, given no additional information, is likely to assume that the victim instigated the shooting and thus "deserved" to be shot. On the other hand, a Black person is more likely to assume that the police officer fired unnecessarily, perhaps because the officer is dispositionally assumed to be a racist (Taylor et al. 2009; Kluegel and Bobo 1993; Bobo and Kluegel 1991).

A related phenomenon has been seen in men's perceptions of women coworkers. Meticulous behavior in a man is perceived positively and is seen by other men as "thorough"; in a woman, the *exact same* behavior is perceived negatively and is considered "picky." Behavior applauded in a man as "aggressive" is condemned in a woman exhibiting the same behavior as "pushy" or "bitchy" (Baumeister and Bushman 2008; Uleman et al. 1996; Wood 1994).

## Social Networks

As already noted, no individual is a member of only one group. Social life is far richer than that. A **social network** is a set of links between individuals, between groups, or between other social units, such as bureaucratic organizations or even entire nations (Aldrich and Ruef 2006; Centeno and Hargittai 2003; Mizruchi 1992). One could say that any given person belongs simultaneously to several networks (Wasserman and Faust 1994). Your group of friends, or all the people on an electronic mailing list to which you subscribe, or all of your Facebook subscribers are social networks.

The network of people you are closest to, rather than those merely linked to you in some impersonal way, is probably most important to you. Numerous research studies indicate that people get jobs via their personal networks more often than through formal job listings, want ads, or placement agencies (Ruef et al. 2003; Petersen et al. 2000; Granovetter 1995, 1974). This is especially true for high-paying, prestigious

This job candidate does a last-minute check of his resume just before being interviewed by a company representative who contacted the job candidate through a social network. Like many others, he was let go from his previous job.

jobs. Getting a job is more often a matter of who you know than what you know. Who you know, and whom they know in turn, is a social network that may have a marked effect on your life and career.

Networks form with all the spontaneity of other forms of human interaction (Mintz and Schwartz 1985; Wasserman and Faust 1994; Knoke 1992). Networks evolve, such as social ties within neighborhoods, professional contacts, and associations formed in fraternal, religious, occupational, and volunteer groups. Networks to which you are only *weakly* tied (you may know only one person in your neighborhood) provide you with access to that entire network, hence the sociological principle that there is "strength in weak ties" (Granovetter 1973; Petersen et al. 2000; Montgomery 1992).

Networks based on race, class, and gender form with particular readiness. This has been especially true of job networks. The person who leads you to a job is likely to have a similar social background. Recent research indicates that the "old boy network"—any network of White, male corporate executives—is less important than it used to be, although it is certainly not by any means gone. The diminished importance of the old boy network is because of the increasing prominence of women and minorities in business organizations. In fact, among African American and Latino individuals, one's family can provide network contacts that can lead to jobs and upward mobility

(Dominguez and Watkins 2003). Still, as we will see later in this chapter, women and minorities are considerably underrepresented in corporate life, especially in high-status jobs (Padavic and Reskin 2002; Green et al. 1999; Collins-Lowry 1997; Gerson 1993). Some recent research shows that despite recent gains on the part of minorities, relative to Whites, Blacks and Latinos are still disproportionately harmed by lack of network contacts (Smith 2007).

Networks can reach around the world, but how big is the world? How many of us, when we discover someone we just met is a friend of a friend, have remarked, "My, it's a small world"? Research into what has come to be known as the *small world problem* has shown that networks make the world a lot smaller than you might think.

Original small world researchers Travers and Milgram wanted to test whether a document could be routed via the U.S. postal system to a complete stranger more than 1000 miles away using only a chain of acquaintances (Travers and Milgram 1969; Lin 1989; Kochen 1989; Watts and Strogatz 1998; Watts 1999). If so, how many steps would be required? The researchers organized an experiment in which approximately 300 senders were all charged with getting a document to one receiver, a complete stranger. (Remember that all this was well before the advent of the desktop computer in the 1980s.) The receiver was a male, Boston stockbroker. The senders were one group of Nebraskans and one group of Bostonians chosen completely at random. Every sender in the study was given the receiver's name, address, occupation, alma mater, year of graduation, wife's maiden name, and hometown. They were asked to send the document directly to the stockbroker if they knew him on a first-name basis. Otherwise, they were asked to send the folder to a friend, relative, or acquaintance known on a first-name basis who might be more likely than the sender to know the stockbroker.

How many intermediaries do you think it took, on average, for the document to get through? (Most people estimate from twenty to hundreds.) *The average number of intermediate contacts was only 6.2!* However, only about one-third of the documents actually arrived at the target. This was quite impressive, considering that the senders did not know the target person—hence the current expression that any given person in the country is on average only about "six degrees of separation" from any other person. In this sense the world is indeed "small."

This original small world research has recently been criticized on two grounds: First, only one-third of the documents actually reached the target person. The 6.2 average intermediaries applied only to these completed chains. Thus two-thirds of the initial documents never reached the target person. For these persons, the world was certainly not "small." Second, the sending chains tended to closely follow occupational, social class, and ethnic lines, just as general network

theory would predict (Wasserman and Faust 1994). Thus, the world may indeed be "small," but only for people in your immediate social network (Ruef et al. 2003; Kleinfeld 2002; Watts 1999).

A study of Black national leaders by Taylor and associates shows that Black leaders form a very closely knit network, one considerably more closely knit than longer-established White leadership networks (Taylor 1992b; Domhoff 2002; Jackson 2000; Jackson et al. 1995, 1994; Alba and Moore 1982; Moore 1979; Kadushin 1974; Mills 1956). The world is indeed quite "small" for America's Black leadership. Included in the study were Black members of Congress, mayors, business executives, military officers (generals and full colonels), religious leaders, civil rights leaders, media personalities, entertainment and sports figures, and others. The study found that when considering only direct personal acquaintances—not indirect links involving intermediaries—one-fifth of the entire *national* Black leadership network know each other directly as a friend or close acquaintance. The Black leadership network is considerably more closely connected than White leadership networks. The Black network had greater *density*. Add only one intermediary, the friend of a friend, and the study estimated that almost three-quarters of the entire Black leadership network are included. Therefore, any given Black leader can generally get in touch with three-quarters of all other Black leaders in the country either by knowing them personally (a "friend") or via only one common acquaintance (a "friend of a friend"). That's pretty amazing when one realizes that the study is considering the population of Black leaders in the entire country.

# Social Influence in Groups

The groups in which we participate exert tremendous influence on us. We often fail to appreciate how powerful these influences are. For example, who decides what you should wear? Do you decide for yourself each morning, or is the decision already made for you by fashion designers, role models, and your peers? Consider how closely your hair length, hair styling, and choice of jewelry have been influenced by your peers. Did you invent your baggy pants, your dreadlocks, or your blue blazer? People who label themselves as nonconformists often conform rigidly to the dress code and other norms of their in-group. This was true of the Beatniks in the 1950s, the hippies of the 1960s and early 1970s, the punk rockers of the 1970s and 1980s, and the grunge kids and goths of the 1990s.

After the rebelliousness of youth has faded, the influences of our youth extend to adulthood. The choices of political party among adults (Republican, Democratic, or Independent) correlate strongly with the party of one's parents, again demonstrating the power of the primary group. Seven out of ten people vote with the political party of their parents, even though these same people insist that they think for themselves when voting (Worchel et al. 2000; Jennings and Niemi 1974). Furthermore, most people share the religious affiliation of their parents, although they will insist that they chose their own religion, free of any influence by either parent.

We all like to think we stand on our own two feet, immune to a phenomenon as superficial as group pressure. The conviction that one is impervious to social influence results in what social psychologist Philip Zimbardo calls the *not-me syndrome:* When confronted with a description of group behavior that is disappointingly conforming and not individualistic, most individuals counter that some people may conform to social pressure, "but not me" (Zimbardo et al. 1977; Taylor et al. 2009). But sociological experiments often reveal a dramatic gulf between what people think they will do and what they actually do. The conformity study by Solomon Asch discussed next is a case in point.

## The Asch Conformity Experiment

We learned in the previous section that social influences are evidently quite strong. Are they strong enough to make us disbelieve our own senses? Are they strong enough to make us misperceive what is objective, actual fact? In a classic piece of work known as the Asch conformity experiment, Solomon Asch showed that even simple objective facts cannot withstand the distorting pressure of group influence (Asch 1955, 1951).

Examine the two illustrations in Figure 6.1. Which line on the right is more nearly equal in length to the line on the left (line S)? Line B, obviously. Could anyone fail to answer correctly?

In fact, Solomon Asch discovered that social pressure of a rather gentle sort was sufficient to cause

an astonishing rise in the number of wrong answers. Asch lined up five students at a table and asked which line in the illustration on the right is the same length as the line on the left. Unknown to the fifth student, the first four were *confederates*—collaborators with the experimenter who only pretended to be participants. For several rounds, the confederates gave correct answers to Asch's tests. The fifth student also answered correctly, suspecting nothing. Then on subsequent trials the first student gave a wrong answer. The second student gave the same wrong answer. Third, wrong. Fourth, wrong. Then came the fifth student's turn.

In Asch's experiment, fully *one-third* of all students in the fifth position gave the same wrong answer as the confederates at least half the time. Forty percent gave "some" wrong answers. Only one-fourth of the students consistently gave correct answers in defiance of the invisible pressure to conform.

Line length is not a vague or ambiguous stimulus. It is clear and objective. Wrong answers from one-third of all subjects is a very high proportion. The subjects fidgeted and stammered while doing it, but they did it nonetheless. Those who did not yield to group pressure showed even more stress and discomfort than those who yielded to the (apparent) opinion of the group.

Would you have gone along with the group? Perhaps, perhaps not. Sociological insight grows when we acknowledge the fact that fully one-third of all participants will yield to the group. The Asch experiment has been repeated many times over the years, with students and nonstudents, old and young, in groups of different sizes, and in different settings (Worchel et al. 2000; Cialdini 1993). The results remain essentially the same. One-third to one-half of the participants make a judgment contrary to fact, yet in conformity with the group. Finally, the Asch findings have consistently revealed a *group size effect:* The greater the number of individuals (confederates) giving an incorrect answer (from five up to fifteen confederates), the greater the number of subjects per group giving an incorrect answer.

## The Milgram Obedience Studies

What are the limits of social pressure? In terms of moral and psychological issues, judging the length of a line is a small matter. What happens if an authority figure demands obedience—a type of conformity—even if the task is something the test subject (the person) finds morally wrong and reprehensible? A chilling answer emerged from the now famous Milgram Obedience Studies done from 1960 through 1973 by Stanley Milgram (Milgram 1974).

In this study, a naive research subject entered a laboratory-like room and was told that an experiment on learning was to be conducted. The subject was to act as a "teacher," presenting a series of test questions to another person, the "learner." Whenever

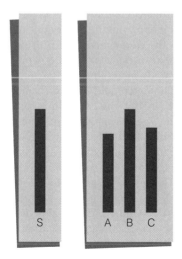

**FIGURE 6.1** *Lines from Asch Experiment*

*Source:* Asch, Solomon, 1956. "Opinion and Social Pressure." *Scientific American 19* (July): 31–36.

the learner gave a wrong answer, the teacher would administer an electric shock.

The test was relatively easy. The teacher read pairs of words to the learner, such as

**blue        box**
**nice        house**
**wild        duck**

The teacher then tested the learner by reading a multiple-choice answer, such as

**blue    sky    ink    box    lamp**

The learner had to recall which term completed the pair of terms given originally, in this case, "blue box."

If the learner answered incorrectly, the teacher was to press a switch on the shock machine, a formidable-looking device that emitted an ominous hum when activated (see Figure 6.2). For each successive wrong answer, the teacher was to increase the intensity of the shock by 15 volts.

The machine bore labels clearly visible to the teacher: Slight Shock, Moderate Shock, Strong Shock, Very Strong Shock, Intense Shock, Extreme Intensity Shock, Danger: Severe Shock, and lastly, XXX at 450 volts. As the voltage rose, the learner responded with squirming, groans, then screams.

(a)

(b)

(c)

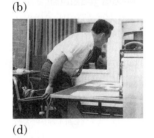

(d)

### FIGURE 6.2 *Milgram's Setup*

*These photographs show how intimidating and authoritative the Milgram experiment must have been. The first picture (a) shows the formidable-looking shock generator. The second (b) shows the role player, who pretends to be getting the electric shock, being hooked up. The third (c) shows an experimental subject (seated) and the experimenter (in lab coat, standing). The fourth picture (d) shows a subject terminating the experiment prematurely, that is, before giving the maximum shock level (voltage) of 450 volts. A large majority (65 percent) of subjects did not do this and actually went all the way to the maximum shock level.*

*Source: Milgram, Stanley. 1974. Obedience to Authority: An Experimental View. New York: Harper & Row, p. 26.*

The experiment was rigged. The learner was a confederate. No shocks were actually delivered. The true purpose of the experiment was to see if any "teacher" would go all the way to 450 volts. If the subject (teacher) tried to quit, the experimenter responded with a sequence of prods:

"Please continue."
"The experiment requires that you continue."
"It is absolutely essential that you continue."
"You have no other choice, you must go on."

In the first experiment, fully 65 percent of the volunteer subjects ("teachers") went *all the way* to 450 volts on the shock machine!

Milgram himself was astonished. Before carrying out the experiment, he had asked a variety of psychologists, sociologists, psychiatrists, and philosophers to guess how many subjects would actually go all the way to 450 volts. The opinion of these consultants was that only one-tenth of 1 percent (one in one thousand) would actually do it.

What would you have done? Remember the "not-me" syndrome. Think about the experimenter saying, "You have no other choice, you must go on." Most people claim they would refuse to continue as the voltage escalated. The importance of this experiment derives in part from how starkly it highlights the difference between what people *think* they will do and what they *actually* do.

Milgram devised a series of additional experiments in which he varied the conditions to find out what would cause subjects *not* to go all the way to 450 volts. He moved the experiment from an impressive university laboratory to a dingy basement to counteract some of the tendency for people to defer to a scientist conducting a scientific study. One learner was then instructed to complain of a heart condition. Still, well over half of the subjects delivered the maximum shock level. Speculating that women might be more humane than men (all prior experiments used only male subjects), Milgram did the experiment again using only women subjects. The results? Exactly the same. Social class background made no difference. Racial and ethnic differences had no detectable effect on compliance rate.

At the time that the Milgram experiments were conceived, the world was watching the trial in Jerusalem of World War II Nazi Adolf Eichmann. Millions of Jews, Gypsies, homosexuals, and communists were murdered between 1939 and 1945 by the Nazi party, led by Adolf Hitler. As head of the Gestapo's "Jewish section," Eichmann oversaw the deportation of Jews to concentration camps and the mass executions that followed. Eichmann disappeared after the war, was abducted in Argentina by Israeli agents in 1961, and transported to Israel, where he was tried and ultimately hanged for crimes against humanity.

The world wanted to see what sort of monster could have committed the crimes of the Holocaust, but a jarring picture of Eichmann emerged. He was slight and mild mannered, not the raging ghoul that everyone expected. He insisted that although he had indeed been a chief administrator in an organization whose product was mass murder, he was guilty only of doing what he was told to do by his superiors. He did not hate Jews, he said. In fact, he had a Jewish half-cousin whom he hid and protected. He claimed, "I was just following orders."

How different was Adolph Eichmann from the rest of us? The political theorist Hannah Arendt dared to suggest in her book *Eichman in Jerusalem* (1963) that evil on a giant scale is banal. It is not the work of monsters, but an accident of civilization. Arendt argued that to find the villain, we need only look into ourselves.

## The Iraqi Prisoners at Abu Ghraib: Research Predicts Reality?

We have just learned that ordinary people will do horrible things to other humans simply because of the influence of the group, because of an authority figure, or because of a combination of both. This has been the lesson of the Asch studies and the Milgram studies. Recent events in the world have once again shown vividly and clearly how accurate such sociological and psychological experiments are in the prediction of actual human behavior.

In the spring of 2004, it was revealed that American soldiers who were military police guards at a prison in Iraq (the prison was named Abu Ghraib) had engaged in severe torture of Iraqi prisoners of war. The torture included sexual abuse of the prisoners—having male prisoners simulate sex with other male prisoners, positioning their mouths next to the genitals of another male prisoner, being forced to masturbate in view of others, and other such acts. Still other acts of torture involved physical abuse such as beatings, stomping on the fingers of prisoners (thus fracturing them), and a large number of other physical acts of torture, including bludgeoning, some allegedly resulting in deaths of prisoners. Such tortures are clearly outlawed by the Geneva Conventions and by clearly stated U.S. principles of war. Both male and female guards participated in these acts of torture, and although most of the Iraqi victims were male, some were female.

The guards later claimed that they were simply following orders, either orders directly given or indirectly assumed. At the time, President George W. Bush and then-Secretary of Defense Donald H. Rumsfeld both claimed that the acts of torture were merely the acts of a "corrupt few" and that the vast majority of American soldiers would never engage in such horrible acts. Since then, it has come to light via CIA memoranda that certain kinds of torture were indeed formal U.S. policy.

Now consider what we know from research. The Milgram studies strongly suggest that many ordinary soldiers who were not at all "corrupt," at least not more than average, would indeed engage in these acts of torture, particularly if they believed that they were under orders to do so, *or* if they believed that they would not be punished in any way if they did. The American soldiers must bear a significant portion of the responsibility for their own behavior. *Nonetheless, the causes of the soldiers' behaviors lie not in their personalities (their "natures") but in the social structure and group pressures of the situation.*

The soldiers (guards) in the Abu Ghraib prison may not have received *direct* orders to torture prisoners. But they did so nonetheless. A now classic study of a simulated prison by Haney, Banks, and Zimbardo (1973) shows this effect quite clearly. In this study, Stanford University students were told by an experimenter to enter a dungeon-like basement. Half were told to pretend to be guards (to *role-play* being a guard) and half were told that they were prisoners (to role-play being a prisoner). Which students were told what was *randomly determined*.

After two or three days, the guards, completely on their own, began to act very sadistically and brutally toward the prisoners—having them strip naked, simulate sex, act subservient, and so on. Interestingly, the prisoners for the most part did just what the guards wanted them to do, no matter how unpleasant the requested act! The experiment was so scary that the researchers terminated the experiment after six days—more than one week early.

Remember that this study was conducted in 1973—thirty-one years *before* Abu Ghraib. Yet, this simulated prison study predicted quite precisely how both "guards" and "prisoners" would act in a prison situation. Group influence effects uncovered by the Asch as well as the Milgram studies ruled in both the simulated prison of 1973 as well as the only too real Iraq prison of 2004.

## Debunking Society's Myths

**Myth:** People in groups are just individuals who make up their own minds about how to think and behave.

**Sociological perspective:** The Asch, Milgram, and simulated prison experiments conclusively show that people are profoundly influenced by group pressure, often causing them to make up their minds contrary to objective fact and even to deliberately cause harm to another person.

## Groupthink

Wealth, power, and experience are apparently not enough to save us from social influences. **Groupthink,** as described by I. L. Janis, is the tendency for group members to reach a consensus opinion, even if that decision is downright stupid (Janis 1982).

Janis reasoned that because major government policies are often the result of group decisions, it would be fruitful to analyze group dynamics that operate at the highest level of government—for instance, in the Office of the President of the United States. The president makes decisions based upon group discussions with his advisers. The president is human and thus susceptible to group influence. To what extent have past presidents and their advisers been influenced by group decision making instead of just the facts?

Janis investigated five ill-fated decisions, all the products of group deliberation:

- The decision of the Naval High Command in 1941 not to prepare for the attack on Pearl Harbor by Japan, which occurred anyway.
- President Harry Truman's decision to send U.S. troops to North Korea in 1950.
- President John F. Kennedy's attempt to overthrow Cuba by launching the ill-fated invasion at the Bay of Pigs in 1961.
- President Lyndon B. Johnson's decision in 1967 to increase the number of U.S. troops in Vietnam.
- The fateful decision by President Richard M. Nixon's advisers in 1972 to break into the Democratic Party headquarters at the Watergate apartment complex, launching the famed Watergate affair.

All the preceding were group decisions, and all were absolute fiascoes. For example, the Bay of Pigs invasion was a major humiliation for the United States—a covert outing so ill conceived it is hard to imagine how it survived discussion by a group of foreign policy experts. Fifteen hundred Cuban exiles trained by the CIA to parachute into heavily armed Cuba landed in an impassibly dense 80-mile swamp far from their planned drop zone, with inadequate weapons and incorrect maps. A sea landing was demolished by well-prepared, warned defenders.

Janis discovered a common pattern of misguided thinking in his investigations of presidential decisions. He surmised that outbreaks of groupthink had several things in common:

1. *An illusion of invulnerability.* "With such a brilliant team, and such a nation, how could any plan fail?" thought those in the group.

2. *A falsely negative impression of those who are antagonists to the group's plans.* Fidel Castro was perceived to be clownish, and Cuban troops were supposed to be patsies. In truth, the defenders at the Bay of Pigs were actually highly trained commandoes. Castro remained in power for many decades after the failed invasion.

3. *Discouragement of dissenting opinion.* As groupthink takes hold, dissent is equated with disloyalty. This can discourage dissenters from voicing their objections.

4. *An illusion of unanimity.* In the aftermath, many victims of groupthink recall their reservations, but at the moment of decision there is a prevailing sense that the entire group is in complete agreement.

We now might ask if groupthink influenced the torture of Iraq prisoners at the Abu Ghraib prison. (For that matter, we might ask if groupthink influenced the Bush administration's decision to enter the war in Iraq in the first place.) The actions of the military guards there were, it seems at least in part, directly or indirectly the result of high-level group decisions among presidential advisers. Groupthink is not inevitable when a team gathers to make a decision, but it is common and appears in all sorts of groups, from student discussion groups to the highest councils of power (Flowers 1977; McCauley 1989; Aldag and Fuller 1993; Kelley et al. 1999; Paulus et al. 2001).

## Debunking Society's Myths

**Myth:** A group of experts brought together in a small group will solve a problem according to their collective expertise.

**Sociological perspective:** Groupthink can lead even the most qualified people to make disastrous decisions because people in groups in the United States tend to seek consensus at all costs.

## Risky Shift

The term *groupthink* is commonly associated with group decision making with consequences that are not merely unexpected but disastrous. Another group phenomenon, **risky shift** (also called *polarization shift*), may help explain why the products of groupthink are frequently calamities. Have you ever found yourself in a group engaged in a high-risk activity that you would not do alone? When you created mischief as a child, were you not usually part of a group? If so, you were probably in the thrall of risky shift—the general tendency for groups to be more risky than individuals taken singly.

Risky shift was first observed by James Stoner (1961). Stoner gave study participants descriptions of a situation involving risk, such as one in which persons seeking a job must choose between job security and a potentially lucrative but risky advancement. The participants were then asked to decide how much risk the person should take. Before performing his study, Stoner believed that individuals in a group would take less risk than individuals alone, but he found the opposite: After his groups had engaged in open discussions, they favored greater risk than they would have before discussion.

Think of a time when you engaged in some risky behavior. What group were you part of, and how did the group influence your behavior? How does this illustrate the concept of *risky shift*? Is there more risky shift with more people in the group? If so, this would illustrate a *group size effect*.

Stoner's research has stimulated literally hundreds of studies using males and females, different nationalities, different tasks, and other variables (Pruitt 1971; Blaskovitch 1973; Johnson et al. 1977; Hong 1978; Worchel et al. 2000; Taylor et al. 2009). The results are complex. Most, but not all, group discussion leads to greater risk-taking. In subcultures that value caution above daring, as in some work groups of Japanese and Chinese firms, group decisions are less risky after discussion than before. The shift can occur in either direction, driven by the influence of group discussion, but there is generally some kind of shift, in one direction or the other, rather than no shift at all (Kerr 1992).

What causes risky shifts? The most convincing explanation is that deindividuation occurs. **Deindividuation** is the sense that one's self has merged with a group. In terms of risk-taking, one feels that responsibility (and possibly blame) is borne not only by oneself but also by the group. This seems to have happened among the American prison guards who tortured prisoners at Abu Ghraib prison: Each

*Streaking, or running nude in a public place—relatively popular among college students in the 1970s and early 1980s and still popular on some campuses—is more common as a group activity than as a strictly individual one. This illustrates how the group can provide the persons in it with deindividuation, or merging of self with group. This allows the individual to feel less responsibility or blame for his or her actions, thus convincing herself or himself that the group must share the blame.*

guard could convince himself or herself that responsibility, hence blame, was to be borne by the group as a whole. The greater the number of people in a group, the greater the tendency toward deindividuation. In other words, deindividuation is a *group size effect.* As groups get larger, trends in risk-taking are amplified.

# Formal Organizations and Bureaucracies

Groups, as we have seen, are capable of greatly influencing individuals. The study of groups and their effects on the individual represent an example of *microanalysis,* to use a concept introduced in Chapter 5. In contrast, the study of formal organizations and bureaucracies, a subject to which we now turn, represents an example of *macroanalysis.* The focus on groups drew our attention to the relatively small and less complex, whereas the focus on organizations draws our attention to the relatively large and structurally more complex.

A **formal organization** is a large secondary group, highly organized to accomplish a complex task or tasks and to achieve goals efficiently. Many of us belong to various formal organizations: work organizations, schools, and political parties, to name a few. Organizations are formed to accomplish particular tasks and are characterized by their relatively large size, compared with a small group such as a family or a friendship circle. Often organizations consist of an array of other organizations. The federal government is a huge organization comprising numerous other organizations, most of which are also vast. Each organization within the federal government is also designed to accomplish specific tasks, be it collecting your taxes, educating the nation's children, or regulating the nation's transportation system and national parks.

Organizations develop cultures and routine practices. The culture of an organization may be reflected in certain symbols, values, and rituals. Some organizations develop their own language and styles of dress. The norms can be subtle, such as men being expected to wear long-sleeve shirts and ties or women being expected to wear stockings, even on hot summer days. It does not take explicit rules to regulate this behavior; comments from coworkers or bosses may be enough to enforce such organizational norms. Some work organizations have instituted a practice called "casual day" or "dress down day" one day per week, usually Friday, when workers can dress less formally.

Organizations tend to be persistent, although they are also responsive to the broader social environment where they are located (DiMaggio and Powell 1991). Organizations are frequently under pressure to respond to changes in the society by incorporating new practices and beliefs into their structure. Business corporations, as an example, have had to respond to increasing global competition; they do so by expanding into new international markets, developing a globally focused workforce, and trimming costs by *downsizing,* that is, by eliminating workers and various layers of management. Another recent response to increased global competition is *outsourcing*—having manufacturing tasks ordinarily performed by the home company (such as the manufacture of athletic shoes or soccer balls) performed instead by foreign workers.

Organizations can be tools for innovation, depending on the organization's values and purpose. Rape crisis centers are examples of organizations that originally emerged from the women's movement because of the perceived need for services for rape victims. Rape crisis centers have, in many cases, changed how police departments and hospital emergency personnel respond to rape victims. By advocating changes in rape law and services for rape victims, rape crisis centers have generated change in other organizations as well (Schmitt and Martin 1999; Fried 1994).

## Types of Organizations

Sociologists Blau and Scott (1974) and Etzioni (1975) classify formal organizations into three categories distinguished by their types of membership affiliation: normative, coercive, and utilitarian.

**Normative Organizations.** People join **normative organizations** to pursue goals that they consider worthwhile. They obtain personal satisfaction, but no monetary reward for membership in such an organization. In many instances, people join the normative organization for the social prestige that it offers. Many are service and charitable organizations and are often called *voluntary organizations.* They include organizations such as the PTA, Kiwanis clubs, political parties, religious organizations, the National Association for the Advancement of Colored People (NAACP), B'nai B'rith, La Raza, and other similar voluntary organizations that are concerned with specific issues. Civic and charitable organizations, such as the League of Women Voters, and political organizations, such as the National Women's Political Caucus, reflect the fact that for decades women have been excluded from traditionally all-male voluntary organizations and political networks, such as the Kiwanis and Lions clubs—organizations that are now less influential than they were two or three decades ago. Like other service and charitable organizations, these groups have been created to meet particular needs, ones that members see as not being served by other organizations.

Gender, class, race, and ethnicity all play a role in who joins what voluntary organization. Social class is reflected in the fact that many people do not join certain organizations simply because they cannot afford to join. Membership in a professional organization, as one example, can cost hundreds of dollars each year. Those who feel disenfranchised, however, may join grassroots organizations—voluntary organizations that spring from specific local needs that people think are unmet. Tenants may form an organization to protest rent increases or lack of services, or a new political party may emerge from people's sense of alienation from existing party organizations. African Americans, Latinos, and Native Americans have formed many of their own voluntary organizations in part because of their historical exclusion from traditional White voluntary organizations—which are now vibrant, ongoing organizations in their own right (such as the African American organizations Delta Sigma Theta and Alpha Kappa Alpha sororities and the fraternities Alpha Phi Alpha, Kappa Alpha Psi, and Omega Psi Phi; see Giddings 1994).

The NAACP, founded in 1909 by W.E.B. Du Bois (recall from Chapter 1), and the National Urban League are two other large national organizations that have historically fought racial oppression on the legal and urban fronts, respectively. La Raza Unida, a Latino organization devoted to civic activities as well as combating racial–ethnic oppression, has a large membership, with Latinas holding major offices. In fact, such voluntary organizations dedicated to the causes of people of color have in recent years had more women in leadership positions than have many standard, White organizations. Similarly, Native American voluntary organizations have boasted increasing numbers of women in leadership positions (Feagin and Feagin 1993; Snipp 1996, 1989).

**Coercive Organizations.** **Coercive organizations** are characterized by membership that is largely involuntary. Prisons are an example of organizations that people are coerced to "join" by virtue of punishment for their crime. Similarly, mental hospitals are coercive organizations: People are placed in them, often involuntarily, for some form of psychiatric treatment. In many respects, prisons and mental hospitals are similar in their treatment of inmates or patients. They both have strong security measures such as guards, locked and barred windows, and high walls (Goffman 1961; Rosenhan 1973). Sexual harassment and sexual victimization are common in both prisons and mental hospitals (Andersen 2003; Chesney-Lind 1992).

The sociologist Erving Goffman has described coercive organizations as total institutions. A **total institution** is an organization that is cut off from the rest of society and one in which resident individuals are subject to strict social control (Goffman 1961). Total institutions include two populations: the "inmates" and the staff. Within total institutions, the staff exercises complete power over inmates, for example, nurses over mental patients and guards over prisoners. The staff administers all the affairs of everyday life, including basic human functions such as eating and sleeping. Rigid routines are characteristic of total institutions, thus explaining the common complaint by those in hospitals that they cannot sleep because nurses repeatedly enter their rooms at night, regardless of whether the patient needs medication or treatment. However, the problem of such rigid routines has eased somewhat in some institutions.

**Utilitarian Organizations.** The third type of organization named is **utilitarian.** These are large organizations, either for-profit or nonprofit, that individuals join for specific purposes, such as monetary reward. Large business organizations that generate profits (in the case of for-profit organizations) and salaries and wages for the organization's employees (as with either for-profit or nonprofit organizations) are utilitarian organizations. Examples of large, for-profit organizations include Microsoft, Amazon.com, and Procter & Gamble. Examples of large nonprofit organizations that pay salaries to employees are colleges and, universities, churches, and organizations such as the National Collegiate Athletic Association (NCAA).

## Bureaucracy

As formal organizations develop, many become a **bureaucracy,** a type of formal organization characterized by an authority hierarchy, a clear division of labor, explicit rules, and impersonality. Bureaucracies are notorious for their unwieldy size and complexity as well as their reputation for being remote and cumbersome organizations that are highly impersonal and machinelike in their operation. The federal government is a good example of a cumbersome bureaucracy that many believe is ineffective because of its sheer size. Numerous other formal organizations have developed into huge bureaucracies: IBM, Disney, many universities, hospitals, state motor vehicle registration systems, and some law firms. Other formal organizations, such as Enron and WorldCom, quickly developed into large bureaucracies, then subsequently collapsed under fraudulent accounting procedures. More recently, large national banks such as Merrill Lynch, now in bankruptcy, and several others have fallen under close scrutiny by Congress for questionable practices such as exorbitant salaries and excess bonuses for top management. Automakers such as General Motors, now in bankruptcy, have been criticized on similar grounds.

The early sociological theorist **Max Weber** (1947/1925) analyzed the classic characteristics of the bureaucracy. These characteristics represent what he called the *ideal type bureaucracy*—a model rarely seen in reality but that defines the principal characteristics of a social form. The characteristics of bureaucracies described as an ideal type are:

1. **High degree of division of labor and specialization.** The notion of the specialist embodies this criterion. Bureaucracies ideally employ specialists in the various positions and occupations, and these specialists are responsible for a specific set of duties. Sociologist Charles Perrow (2007, 1994, 1986) notes that many modern bureaucracies have hierarchical authority structures and an elaborate division of labor.

2. **Hierarchy of authority.** In bureaucracies, positions are arranged in a hierarchy so that each is under the supervision of a higher position. Such hierarchies are often represented in an *organization chart*, a diagram in the shape of a pyramid that shows the relative rank of each position plus the lines of authority between each. These lines of authority are often called the "chain of command," and they show not only who has authority, but also who is responsible to whom and how many positions are responsible to a given position.

3. **Rules and regulations.** All the activities in a bureaucracy are governed by a set of detailed rules and procedures. These rules are designed, ideally, to cover almost every possible situation and problem that might arise, including hiring, firing, salary scales, and rules for sick pay and absences.

4. **Impersonal relationships.** Social interaction in the (ideal) bureaucracy is supposed to be guided by *instrumental* criteria, such as the organization's rules, rather than by *expressive needs*, such as personal attractions or likes and dislikes. The ideal is that the objective application of rules will minimize matters such as personal favoritism—giving someone a promotion simply because you like him or her or firing someone because you do not like him or her. Of course, as we will see, sociologists have pointed out that bureaucracy has "another face"—the *informal* social interaction that keeps the bureaucracy working and often involves interpersonal friendships and social ties, typically among people taken for granted in these organizations, such as the support staff.

5. **Career ladders.** Candidates for the various positions in the bureaucracy are supposed to be selected on the basis of specific criteria, such as education, experience, and standardized examinations. The idea is that advancement through the organization becomes a career for the individual. Some organizations, such as some universities and some law firms, have a policy of **tenure**—a guarantee of continued employment until one's retirement from the organization.

6. **Efficiency.** Bureaucracies are designed to coordinate the activities of many people in pursuit of organizational goals. Ideally, all activities have been designed to maximize this efficiency. The whole system is intended to keep social–emotional relations and interactions at a minimum and instrumental interaction at a maximum.

## Bureaucracy's Other Face

All the characteristics of Weber's "ideal type" are general defining characteristics. Rarely do actual bureaucracies meet this exact description. A bureaucracy has, in addition to the ideal characteristics of structure, an *informal structure*. This includes social interactions, even network connections, in bureaucratic settings that ignore, change, or otherwise bypass the formal structure and rules of the organization. This informal structure often develops among those who are taken for granted in organizations, such as secretaries and administrative assistants—who are most often women. Sociologist Charles Page (1946) coined the phrase *bureaucracy's other face* to describe this condition.

This other face is informal culture. It has evolved over time as a reaction to the formality and impersonality of the bureaucracy. Thus, administrative assistants and secretaries will sometimes "bend the rules a bit" when asked to do something more quickly than usual for a boss they like and bend the rules in another direction for a boss they do not like by slowing down or otherwise sabotaging the boss's work. Researchers have noted, for example, that secretaries and assistants have more authority than their job titles and salaries suggest. As a way around the cumbersome formal communication channels within the organization, the informal network, or "grapevine," often works better, faster, and sometimes even more accurately than the formal channels. As with any culture, the informal culture in the bureaucracy has its own norms or rules. One is not supposed to "stab friends in the back," such as by "ratting on" them to a boss or spreading a rumor about them that is intended to get them fired. Yet, just as with any norms, there is deviation from the norms, and "back-stabbing" and "ratting" does happen.

Bureaucracy's other face can also be seen in the workplace subcultures that develop, even in the largest bureaucracies. Some sociologists interpret the subcultures that develop within bureaucracies as people's attempts to humanize an otherwise impersonal organization. Keeping photographs of family and loved ones in the office, placing personal decorations on one's desk (if you are allowed), and organizing office parties are some ways people resist the impersonal culture of bureaucracies. Of course, this informal culture can also become exclusionary, increasing the isolation that some workers feel at work. Gay and lesbian workers may feel left out when other workers gossip about people's heterosexual dates; minority workers may be excluded from the casual conversations in the workplace that connect nonminority people to one another.

The informal norms that develop within the modern day bureaucracy often cause worker productivity to go up or down, depending on the norms and how they are informally enforced. The classic 1930s Hawthorne Studies, so named because they were carried out at the Western Electric telephone plant in Hawthorne, Illinois (Roethlisberger and Dickson 1939), discovered that small groups of workers developed their own ideas—their own norms—about how much work they should produce each day. If someone produced too many completed tasks in a day, he would make the rest of the workers "look bad" and run the risk of having the organization raise its expectations of how much work the group might be expected to produce. Because of this, anyone producing too much was informally labeled a "rate buster," and that person was punished by some act, such as punches on the shoulder (called "binging") or by group ridicule (called "razzing"). By the same token, one could be accused of producing too little, in which case he was labeled a "chiseler" and punished in the same way by either binging or razzing. This informal culture of bureaucracy's other face continues today in a manner similar to the culture initially discovered in the early Hawthorne studies (Ritzer 2007; Perrow 2007, 1986).

## Problems of Bureaucracies

In contemporary times, problems have developed that grow out of the nature of the complex bureaucracy. Two problem areas already discussed are the occurrence of risky shift in work groups and the development of groupthink. Additional problems include a tendency to *ritualism* and the potential for *alienation* on the part of those within the organization.

**Ritualism.** Rigid adherence to rules can produce a slavish following of them, regardless of whether it accomplishes the purpose for which the rule was originally designed. The rules become ends in themselves rather than means to an end: This is ritualism.

Two now classic examples of the consequences of *organizational ritualism* have come to haunt us: the explosion of the space shuttle *Challenger* on January 28, 1986, and, to our horror, the breakup of yet another space shuttle, the *Columbia,* on February 1, 2003. People in the United States became bound together at the moment of the *Challenger* accident. Many remember where they were and exactly what they were doing when they heard about the tragedy. The failure of the essential O-ring gaskets on the solid fuel booster rockets of the *Challenger* shuttle caused the catastrophic explosion. It was revealed later that the O-rings became brittle at below-freezing temperatures, as was the temperature at the launch pad the evening before the *Challenger* lifted off.

Why did the managers and engineers at NASA (National Aeronautics and Space Administration) allow the shuttle to lift off given these prior conditions? The managers had all the information about the O-rings before the launch. Furthermore, engineers had warned them against the danger. In a detailed analysis of the decision to launch, sociologist Diane Vaughan (1996) uncovered both risky shift and organizational ritualism within the organization. The NASA insiders, confronted with signals of danger, proceeded as if nothing was wrong when they were repeatedly faced with the evidence that something was

The horror of the explosion of the space shuttle Challenger in 1986 is seen in the faces of the observers here. All seven astronauts died in the explosion (top right). Sociologist Diane Vaughan (1996) attributes the disaster to an ill-formed launch decision in the bureaucracy of NASA based on group interaction phenomena such as risky shift, ritualism, groupthink, and the normalization of deviance. Tragedy struck again in February 2003, when the space shuttle Columbia broke up upon reentry into the atmosphere, killing all seven of the astronauts on board (bottom right).

indeed *very* wrong. They in effect *normalized* their own behavior so that their actions became acceptable to them, representing nothing out of the ordinary. This is an example of organizational ritualism, as well as what Vaughan calls the "normalization of deviance."

Unfortunately, history repeated itself on February 1, 2003, when the space shuttle *Columbia,* upon its return from space, broke up in a fiery descent into the atmosphere above Texas, killing all who were aboard. The evidence shows that a piece of hard insulating foam separated from an external fuel tank during launch and struck the shuttle's left wing, damaging it and dislodging its heat-resistant tiles that are necessary for reentry. The absence of these tiles caused a burn-up upon reentry into the atmosphere. With eerie similarity to the earlier 1986 *Challenger* accident, a recent research report concludes that a "flawed institutional culture" and—citing sociologist Diane Vaughan—a normalization of deviance accompanying a gradual erosion of safety margins were among the causes of the *Columbia* accident (Schwartz and Wald 2003).

No single individual was at fault in either accident. The story is not one of evil but rather of the ritualism of organizational life in one of the most powerful bureaucracies in the United States. It is a story of rigid group conformity within an organizational setting and of how deviant behavior is redefined, that is, socially constructed, to be perceived as normal. Organizational procedures in this case, or rituals, dominate so much that the means toward goals become the goals themselves. A critical decrease in overall safety and a dramatic increase in risk are the results. Vaughan's analysis is a powerful warning about the hidden hazards of bureaucracy in a technological age.

**Alienation.** The stresses on rules and procedures within bureaucracies can result in a decrease in the overall cohesion of the organization. This often psychologically separates a person from the organization and its goals. This state of *alienation* results in increased turnover, tardiness, absenteeism, and overall dissatisfaction with the organization.

Alienation can be widespread in organizations where workers have little control over what they do or where workers themselves are treated like machines employed on an assembly line, doing the same repetitive action for an entire work shift. Alienation is not restricted to manual labor, however. In organizations where workers are isolated from others, where they are expected only to implement rules, or where they think they have little chance of advancement, alienation can be common. As we will see, some organizations have developed new patterns of work to try to minimize worker alienation and thus enhance their productivity.

## The McDonaldization of Society

Sometimes the problems and peculiarities of bureaucracy can have effects on the total society. This has been the case with what George Ritzer (2007) has called the **McDonaldization,** a term coined from the well-known fast-food chain. In fact, each month 90 percent of the children in the United States between ages 3 and 9 visit McDonald's! Ritzer noticed that the principles that characterize fast-food organizations are increasingly dominating more aspects of U.S. society, indeed, of societies around the world. McDonaldization refers to the increasing and ubiquitous presence of the fast-food *model* in most organizations that shape daily life. Work, travel, leisure, shopping, health care, politics, and even education, have all become subject to McDonaldization. Each industry is based on a principle of high and efficient productivity, which translates into a highly rational social organization, with workers employed at low pay but with customers experiencing ease, convenience, and familiarity.

Ritzer argues that McDonald's has been such a successful model of business organization that other industries have adopted the same organizational characteristics, so much so that their nicknames associate them with the McDonald's chain: McPaper for *USA Today,* McChild for child-care chains like KinderCare,

and McDoctor for the drive-in clinics that deal quickly and efficiently with minor health and dental problems. Finally, the efficiency and predictability characteristic of the various Starbuck coffee shops represent what Ritzer calls "Starbuckization"—a type of McDonaldization.

Based in part upon Max Weber's concept of the ideal bureaucracy mentioned earlier, Ritzer identifies four dimensions of the McDonaldization process: efficiency, calculability, predictability, and control:

1. **Efficiency** means that things move from start to finish in a streamlined path. Steps in the production of a hamburger are regulated so that each hamburger is made exactly the same way—hardly characteristic of a home-cooked meal. Business can be even more efficient if the customer does the work once done by an employee. In fast-food restaurants, the claim that you can "have it your way" really means that you assemble your own sandwich or salad.

2. **Calculability** means there is an emphasis on the quantitative aspects of products sold: size, cost, and the time it takes to get the product. At McDonald's, branch managers must account for the number of cubic inches of ketchup used per day; likewise, ice cream scoopers in chain stores measure out predetermined and exact amounts of ice cream. Workers are monitored for how long it takes them to complete a transaction; every bit of food and drink is closely monitored by computer, and everything has to be accounted for.

3. **Predictability** is the assurance that products will be exactly the same, no matter when or where they are purchased. Eat an Egg McMuffin in New York, and it will likely taste just the same as an Egg McMuffin in Los Angeles or Paris! Ditto for a Decaf Tall Cappuccino from Starbucks: It will taste the same in whatever town or city you are drinking it.

4. **Control** is the primary organizational principle that lies behind McDonaldization. Behavior of the customers and workers is reduced to a series of machinelike actions. Ultimately, efficient technologies replace much of the work that humans once performed.

McDonaldization—and Starbuckization—clearly brings many benefits. There is a greater availability of goods and services to a wide proportion of the population; instantaneous service and convenience to a public with less free time; predictability and familiarity in the goods bought and sold; and standardization of pricing and uniform quality of goods sold, to name a few benefits. However, this increasingly rational system of goods and services also spawns irrationalities. For example, the majority of workers at McDonald's lack full-time employment, have no worker benefits, have no control over their workplace, and quit on average after only four or five months. Ritzer argues

*Evidence of the "McDonaldization of society" can be seen everywhere, perhaps including on your own campus. Shopping malls, food courts, sports stadiums, even cruise ships reflect this trend toward standardization.*

Tony Dejak/AP Photo

that, as we become more dependent on the familiar and that which is taken for granted, there is the danger of dehumanization. People lose their creativity, and there is little concern with the quality of goods and services, thereby disrupting something fundamentally human—the capacity for error, surprise, and imagination.

# Diversity: Race, Gender, and Class in Organizations

The hierarchical structuring of positions within organizations results in the concentration of power and influence with a few individuals at the top. Since organizations tend to reflect patterns within the broader society, this hierarchy, like that of society, is marked by inequality in race, gender, and class relations. Although the concentration of power in organizations is incompatible with the principles of a democratic society, discrimination against women and minorities still occurs (Perrow 2007, 1994). There have been widespread disparities in the promotion rates for White and Black workers, with Whites more likely to be promoted and promoted more quickly—a pattern repeated in many work organizations (Perrow 2002; Eichenwald 1996; McGuire and Reskin 1993; Collins 1989).

Traditionally, within organizations the most powerful positions are held by White men of upper social class status. Women and minorities, on average, occupy lower positions in the organization. Although very small numbers of minorities and women do get promoted, there is typically a "glass ceiling" effect, meaning that women and minorities may be promoted but only up to a point. The glass ceiling acts as a barrier to the promotion of women and minorities into higher ranks of management, as discussed further in Chapters 10 and 11. Over the last five years, promotions of minorities and women in the organization have become slightly more common, but the overall picture is still one of discrimination and a glass ceiling.

What then are the barriers that prevent more inclusiveness in the higher ranks of organizations? Sociological research finds that organizations are sensitive to the climate in which they operate. The more egalitarian the environment in which a firm operates, the more equitable is its treatment of women and minorities.

Yet studies find that patterns of race and gender discrimination persist throughout organizations even to this day, even when formal barriers to advancement have been removed. Many minorities are now equal to Whites in education, particularly in organizational jobs that require advanced graduate degrees such as the master of business administration (MBA). Still, White men in organizations are somewhat more likely to receive promotions than African American, Hispanic, and Native American workers *with the same education* (Smith 2007: DeWitt 1995; Zwerling and Silver 1992). The same thing often happens to both White and minority women in organizations: Women are less likely to receive promotions than a White male with the same education, and sometimes even less education. Studies consistently find that women are held to higher promotion standards than men; for men, the longer they are in a position in an organization, the more likely they will be promoted, but the same is not true for women. Studies find that women change jobs more frequently within organizations than do men, but these tend to be lateral moves. For men, job changes are more likely to mark a jump from

*Few organizational boards and executive committees contain minorities and women: when present, they are often tokens.*

a lower level to a higher level in the organization, thus constituting a promotion.

Things work the same way with respect to people being discharged or fired. Studies show quite clearly that Black federal employees (men and women) were more than *twice as likely* to be dismissed as their White counterparts (DeWitt 1995; Zwerling and Silver 1992). This disparity occurred regardless of education and regardless of occupational category, pay level, type of federal agency, age, performance rating, seniority, or attendance record. The main reasons cited in the studies for such disparities were lack of network contacts with the old boy network and racial bias within the organization (Smith 2007). These studies were particularly well designed because they took into account quite a few factors besides race–ethnicity that are often given as reasons for not promoting minorities. The studies showed quite conclusively that with all factors taken into account, it is still race that is an important reason for the way people are treated in organizations today. Even though there has been some improvement in recent years, these studies strongly suggest that racism still thrives in the bureaucracy. Will things change as the result of having a Black man in the highest office of the United States? Some would say yes, because President Obama is an inspiring role model, but sociological processes occur beyond the influence of any one individual, so change requires more than the influence of one person. What do you think?

## Debunking Society's Myths

**Myth:** Programs designed to enhance the number of women and minorities in organizational leadership are no longer needed because discriminatory barriers have been removed.

**Sociological perspective:** Research right up to the present continues to find significant differences in the promotion rates for women and minorities in most organizational settings. Even with the removal of formal discriminatory barriers, organizational practices persist that block the mobility of these workers.

A classic study by Rosabeth Moss Kanter (1977) shows how the structure of organizations leads to obstacles in the advancement of groups that are tokens—rarely represented—in the organizational environment. Kanter demonstrated how the hierarchical structure of the bureaucracy negatively affects both minorities and women who are underrepresented in the organization. In such cases, they represent *token* minorities or women; they feel put "out front" and under the all-too-watchful eyes of their superiors as well as coequals. As a result—as research since Kanter's has shown—they often suffer severe stress

(Smith 2007; Jackson 2000; Jackson et al. 1995, 1994; Yoder 1991; Spangler et al. 1978). Coworkers often accuse women and minorities of getting a position simply because they are women, minorities, or both. It is a fairly widespread phenomenon in universities and colleges that not only minorities, but women as well, are often accused of being admitted simply because of their gender and/or their race, *even in instances where the person has had superior admissions qualifications*. This is stressful for the person and shows that tokenism can have very negative consequences.

Social class, in addition to race and gender, plays a part in determining people's place within formal organizations. Middle- and upper-class employees in organizations make higher salaries and wages and are more likely to get promoted than are people of lower social class status, even for individuals who are of the same race or ethnicity. This even holds for people coming from families of lower social class status who are as well educated as their middle- and upper-class coworkers. Thus, their lower salaries and lack of promotion cannot necessarily be attributed to a lack of education. In this respect, their treatment in the bureaucracy only perpetuates rather than lessens the negative effects of the social class system in the United States.

The social class stratification system in the United States produces major differences in the opportunities and life chances of individuals, and the bureaucracy simply carries these differences forward. Class stereotypes also influence hiring practices in organizations. Personnel officers look for people with "certain demeanors," a code phrase for those who convey middle-class or upper-middle-class standards of dress, language, manners, and so on, which some people may be unable to afford or may not possess.

Patterns of race, class, and gender inequality in organizations persist at the same time that many organizations have become more aware of the need for a more diverse workforce. Responding to the simple fact of more diversity within the working-age population, organizations have developed human relations experts who work within organizations to enhance sensitivity to diversity. Such diversity training has become commonplace in many large organizations.

# Functional, Conflict, and Symbolic Interaction: Theoretical Perspectives

All three major sociological perspectives—functional, conflict, and symbolic interaction—are exhibited in the analysis of formal organizations and bureaucracies (see Table 6.1). The functional perspective, based in this case on the early writing of Max Weber, argues

| table6.1 | Theoretical Perspective on Organizations | | |
|---|---|---|---|
| | **Functionalist Theory** | **Conflict Theory** | **Symbolic Interaction Theory** |
| *Central Focus* | Positive functions (such as efficiency) contribute to unity and stability of the organization. | Hierarchical nature of bureaucracy encourages conflict between superior and subordinate, men and women, and people of different racial or class backgrounds. | Stresses the role of self in the bureaucracy and how the self develops and changes. |
| *Relationship of Individual to the Organization* | Individuals, like parts of a machine, are only partly relevant to the operation of the organization. | Individuals subordinated to systems of power and experience stress and alienation as a result. | Interaction between superiors and subordinates forms the structure of the organization. |
| *Criticism* | Hierarchy can result in dysfunctions such as ritualism and alienation. | De-emphasizes the positive ways that organizations work. | Tends to downplay overall social organization. |

that certain functions, called *eufunctions* (that is, positive functions), characterize bureaucracies and contribute to their overall unity. The bureaucracy exists to accomplish these eufunctions, such as efficiency, control, impersonal relations, and a chance for the individual to develop a career within the organization. As we have seen, however, bureaucracies develop the "other face" (informal interaction and culture, as opposed to formal or bureaucratic interaction and culture) as well as the problems of ritualism and alienation of the person from the organization. These latter problems are called *dysfunctions* (negative functions), which have the consequence of contributing to the disunity, lack of harmony, and less efficiency in the bureaucracy.

The conflict perspective argues that the hierarchical or stratified nature of the bureaucracy in effect encourages rather than inhibits conflict among the individuals within it. These conflicts are between superior and subordinate, as well as between racial and ethnic groups, men and women, and people of different social class backgrounds, hampering the smooth and efficient running of the bureaucracy.

Consider the symbolic interaction perspective as underlying two management theories, those of Argyris (1990) and of Ouchi (1981). Symbolic interaction stresses the role of the self in any group and especially how the self develops as a product of social interaction. Argyris's theory advocates increased involvement of the self within the organization as a way of "actualizing" the self. This helps reduce the disconnection between individual and organization as well as other organizational problems and dysfunctions. Ouchi's theory argues that increased interaction between superior and subordinate, based on the Japanese organization model of executives "walking around" and interacting more on a primary group basis, will reduce organizational dysfunction.

# Chapter Summary

- ## *What are the types of groups?*
  Groups are a fact of human existence and permeate virtually every facet of our lives. Group size is important, as is the otherwise simple distinction between dyads and triads. *Primary groups* form the basic building blocks of social interaction in society. *Reference groups* play a major role in forming our attitudes and life goals, as do our relationships with in-groups and out-groups. *Social networks* partly determine things such as who we know and the kinds of jobs we get. Networks based on race–ethnicity, social class, and

other social factors are extremely closely connected—very dense.

- *How strong is social influence?*

  The social influence groups exert on us is tremendous, as seen by the Asch conformity experiments. The Milgram experiments demonstrated that the interpersonal influence of an authority figure can cause an individual to act against his or her deep convictions. The torture and abuse of Iraqi prisoners of war by American soldiers as prison guards serves as testimony to the powerful effects of both social influence and authority structures.

- *What is the importance of groupthink and risky shift?*

  *Groupthink* can be so pervasive that it adversely affects group decision making. *Risky shift* similarly often compels individuals to reach decisions that are at odds with their better judgment.

- *What are the types of formal organizations and bureaucracies, and what are some of their problems?*

  There are several types of *formal organizations,* such as *normative, coercive,* or *utilitarian.* Weber typified *bureaucracies* as organizations with an efficient division of labor, an authority hierarchy, rules, impersonal relationships, and career ladders. Bureaucratic rigidities often result in organizational problems such as ritualism and resulting "normalization of deviance," which may have been significantly responsible for the space shuttle *Challenger* explosion in 1986 and the space shuttle *Columbia* breakup in 2003. The **McDonaldization** of society has resulted in greater efficiency, calculability, and control in many industries, probably at the expense of some individual creativity.

- *What are the problems of diversity in organizations?*

  Formal organizations perpetuate society's inequalities on the basis of race–ethnicity, gender, and social class. Even today, Blacks, Hispanics, and Native Americans are less likely to get promoted, and more likely to get fired, than Whites of comparable education and other qualifications. Women experience similar effects of inequality, especially negative effects of tokenism, such as stress and lowered self-esteem. Finally, persons of less than middle-class origins make less money and are less likely to get promoted than a middle-class person of comparable education.

- *What do the functional, conflict, and symbolic interaction theories say about organizations?*

  Functional, conflict, and symbolic interaction theories highlight and clarify the analysis of organizations by specifying both organizational functions and dysfunctions (*functional theory*); by analyzing the consequences of hierarchical, gender, race, and social class conflict in organizations (*conflict theory*); and, finally, by studying the importance of social interaction and integration of the self into the organization (*symbolic interaction theory*).

# Key Terms

# Online Resources

## *Sociology: The Essentials* Companion Website

**www.cengage.com/sociology/andersen**

Visit your book companion website where you will find more resources to help you study and write your research papers. Resources include web links, learning objectives, Internet exercises, quizzing, and flash cards.

 **is an easy-to-use online resource that helps you study in less time to get the grade you want NOW.**

**www.cengage.com/login**

Need help studying? This site is your one-stop study shop. Take a Pre-Test and Cengage NOW will generate a Personalized Study Plan based on your test results. The Study Plan will identify the topics you need to review and direct you to online resources to help you master those topics. You can then take a Post-Test to determine the concepts you have mastered and what you still need to work on.

Chapter seven
CHAPTER SEVEN
Chapter

# Deviance and Crime

[ *In the early* 1970s, an airplane carrying forty members of an amateur rugby team crashed in the Andes Mountains in South America. The twenty-seven survivors were marooned at 12,000 feet in freezing weather and deep snow. There was no food except for a small amount of chocolate and some wine. A few days after the crash, the group heard on a small transistor radio that the search for them had been called off.

Scattered in the snow were the frozen bodies of dead passengers. Preserved by the freezing weather, these bodies became, after a time, sources of food. At first, the survivors were repulsed by the idea of eating human flesh, but as the days wore on, they agonized over the decision about whether to eat the dead crash victims, eventually concluding that they had to eat if they were to live.

In the beginning, only a few ate the human meat, but soon the others began to eat too. The group experimented with preparations as they tried different parts of the body. They developed elaborate rules about how, what, and whom they would eat. Some could not bring themselves to cut the meat from the human body, but would slice it once someone else had cut off large chunks. They all refused to eat certain parts—the lungs, skin, head, and genitals.

After two months, the group sent out an expedition of three survivors to find help. The group was rescued, and the world learned of their ordeal. Their cannibalism (the eating of other human beings) was generally accepted as something they had to do to survive. Although people might have been repulsed by the story, the survivors' behavior was understood as a necessary

*continued*

Nic Cleave Photography/Alamy

adaptation to their life-threatening circumstances. The survivors also maintained a sense of themselves as good people even though what they did profoundly violated ordinary standards of socially acceptable behavior in most cultures in the world (Read 1974; Miller 1991; Henslin 1993).

Was the behavior of the Andes crash survivors socially deviant? Were the people made crazy by their experience, or was this a normal response to extreme circumstances?

Compare the Andes crash to another case of human cannibalism. In 1991, in Milwaukee, Wisconsin, Jeffrey Dahmer pled guilty to charges of murdering at least fifteen men in his home. Dahmer lured the men—eight of them African American, two White, and one a fourteen-year-old Laotian (Asian) boy—to his apartment, where he murdered and dismembered them, then cooked and ate some of their body parts. For those he considered most handsome, he boiled the flesh from their heads so that he could save and admire their skulls. Dahmer was seen as a total social deviant, someone who violated every principle of human decency. Even hardened criminals were disgusted by Dahmer. In fact, he was killed in prison by another inmate in 1994.

Why was Dahmer's behavior considered so deviant when that of the Andes survivors was not? The answer can be found by looking at the situation in which these behaviors occurred. For the Andes survivors, eating human flesh was essential for survival. For Dahmer, however, it was murder. From a sociological perspective, the deviance of cannibalism resides *not just in the act itself but also in the social context in which it occurs*. The exact same behavior—eating other human beings—is considered reprehensible in one context and acceptable in another. That is the essence of the sociological explanation: The nature of deviance is not only in the personality of the deviant person, nor is it inherently in the deviant act itself, but instead it is a significant part and product of the social structure.

# Defining Deviance

Sociologists define **deviance** as *behavior that is recognized as violating expected rules and norms*. Deviance is more than simple nonconformity; it is behavior that departs significantly from social expectations. In the sociological perspective on deviance, there are four main identifying characteristics:

- Deviance emerges in a social context, not just the behavior of individuals; sociologists see deviance in terms of group processes and judgments.

- Not all behaviors are judged similarly by all groups; what is deviant to one group may be normative (not deviant) to another.

- Established rules and norms are socially created, not just morally decided or individually imposed.

- Deviance lies not just in behavior itself but in the social responses of groups to behavior by others.

## Sociological Perspectives on Deviance

Strange, unconventional, or nonconformist behavior is often understandable in its sociological context. Consider suicide. Are people who commit suicide mentally disturbed, or might their behavior be explained by social factors? Are there conditions under which suicide is acceptable behavior—for example, someone who commits suicide in the face of a terminal illness compared to a despondent person who jumps from a window?

Sociologists distinguish two types of deviance: formal and informal. *Formal deviance* is behavior that breaks laws or official rules. Crime is an example. There are formal sanctions against formal deviance, such as imprisonment and fines. *Informal deviance* is behavior that violates customary norms (Schur 1984). Although such deviance may not be specified in law, it is judged to be deviant by those who uphold the society's norms.

The study of deviance can be divided into the study of why people violate laws or norms and the study of how society reacts. *Labeling theory* is discussed in detail later, but it recognizes that deviance is not just in the breaking of norms or rules but it includes how people react to those behaviors. Social groups actually *create* deviance "by making the rules whose infraction constitutes deviance, and by applying those rules to particular people and labeling them as outsiders" (Erikson 1966; Becker 1963 : 9).

**The Context of Deviance.** Even the most unconventional behavior can be understood if we know the context in which it occurs. Behavior that is deviant in one circumstance may be normal in another, or behavior may be ruled deviant only when performed by certain people. For example, people who break gender stereotypes may be judged as deviant even though their behavior is considered normal for the other sex. Heterosexual men and women who kiss in public are the image of romance; lesbians and gay men who even dare to hold hands in public are often seen as flaunting their sexual orientation.

The definition of deviance can also vary over time. Acquaintance rape (also called "date rape"), for example, was not considered social deviance until fairly recently. Women have been presumed to mean yes when they said no, and men were expected to "seduce" women through aggressive sexual behavior. Even now, women who are raped by someone they know may not think of it as rape.

If they do, they may find that prosecuting the offender is difficult because others do not think of it as rape, especially under certain circumstances, such as the woman being drunk. What is in fact rape may not be seen as such by everyone.

The sociologist Emile Durkheim argued that one reason acts of deviance are publicly punished is that the social order is threatened by deviance. Judging those behaviors as deviant and punishing them confirms general social standards. Therein lies the value of widely publicized trials, public executions, or the historical practice of displaying a wrongdoer in the stocks, which held one's feet fast, or the pillory, which held the hands and head. Passersby were permitted to hurl both stones and large rocks at those persons so immobilized. The punishment affirms the collective beliefs of the society, reinforces social order, and inhibits future deviant behavior, especially as defined by those with the power to judge others.

# Debunking Society's Myths

**Myth:** Deviance is bad for society because it disrupts normal life.

**Sociological perspective:** Deviance tends to stabilize society. By defining some forms of behavior as deviant, people are affirming the social norms of groups. In this sense, society actually to some extent *creates* deviance.

*This widely distributed photo of a woman being executed by the Taliban in Afghanistan illustrates the extreme sanctions that can be brought against those defined as deviant by a powerful group. In this case, the photo also mobilized world condemnation of the Taliban regime for its treatment of women.*

© RAWA/WorldPicture News

Durkheim argued that societies actually *need* deviance to know what presumably normal behavior is. In this sense, Durkheim considered deviance "functional" for society (Durkheim 1951/1897; Erikson 1966). You could observe Durkheim's point in the aftermath of the terrorist attacks of September 11, 2001. Horrified by the sight of hijacked planes flying into the World Trade Center and the Pentagon and crashing in a Pennsylvania field, U.S. citizens responded through publicly demonstrating strong patriotism. Durkheim would interpret these terrorist acts as deviance producing strong social solidarity. This was one of Durkheim's most important insights: *Deviance produces social solidarity. Instead of breaking society up, deviance produces a pulling together, or social solidarity.*

**The Influence of Social Movements.** The perception of deviance may also be influenced by social movements, which are networks of groups that organize to support or resist changes in society (see Chapter 16). With a change in the social climate, formerly acceptable behaviors may be newly defined as deviant. Smoking, for instance, was once considered glamorous, sexy, and "cool." Now, smokers are widely scorned as polluters and, despite strong lobbying by the tobacco industry, regulations against smoking have proliferated.

Whereas in 1987 only 17 percent of the public thought that smoking should be banned in restaurants, by 2008 over half (60 percent) thought so (Gallup Organization 2008). The increase in public disapproval of smoking results as much from social and political movements as it does from the known health risks. The success of the antismoking movement has come from the mobilization of constituencies able to articulate to the public that smoking is dangerous. Note that the key element here is the ability of people to mobilize—not just the evidence of risk. In other words, there has to be a social response for deviance to be defined as such; scientific evidence of harm in and of itself is not enough.

**The Social Construction of Deviance.** Perhaps because it violates social conventions or because it sometimes involves unusual behavior, deviance captures the public imagination. Commonly, however, the public understands deviance as the result of individualistic or personality factors. Many people see deviants as crazy, threatening, "sick," or in some other ways inferior, but sociologists see deviance as influenced by society—the same social processes and institutions that shape all social behavior.

Deviance, for example, is not necessarily irrational or "sick" and may be a positive and rational adaptation to a situation. Think of the Andes survivors discussed in this chapter's opener. Was their action (eating human flesh) irrational, or was it an inventive and rational response to a dreadful situation? To use another example, are gangs the result of the irrational

*Once considered "cool," smokers are now considered to be deviants, scorned as polluters, and often banished to outside office buildings, as here.*

behavior of maladjusted youth, or are they rational responses to social situations?

Sociological studies of gangs in the United States shed light on this question. The family situations of gang members are often problematic, although girls in gangs tend to be more isolated from their families than are boys in gangs (Fleisher 2000; Esbensen-Finn et al. 1999). Given the class, race, and gender inequality faced by minority youth, many turn to gangs for the social support they lack elsewhere (Walker-Barnes and Mason 2001; Moore and Hagedorn 1996). For example, some poor, young Puerto Rican girls live in relatively confined social environments with little opportunity for educational or occupational advancement. Their community expects them to be "good girls" and to remain close to their families. Joining a gang is one way to reject these restrictive roles (Messerschmidt 1997; Campbell 1987). Are these young women irrational or just doing the best they can to adapt to their situation? Sociologists interpret their behavior as an understandable adaptation to conditions of poverty, racism, and sexism.

Also, in some subcultures or situations, deviant behavior is encouraged and praised. Have you ever been egged on by friends to do something that you thought was deviant, or have you done something you knew was wrong? Many argue that the reason so many college students drink excessively is that the student subculture encourages them to do so—even though students know it is harmful. Similarly, the juvenile delinquent regarded by school authorities as defiant and obnoxious is rewarded and praised by peers for the very behaviors that school authorities loathe. Much deviant behavior occurs, or escalates, because of the social support received from others.

Some behavior patterns defined as deviant are also surprisingly similar to so-called normal behavior.

Is a heroin addict who buys drugs with whatever money he can find so different from a business executive who spends a large proportion of his discretionary income on alcohol? Each may establish a daily pattern that facilitates drug use; each may select friends based on shared interests in drinking or taking drugs; and each may become so physically, emotionally, and socially dependent on their "fix" that life seems unimaginable without it. Which of the two is more likely to be considered deviant?

The point is that deviance is both created and defined within a social context. It is not just weird, pathological, or irrational behavior. Sociologists who study deviance understand it in the context of social relationships and society. They define deviance in terms of existing social norms and the social judgments people make about one another. Indeed, deviant behavior can sometimes be indicative of changes that are taking place in the cultural folkways. Thus, whereas only a few years ago body piercing and tattooing were associated with gangs and disrespectable people, now it is considered fashionable among young, middle-class people.

In sum, a sociological perspective on deviance asks: Why is deviance more common in some groups than others? Why are some more likely to be labeled deviant than others, even if they engage in the exact same behavior? How is deviance related to patterns of inequality in society? Sociologists do not ignore individual psychology but integrate it into an explanation of deviance that focuses on the social conditions surrounding the behavior, going beyond explanations of deviance that root it in the individual personality.

## The Medicalization of Deviance

Commonly, people will say that someone who commits a very deviant act is "sick." This common explanation is what sociologists call the **medicalization of deviance** (Conrad and Schneider 1992). Medicalizing deviance attributes deviant behavior to a "sick" state of mind, where the solution is to "cure" the deviant through therapy or other psychological treatment.

An example is found in alcoholism. There is some evidence that there may be a genetic basis to alcoholism, and certainly alcoholism must be understood at least in part in medical terms, but viewing alcoholism *solely* from a medical perspective ignores the social causes that influence the development and persistence of this behavior. Practitioners know that medical treatment alone does not solve the problem. The social relationships, social conditions, and social habits of alcoholics must be altered, or the behavior is likely to recur.

*thinkingsociologically*

Ask some of your friends to explain why rape occurs. What evidence of the *medicalization of deviance* exists in your friends' answers?

Sociologists criticize the medicalization of deviance for ignoring the effects of social structures on the development of deviant behavior. From a sociological perspective, deviance originates in society, not just in individuals. Changing the incidence of deviant behavior requires changes in society in addition to changes in individuals. Deviance, to most sociologists, is not a pathological state but an *adaptation to the social structures* in which people live. Factors such as family background, social class, racial inequality, and the social structure of gender relations in society produce deviance, and these factors must be considered in order to explain it.

# Sociological Theories of Deviance

Sociologists have drawn on several major theoretical traditions to explain deviant behavior, including functionalism, conflict theory, and symbolic interaction theory.

## Functionalist Theories of Deviance

Recall that functionalism is a theoretical perspective that interprets all parts of society, even those that may seem dysfunctional, as instead contributing to the stability of the whole. At first glance, deviance seems to be dysfunctional for society. Functionalist theorists argue otherwise (see Table 7.1). They contend that deviance is functional *because it creates social cohesion.* Branding certain behaviors as deviant provides contrast with behaviors that are considered normal, giving people a heightened sense of social order. Norms are meaningless unless there is deviance from them; thus, deviance is necessary to clarify what society's norms are. Group coherence then comes from sharing a common definition of legitimate, as well as deviant, behavior. The collective identity of the group is affirmed when those who are defined as deviant are ridiculed or condemned by group members (Erikson 1966).

To give an example, think about how many people define gay men as deviant. Although lesbians and gay men have rejected this label, labeling homosexuality as deviant is one way of affirming the presumed normality of heterosexual behavior. Labeling someone else an outsider is, in other words, a way of affirming one's "insider" identity.

**Durkheim: The Study of Suicide.** The functionalist perspective on deviance stems originally from the work of **Emile Durkheim.** Recall that one of Durkheim's central concerns was how society maintains its coherence (or social order). Durkheim saw deviance as functional for society because it produces solidarity among society's members. He developed his analysis of deviance in large part through his analysis of suicide. Through this work, he discovered a number of important sociological points. First, he criticized the usual psychological interpretations of why people commit suicide, turning instead to sociological explanations with data to back them up. Second, he emphasized the role of social structure in producing deviance. Third, he pointed to the importance of people's social attachments to society in understanding deviance. Finally, he elaborated the functionalist view that deviance provides the basis for social cohesion. His studies of suicide illustrate these points.

Durkheim was the first to argue that the causes of suicide were to be found in social factors, not individual personalities. Observing that the rate of suicide in a society varied with time and place, Durkheim looked for causes linked to these factors other than emotional stress. Durkheim argued that suicide rates are affected by the different social contexts in which they emerge. He looked at the degree to which people feel integrated into the structure of society and their social surroundings as social factors producing suicide.

Durkheim analyzed three types of suicide: anomic suicide, altruistic suicide, and egoistic suicide. **Anomie,** as defined by Durkheim, is the condition that exists when social regulations in a society break down: The controlling influences of society are no longer effective, and people exist in a state of relative normlessness.

| *table 7.1* | *Sociological Theories of Deviance* | |
|---|---|---|
| **Functionalist Theory** | **Symbolic Interaction Theory** | **Conflict Theory** |
| Deviance creates social cohesion. | Deviance is a learned behavior, reinforced through group membership. | Dominant classes control the definition of and sanctions attached to deviance. |
| Deviance results from structural strains in society. | Deviance results from the process of social labeling, regardless of the actual commission of deviance. | Deviance results from social inequality in society. |
| Deviance occurs when people's attachment to social bonds is diminished. | Those with the power to assign deviant labels themselves produce deviance. | Elite deviance and corporate deviance go largely unrecognized and unpunished. |

The term *anomie* refers not to an individual's state of mind, but instead to social conditions.

**Anomic suicide** occurs when the disintegrating forces in the society make individuals feel lost or alone. Teenage suicide is often cited as an example of anomic suicide. Studies of college campuses, for example, trace the cause of campus suicides to feelings of depression and hopelessness (Langhinrichsen-Rohling et al. 1998). These feelings are, however, more likely to arise in certain sociological contexts. Thus, suicide is more likely committed by those who have been sexually abused as children or by those whose parents are alcoholics (Thakkar et al. 2000; Bryant and Range 1997).

**Altruistic suicide** occurs when there is excessive regulation of individuals by social forces. An example is someone who commits suicide for the sake of a religious or political cause. For example, after hijackers took control of four airplanes—crashing two into the World Trade Center in New York, one into the Pentagon, and, through the intervention of passengers, one in a Pennsylvania field—many wondered how anyone could do such a thing, killing themselves in the process. Although sociology certainly does not excuse such behavior, it can help explain it. Terrorists and *suicide bombers* are so regulated by their extreme beliefs that they are willing to die to kill as many people as possible to achieve their goals. As Durkheim argued, altruistic suicide results when individuals are excessively dominated by the expectations of their social group. People who commit altruistic suicide subordinate themselves to collective expectations, even when death is the result.

**Egoistic suicide** occurs when people feel totally detached from society. This helps explain the high rate of suicide among the elderly in the United States. People over seventy-five years of age have one of the highest rates of suicide, presumably because the elderly lose many of their functional ties to society (National Center for Health Statistics 2008). Ordinarily, people are integrated into society by work roles, ties to family and community, and other social bonds. When these bonds are weakened through retirement or loss of family and friends, the likelihood of egoistic suicide increases. Suicide is also more likely to occur among people who are not well integrated into social networks (Berkman et al. 2000). Thus, it should not be surprising that women have lower suicide rates than men (National Center for Health Statistics 2008). Sociologists explain this fact as a result of men being less embedded in social relationships of care and responsibility than women (Watt and Sharp 2001).

Durkheim's major point is that suicide is a social, not just an individual, phenomenon. Recall from Chapter 1 that Durkheim sees sociology as the discovery of the social forces that influence human behavior. One recent study shows that these social forces that affect behavior such as suicides among youths are *multilevel*: The higher the degree of integration of the

Strong ties among the Navajo produce social integration, resulting in the fact that the Navajo have one of the lowest suicide rates of any group in the United States, and also lowest among other Native American tribal groups.

individual into structural "levels," such as the family, the peer group, religion, the neighborhood, and the school, then the lower the risk of suicide (Mainon and Kuhl 2008). As individualistic as suicide might seem, Durkheim uncovered the influence of social structure even here. In fact, suicide also varies considerably by state (see Map 7.1)—another structural "level."

Durkheim's theory of suicide can help you understand such horrific acts as the Virginia Tech student massacre in 2007. Seung-Hui Cho, a college student, armed with two semiautomatic pistols, shot and killed thirty-two people at Virginia Tech University, wounded fourteen others, and then killed himself, bringing the total killed to thirty-three. This act shocked the nation, and the media instantly dubbed it the largest mass rampage killing in U.S. history. There are social–structural elements that are common to both the Virginia Tech rampage and other "school shootings," such as the rampage killings at Columbine High School in Littleton, Colorado, in 1999. Both acts were committed by individuals who could be characterized as extremely socially isolated and utterly outside a network of peers. All three perpetrators (Cho in the case of Virginia Tech and Dylan Klebold and Eric Harris in the case of Columbine High School) were social isolates, and all three committed suicide immediately after their carnage. In Durkheim's sense, all three instances represented examples of egoistic suicide, given the attributes of social isolation, lack of integration into society, troubled individual histories, and a desire to "make their mark" in history by killing the largest number of individuals possible in a single attack (Newman 2006).

**Merton: Structural Strain Theory.** The functionalist perspective on deviance has been further elaborated by the sociologist **Robert Merton**

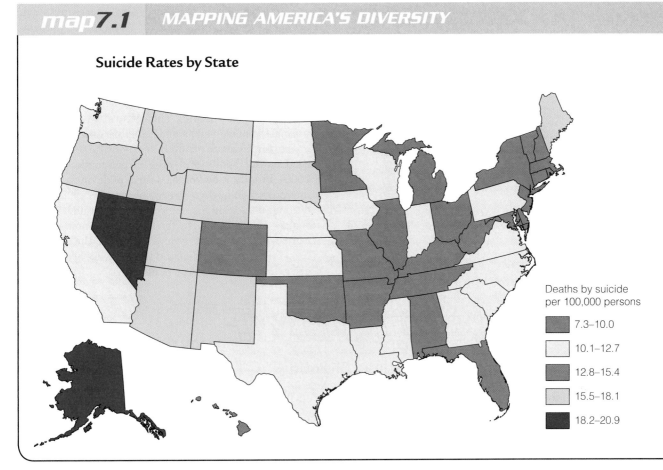

*Many factors can influence the suicide rate in different contexts. As discussed in the text, suicides can be caused by a multiple of structural and cultural factors, and sometimes these factors may be differently distributed by state or region. What are some of the social facts about the different states and regions that might affect the different rates of suicide you see in this map? What, in particular, might you guess about such social facts characterizing the states with the highest suicide rates?*

*Data:* U.S. Census Bureau, 2008. *The 2007 Statistical Abstract: National Data Book.* Washington, DC: U.S. Government Printing Office.

(1910–2003). Merton's **structural strain theory** traces the origins of deviance to the tensions caused by the gap between cultural goals and the means people have available to achieve those goals. Merton noted that societies are characterized by both culture and social structure. Culture establishes goals for people in society; social structure provides, or fails to provide, the means for people to achieve those goals. In a well-integrated society, according to Merton, people use accepted means to achieve the goals society establishes. In other words, the goals and means of the society are in balance. When the means are out of balance with the goals, deviance is likely to occur. According to Merton, this imbalance, or disjunction, between cultural goals and structurally available means can actually compel the individual into deviant behavior (Merton 1968).

To explain further, a collective goal in U.S. society is the achievement of economic success. The legitimate means to achieve such success are education and jobs, but not all groups have equal access to those means. The result is structural strain that produces deviance.

According to Merton, lower-class individuals are most likely to experience these strains because they internalize the same goals and values as the rest of society but have blocked opportunities for success. Structural strain theory therefore helps explain the high correlation that exists between unemployment and crime.

Figure 7.1 illustrates how strain between cultural goals and structurally available means can produce deviance. *Conformity* is likely to occur when the goals are accepted and the means for attaining the goals are made available to the individual by the social structure. If this does not occur, then cultural–structural strain exists, and at least one of four possible forms of deviance is likely to result: innovative deviance, ritualistic deviance, retreatism deviance, or rebellion.

Consider the case of female prostitution: The prostitute has accepted the cultural values of the dominant society—obtaining economic success and material wealth. Yet if she is poor, then the structural means to attain these goals are less available to her and turning to prostitution may result.

| | Cultural goals accepted? | Institutionalized means toward goal available? |
|---|---|---|
| Conformity | Yes | Yes |
| Innovative deviance | Yes | No |
| Ritualistic deviance | No | Yes |
| Retreatism deviance | No | No |
| Rebellion | No (old goals) Yes (new goals) | No (old means) Yes (new means) |

**FIGURE 7.1** *Merton's Structural Strain Theory*

Other forms of deviance also represent strain between goals and means. *Retreatism deviance* becomes likely when neither the goals nor the means are available. Examples of retreatism are the severe alcoholic or the homeless person or the hermit. *Ritualistic deviance* is illustrated in the case of some eating disorders among college women, such as *bulimia* (purging oneself after eating). The cultural goal of extreme thinness is perceived as unattainable, even though the means for trying to attain it are plentiful, for example, good eating habits and proper diet methods (Sharp 2000). Finally, *rebellion* as a form of deviance is likely to occur when new goals are substituted for more traditional ones, and also new means are undertaken to replace older ones, as by force or armed combat. Many right-wing extremist groups, such as the American Nazi Party, "skinheads," and the Ku Klux Klan (KKK), are examples of this type of deviance.

# what would they say now?

## Classical Theorists Reflect on School Shootings

Sociological theory can help explain the underlying causes of current events. Were some of the classical theorists to be brought back to life, what might they say about school shootings?

**Emile Durkheim:** As with suicide, people tend to think of most acts of deviance in individualistic terms, thus missing some important sociological dimensions even to horrific individual crimes. Shooters who go on a rampage are often alienated people, living outside a strong support system of peers. Often they are people who have been identified as "deviant" by peers because of their lack of integration into peer networks. The public mourning that follows school shootings, though certainly marked by great individual and collective sadness, can also be seen as a process of social cohesion that unites communities, even in their great sorrow.

**Max Weber:** School shootings involve the interplay of cultural factors with social structural realities. As a culture, U.S. society has become quite bureaucratic and this can be quite dehumanizing; how else could a person kill so many other human beings, unless the culture has made him numb to his actions? But, at the same time, there is an economic ethic in this society—one that tells people they are most valued when they are successful. Young people facing such an interplay of culture and the economic structure may feel so devalued that they can be led by these multiple social forces into behaviors that would otherwise be unimaginable.

**Karl Marx:** Guns, and violence more generally, are highly profitable businesses in this society. Just look at the sales figures for things like Grand Theft Auto—the video game where people spend money to shoot and rape people for fun. Why would we not expect this to shape actual behavior? Ultimately, a capitalist society has to treat people like things because what really drives the society is a system of profit—here people are mere cogs in the capitalist system. Only by knowing this can you understand how people could go on such angry rampages as has happened in school shootings!

**W.E.B. Du Bois:** It is no accident that most of the mass school shootings have been committed by young, White men. I think they are, in part, angry about their class and race status in society. In the contemporary culture of White youth, "Black" is cool, White is not. And note that some of the targets of school shootings were "preppies," suggesting that class anger is part of the context of these terrible events. Of course, gun violence is also a major social problem in African American, low-income communities, but it takes a different form than we have seen in mass school shootings and rarely generates the kind of sympathy and empathy that has followed mass school shootings.

**Social Control Theory.** Taking functionalist theory in another direction, Travis Hirschi has developed social control theory to explain deviance. **Social control theory,** a type of functionalist theory, suggests that deviance occurs when a person's (or group's) attachment to social bonds is weakened (Hirschi 1969; Gottfredson and Hirschi 1995, 1990). According to this view, people internalize social norms because of their attachments to others. People care what others think of them and therefore conform to social expectations because they accept what people expect. You can see here that social control theory, like the functionalist framework from which it stems, assumes the importance of the socialization process in producing conformity to social rules. When that conformity is broken, deviance occurs.

Social control theory assumes there is a common value system within society, and breaking allegiance to that value system is the source of social deviance. This theory focuses on how deviants are attached (or not) to common value systems and what situations break people's commitment to these values. Social control theory suggests that most people probably feel some impulse toward deviance at times but that the attachment to social norms prevents them from actually participating in deviant behavior. Sociologists find that juveniles whose parents exercise little control over violent behavior and who learn violence from aggressive peers are most likely to engage in violent crimes (Heimer 1997), as was the case with the two teenagers who killed twelve students and a teacher at Columbine High School (Newman 2006).

**Functionalism: Strengths and Weaknesses.** Functionalism emphasizes that social structure, not just individual motivation, produces deviance. Functionalists argue that social conditions exert pressure on individuals to behave in conforming or nonconforming ways. Types of deviance are linked to one's place in the social structure; thus, a poor person blocked from economic opportunities may use armed robbery to achieve economic goals, whereas a stockbroker may use insider trading to achieve the same. Functionalists acknowledge that people choose whether to behave in a deviant manner but believe that they make their choice from among socially prestructured options. The emphasis in functionalist theory is on social structure, not individual action. In this sense, functionalist theory is highly sociological.

Functionalists also point out that what appears to be dysfunctional behavior may actually be functional for the society. An example is the fact that most people consider prostitution to be dysfunctional behavior; from the point of view of an individual, that is true: It demeans the women who engage in it, puts them at physical risk, and subjects them to sexual exploitation. From the view of functionalist theory, however, prostitution supports and maintains a social system that links women's gender roles with sexuality, associates sex with commercial activity, and defines women as passive sexual objects and men as sexual aggressors. In other words, what appears to be deviant may actually serve various purposes for society.

Critics of the functionalist perspective argue that it does not explain how norms of deviance are first established. Despite its analysis of the ramifications of deviant behavior for society as a whole, functionalism does little to explain why some behaviors are defined as normative and others as illegitimate. Who determines social norms and on whom such judgments are most likely to be imposed are questions seldom asked by anyone using a functionalist perspective. Functionalists see deviance as having stabilizing consequences in society, but they tend to overlook the injustices that labeling someone deviant can produce. Others would say that the functionalist perspective too easily assumes that deviance has a positive role in society; thus, functionalists rarely consider the differential effects that the administration of justice has on different groups. The tendency in functionalist theory to assume that the system works for the good of the whole too easily ignores the inequities in society and how these inequities are reflected in patterns of deviance. These issues are left for sociologists who work from the perspectives of conflict theory and symbolic interaction.

## Conflict Theories of Deviance

Recall that conflict theory emphasizes the unequal distribution of power and resources in society. It links the study of deviance to social inequality. Based on the work of Karl Marx (1818–1883; see Chapter 1), conflict theory sees a dominant class as controlling the resources of society and using its power to create the institutional rules and belief systems that support its power. Like functionalist theory, conflict theory is a *macrostructural* approach; that is, both theories look at the structure of society as a whole in developing explanations of deviant behavior.

Because some groups of people have access to fewer resources in capitalist society, they are forced into crime to sustain themselves. Conflict theory posits that the economic organization of capitalist societies produces deviance and crime. The high rate of crime among the poorest groups, especially economic crimes such as theft, robbery, prostitution, and drug selling, are a result of the economic status of these groups. Rather than emphasizing values and conformity as a source of deviance as do functional analyses, conflict theorists see crime in terms of power relationships and economic inequality (Grant and Martínez 1997).

The upper classes, conflict theorists point out, can also better hide crimes they commit because affluent groups have the resources to mask their deviance and crime. As a result, a working-class man who beats his wife is more likely to be arrested and prosecuted than an upper-class man who engages in the same behavior. In addition, those with greater resources can afford to buy their way out of trouble by paying bail, hiring expensive attorneys, or even resorting to bribes.

*Corporate crime* is crime committed within the legitimate context of doing business. Conflict theorists expand our view of crime and deviance by revealing the significance of such crimes. They argue that appropriating profit based on exploitation of the poor and working class is inherent in the structure of capitalist society. **Elite deviance** refers to the wrongdoing of wealthy and powerful individuals and organizations (Simon 2007). Elite deviance includes what early conflict theorists called *white-collar crime* (Sutherland 1940; Sutherland and Cressey 1978). Elite deviance includes tax evasion; illegal campaign contributions; corporate scandals, such as fraudulent accounting practices that endanger or deceive the public but profit the corporation or individuals within it; and even government actions that abuse the public trust. Several examples of elite deviance are covered in detail later in this chapter.

The ruling groups in society develop numerous mechanisms to protect their interests according to conflict theorists who argue that law, for example, is created by elites to protect the interests of the dominant class. Thus law, supposedly neutral and fair in its form and implementation, works in the interest of the most well-to-do (Weisburd et al. 2001, 1991; Spitzer 1975). Another way that conflict theorists see dominant groups as using their power is through the excessive regulation of populations that are a potential threat to affluent interests. Periodically sweeping the homeless off city streets, especially when there is a major political event or other elite event occurring, is a good example.

Conflict theory emphasizes the significance of social control in managing deviance and crime. **Social control** is the process by which groups and individuals within those groups are brought into conformity with dominant social expectations. Social control, as we saw in Chapter 4, can take place simply through socialization, but dominant groups can also control the behavior of others through marking them as deviant. An example is the historic persecution of witches during the Middle Ages in Europe and during the early colonial period in America (Ben-Yehuda 1986; Erikson 1966). Witches often were women who were healers and midwives—those whose views were at odds with the authority of the exclusively patriarchal hierarchy of the church, then the ruling institution. "Witch hunt" is a term still used today to refer to the aggressive pursuit of those who dissent from prevailing political and social norms.

One implication of conflict theory, especially when linked with labeling theory, is that the power to define deviance confers an important degree of social control. **Social control agents** are those who regulate and administer the response to deviance, such as the police and mental health workers. Members of powerless groups may be defined as deviant for even the slightest infraction against social norms, whereas others may be free to behave in deviant ways without consequence. Oppressed groups may actually engage in more deviant behavior, but it is also true that they have a greater likelihood of being labeled deviant and incarcerated or institutionalized, whether or not they have actually committed an offense. This is evidence of the power wielded by social control agents.

When powerful groups hold stereotypes about other groups, the less powerful people are frequently assigned deviant labels. As a consequence, the least powerful groups in society are subject most often to social control. You can see this in the patterns of arrest data. Poor people are more likely to be considered criminals and therefore more likely to be arrested, convicted, and imprisoned than middle- and upper-class people. The same is true of Latinos, Native Americans, and African Americans. Sociologists point out that this does not necessarily mean that these groups are somehow more criminally prone; rather, they take it as evidence of the differential treatment of these groups by the criminal justice system.

**Conflict Theory: Strengths and Weaknesses.** The strength of conflict theory is its insight into the significance of power relationships in the definition, identification, and handling of deviance. It links the commission, perception, and treatment of crime to inequality in society and offers a powerful analysis of how the injustices of society produce crime and result in different systems of justice

*From the point of view of conflict theory, social control agents play a significant role in defining and causing defiant behavior, as in this case of cocaine use.*

© David Young-Wolff/PhotoEdit

for disadvantaged and privileged groups. Not without its weaknesses, however, critics point out that laws protect most people, not just the affluent, as conflict theorists argue.

In addition, although conflict theory offers a powerful analysis of the origins of crime, it is less effective in explaining other forms of deviance. For example, how would conflict theorists explain the routine deviance of middle-class adolescents? They might point out that much of middle-class deviance is driven by consumer marketing. Profits are made from the accoutrements of deviance—rings in pierced eyebrows, "gangsta" rap music, and so on—but economic interests alone cannot explain all the deviance observed in society. As Durkheim argued, deviance is functional for the whole of society, not just those with a major stake in the economic system.

## Symbolic Interaction Theories of Deviance

Whereas functionalist and conflict theories are *macrosociological* theories, certain *microsociological* theories of deviance look directly at the interactions people have with one another as the origin of social deviance. *Symbolic interaction theory* holds that people behave as they do because of the meanings people attribute to situations (see Chapter 1). This perspective emphasizes the meanings surrounding deviance, as well as how people respond to those meanings. Symbolic interaction emphasizes that deviance originates in the interaction between different groups and is defined by society's reaction to certain behaviors. Symbolic interactionist theories of deviance originate in the perspective of the Chicago School of sociology.

**W. I. Thomas and the Chicago School.**
**W. I. Thomas** (1863–1947), one of the early sociologists from the University of Chicago, was among the first to develop a sociological perspective on social deviance. Thomas explained deviance as *a normal response to the social conditions in which people find themselves.* Thomas was one of the first to argue that delinquency was caused by the social disorganization brought on by slum life and urban industrialism; he saw deviance as a problem of social conditions, not individual character.

**Differential Association Theory.** Thomas's work laid the foundation for a classic theory of deviance: differential association theory. **Differential association theory,** a type of symbolic interaction theory, interprets deviance, including criminal behavior, as behavior one learns through interaction with others (Sutherland 1940; Sutherland and Cressey 1978). Edwin Sutherland argued that becoming a criminal or a juvenile delinquent is a matter of learning criminal ways within the primary groups to which one belongs. To Sutherland, people become criminals when they are more strongly socialized to break the law than to

obey it. Differential association theory emphasizes the interaction people have with their peers and others in their environment. Those who "differentially associate" with delinquents, deviants, or criminals learn to value deviance. The greater the frequency, duration, and intensity of their immersion in deviant environments, the more likely it is that they will become deviant.

Consider the career path of con artists and hustlers. Hustlers seldom work alone. Like any skilled worker, they have to learn the "tricks of the trade." A new recruit becomes part of a network of other hustlers who teach the recruit the norms of the deviant culture (Prus and Sharper 1991). Crime also tends to run in families. This does not necessarily mean that crime is passed on in genes from parent to child. It means that youths raised in deviant families are more likely socialized to become deviant themselves (Miller 1986). Differential association theory offers a compelling explanation for how deviance is culturally transmitted—that is, people pass on deviant expectations through the social groups in which they interact, of which the family is but one.

Critics of differential association theory have argued that this perspective tends to blame deviance on the values of particular groups. Differential association has been used, for instance, to explain the higher rate of crime among the poor and working class, arguing that this higher rate of crime occurs because they do not share the values of the middle class. Such an explanation, critics say, is class-biased, because it overlooks the deviance that occurs in the middle-class culture and among elites. Disadvantaged groups may share the values of the middle class but cannot necessarily achieve them through legitimate means (a point, you will remember, made by Merton's structural strain theory). Still, differential association theory offers a good explanation of why deviant activity may be more common in some groups than others, and it emphasizes the significant role that peers play in encouraging deviant behavior.

**Labeling Theory.** **Labeling theory,** a branch of symbolic interaction theory, interprets the responses of others as the most significant factor in understanding how deviant behavior is both created and sustained (Becker 1963). Labeling theory stems from the work of W. I. Thomas, who it will be recalled wrote, "If men define situations as real, they are real in their consequences" (Thomas and Thomas 1928: 572). A *label* is the assignment or attachment of a deviant identity to a person by others, including by agents of social institutions; therefore, people's reactions, not the action itself, produce deviance as a result of the labeling process. Once applied, the deviant label is difficult to shed.

Linked with conflict theory, labeling theory shows how those with the power to label an act or a person deviant and to impose sanctions—such as police, court officials, school authorities, experts, teachers, and official agents of social institutions—wield great power in determining societal understandings of deviance. When they apply the "deviant" label, it sticks. Furthermore, because deviants are handled through bureaucratic organizations, bureaucratic workers "process" people according to rules and procedures, seldom questioning the basis for those rules or willing or able to challenge them (Cicourel 1968; Kitsuse and Cicourel 1963; Margolin 1992; Montada and Lerner 1998).

Once the label is applied, it is difficult for the deviant to recover a nondeviant identity. To give an example, once a social worker or psychiatrist labels a client mentally ill, that person will be treated as mentally ill, regardless of his or her actual mental state. Pleas by the accused that he or she is mentally sound are typically taken as further evidence of mental illness! Once labeled, a person may have great difficulty changing his or her classification; the label itself has consequences.

A person need not have actually engaged in deviant behavior to be labeled deviant; yet, once applied, the label has social consequences. Labeling theory helps explain why convicts released from prison have such high rates of *recidivism* (return to criminal activities). Convicted criminals are formally and publicly labeled wrongdoers. They are treated with suspicion ever afterward and have great difficulty finding legitimate employment: The label "ex-con" defines their future options.

It is in fact exceedingly difficult for an ex-con to find employment after release from prison, even more so if the person is male and Black or Hispanic. In a clever study, Pager (2007) had pretrained role-players pose as ex-cons looking for a job. These role-players went into the job market and were interviewed for various jobs; all of them used the same preset script during the interview. The idea of the study was to see how many of them would be invited back for another interview. The results were staggering: A very small percentage of the male Black and Hispanic role-players were invited back for interviews, yet a large percentage of the male White role-players were. Blacks who were *not* ex-cons were *less* likely to be invited back for the job interview than were Whites who *were* ex-cons! So the effect of race alone exceeded the effect of incarceration alone. These upsetting differences could not be attributed to differences in interaction displayed during the interview, because everyone used the exact same prepared script.

Researchers Bruce Western (2006) and Jeffrey Reiman (2007) note that the prison system in the United States is in effect designed to *train and socialize* prisoners into a career of secondary deviance and to tell the public that crime is a threat primarily from the poor (see the box, "Understanding Diversity: The Rich Get Richer and the Poor Get Prison," on page 171). Reiman sees that the goal of the prison system is not to reduce crime but to impress upon the public

that crime is inevitable and that it originates only from the lower classes. Prisons accomplish this, even if unintentionally, by demeaning prisoners, not training them in marketable skills, and stigmatizing them as different from "decent citizens." As a consequence, the person will never be able to pay his or her debt to society, and the prison system has created the very behavior it intended to eliminate.

Labeling theory suggests that deviance refers not just to something one does but to something one becomes. **Deviant identity** is the definition a person has of himself or herself as a deviant. Most often, deviant identities emerge over time (Lemert 1972; Simon 2007). A drug addict, for example, may not think of herself as a junkie until she realizes she no longer has non-using friends. The formation of a deviant identity, like other identities, involves a process of social transformation in which a new self-image and new public definition of a person emerges. This is a process that involves how people view the deviant and how the deviant views himself or herself. Studies of tattoo "collectors" (that is, those who are very heavily tattooed) find, for example, that if collectors first learn to interpret tattooing as a desirable thing, they then begin to feel connected to a subculture of other collectors and eventually come to see their tattoos as part of themselves (Irwin 2001; Vail 1999; Montada and Lerner 1998; Scheff 1984).

*thinking sociologically*

Perform an experiment by doing something deviant for a period, such as carrying around a teddy bear doll and treating it as a live baby or standing in the street and looking into the air, as though you are looking at something up there. Make a record of how others respond to you, and then ask yourself how *labeling theory* is important to the study of *deviance*. Then take your experiment a step further and ask yourself how people's reactions to you might have differed had you been of another race or gender. You might want to structure this question into your experiment by teaming up with a classmate of another race or gender. You could then compare responses to the same behavior by both of you. *A note of caution:* Do not do anything illegal or dangerous; even the most seemingly harmless acts of deviance can generate strong (and sometimes hostile) reactions, so be careful in planning your experiment!

**Deviant Careers.** In the ordinary context of work, a career is the sequence of movements a person makes through different positions in an occupational system (Becker 1963). A **deviant career**—a direct outgrowth of the labeling process—is the sequence of movements people make through a particular subculture of deviance. Deviant careers can be studied sociologically, like any other career. Within deviant careers, people are socialized into new "occupational" roles and encouraged, both materially and psychologically, to engage in deviant behavior. The concept of a deviant career emphasizes that there is a progression through deviance: Deviants are recruited, given or denied rewards, and promoted or demoted. As with legitimate careers, deviant careers involve an evolution in the person's identity, values, and commitment over time. Deviants, like other careerists, may have to demonstrate their commitment to the career to their superiors, perhaps by passing certain tests of their mettle, such as when a gang expects new members to commit a crime, perhaps even shoot someone.

Within deviant careers, there may be rites of passage that bring increased social status among peers. Punishments administered by the authorities may even become badges of honor within a deviant community. Similarly, labeling a teenager "bad" for behavior that others think is immoral may actually encourage the behavior to continue because the juvenile may take this as a sign of success as a deviant.

**Deviant Communities.** The preceding discussion continues to indicate an important sociological point: Deviant behavior is not just the behavior of maladjusted individuals; it often takes place within a group context and involves group response. Some groups are actually organized around particular forms of social deviance; these are called **deviant communities** (Becker 1963; Erikson 1966; Blumer 1969; Mizruchi 1983).

Like subcultures and countercultures, deviant communities maintain their own values, norms, and rewards for deviant behavior. Joining a deviant community closes one off from conventional society and tends to solidify deviant careers because the deviant individual receives rewards and status from the in-group. Disapproval from the out-group may only enhance one's status within. Deviant communities also create a worldview that solidifies the deviant identity of their members. They may develop symbolic systems such as emblems, forms of dress, publications, and other symbols that promote their identity as a deviant group. Gangs wear their "colors," prostitutes have their own vocabulary of *tricks* and *johns;* skinheads have their insignia and music. All are examples of deviant communities. Ironically, subcultural norms and values reinforce the deviant label both inside and outside the deviant group, thereby reinforcing the deviant behavior.

Some deviant communities are organized specifically to provide support to those in presumed deviant categories. Groups such as Alcoholics Anonymous, Weight Watchers, and various twelve-step programs help those identified as deviant overcome their deviant behavior. These groups, which can be quite effective, accomplish their mission by encouraging members to accept their deviant identity as the first step to recovery.

**A Problem with Official Statistics.** Because labeling theorists see deviance as produced by those with

Jim West/Alamy

*Some deviance develops in deviant communities, such as the Neo-Nazis/"skin-heads" shown marching here. Such right-wing extremist groups have remained relatively constant in numbers for the last several years.*

the power to assign labels, they question the value of official statistics as indicators of the true extent of deviance. *Reported rates of deviant behavior are themselves the product of socially determined behavior, specifically the behavior of identifying what is deviant.* Official rates of deviance are produced by people in the social system who define, classify, and record certain behaviors as deviant and others as legitimate. Labeling theorists are more likely to ask how behavior becomes labeled deviant than they are to ask what motivates people to become deviant (Best 2001; Kitsuse and Cicourel 1963).

For example, in the aftermath of the terrorist attacks on the World Trade Center, officials debated whether to count the deaths of thousands as murder or as a separate category of terrorism. The decision would change the official rate of deviance by inflating or deflating the reported crime rate of murder in New York City in that year. In the end, these deaths were not counted in the murder rate. Labeling theorists think that official rates of deviance do not necessarily reflect the actual commission of crimes or deviant acts; instead, the official rates reflect social judgments.

In another example, official rape rates are underestimates of the actual extent of rape, largely due to victims' reluctance to report. Also, some rapes are less likely to be "counted" as rape by police, such as if the victim is a prostitute, was drunk at the time of the assault, or had a previous relationship with the assailant. Moreover, rapes resulting in death are classified as homicides and therefore do not appear in the official statistics on rape. Discrimination by the police can also influence official statistics; thus, higher arrest rates for African American men tell us as much about police behavior as it does the behavior of African American men (Babbie 2007; DeFleur 1975). Given such problems, any official statistics must be interpreted with caution.

**Labeling Theory: Strengths and Weaknesses.** The strength of labeling theory is its recognition that the judgments people make about presumably deviant behavior have powerful social effects. Labeling theory does not, however, explain why deviance occurs in the first place. It may illuminate the consequences of a young man's violent behavior, but it does not explain the actual origins of the behavior. Put bluntly, it does not explain why some people become deviant and others do not.

# Forms of Deviance

Although there are many forms of deviance, the sociology of deviant behavior has focused heavily on subjects such as mental illness, social stigmas, and crime. As we review each, you will also see how the different sociological theories about deviance contribute to understanding each subject. In addition, you will see how the social context of race, class, and gender relationships shape these different forms of deviance.

## Mental Illness

Sociological explanations of mental illness look to the social systems in which mental illness is defined, identified, and treated, even though it is typical for many to think of mental illness only in psychological terms. This has several implications for understanding mental illness. Functionalist theory suggests, for example, that by recognizing mental illness, society also upholds normative values about more conforming behavior. Symbolic interaction theory tells us that mentally ill people are not necessarily "sick," but rather are the victims of societal reactions to their behavior. Some go so far as to say there is no such thing as mental illness, only people's reactions to unusual behavior. From this point of view, people learn faulty self-images and then are cast into the role of patient when they are treated

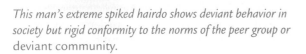
© Keith Erskine/Alamy

*This man's extreme spiked hairdo shows deviant behavior in society but rigid conformity to the norms of the peer group or deviant community.*

by therapists. Once someone is labeled as a "patient," he or she is forced into the "sick" role, as expected by those who reinforce it, and it becomes difficult to get out of the role (Szasz 1974).

Labeling theory, combined with conflict theory, suggests that those people with the fewest resources are most likely to be labeled mentally ill. Women, racial minorities, and the poor all suffer higher rates of reported mental illness and more serious disorders than do groups of higher social and economic status. Furthermore, research over the years has consistently shown that middle- and upper-class persons are more likely to receive some type of psychotherapy for their illness. Poorer individuals and minorities are more likely to receive only physical rehabilitation and medication, with no accompanying psychotherapy (Hollingshead and Redlich 1958; Simon 2007).

## Debunking Society's Myths

**Myth:** Mental illness is an abnormality best studied exclusively by psychologists and physicians.

**Sociological perspective:** Mental illness follows patterns associated with race, class, and gender relations in society and is subject to a significant labeling effect. Those who study and treat mental illness benefit from combining a sociological perspective with both medical and psychological knowledge.

Sociologists give two explanations for the correlation between social status and mental illness. On the one hand, the stresses of being in a low-income group, being a racial minority, or being a woman in a sexist society all contribute to higher rates of mental illness; the harsher social environment is a threat to mental health. On the other hand, the same behavior that is labeled mentally ill for some groups may be tolerated and not so labeled in others. For example, behavior considered crazy in a homeless woman (who is likely to be seen as "deranged") may be seen as merely eccentric or charming when exhibited by a rich person.

## Social Stigmas

A **stigma** is an attribute that is socially devalued and discredited. Some stigmas result in people being labeled deviant. The experiences of people who are disabled, disfigured, or in some other way stigmatized are studied in much the same way as other forms of social deviance. Like other deviants, people with stigmas are stereotyped and defined only in terms of their presumed deviance.

Think, for example, of how disabled people are treated in society. Their disability can become a master status (Chapter 5), a characteristic of a person that overrides all other features of the person's identity (Goffman 1963). Physical disability can become a master status when other people see the disability as the defining feature of the person; a person with a disability becomes "that blind woman" or "that paralyzed guy." People with a particular stigma are often seen to be all alike. This may explain why stigmatized individuals of high visibility are often expected to represent the whole group.

People who suddenly become disabled often have the alarming experience of their new master status rapidly erasing their former identity. They may be treated and seen differently by people they know. A master status may also prevent people from seeing other parts of a person. A person with a disability may be assumed to have no meaningful sex life, even if the disability is unrelated to sexual ability or desire. Sociologists have argued that the negative judgments made about people with stigmas tend to confirm the "usualness" of others (Goffman 1963: 3). For example, when welfare recipients are stigmatized as lazy and undeserving of social support, others are indirectly promoted as industrious and deserving.

Stigmatized individuals are measured against a presumed norm and may be labeled, stereotyped, and discriminated against. In Goffman's words, people with stigmas are perceived to have a "spoiled identity." Seen by others as deficient or inferior, they are caught in a role imposed by the stigma.

Sometimes, people with stigmas bond with others, perhaps even strangers. This can involve an acknowledgment of "kinship" or affiliation that can be as subtle as an understanding look, a greeting that makes a connection between two people, or a favor extended to a stranger who the person sees as sharing the presumed stigma. Public exchanges are common between various groups that share certain forms of disadvantage, such as people with disabilities, lesbians and gays, or members of other minority groups.

## Substance Abuse: Drugs and Alcohol

As with mental illness and stigmas, sociologists study the social factors that influence drug and alcohol use. Who uses what and why? How are users defined by others? These questions guide sociological research on substance abuse.

One of the first things to ask when thinking about drugs and alcohol is why using one substance is considered deviant and stigmatizing and using another is not. How do such definitions of deviance change over time?

For example, alcohol is a legal drug. Whether one is labeled an alcoholic depends in large part on the social context in which one drinks, not solely on the amount of alcohol consumed. For years, the businessman's lunch where executives drank two or three martinis was viewed as normative. Drinking wine from a bottle in a brown bag on the street corner is considered highly deviant; having martinis in a posh bar is seen as cool—even though one martini contains considerably more alcoholic content than a glass of wine.

Sociological understandings challenge views of drug and alcohol use as stemming solely from inherent individual propensities that lead to substance abuse. Patterns of use vary by factors such as age, gender, and race (see Figure 7.2). Age is one significant predictor of illegal drug use. Young people are on average more likely to use marijuana and cocaine and binge drink than are people who are somewhat older, though there are, of course, exceptions.

# Crime and Criminal Justice

The concept of deviance in sociology is a broad one, encompassing many forms of behavior—both legal and illegal, ordinary and unusual. **Crime** is one form of deviance, specifically behavior that violates

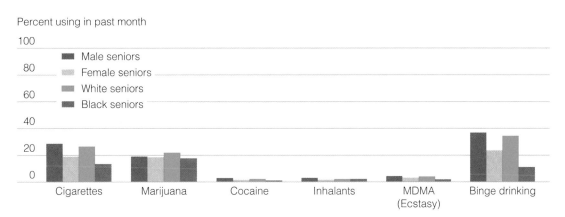

*FIGURE 7.2* *Use of Selected Substances by High School Seniors*

*Source:* National Center for Health Statistics. 2008. *Health United States 2008.* Hyattsville, MD: U.S. Department of Health and Human Services.

particular criminal laws. Not all deviance is crime. Deviance becomes crime when it is designated by the institutions of society as violating a law or laws. *Deviance* is behavior that is recognized as violating rules and norms of society. Those rules may be formal laws, in which case the deviant behavior would be called *crime,* or informal customs or habits, in which case the deviant behavior would not be called crime.

**Criminology** is the study of crime from a scientific perspective. Criminologists include social scientists such as sociologists who stress the societal causes and treatment of crime. All the theoretical perspectives on deviance that we examined earlier contribute to our understanding of crime (see Table 7.2). According to the functionalist perspective, crime may be *necessary* to hold society together—a profound hypothesis. By singling out criminals as socially deviant, others are defined as good. The nightly reporting of crime on television is a demonstration of this sociological function of crime. Conflict theory suggests that disadvantaged groups are more likely to become criminal; it also sees the well-to-do as better able to hide their crimes and less likely to be punished. Symbolic interaction helps us understand how people learn to become criminals or come to be accused of criminality, even when they may be innocent. Each perspective traces criminal behavior to social conditions rather than only to the intrinsic tendencies or personalities of individuals.

## Measuring Crime: How Much Is There?

Is crime increasing in the United States? One would certainly think so from watching the media. Images of violent crime abound and give the impression that crime is a constant threat and is on the rise. Data on crime actually show that violent crime peaked in 1990, but *decreased* through the 1990s and leveled off a bit through 2005–2007 (see Figure 7.3). Assault and robbery, in particular, decreased quite significantly through the 1990s. Murder and rape remained more constant, though they too have shown some decline since the 1990s.

Data about crime come from the Federal Bureau of Investigation (FBI) based on reports from police departments across the nation. The data are distributed annually in the *Uniform Crime Reports* and are the basis for official reports about the extent of crime and its rise and fall over time. *These data show that although media coverage of crime—especially as reported in TV news—has remained high and about the same, the officially reported rate of crime has decreased.*

A second major source of crime data is the *National Crime Victimization Surveys* published by the Bureau of Justice Statistics in the U.S. Department of Justice. These data are based on surveys in which national samples of people are periodically asked if they have been the victims of one or more criminal acts (see Figures 7.4 and 7.5 on pages 171–172). These surveys also show that violent crime, including rape, assault, robbery, and murder, declined by 15 percent over the 1990s.

Both of these sources of data—the *Uniform Crime Reports* and the *National Crime Victimization Surveys*—are subject to the problem of underreporting. About half to two-thirds of all crimes may not be reported to police, meaning that much crime never shows up in the official statistics. Certain serious crimes, such as rape, are significantly underreported, as we have already noted. Victims may be too upset to report a rape to the police, or they may believe that the police will not believe a rape has occurred. Equally significant, the victim may not want to undergo the continued emotional stress of an investigation and trial. Recall from earlier in this chapter that certain kinds of noncriminal deviance, such as suicide, are also underreported, particularly by upper-income families, because of embarrassment to the deceased person's family.

Another problem arises in the attempt to measure crime by means of official statistics. The FBI's *Uniform Crime Reports* stress what are called **index crimes,** which include the violent crimes of murder, manslaughter, rape, robbery, and aggravated assault, plus property crimes of burglary, larceny-theft, and motor

| *table7.2* | *Sociological Theories of Deviance* |

| Functionalist Theory | Symbolic Interaction Theory | Conflict Theory |
|---|---|---|
| Societies require a certain level of crime in order to clarify norms. | Crime is behavior that is learned through social interaction. | The lower the social class, the more the individual is *forced* into criminality. |
| Crime results from social structural strains (such as class inequality) within society. | Labeling criminals tends to reinforce rather than deter crime. | Inequalities in society by race, class, gender, and other forces tend to produce criminal activity. |
| Crime may be functional to society, thus difficult to eradicate. | Institutions with the power to label, such as prisons, actually produce rather than lessen crime. | Reducing social inequality in society is likely to reduce crime. |

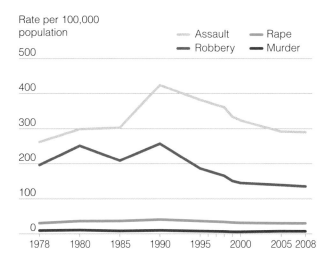

**FIGURE 7.3** *Violent Crime in the United States*

*Source:* Federal Bureau of Investigation, 2009. *Uniform Crime Reports.* Washington, DC: U.S. Department of Justice. **http://www.fbi.gov**

vehicle theft. These crimes are committed mostly by individuals who are disproportionately Black, Hispanic, and poor. Statistics based on these offenses do not reflect the crimes that tend to be committed by middle-class and upper-class persons, such as tax violations, insider trading, fraudulent investment and accounting schemes, embezzlement, and other so-called elite crimes. The official statistics provide a relatively inflated picture for index crimes but an underreported picture of elite crimes, giving a biased picture of crime.

A final result is, unfortunately, that the public sees the stereotypic "criminal" as a lower-class person, most likely an African American or Latino male, not as a middle- or upper-class White person who has committed tax fraud. The official statistics give biased support to the stereotype. This in turn perpetuates the public belief that the "typical" criminal is lower class and minority instead of upper class and nonminority.

## a sociological eye on the media

### Images of Violent Crime

The media routinely drive home two points to the consumer: violent crime is always high and may be increasing over time and there is much random violence constantly around us. The media bombard us with stories of "wilding," in which bands of youths kill random victims. Many of us think road rage is extensive (which it is not) and completely random. The media vividly and routinely report such occurrences as pointless, random, and probably increasing.

The evidence shows that although violent crime in the United States increased during the 1970s and 1980s, it nonetheless began to decrease in 1990 and continues to decrease nationally through the present. For example, both robbery and physical assaults have declined dramatically since 1990 (see Figure 7.3). Yet according to research (Best 2007, 1999; Glassner 1999), the media have consistently given a picture that violent crime has increased during this same period and, furthermore, that the violence is completely unpatterned and random.

No doubt there are occasions when victims are indeed picked at random. But the statistical rule

of randomness could not possibly explain what has come to be called *random violence,* a vision of patternless chaos that is advanced by the media. If randomness truly ruled, *then each of us would have an equal chance of being a victim*—and of being a criminal. This is assuredly not the case. The notion of random violence, and the notion that it is increasing, ignores virtually everything that criminologists, psychologists, sociologists, and extensive research studies know about crime: It is highly patterned and significantly predictable, beyond sheer chance, by taking into account the social structure, social class, location, race–ethnicity, gender, labeling, age, whom one's family members are, and other such variables and forces in society that affect both criminal and victim. The broad picture, then, is clearly not conveyed in the media. Some have speculated that the picture maintained in the media of increasing crime is simply a tool to increase viewer ratings. But criminal violence is not increasing, but decreasing, and it is not random, but highly patterned and even predictable.

**Personal and Property Crimes.** The *Uniform Crime Reports* are subject to the same biases in official statistics mentioned earlier, but they are the major source of information on patterns of crime and arrest, with crimes classified into four categories. **Personal crimes** are violent or nonviolent crimes directed against people. Included in this category are murder, aggravated assault, forcible rape, and robbery. As we see in Figure 7.3, aggravated assault is the most frequently reported personal crime.

**Hate crimes** refer to assaults and other malicious acts (including crimes against property) motivated by various forms of social bias, including that based on race, religion, sexual orientation, ethnic/national origin, or disability. This form of crime has been increasing in recent years, especially against gays and lesbians (Jenness and Broad 2002).

**Property crimes** involve theft of property without threat of bodily harm. These include burglary (breaking and entering), larceny (the unlawful taking of property, but without unlawful entry), auto theft, and arson. Property crimes are the most frequent criminal infractions.

Finally, **victimless crimes** violate laws but are not listed in the FBI's serious crime index. These include illicit activities, such as gambling, illegal drug use, and prostitution, in which there is no complainant. Nonetheless, there is clearly at least some degree of victimization in such crimes: Some researchers see in many instances prostitution as containing at least one victim—the prostitute herself. Enforcement of these crimes is typically not as rigorous as the enforcement of crimes against persons or property, although periodic crackdowns occur, such as the current policy of mandatory sentencing for drug violations.

**Elite and White-Collar Crime.** Sociologists use the term *white-collar crime* to refer to criminal activities by people of high social status who commit their crimes in the context of their occupation (Sutherland 1940; Sutherland and Cressey 1978). White-collar crime includes activities such as embezzlement (stealing funds from one's employer), involvement in illegal stock manipulations (insider trading), and a variety of violations of income tax law, including tax evasion. Also included are manipulations of accounting practices to make one's company appear profitable, thus artificially increasing the value of the company's stock.

Until very recently, white-collar crime seldom generated great concern in the public mind—far less than the concern directed at street crime. In terms of total dollars, however, white-collar crime is even more consequential for society. Scandals involving prominent white-collar criminals come to the public eye occasionally, such as the Ponzi scheme by white-collar criminal Bernard Madoff in 2009. Madoff ran a **Ponzi scheme**—*a con game* whereby a central person (Mr. Madoff) collects money from a large number of people, including friends and relatives, and then promises to invest their dollars with a high rate of interest for them. In Madoff's case, he promised a 10 percent rate of annual return, a very high rate, even while the U.S. economy was souring. Actually, the money was never invested at all, but was used to pay off earlier investors. This is the key principle of a Ponzi scheme. In the Madoff case, investors were led to believe that their money was under the competent control of Madoff himself, and because they trusted him, they never saw any records or stock certificates. For the scheme to work, Madoff had to convince new recruits that they could make a great deal of money if they just "left it to him." In the meantime Madoff siphoned off a portion of the collected funds for himself and lived lavishly.

Such schemes are often called *pyramid schemes*, with large numbers of recent investors at the bottom of the pyramid and smaller numbers of the older (original) investors at the top. Such illegal schemes are named for one Carlo Ponzi, an immigrant who invented and perfected it in the 1920s in the United States.

When arrested early in 2009, Madoff had processed over the years about $50 billion—that is $50 *billion*, not $50 million! Some (not all) of the early investors received annual interest, but the vast majority of all investors were simply told by Madoff that their money was safe with him. Madoff will spend the rest of his life in prison for his efforts. His scheme has been called the largest Ponzi scheme ever perpetrated in United States history. Madoff leaves in his crumbled wake hundreds of former friends and clients, several of whom are quite famous, such as New Jersey Senator Frank

*Bernard Madoff, master-mind of a massive "Ponzi" investment scam that bilked over $50 billion from unsuspecting investors.*

Brendan McDermid/Reuters/Landov

Lautenberg, Hall of Fame baseball pitcher Sandy Koufax, and actor John Malkovitch (*The New York Times* 2009). Many former clients lost everything—their life savings, retirement accounts, and other investments—so much so that many universities, charities, and other organizations have felt the weight of the pyramid's collapse.

## Organized Crime

The structure of crime and criminal activity in the United States often takes on an organized, almost institutional character. This is crime in the form of mob activity and racketeering, known as organized crime. Also, there are crimes committed by bureaucracies, known as corporate crime. Both types of crime are so highly organized, complex, and sophisticated that they take on the nature of social institutions.

**Organized crime** is crime committed by structured groups typically involving the provision of illegal goods and services to others. Organized crime syndicates are typically stereotyped as the Mafia, but the term can refer to any group that exercises control over large illegal enterprises, such as the drug trade, illegal gambling, prostitution, weapons smuggling, or money laundering. These organized crime syndicates are often based on racial, ethnic, or family ties, with different groups dominating and replacing each other in different criminal "industries," at different periods in U.S. history.

A key concept in sociological studies of organized crime is that these industries are organized along the same lines as legitimate businesses; indeed, organized crime has taken on a corporate form (Best 2007; Carter 1999). There are likely senior partners who control the profits of the business, workers who manage and provide the labor for the business, and clients who buy the services that organized crime provides, such as prostitution and drug dealing. In-depth studies of the organized-crime underworld are difficult, owing to its secretive nature and dangers. As organized crime has moved into seemingly legitimate corporate organizations, it is even more difficult to trace, although some sociologists have penetrated underworld networks and provided fascinating accounts of how these crime networks are organized (Carter 1999).

## Corporate Crime and Deviance: Doing Well, Doing Time

Corporations and even entire governments may engage in deviance—behavior that can be very costly to society. Sociologists estimate that the costs of corporate crime may be as high as $200 billion every year, dwarfing the take from street crime (roughly $15 billion), which most people imagine is the bulk of criminal activity. Tax cheaters in business alone probably skim $50 billion a year from the IRS, three times the value of street crime. Taken as a whole, the cost of corporate crime is almost 6000 times the amount taken in bank robberies in a given year and 11 times the total amount for all theft in a year (Reiman 2007).

*Corporate crime and deviance* is wrongdoing that occurs within the context of a formal organization or bureaucracy and is actually sanctioned by the norms and operating principles of the bureaucracy (Simon 2007).

*This dinner gathering of HBO's long-running "Sopranos" gang illustrates both the hierarchy and group cohesion that characterizes organized crime.*

This can occur within any kind of organization—corporate, educational, governmental, or religious. It exists once deviant behavior becomes institutionalized in the routine procedures of an organization. Sociological studies of corporate deviance show that this form of deviance is embedded in the ongoing and routine activities of organizations (Punch 1996; Lee and Ermann 1999). Individuals within the organization may participate in the deviant behavior with little awareness that their behavior is illegitimate. In fact, their actions are likely to be defined as in the best interests of the organization—business as usual. New members who enter the organization learn to comply with the organizational expectations or leave.

Instead of conceptualizing organizational deviance as merely the behavior of bad individuals, sociologists see it as the result of employees following rules and making decisions in more ordinary ways.

A recent example of corporate and accounting malfeasance involved the WorldCom Corporation, a telecommunications company of worldwide repute. The company engaged in a multimillion dollar accounting fraud that disguised mounting losses from early in the year 2000 through the summer of 2002. By incorrectly reporting its operating expenses as though they were capital gains—again, employing illegal accounting—the company was able to inflate the value of its own stock even though its own finances were rapidly deteriorating (Eichenwald 2002; Costello 2004).

## Race, Class, Gender, and Crime

Arrest data show a clear pattern of differential arrests along lines of race, gender, and class. To sociologists the central question posed by such data is whether this reflects actual differences in the extent of crime among different groups or whether this reflects differential treatment by the criminal justice system. The answer is "both" (D'Alissio and Stolzenberg 2003).

Certain groups are more likely to commit crime than others, because crime is distinctively linked to patterns of inequality in society. Unemployment, for example, is one correlate of crime, as is poverty. For example, there is a clear link between the likelihood of lethal violence and the socioeconomic conditions for Latinos in urban areas (Martinez 2002).

Sociologists also show that prosecution by the criminal justice system is significantly related to patterns of race, gender, and class inequality. We see this in the bias of official arrest statistics, in treatment by the police, in patterns of sentencing, and in studies of imprisonment.

Arrest statistics show a strong correlation between social class and crime, the poor being more likely than others to be arrested for crimes. Does this mean that the poor commit more crimes? To some extent, yes. Unemployment and poverty are related to crime (Best 2007; Reiman 2007; Scarpitti et al. 1997; Hagan 1993; Britt 1994; M. Smith et al. 1992). The reason is simple: Those who are economically deprived often see no alternative to crime, as Merton's structural strain theory would predict.

Moreover, law enforcement is concentrated in lower income and minority areas. People who are better off are further removed from police scrutiny and better able to hide their crimes. When and if white-collar criminals are prosecuted and convicted, with few exceptions they typically receive light sentences—often a fine or community service instead of imprisonment. Middle- and upper-income people may be perceived as being less in need of imprisonment because they likely have a job and high-status people to testify for their good character. And, white-collar crime is simply perceived as less threatening than crimes by the poor. Class also predicts who most likely will be victimized by crime, with those at the highest ends of the socioeconomic scale least likely to be victims of violent crime (see Figure 7.4).

Research shows that African Americans and Hispanics are more than twice as likely to be arrested for a crime than are Whites. Native Americans and Asians are exceptions, with both groups having relatively low rates of arrest for crime (Federal Bureau of Investigation 2006).

Bearing in mind the factors that affect the official rates of arrest and conviction—bias of official statistics, influence of powerful individuals, discrimination in patterns of arrest, differential policing—there remains evidence that the actual commission of crime varies by race. Why? Again, sociologists find a compelling explanation in social structural conditions. Racial minority groups are far more likely than Whites to be poor, unemployed, and living in single-parent families. These social facts are all predictors of a higher rate of crime. Note, too, as Figure 7.5 shows, that African Americans are generally more likely to be victimized by crime.

Generally, women commit fewer crimes than do men. Why? Although the number of women arrested for crime has increased slightly in recent years, the numbers are still small relative to men, except for a few crimes such as fraud, embezzlement, and prostitution. Some argue that women's lower crime participation reflects their socialization into less risk-taking roles; others say that women commit crimes that are extensions of their gender roles—this would explain why the largest number of arrests of women are for crimes such as shoplifting, credit card fraud, and passing bad checks.

Nonetheless, women's participation in crime has been increasing in recent years, the result of several factors. Women are now more likely to be employed in jobs that present opportunities for crimes, such as property theft, embezzlement, and fraud. Violent crime by women has also increased notably since the early 1980s, possibly because the images that women have of themselves are changing, making new behaviors possible. Most significant, crime by women is related to their continuing disadvantaged status in society. Just

Rate per 1000 persons
(age 12 and over)

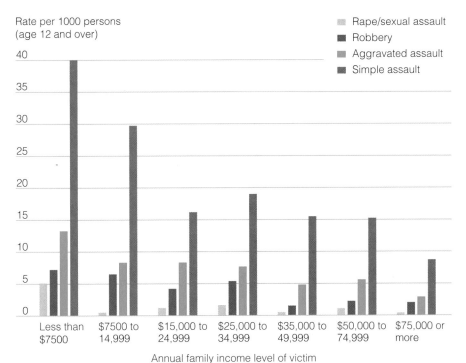

Legend:
- Rape/sexual assault
- Robbery
- Aggravated assault
- Simple assault

Annual family income level of victim

Income levels: Less than $7500, $7500 to 14,999, $15,000 to 24,999, $25,000 to 34,999, $35,000 to 49,999, $50,000 to 74,999, $75,000 or more

**FIGURE 7.4** *Victimization in Crime: A Class Phenomenon*

*Source:* U.S Bureau of Justice Statistics, 2008.

as crime is linked to socioeconomic status for men, so it is for women (Belknap 2001; Miller 1986).

Despite recent achievements, many women remain in disadvantaged, low-wage positions in the labor market. At the same time, changes in the social structure of families mean that more women are economically responsible for their children without the economic support of men. Disadvantaged women may turn to illegitimate means of support, a trend that may be exacerbated by reductions in welfare support.

## understanding diversity

## The Rich Get Richer and the Poor Get Prison

Jeffrey H. Reiman (2007) notes that the prison system in the United States, instead of serving as a way to rehabilitate criminals, is in effect designed to train and socialize inmates into a career of crime. It is also designed in such a way as to assure the public that crime is a threat primarily from the poor and that it originates at the lower rungs of society. This observation has also been made by Bruce Western (Reiman 2007). Reiman and Western note that prisons contain elements that seem designed to accomplish this view. One can "construct" a prison that ends up looking like a U.S. prison.

First, continue to label as criminals those who engage in crimes that have no unwilling victim, such as prostitution or gambling. Second, give prosecutors and judges broad discretion to arrest, convict, and sentence based on appearance, dress, race, and apparent social class. Third, treat prisoners in a painful and demeaning manner, as one might treat children. Fourth, make certain that prisoners are not trained in a marketable skill that would be useful upon their release. And, finally, assure that prisoners will forever be labeled and stigmatized as different from "decent citizens," even after they have paid their debt to society. Once an ex-con, always an ex-con. One has thus socially constructed a U.S. prison, an institution that will continue to generate the very thing that it claims to eliminate.

*Sources:* Reiman, Jeffrey H. 2007. *The Rich Get Richer and the Poor Get Prison.* 8th edition. Boston, MA: Allyn and Bacon; Western, Bruce. 2007. *Punishment and Inequality in America.* New York: Russell Sage Foundation.

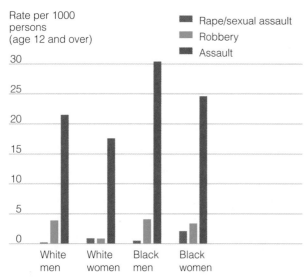

**FIGURE 7.5** *Crime Victimization (by race and gender)*

*Source:* U.S. Bureau of Justice Statistics. 2008.

Women are less likely than men to be victimized by crime, although victimization by crime among women varies significantly by race and age. Black women are much more likely than White women to be victims of violent crime; young Black women are especially vulnerable. Divorced, separated, and single women are more likely than married women to be crime victims.

For all women, victimization by rape is probably the greatest fear. Although rape is the most underreported crime, until recently it has been one of the fastest growing—something criminologists explain as the result of a greater willingness to report *and* an actual increase in the extent of rape (Federal Bureau of Investigation 2006). More than 200,000 rapes (including attempted rapes) are reported to the police annually. Officials estimate that this is probably only about one in four of all rapes committed. Many women are reluctant to report rape because they fear the consequences of having the criminal justice system question them. Rape victims are least likely to report the assault when the assailant is someone known to them, even though a large number of rapes are committed by someone the victim knows.

A disturbingly frequent form of rape is *acquaintance rape*—rape committed by an acquaintance or someone the victim has just met. The extent of acquaintance rape is difficult to measure. The Bureau of Justice Statistics finds that 3 percent of college women experience rape or attempted rape in a given college year; 13 percent report being stalked (Fisher et al. 2000). Research finds that acquaintance rape is linked to men's acceptance of various rape myths (such as believing that a woman's "no" means "yes"), the use of alcohol, and the peer support that men receive in some all-male groups and organizations,

such as fraternities (Taylor et al. 2006; Ullman et al. 1999; Boeringer 1999; Belknap et al. 1999).

Sociologists have argued that the causes of rape lie in women's status in society—that women are treated as sexual objects for men's pleasure. The relationship between women's status and rape is also reflected in data revealing who is most likely to become a rape victim. African American women, Latinas, and poor women have the highest likelihood of being raped, as do women who are single, divorced, or separated. Young women are also more likely to be rape victims than older women (U.S. Bureau of Justice Statistics 2008). Sociologists interpret these patterns to mean that the most powerless women are also most subject to this form of violence.

## The Criminal Justice System: Police, Courts, and the Law

Whether it is in the police station, the courts, or prison, the factors of race, class, and gender are highly influential in the administration of justice in this society. Those in the most disadvantaged groups are more likely to be defined and identified as deviant independently of their behavior and, having encountered these systems of authority, are more likely to be detained and arrested, found guilty, and punished.

## Debunking Society's Myths

**Myth:** The criminal justice system treats all people according to the neutral principles of law.

**Sociological perspective:** Race, class, and gender continue to have an influential role in the administration of justice. For example, even when convicted of the same crime as Whites, African American and Latino male defendants with the *same* prior arrest record as Whites are more likely to be arrested, sentenced, and to be sentenced for longer terms than White defendants.

**The Policing of Minorities.** There is little question that minority communities are policed more heavily than White neighborhoods; moreover, policing in minority communities has a different effect from that in White, middle-class communities. To middle-class Whites, the presence of the police is generally reassuring, but for African Americans and Latinos an encounter with a police officer can be terrifying. Regardless of what they are doing at the time, minority people, men in particular, are perceived as a threat, especially if they are observed in communities where they "don't belong."

Racial profiling has recently come to the public's attention, although it is a practice that has a long history. Often referred to half in jest by African Americans as the offense of "DWB," or "driving while Black," **racial profiling** on the part of a police officer is the use of race alone as the criterion for deciding whether to stop and detain someone on suspicion of their having committed a crime. The police argue that racial profiling is justified because a high proportion of Blacks and Hispanics commit crimes; but, although the crime rate for Blacks and Hispanics is higher than that of Whites, race is a particularly bad basis for suspicion because the vast majority of Blacks and Hispanics, like the vast majority of Whites, do not commit any crime at all. As evidence of this, studies have found that *eight out of every ten* automobile searches carried out by state troopers on the New Jersey Turnpike over ten years were conducted on vehicles driven by Blacks and Hispanics; the vast majority of these searches turned up no evidence of contraband or crimes of any sort (Kocieniewski and Hanley 2000; Cole 1999).

Racial minorities are also more likely than the rest of the population to be victims of excessive use of force by the police, also called police brutality. Most cases of police brutality involve minority citizens, and there is usually no penalty for the officers involved. Increasing the number of minority police officers has some effect on how the police treat minorities. Simply increasing the number of African Americans in police departments does not, however, reduce crime dramatically, because it does not change the material conditions that create crime to begin with (Cashmore 1991).

**Race and Sentencing.** What happens once minority citizens are arrested for a crime? Bail is set higher for African Americans and Latinos than for Whites, and minorities have less success with plea bargains. Once on trial, minority defendants are found guilty more often than White defendants. At sentencing, African Americans and Hispanics are likely to get longer sentences than Whites, even when they have the same number of prior arrests and socioeconomic background as Whites. Young African American men, as well as Latino men, are sentenced more harshly than any other group, and once sentenced they are less likely to be released on probation (Western 2007; Steffensmeier and Demuth 2000; Mauer 1999; Steffensmeier et al. 1998; Chambliss and Taylor 1989; Bridges and Crutchfield 1988). In fact Blacks and Hispanics who have *already received* the death penalty are more likely to be executed, rather than being pardoned or having the execution postponed, than are Whites who have committed the same crime (Jacobs et al. 2007). Any number of factors influence judgments about sentencing, including race of the judge, severity of the crime, race of the victim, and the gender of the defendant, but throughout these studies, race is shown to consistently matter—and matter a lot.

**Prisons: Rehabilitation or Mass Racialized Incarceration?** Racial minorities account for *more than half* of the federal and state male prisoners in the United States. Blacks have the highest rates of imprisonment, followed by Hispanics, then Native Americans and Asians. (Native Americans and Asian Americans together are less than 1 percent of the total prison population.) Hispanics are the fastest growing minority group in prison (U.S. Bureau of Justice Statistics 2008). Native Americans, though a small proportion of the prison population, are still overrepresented in prisons. In theory, the criminal justice system is supposed to be unbiased, able to objectively weigh guilt and innocence. The reality is that the criminal justice system reflects the racial and class stratification and biases in society.

The United States and Russia have the highest rate of incarceration in the world (see Figure 7.6). In the United States, the rate of imprisonment has been rapidly growing (see Figure 7.7). By all signs, the population of state and federal prisons continues to grow, with the population in prisons exceeding the capacity of the facilities. The cost to the nation of keeping people behind bars is at least $160 billion (U.S. Bureau of Justice Statistics 2008).

Although it is certainly true that, as we have already noted, Blacks and Hispanics themselves commit proportionately more crime than Asians and Native American Indians, it is nonetheless *also* demonstrably true that the structure of the U.S. criminal justice system disproportionately *propels* Blacks and Hispanics into prison at a greater rate than same-aged Whites who have the same criminal record. This is because unemployment is much higher for Blacks and Hispanics. Also, federal and state officials have traditionally been more hostile to persons of color who run afoul of the criminal justice system than to Whites who do so. Finally, the "three strikes" law (giving mandatory long sentences if caught three times for the same drug offense) disproportionately affects minorities of color. The situation is so severe and there are so many minority persons now in prison that sociologist Bruce Western calls them a *new color caste* in U.S. society—in other words, a society unto itself (Western 2007).

The picture of incarceration in the United States seems contradictory. The overall violent crime rate has declined (see Figure 7.3); this would cause us to expect that the rate of admissions to prison would also decline. Yet, at the same time, the numbers of individuals in state and federal prisons have been increasing (Figure 7.7). Why is there such growth in the prison population when the crime rate has been declining? A major reason for the increasing number of individuals behind bars is the increased enforcement of drug offenses and the mandatory sentencing that has been introduced. Nearly one-quarter of those in state prisons are serving a drug sentence (U.S. Bureau of Justice Statistics 2008).

Women in prison face unique problems, in part because they are in a system designed for men and run mostly by men, which tends to ignore the particular needs of women. For example, 25 percent of the women entering prison are pregnant or have just given birth,

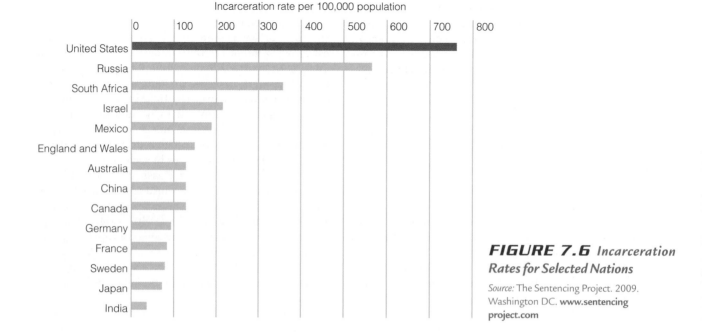

Incarceration rate per 100,000 population

***FIGURE 7.6*** *Incarceration Rates for Selected Nations*

*Source:* The Sentencing Project. 2009. Washington DC. **www.sentencing project.com**

but they often get no prenatal or obstetric care. Male prisoners are trained for such jobs as auto mechanics, whereas women are more likely to be trained in relatively lower-status jobs such as beauticians and launderers. The result is that few women offenders are rehabilitated by their experience in prison.

The United States, then, is putting offenders in prison at a record pace. Is crime being deterred? Are prisoners being rehabilitated? Or are they simply being *warehoused*—put on a shelf? If the deterrence argument were correct, we would expect that increasing the risk of imprisonment would lower the rate of crime. For example, we would expect drug use to decline as enforcement of drug laws increases. In the past few years, there has been a marked increase in drug law enforcement but not the expected decrease in drug use. Using drugs as an example, then, it appears that the threat of imprisonment does not deter crime (Mauer 1999).

There is also little evidence that the criminal justice system rehabilitates offenders. Using drugs as the example again, only about 20 percent of those

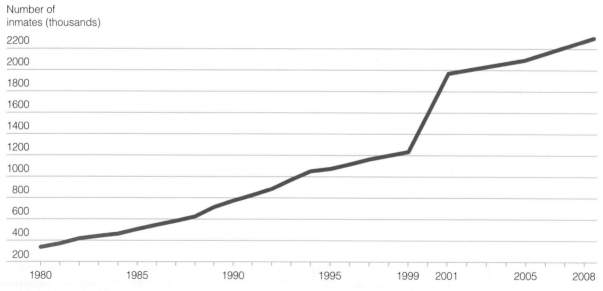

***FIGURE 7.7*** *State and Federal Prison Population, 1980–2008*

*Source:* U.S. Bureau of Justice Statistics. 2008. *"Prison and Jail Inmates."* **www.ojp.usdoj.gov/bjs/prisons.html**

imprisoned for drug offenses ever receive drug treatment. If the criminal justice system fails to reduce crime, what does it do? Some sociologists contend that the criminal justice system is not meant to reduce crime but has other *functions*, namely, to reinforce an image of crime as a threat from the poor and from racial groups.

# Terrorism as International Crime: A Global Perspective

Crime now crosses international borders and has become global, as we see with terrorism.

The FBI includes *terrorism* in its definition of crime, seeing it as violent action to achieve political ends (White 2002). Thus, terrorism is a crime that violates both international and domestic laws. It is a crime that crosses national borders and to understand it requires a global perspective.

Terrorism is globally linked to other forms of international crime. A case in point was Osama bin Laden's role in the international opium trade. Afghanistan, where bin Laden's terrorist al Qaeda organization was headquartered, was the world's largest grower of opium-producing poppies. It is suspected that profits from the international drug trade helped finance the September 11 terrorist attacks. Therefore, a global perspective on crime involves recognizing the global basis of some international crime networks that cross national borders (Binns 2003).

Many nations have long experienced terrorism in the form of bombings, hijackings, suicide attacks, and other terrorist crimes. But the attacks of September 11 focused the world's attention on the problem of terrorism in new ways, including increased fears of **bioterrorism**—the form of terrorism involving the dispersion of chemical or biological substances intended to cause widespread disease and death.

*Terrorists crashed two jets into the World Trade Center on September of 2001, causing the total collapse of both towers and killing over 3,000 people.*

Moshe Bursuker/AP Photo

Another form of terrorism, and thus cause for international concern, is **cyberterrorism,** the use of the computer to commit one or more terrorist acts. Terrorists may use computers in a number of ways. Data-destroying computer viruses may be implanted electronically in an enemy's computer. Another use would be to employ "logic bombs" that lie dormant for years until they are electronically instructed to overwhelm a computer system. The use of the Internet to serve the needs of international terrorists has already become a reality (Jucha 2002).

Without understanding the political, economic, and social relations from which terrorist groups originate, terrorist acts seem like the crazed behavior of violent single individuals. Although sociologists in no way excuse such acts, they look to the social structure of conflicts from which terrorism emerges as the cause of such criminal and deviant behavior.

# Chapter Summary

- ### What is the difference between deviance and crime?

  *Deviance* is behavior that violates norms and rules of society, and *crime* is a type of deviant behavior that violates the formal criminal law. *Criminology* is the study of crime from a scientific perspective.

- ### How do sociologists conceptualize and explain deviance and crime?

  Deviance is behavior that is recognized as violating expected rules and norms and that should be understood in the social context in which it occurs. Psychological explanations of deviance place the cause of deviance primarily within the individual. Sociologists emphasize the total social context in which deviance occurs. Sociologists see deviance more as the result of group and institutional, not individual, behavior.

- **What does sociological theory contribute to the study of deviance and crime?**

  *Functionalist theory* sees both deviance and crime as functional for the society because it affirms what is acceptable by defining what is not. *Structural strain theory,* a type of functionalist theory, predicts that societal inequalities actually force and compel the individual into deviant and criminal behavior. *Conflict theory* explains deviance and crime as a consequence of unequal power relationships and inequality in society. *Symbolic interaction theory* explains deviance and crime as the result of meanings people give to various behaviors. *Differential association theory,* a type of symbolic interaction theory, interprets deviance as behavior learned through social interaction with other deviants. *Labeling theory,* also a type of symbolic interaction theory, argues that societal reactions to behavior produce deviance, with some groups having more power than others to assign deviant labels to people.

- **What are the major forms of deviance?**

  Mental illness, *stigma,* and substance abuse are major forms of deviance studied by sociologists, although deviance comprises many different forms of behavior. Sociological explanations of mental illness focus on the social context in which mental illness develops and is treated. Social *stigmas* are attributes that are socially devalued. Substance abuse includes alcohol and drug abuse but is not limited to these two forms.

- **What are the connections between inequality, deviance, and crime?**

  Sociological studies of crime analyze the various types of crimes, such as *elite crime, organized crime, corporate crime,* and *personal* and *property crimes.* Many types of crimes are underreported, such as rape and certain elite and corporate crimes. Sociologists study the conditions, including race, class, and gender inequality, that produce crime and shape how different groups are treated by the criminal justice system, such as showing group differences in sentencing.

- **How is crime related to race, class, and gender?**

  In general, crime rates for a variety of crimes are higher among minorities than among Whites, among poorer persons than among middle- or upper-class persons, and among men than among women. Women, especially minority women, are more likely to be victimized by serious crimes such as rape or violence from a spouse or boyfriend.

- **How is globalization affecting the development of deviance and crime?**

  International *terrorism* is a crime, and crime is thus global. Other global crimes of significance are *bioterrorism* and *cyberterrorism.* Osama bin Laden's al Qaeda organization, assumed to be the organization that destroyed the World Trade Center and killed over 3000 individuals, was centered in Afghanistan and was central to the international drug trade. Thus, crimes are clearly not just the acts of a crazed individual or small group of individuals, but the result of structural and cultural conditions.

# Key Terms

altruistic suicide  156
anomic suicide  156
anomie  155
bioterrorism  175
crime  165
criminology  166
cyberterrorism  175
deviance  152
deviant career  162
deviant communities  163
deviant identity  162

differential association
  theory  161
egoistic suicide  156
elite deviance  160
hate crime  168
index crimes  166
labeling theory  161
master status  165
medicalization of deviance  154
organized crime  169
personal crimes  168

Ponzi scheme  168
property crimes  168
racial profiling  172
social control  160
social control agents  160
social control theory  159
stigma  164
structural strain theory  157
victimless crimes  168

## Online Resources

### *Sociology: The Essentials* Companion Website

**www.cengage.com/sociology/andersen**
Visit your book companion website where you will find more resources to help you study and write your research papers. Resources include web links, learning objectives, Internet exercises, quizzing, and flash cards.

 **is an easy-to-use online resource that helps you study in less time to get the grade you want NOW.**

**www.cengage.com/login**
Need help studying? This site is your one-stop study shop. Take a Pre-Test and Cengage NOW will generate a Personalized Study Plan based on your test results. The Study Plan will identify the topics you need to review and direct you to online resources to help you master those topics. You can then take a Post-Test to determine the concepts you have mastered and what you still need to work on.

8

Chapter eight
CHAPTER EIGHT
chapter

# Social Class and Social Stratification

*Beth A. Keiser/AP Photo*

[ *One afternoon in* a major U.S. city, two women go shopping. They are friends—wealthy, suburban women who shop for leisure. They meet in a gourmet restaurant and eat imported foods while discussing their children's private schools. They also talk about the volunteer work they do in the local hospital, but they don't worry too much about their own health care, at least not financially, because both are fully covered through ample health insurance policies. After lunch, they spend the afternoon in exquisite stores—some of them large, elegant department stores; others, intimate boutiques where the staff know them by name. When one of the women stops to use the bathroom in one store, she enters a beautifully furnished room with an upholstered chair, a marble sink with brass faucets, fresh flowers on a wooden pedestal, shining mirrors, an ample supply of hand towels, and jars of lotion and soaps. The toilet is in a private stall with solid doors. In the stall there is soft toilet paper and another small vase of flowers.

The same day, in a different part of town, another woman goes shopping. She lives on a marginal income earned as a stitcher in a textiles factory. Her daughter badly needs a new pair of shoes because she has outgrown last year's pair. The woman goes to a nearby discount store where she hopes to find a pair of shoes for under $15, but she dreads the experience. She knows her

*continued*

daughter would like other new things—a bathing suit for the summer, a pair of jeans, and a blouse. But this summer the daughter will have to wear hand-me-downs because medical bills over the winter have depleted the little money left after food and rent. For the mother, shopping is not recreation but a bitter chore reminding her of the things she is unable to get for her daughter.

While this woman is shopping, she, too, stops to use the bathroom. She enters a vast space with sinks and mirrors lined up on one side of the room and several stalls on the other. The tile floor is gritty and gray. The locks on the stall doors are missing or broken. Some of the overhead lights are burned out, so the room has dark shadows. In the stall, the toilet paper is coarse. When the woman washes her hands, she discovers there is no soap in the metal dispensers. The mirror before her is cracked. She exits quickly, feeling as though she is being watched.

Two scenarios, one society. The difference is the mark of a society built upon class inequality. The signs are all around you. Think about the clothing you wear. Are some labels worth more than others? Do others in your group see the same marks of distinction and status in clothing labels? Do some people you know never seem to wear the "right" labels? Whether it is clothing, bathrooms, schools, homes, or access to health care, the effect of class inequality is enormous, giving privileges and resources to some and leaving others struggling to get by.

Great inequality divides society. Nevertheless, most people think that in the United States equal opportunity exists for all. The tendency is to blame individuals for their own failure or attribute success to individual achievement. Many people think the poor are lazy and do not value work. At the same time, the rich are often admired for their supposed initiative, drive, and motivation. Neither is an accurate portrayal. There are many hard-working individuals who are poor, and most rich people have inherited their wealth rather than earned it themselves.

Observing and analyzing class inequality is fundamental to sociological study. What features of society cause different groups to have different opportunities? Why is there such an unequal allocation of society's resources? Sociologists respect individual achievements but have found the greatest cause for the disparities in material success is the organization of society. Instead of understanding inequality as the result of individual effort, sociologists thus study the social structural origins of inequality.

# Social Differentiation and Social Stratification

All social groups and societies exhibit social differentiation. **Status,** as we have seen earlier, is a socially defined position in a group or society. **Social differentiation** is the process by which different statuses develop in any group, organization, or society. Think of a sports organization. The players, the owners, the managers, the fans, the cheerleaders, and the sponsors all have a different status within the organization. Together they constitute a whole social system, one that is marked by social differentiation.

## *thinking sociologically*

Take a shopping trip to different stores and observe the appearance of stores serving different economic groups. What kinds of bathrooms are there in stores catering to middle-class clients? The rich? The working class? The poor? Which ones allow the most privacy or provide the nicest amenities? What fixtures are in the display areas? Are they simply utilitarian with minimal ornamentation, or are they opulent displays of consumption? Take detailed notes of your observations, and write an analysis of what this tells you about *social class* in the United States.

Status differences can become organized into a hierarchical social system. Social stratification is a relatively fixed, hierarchical arrangement in society by which groups have different access to resources, power, and perceived social worth. **Social stratification** is a system of structured social inequality. Using sports as an example again, you can see that many of the players earn extremely high salaries, although most do not. Those who do are among the elite in this system of inequality. But it is the owners who control the resources of the teams and hold the most power in this system. Sponsors (including major corporations and media networks) are the economic engines on which this system of stratification rests; fans are merely observers who pay to watch the teams play, but the revenue they generate is essential for keeping this system intact. Altogether, sports are systems of stratification because the groups that constitute the organization are arranged in a hierarchy where some have more resources and power than others. Some provide resources; others take them. And, even within the field of sports, there are huge differences in which teams—and which sports—are among the elite.

All societies seem to have a system of social stratification, although they vary in the degree and complexity of stratification. Some societies stratify only along a single dimension, such as age, keeping the stratification system relatively simple. Most contemporary societies are more complex, with many factors interacting to create different social strata. In the United States,

| **table8.1** | **Inequality in the United States** |
|---|---|

Almost one in five (18 percent) children in the United States lives in poverty, including 35 percent of African American children, 29 percent of Hispanic children, 10 percent of White children, and 12 percent of Asian American children (DeNavas-Walt et al. 2008).

The rate of poverty among people in the United States has been steadily increasing since 2000 (DeNavas-Walt et al. 2008).

Among women heading their own households, 31 percent live below the poverty line (DeNavas-Walt et al. 2008).

One percent of the U.S. population controls 33 percent of the total wealth in the nation; the bottom 20 percent owe more than they own (Mishel et al. 2007).

When Leona Helmsley (the hotel financier) died, she left a $12 million inheritance to her dog, with the provision that the dog should eventually be buried in a mausoleum with Helmsley—a mausoleum that would be steam-cleaned once per week in perpetuity.

The average CEO of a major company has a salary of $13.1 million per year; workers earning the minimum wage make $10,712 per year if they work 40 hours a week for 52 weeks and hold only one job (Lavelle 2001).

social stratification is strongly influenced by class, which is in turn influenced by matters such as one's occupation, income, and education, along with race, gender, and other influences such as age, region of residence, ethnicity, and national origin (see Table 8.1).

## Estate, Caste, and Class

Stratification systems can be broadly categorized into three types: estate systems, caste systems, and class systems. In an **estate system** of stratification, the ownership of property and the exercise of power is monopolized by an elite who have total control over societal resources. Historically, such societies were feudal systems where classes were differentiated into three basic groups—the nobles, the priesthood, and the commoners. Commoners included peasants (usually the largest class group), small merchants, artisans, domestic workers, and traders. The nobles controlled the land and the resources used to cultivate the land, as well as all the resources resulting from peasant labor.

Estate systems of stratification are most common in agricultural societies. Although such societies have been largely supplanted by industrialization, there are still examples of societies that have a small but powerful landholding class ruling over a population that works mainly in agricultural production. Unlike the feudal societies of the European Middle Ages, however, contemporary estate systems of stratification display the influence of international capitalism. The "noble class" comprises not knights who conquered lands in war, but international capitalists or local elites who control the labor of a vast and impoverished group of people, such as in some South American societies where landholding elites maintain a dictatorship over peasants who labor in agricultural fields.

In a **caste system,** one's place in the stratification system is an *ascribed status* (see Chapter 5), meaning it is a quality given to an individual by circumstances of birth. The hierarchy of classes is rigid in caste systems and is often preserved through formal law and cultural practices that prevent free association and

*Social class differences make it seem as if some people are practically living in two different societies.*

© Tony Freeman/PhotoEdit

SUNNYphotography.com/Alamy

movement between classes. The system of *apartheid* in South Africa was a stark example of a caste system. Under apartheid, the travel, employment, associations, and place of residence of Black South Africans were severely restricted. Segregation was enforced using a pass system in which Black South Africans could not be in White areas unless for purposes of employment; those found without passes were arrested, often sent to prison without ever seeing their families again. Interracial marriage was illegal. Black South Africans were prohibited from voting; the system was one of total social control where anyone who protested was imprisoned. The apartheid system was overthrown in 1994 when Nelson Mandela, held prisoner for 27 years of his life, was elected president of the new nation of South Africa; a new national constitution guaranteeing equal rights to all was ratified in 1996.

In **class systems,** stratification exists, but a person's placement in the class system can change according to personal achievements; that is, class depends to some degree on *achieved status,* defined as status that is earned by the acquisition of resources and power, regardless of one's origins. Class systems are more open than caste systems because position does not depend strictly on birth, and classes are less rigidly defined than castes because the divisions are blurred by those who move between one class and the next.

Despite the potential for movement from one class to another, in the class system found in the United States, class placement still depends heavily on one's social background. Although ascription (the designation of ascribed status according to birth) is not the basis for social stratification in the United States, the class a person is born into has major consequences for that person's life. Patterns of inheritance; access to exclusive educational resources; the financial, political, and social influence of one's family; and similar factors

all shape one's likelihood of achievement. Although there is no formal obstacle to movement through the class system, individual achievement is very much shaped by an individual's class of origin.

## Defining Class

In common terms, *class* refers to style or sophistication. In sociological use, **social class** (or *class*) is the social structural position groups hold relative to the economic, social, political, and cultural resources of society. Class determines the access different people have to these resources and puts groups in different positions of privilege and disadvantage. Each class has members with similar opportunities who tend to share a common way of life. Class also includes a cultural component in that class shapes language, dress, mannerisms, taste, and other preferences. *Class is not just an attribute of individuals; it is a feature of society.*

The social theorist Max Weber described the consequences of stratification in terms of **life chances,** meaning the opportunities that people have in common by virtue of belonging to a particular class. Life chances include the opportunity for possessing goods, having an income, and having access to particular jobs. Life chances are also reflected in the quality of everyday life. Whether you dress in the latest style or wear another person's discarded clothes, have a vacation in an exclusive resort, take your family to the beach for a week, or have no vacation at all, these life chances are the result of being in a particular class.

Class is a structural phenomenon; it cannot be directly observed. Nonetheless, you can "see" class through various displays that people project, often unintentionally, about their class status. What clothing do you wear? Do some worn objects project higher class status than others? How about cars? What class status is displayed through the car you drive or, for that

*Recovery from Hurricane Katrina was not easy for anyone, but the likelihood of recovery was shaped by race in in combination with class, evidenced in the progress in different neighborhoods, even several years after this massive disaster.*

Carolyn Kaster/AP Photo

Eric Gay/AP Photo

matter, whether you even have a car or use a bus to get to work? In these and myriad other ways, class is projected to others as a symbol of our presumed worth in society.

Social class can be observed in the everyday habits and presentations of self that people project. Common objects, such as clothing and cars, become symbols of one's class status. As such, they can be ranked not only in terms of their economic value, but also in terms of the status that various brands and labels carry. The interesting thing about social class is that a particular object may be quite ordinary, but with the right "label" it becomes a *status symbol* and thus becomes valuable. Take the example of Vera Bradley bags. These paisley bags are made of ordinary cotton with batting. Not long ago, such cloth was cheap and commonplace, associated with rural, working-class women. If such a bag were sewn and carried by a poor person living on a farm, the bag (and perhaps the person!) would be seen as ordinary, almost worthless. But, transformed by the right label (and some good marketing), Vera Bradley bags have become status symbols, selling for a high price (often a few hundred dollars—a price one would never pay for a simple cotton purse). Presumably, having such a bag denotes the status of the person carrying it. (See also the box "See for Yourself: Status Symbols in Everyday Life.")

Jeff Greenberg/Alamy

*Status symbols connote class status because of the meaning people attach to them, not necessarily their actual value.*

is income; other common indicators are education, occupation, and place of residence. These indicators alone do not define class, but they are often accurate measures of the class standing of a person or group. We will see that these indicators tend to be linked. A good income, for example, makes it possible to afford a house in a prestigious neighborhood and an exclusive education for one's children. In the sociological study of class, indicators such as income and education have had enormous value in revealing the outlines and influences of the class system.

## The Class Structure of the United States

The class structure of the United States is elaborate, arising from the interactions of old wealth, new wealth, intensive immigration, a culture of entrepreneurship and individualism, and in recent times, vigorous globalization. One can conceptualize the class system as a ladder, with different class groups arrayed up and down the rungs, each rung corresponding to a different level in the class system. Conceptualized this way, social class is the common position groups hold in a status hierarchy (Wright 1979; Lucal 1994); class is indicated by factors such as levels of income, occupational standing, and educational attainment. People are relatively high or low on the ladder depending on the resources they have and whether those resources are education, income, occupation, or any of the other factors known to influence people's placement (or ranking) in the stratification system. Indeed, an abundance of sociological research has stemmed from the concept of **status attainment,** the process by which people end up in a given position in the stratification

### SEE *FOR YOURSELF*

#### *STATUS SYMBOLS IN EVERYDAY LIFE*

You can observe the everyday reality of social class by noting the status that different ordinary objects have within the context of a class system. Make a list of every car brand you can think of—or, if you prefer, every clothing label. Then rank your list with the highest status brand (or label) at the top of the list, going down to the lowest status. Then answer the following questions:

1. Where does the presumed value of this object come from? Does the value come from the actual cost of producing the object or something more subjective?

2. Do people make judgments about people wearing or driving the different brands you have noted? What judgments do they make? Why?

3. What consequences do you see (positive and negative) of the ranking you have observed? Who benefits from the ranking and who does not?

What does this exercise reveal about the influence of *status symbols* in society?

Because sociologists cannot isolate and measure social class directly, they use other indicators to serve as measures of class. A prominent indicator of class

# seeing society in *everyday life*

## Social Inequality

If you use your sociological imagination, you will begin to see the signs of social inequality in many places, including commonplace locations, such as shopping. Sociologist Christine Williams noted this in her research for the book, *Inside Toyland*, where she studied the influence of class, race, and gender in the different experiences of shopping in a "big box" toy store compared with shopping in a boutique toy store. Where do you see class inequality in your everyday life?

Thomas Barwick/Getty Images

Don Ryan/AP Photo

### How does the experience of shopping vary by social class?

Of course, everybody loves a bargain, but social class inequality means that people will have very different experiences. For some, shopping is a cruel reminder of their class status; for others, it may be a form of leisure and a mark of their higher status. For the upper-class shopper, shopping is likely to be more personal and accommodating.

Rob Kim/Landov

Richard Vogel/AP Photo

### How are status symbols related to the process of globalization?

Although globalization may not be immediately visible, many of the products by which people in one place accrue status are linked to the low status of workers in other nations. This is known as the global assembly line.

Michael Newman/PhotoEdit

Satchan/zefa/Corbis

**How does social class shape the *division of labor* in the workplace?**

Race and gender intersect with class to shape the division of labor. You can see this if you pay attention to who works where and in what capacity.

Andrew Holbrooke/Corbis News/Corbis

**How wide is the class gap in U.S. society?**

Differences in how people live are shaped by social class; class inequality has been growing in recent years, evidenced in part by differences in where and how people live.

Kareem Black/Getty Images

system. Status attainment research describes how factors such as class origins, educational level, and occupation produce class location.

This laddered model of class suggests that in the United States stratification is hierarchical but somewhat fluid. That is, the assumption is that people can move up and down different "rungs" of the ladder—or class system. In a relatively *open class system* such as the United States, people's achievements do matter, although the extent to which people rise rapidly and dramatically through the stratification system is less than the popular imagination envisions. Some people do begin from modest origins and amass great wealth and influence (celebrities such as Bill Gates, Oprah Winfrey, and millionaire athletes), but these are the exceptions, not the rule. Some people move down in the class system, but as we will see, most people remain relatively close to their class of origin. When people rise or fall in the class system, the distance they travel is usually relatively short, as we will see further in the section on social mobility.

The image of stratification as a laddered system, with different gradients of social standing, emphasizes that one's **socioeconomic status (SES)** is derived from certain factors. Income, occupational prestige, and education are the three measures of socioeconomic status that have been found to be most significant in determining people's placement in the stratification system.

**Income** is the amount of money a person receives in a given period. As we will see, income is distinct from **wealth,** which is the total value of what one owns, minus one's debts. The **median income** for a society is the midpoint of all household incomes. In other words, half of all households earn more than the median income; half earn less. In 2007, median household income in the United States was $50,233 (see Figure 8.1; DeNavas-Walt et al. 2008). Those bunched around the median income level are considered middle class, although sociologists debate which income brackets constitute middle-class standing because the range of what people think of as "middle class" is quite large. Nonetheless, income is a significant indicator of social class standing, although not the only one. Map 8.1 provides a visual image of regional differences in the distribution of income by showing median income in different parts of the country, organized by county.

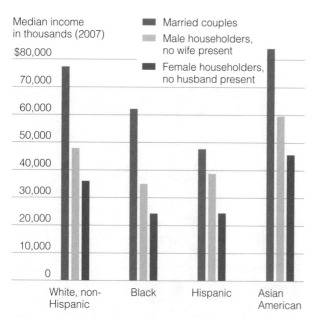

**FIGURE 8.1** *Median Annual Income by Race and Household Status*

*As illustrated in this graph, married couple households have the highest median income in all racial–ethnic groups; female-headed households, the least. The only households that reach median income status are White (non-Hispanic), African American, and Asian married households.*

Source: U.S. Census Bureau. 2008. *Current Population Survey,* Table FINC-02. Age of Reference Person, by Total Money Income in 2007, Type of Family, Race and Hispanic Origin of Reference Person. **www.census.gov**

## SEE *FOR YOURSELF*

### *INCOME DISTRIBUTION: SHOULD GRADES BE THE SAME?*

Figure 8.2 shows the income distribution with in the United States. Imagine that grades in your class were distributed based on the same curve. Let's suppose that after students arrived in class and sat down, different groups received their grades based on where they were sitting in the room and in the same proprtion as the U.S. income distribution. Only students in the front receive As; the back, Ds and Fs. The middle of the room gets the Bs and Cs. Write a short essay answering the following questions based on this hypothetical scenario.

1. How many students would receive As, Bs, Cs, Ds, and Fs?

2. Would it be fair to distribute grades this way? Why or why not?

3. Which groups in the class might be more likely to support such a distribution? Who would think the system of grade distribution should be changed?

4. What might different groups do to preserve or change the system of grade distribution? What if you really needed an A, but got one of the Fs? What might you do?

5. Are there circumstances in actual life that are beyond the control of people and that shape the distribution of income?

6. How is social stratification maintained by the beliefs that people have about merit and fairness?

*Adapted from:* Brislen, William, and Clayton D. Peoples. 2005. "Using a Hypothetical Distribution of Grades to Introduce Social Stratification." *Teaching Sociology* 33 (January): 74–80.

Percent of population
in each income quintile

Radius Images/PhotoLibrary

Ric Feld/AP Photo

*"It's a dog's life," or so the saying goes. But even dogs have their experiences shaped by the realities of social class.*

**FIGURE 8.2** *Income Distribution in the United States*

*This graph shows the percentage of the population that falls into each of the five income brackets.*

*Source:* DeNavas-Walt, Carmen, Bernadette Proctor, and Jessica C. Smith. 2008. *Income, Poverty, and Health Insurance Coverage in the United States: 2007.* Washington, DC: U.S. Census Bureau, #P60-235.

*Occupational prestige* is a second important indicator of socioeconomic status. **Prestige** is the value others assign to people and groups. **Occupational prestige** is the subjective evaluation people give to jobs. To determine occupational prestige, sociological researchers typically ask nationwide samples of adults to rank the general standing of a series of jobs. These subjective ratings provide information about how people perceive the worth of different occupations. People tend to rank professionals, such as physicians, professors, judges, and lawyers highly, with occupations such as electrician, insurance agent, and police officer falling in the middle. Occupations with low occupational prestige are maids, garbage collectors, and shoe-shiners (Nakao and Treas 2000; Davis and Smith 1984). These rankings do not reflect the worth of people within these positions but are indicative of the judgments people make about the worth of these jobs.

The final major indicator of socioeconomic status is **educational attainment,** typically measured as the total years of formal education. The more years of education attained, the more likely a person will have higher class status. The prestige attached to occupations is strongly tied to the amount of education the job requires; the more education people think is needed for a given occupation, the more occupational prestige people attribute to that job (Blau and Duncan 1967; MacKinnon and Langford 1994; Ollivier 2000).

## Layers of Social Class

Taken together, income, occupation, and education are good indicators of people's class standing. How

then do sociologists understand the array of classes in the United States? Most sociologists describe the class system in the United States as being divided into several classes: upper, upper middle, middle, lower middle, and lower class. The different classes are arrayed up and down, like a ladder, with those with the most money, education, and prestige on the top rungs and those with the least at the bottom.

In the United States, the *upper class* owns the major share of corporate and personal wealth; it includes those who have held wealth for generations as well as those who have recently become rich. Only a very small proportion of people actually constitute the upper class, but they control vast amounts of wealth and power in the United States. Those in this class are elites who exercise enormous control throughout society. Some wealthy individuals can wield as much power as entire nations (Friedman 1999).

Each year, the business magazine *Forbes* publishes a list of the 400 wealthiest families and individuals in the country. By 2007, you had to have at least $1.3 billion to be on the list! Bill Gates and Warren Buffet compete for being the richest person on this list; Gates has an estimated worth of $57 billion; Buffet, $50 billion, though some say now over $60 billion. Of all the wealth represented on the *Forbes 400* list, most is inherited, although there has been some increase in the number of people on the list with self-created wealth (Miller and Greenberg 2008). Still, the best predictor of future wealth is the family into which you are born.

Those in the upper class with newly acquired wealth are known as the *nouveau riche.* Luxury vehicles, high-priced real estate, and exclusive vacations may mark the lifestyle of the newly rich. Larry Ellison, who made his fortune as the founder of the software company Oracle, is the third wealthiest person in the United States; he has a megayacht that is 482

## map8.1 MAPPING AMERICA'S DIVERSITY

### Median Income in the United States

Median income range
measured in dollars
(2003)

- $9,243–23,750
- $23,848–33,006
- $33,026–41,183
- $41,201–53,804
- $53,945–82,929

*If you look closely at this map, you will see that median income tends to be higher in more urban areas. Thus, in 2007, median income inside metropolitan areas was $51,831 and outside such areas, $40,615. What the map does not show, however, are differences within cities. Median income inside central cities is substantially lower ($44,205) than the median income within metropolitan areas out of the center city ($57,444)—that is, in suburban areas. Given this, what do you conclude about the significance of residence in the structure of the class system?*

*Data:* U.S. Census Bureau. 2004. *American Fact Finder.* **www.census.gov.** U.S. Census Bureau. 2008. *Statistical Abstract of the United States 2008.* Washington, DC: U.S. Department of Commerce.

feet long, five stories high, with 82 rooms inside. The megayacht also includes an indoor swimming pool, a cinema, a space for a private submarine, and a basketball court that doubles as a helicopter launch pad.

The *upper middle-class* includes those with high incomes and high social prestige. They tend to be well-educated professionals or business executives. Their earnings can be quite high indeed, even millions of

*Social class influences many things, including the leisure time people experience. Few can even imagine having something like the yacht pictured on the left, owned by Larry Ellison, founder of Oracle.*

dollars a year. It is difficult to estimate exactly how many people fall into this group because of the difficulty of drawing lines between the upper, upper middle, and middle classes. Indeed, the upper middle-class is often thought of as "middle class" because their lifestyle sets the standard to which many aspire, but this lifestyle is actually unattainable by most. A large home full of top-quality furniture and modern appliances, two or three relatively new cars, vacations every year (perhaps a vacation home), high-quality college education for one's children, and a fashionable wardrobe are simply beyond the means of a majority of people in the United States.

The *middle-class* is hard to define in part because being "middle class" is more than just economic position. A very large portion of Americans identify themselves as middle class even though they vary widely in lifestyle and in resources at their disposal. But the idea that the United States is an open class system leads many to think that the majority have a middle-class lifestyle; thus, the middle class becomes the ubiquitous norm even though many who call themselves middle class have a tenuous hold on this class position.

The *lower middle-class* includes workers in the skilled trades and low-income bureaucratic workers, many of whom may actually think they are middle class. Also known as the *working class,* this class includes blue-collar workers (those in skilled trades who do manual labor) and many service workers, such as secretaries, hair stylists, food servers, police, and firefighters. A medium to low income, education, and occupational prestige define the lower middle-class relative to the class groups above it. The term *lower* in this class designation refers to the relative position of the group in the stratification system, but it has a pejorative sound to many people, especially to people who are members of this class, many of whom think of themselves as middle class.

The *lower class* is composed primarily of displaced and poor. People in this class have little formal education and are often unemployed or working in minimum-wage jobs. People of color and women make up a disproportionate part of this class. The poor include the *working poor*—those who work at least 27 hours a week but whose wages fall below the federal poverty level. Six percent of all working people now live below the poverty line, a proportion that has generally increased over time. Among White workers, men and women are nearly equivalent in the likelihood of being among the working poor, but among African American workers, Black women are almost twice as likely as Black men to be among the working poor (U.S. Bureau of Labor Statistics 2008).

The concept of the **urban underclass** has been added to the lower class (Wilson 1987). The underclass includes those who are likely to be permanently unemployed and without much means of economic support. The underclass has little or no opportunity for movement out of the worst poverty. Rejected from the economic system, those in the underclass may become dependent on public assistance or illegal activities. Structural transformations in the economy have left large groups of people, especially urban minorities, in these highly vulnerable positions. The growth of the urban underclass has exacerbated the problems of urban poverty and related social problems (Wilson 1996, 1987).

## Class Conflict

Derived from the early work of Karl Marx, sociologists also analyze class according to the perspective of conflict theory. Conflict theory defines classes in terms of their structural relationship to other classes and their relationship to the economic system. The analysis of class from this sociological perspective interprets inequality as resulting from the unequal distribution of power and resources in society (see Chapter 1). Sociologists who work from a conflict perspective see the classes as facing off against each other, with elites exploiting and dominating others. The key idea in this model is that class is not simply a matter of what individuals possess in terms of income and prestige; instead, class is defined by the relationship of the classes to the larger system of economic production (Vanneman and Cannon 1987; Wright 1985).

From a conflict perspective, the middle class, or the *professional–managerial class,* includes managers, supervisors, and professionals. Members of this group have substantial control over other people, primarily through their authority to direct the work of others, impose and enforce regulations in the workplace, and determine dominant social values. Although, as Marx argued, the middle class is controlled by the ruling class, members of this class tend to identify with the interests of the elite. The professional–managerial class, however, is caught in a contradictory position between elites and the working class. Like elites, those in this class have some control over others, but like the working class, they have minimal control over the economic system (Wright 1979). Karl Marx argued that as capitalism progresses, more and more of those in the middle class drop into the working class as they are pushed out of managerial jobs into working-class jobs or as professional jobs become organized more along the lines of traditional working-class employment.

Has this happened? Not to the extent Marx predicted. He thought that ultimately there would be only two classes—the capitalist and the proletariat. To some extent, however, this is occurring. Classes have become more polarized, with the well-off accumulating even more resources and the middle class seeing their income as either flat or falling, measured in constant dollars (Mishel et al. 2007). Rising levels of debt among the middle class have contributed to this growing inequality. Many now have a fragile hold on being middle class: The loss of a job, a family emergency, such as the death of a working parent, divorce, disability, or a prolonged illness, can quickly leave middle- and working-class families in a precarious financial state. At the same time, high salaries for CEOs, tax loopholes that favor the rich, and sheer greed are concentrating more wealth in the hands of a few.

Members of the working class have little control over their own work lives; instead, they generally have to take orders from others. This concept of the working class departs from traditional blue-collar definitions of working-class jobs because it includes many so-called white-collar workers (secretaries, salespeople, and nurses), any group working under the rules imposed by managers. The middle class may exercise some autonomy at work, but the working class has little power to challenge decisions of those who supervise them, except insofar as they can organize collectively, as in unions, strikes, or other collective work actions.

Whether you see the class system as a ladder or as a system of conflict, you can see that the class structure in the United States is hierarchical. Class position gives different people access to jobs, income, education, power, and social status, all of which bestow further opportunities on some and deprive others of success. People sometimes move from one class to another (although this is not the norm), but the class structure is a system with boundaries built into it, generating class conflict. The middle and working classes shoulder much of the tax burden for social programs, producing resentment by these groups toward the poor. At the same time, corporate taxes have declined and tax loopholes for the rich have increased, an indication of the privilege that is perpetuated by the class

Labor unions, traditionally dominated by White men in the skilled trades, are not only more diverse, but also represent workers in occupations typically thought of as "white-collar" work.

system. Whatever features of the class system different sociologists study, they see class stratification as a dynamic process—one involving the interplay of access to resources, judgments about different groups, and the exercise of power by a few.

## Growing Inequality and the Distribution of Wealth and Income

*Income* is the amount of money brought into a household from various sources (wages, investment income, dividends, and so on) during a given period. In recent years, income growth has been greatest for those at the top of the population (see Figure 8.3); for everyone else, income (controlling for the value of the dollar) has been relatively flat. This has contributed to growing inequality in the United States. But inequality becomes even more apparent when you consider both wealth and income.

*Wealth* is the monetary value of everything one actually owns. It is calculated by adding all financial assets (stocks, bonds, property, insurance, savings, value of investments, and so on) and subtracting debts, which gives a dollar amount that is one's **net worth.** Wealth allows you to accumulate assets over generations, giving advantages to subsequent generations that they might not have had on their own. Unlike income, wealth is cumulative—that is, its value tends to increase through investment; it can be passed on to the next generation, giving those who inherit wealth a considerable advantage in accumulating more resources.

To understand the significance of wealth compared to income in determining class location, imagine two college graduates graduating in the same year, from the same college, with the same major and same grade point average. Imagine further that upon graduation, both get jobs with the same salary in the same organization. Yet, in one case parents paid all the student's college expenses and gave her a car upon graduation. The other student worked while in school and graduated with substantial debt from student loans. This student's family has no money with which to help support the new worker. Who is better off? Same salary, same credentials, but wealth (even if modest) matters. It gives one person an advantage that will be played out many times over as the young worker buys a home, finances her own children's education, and possibly inherits additional assets.

Where is all the wealth? The wealthiest 1 percent own 33 percent of all net worth; the bottom 80 percent control only 16 percent. The top 10 percent also own 88 percent of all stock; the bottom 40 percent own less than 1 percent of total stock holdings. Moreover, there has been an increase in the concentration of wealth since the 1980s, making the United States one of the most "unequal" nations in the world (Mishel et al. 2007). The growth of wealth by a select few, though long a feature of the U.S. class system, has also reached historic levels. As just one example,

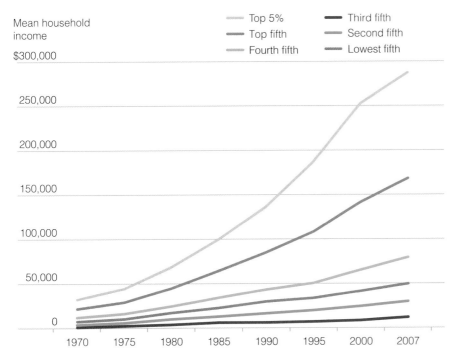

**FIGURE 8.3** *Mean Household Income Received by Different Income Groups, 1970–2007*

*As you can see in this graph, for most income groups in the United States, income (adjusted for rate of inflation) has remained relatively flat in recent years. The top groups, however, have seen huge increases in income, a trend resulting in growing inequality in the United States.*

*Source:* U.S. Census Bureau. 2008. *Historical Income Tables Households, Table H-3.* **www.census.gov**

John D. Rockefeller is typically heralded as one of the wealthiest men in U.S. history. But comparing Rockefeller with Bill Gates, controlling for the value of today's dollars, Gates has far surpassed Rockefeller's riches (Myerson 1998).

In contrast to the vast amount of wealth and income controlled by elites, a very large proportion of Americans have hardly any financial assets once debt is subtracted. Figure 8.4 shows the net worth of different income brackets in the United States, and you can see that most of the population has very low net worth. Moreover, 18 percent of the population have zero or negative net worth, usually because their debt exceeds their assets. The American Dream of owning a home, a new car, taking annual vacations, and sending one's children to good schools—not to mention saving for a comfortable retirement—is increasingly unattainable by many. When you see the amount of income and wealth controlled by a small segment of the population, a sobering picture of class inequality emerges.

Despite the prominence of rags-to-riches stories in American legend, most wealth in this society is inherited. A few individuals make their way into the elite class by virtue of their own success, but this is rare. The upper class is also overwhelmingly White and Protestant. The wealthy also exercise tremendous political power by funding lobbyists, exerting their social and personal influence on other elites, and contributing heavily to political campaigns. Studies of elites also find that they tend to be politically quite conservative (Burris 2000; Zweigenhaft and Domhoff 2006). They travel in exclusive social networks that tend to be open only to those in the upper class. They tend to intermarry, their children are likely to go to expensive schools, and they spend their leisure time in exclusive resorts.

Race also influences the pattern of wealth distribution in the United States; for every dollar of wealth held by White Americans, Black Americans have only 26 cents. Overall, White families have ten times the wealth of Black households. And, at all levels of income, occupation, and education, Black families have lower levels of wealth than similarly situated White families. Being able to draw on assets during times of economic stress means that families with some resources can better withstand difficult times

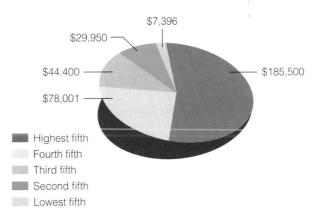

**FIGURE 8.4** *Median Net Worth by Household Income*

*Recall that one's net worth is the value of everything owned minus one's debt. You can see here the vast differences in wealth across different income groups. Remember that median is the midpoint; thus, in each of these groups, half of those in the group have more wealth; half, less.*

*Source:* Orzechowski, Shawna, and Peter Sepielli. 2003. *Net Worth and Asset Ownership of Households: 1998 and 2000.* Washington, DC: U.S. Census Bureau, P70–88.

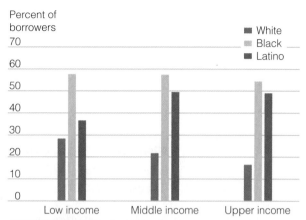

**FIGURE 8.5** *Percentage of Borrowers with High-Cost Home Purchase Loans by Race and Income*

Source: ACORN. 2007. *Foreclosure Exposure: A Study of Racial and Income Disparities in Home Mortgage Lending in 172 American Cities.* Reprinted with permission. **www.acorn.org**

than those without assets. Even small assets, such as home ownership or a savings account, provide protection from crises such as increased rent, a health emergency, or unemployment. Because the effects of wealth are intergenerational—that is, they accumulate over time—just providing equality of opportunity in the present does not address the differences in class status that Black and White Americans experience (Oliver and Shapiro 2006; Mishel et al. 2007).

What explains the disparities in wealth by race? Wealth accumulates over time. Thus, government policies in the past have prevented Black Americans from being able to accumulate wealth. Discriminatory housing policies, bank lending policies, tax codes, and so forth have disadvantaged Black Americans, resulting in the differing assets Whites and Blacks in general hold now. Even though some of these discriminatory policies have ended, many continue. Either way, their effects persist, resulting in what sociologists Melvin Oliver and Thomas Shapiro call the *sedimentation of racial inequality.*

Understanding the significance of wealth in shaping life chances for different groups also challenges the view that all Hispanics have similar experiences and wealth. Cuban Americans and Spaniards are similar to Whites in their wealth holdings, whereas Mexicans, Puerto Ricans, Dominicans, and other Hispanic groups more closely resemble African Americans on the various indicators of wealth and social class. Likewise, one can better understand differences in class status among Asian American groups by carefully considering the importance not just of income, education, and occupation, but also patterns in the net assets of different groups (Oliver and Shapiro 2006).Without significant wealth holdings, families of any race are less able to transmit assets from previous generations to the next generation, one main support of social mobility.

Patterns of wealth contribute heavily to class inequality in the United States—inequality that is growing. Despite beliefs to the contrary, class divisions in the United States are real and becoming more pronounced. The elite are becoming better off, whereas many in the middle class, working class, and the poor seem to be struggling. Indeed, many middle-class people feel that their way of life is slipping away. Many factors have contributed to growing inequality in the United States, including the profound effects of national and global economic changes—changes that recently produced a so-called economic downturn. While some see the economic problems of the nation as stemming from individual greed on Wall Street, the problems are systemic, even though individual greed likely plays a role.

The structural problem is referred to as **economic restructuring,** referring to the decline of manufacturing jobs in the United States, the transformation of the economy by technological change, and the process of globalization. We examine economic restructuring more in Chapter 15 on the economy, but the point here is that these structural changes are having a profound effect on the life chances of people in different social classes. Many in the working class, for example, once largely employed in relatively stable manufacturing jobs with decent wages and good benefits, now likely work, if they work at all, in lower-wage jobs with fewer benefits, such as pensions or health care. Middle-class families may have amassed large sums of debt, sometimes to support a middle-class lifestyle, but also perhaps to pay for their children's education.

Economists have their explanations of why the nation has encountered such huge economic problems, but sociologists have their own way of thinking about this, namely, that economic problems are not purely economic: They are social, both in their origins and their consequences. Take home ownership as an example. Home ownership is one of the main components of the

*The foreclosure crisis that unfolded in 2009 affected many, including whole communities, especially those of working class and minority residents.*

# >doing sociological research

## The Fragile Middle Class

*Research Question:* The hallmark of the middle class in the United States is its presumed stability. Home ownership, a college education for children, and other accoutrements of middle-class status (nice cars, annual vacations, an array of consumer goods) are the symbols of middle-class prosperity. But the rising rate of bankruptcy among the middle class shows that the middle class is not as secure as it is presumed to be (see Figure 8.4). Personal bankruptcy has risen dramatically with now more than one million filings for bankruptcy per year. How can this be happening in such a prosperous society? This is the question examined by Teresa Sullivan, Elizabeth Warren, and Jay Lawrence Westbrook in their study of bankruptcy and debt among the middle class.

*Research Method:* They based their study on an analysis of official records of bankruptcy in five states, as well as on detailed questionnaires given to individuals who filed for bankruptcy.

*Research Results:* Their findings debunk the idea that bankruptcy is most common among poor people. Instead, they found bankruptcy is mostly a middle-class phenomenon representing a cross-section of those in this class (meaning that those who are bankrupt are matched on the demographic characteristics of race, age, and gender with others in the middle class). They also debunk the notion that bankruptcy is rising because it is so easy to file. Rather, they found many people in the middle class so overwhelmed with debt that they cannot possibly pay it off. Most often people file for bankruptcy as a result of job loss and lost wages. But divorce, medical problems, housing expenses, and credit card debt also drive many to bankruptcy court.

*Conclusions and Implications:* Sullivan and her colleagues explain the rise of bankruptcy as stemming from structural factors in society that fracture the stability of the middle class. The volatility of jobs under modern capitalism is one of the biggest factors, but add to this the "thin safety net"—no health insurance for many, but rising medical costs. Also, the American Dream of owning one's own home means many are "mortgage poor"—extended beyond their ability to keep up.

In addition, the United States is a credit-driven society. Credit cards are routinely mailed to people in the middle class, encouraging them to buy beyond their means. You can now buy virtually anything on credit: cars, clothes, doctor's bills, entertainment, groceries. You can even use one credit card to pay off other credit cards. Indeed, it is difficult to live in this society without credit cards. Increased debt is the result. Many are simply unable to keep up with compounding interest and penalty payments, and debt takes on a life of its own as consumers cannot keep up with even the interest payments on debt.

Sullivan, Warren, and Westbrook conclude that increases in debt and uncertainty of income combine to produce the fragility of the middle class. Their research shows that "even the most secure family may be only a job loss, a medical problem, or an out-of-control credit card away from financial catastrophe" (2000: 6).

### Questions to Consider

1. Have you ever had a credit card? If so, how easy was it to get? Is it possible to get by without a credit card?

2. What evidence do you see in your community of the fragility or stability of different social class groups?

*Source:* T. A. Sullivan, E. Warren, and J. L. Westbrook, *The Fragile Middle Class: Americans in Debt.* Copyright © 2000 by Yale University Press.

---

American Dream. For most Americans, owning one's own home is the primary means of attaining economic security. It is also the key to other resources—good schools, cleaner neighborhoods, and an investment in the future. Likewise, losing your home is more than just a financial crisis—it reverberates through various aspects of your life.

Housing foreclosure is a trauma for anyone who experiences it, but foreclosure has hit some groups especially hard. Studies also find that one in ten African Americans will experience foreclosure, compared to one in twenty-five White Americans (Oliver and Shapiro 2008). Furthermore, entire communities have been affected by this crisis, with a strong correlation between foreclosure rates and the proportion of Black people living in a particular area (Bostic and Lee 2008). Why?

Some might argue that this occurred because individual people made bad decisions—buying homes beyond their means. Sociologists explain this as the result of institutional lending practices that target particular groups, making them more vulnerable to the economic forces that can shatter individual lives. One way institutions do this is through subprime loans—loans that carry interest rates higher than is conventional and that may also include adjustable interest rates that increase sharply over time. African Americans are 2.7 times more likely than White Americans to hold subprime mortgage loans; Latinos, 2.3 times more likely. Even more telling, these disparities exist even when the mortgage holders are at the same income level; upper-income African Americans and Latinos are *three times more likely* than White Americans in the same income bracket to hold subprime loans (ACORN 2007; Rivera at al. 2008). These facts reveal that there is a racial dimension to the foreclosure crisis that is not understood solely by individual economic decisions. Lenders may see African Americans as a greater credit risk, but they also know that the value of real estate is less in racially segregated neighborhoods. And, discriminatory practices in the housing market have been well documented (Oliver and Shapiro 2006; Squires 2007).

The sociological point is that economic problems have a sociological dimension and cannot be explained by individual decisions alone. Economic policies also have different effects for different groups—sometimes intended, sometimes not. Tax policies, for example, distribute economic benefits unevenly and according to specific sociological patterns. Corporations benefit the most from the tax structure, as corporate taxes have fallen in recent years; while most individual Americans are paying more in federal tax than ever before (an increase from 13 to 15 cents per dollar of income earned since 1990), corporate taxes since 1990 have fallen from 26 cents on the dollar to 20 cents, even though corporate profits were up 252 percent in that period (Johnston 2000). Tax policies also benefit those at the upper ends of the class system who can take advantage of numerous tax benefits and loopholes. And, as many in the public understood, the Congressional bailouts of recent years have had far more benefit for corporations than for the individuals suffering from the financial crisis.

## Diverse Sources of Stratification

Class is only one basis for stratification in the United States. Factors such as age, ethnicity, and national origin have a tremendous influence on stratification. Race and gender are two primary influences in the stratification system in the United States. In fact, analyzing class without also analyzing race and gender can be misleading. Race, class, and gender, as we are seeing throughout this book, are overlapping systems of stratification that people experience simultaneously. A working-class Latina, for example, does not experience herself as working class at one moment, Hispanic at another moment, and a woman the next. At any given point in time, her position in society is the result of her race, class, *and* gender status. In other words, class position is manifested differently, depending on one's race and gender, just as gender is experienced differently depending on one's race and class, and race is experienced differently depending on one's gender and class. Depending on one's circumstances, race, class, or gender may seem particularly salient at a given moment in a person's life. For example, a Black middle-class man stopped and interrogated by police when driving through a predominantly White middle-class neighborhood may at that moment feel his racial status as his single most outstanding characteristic, but at all times his race, class, and gender influence his life chances. As social categories, race, class, and gender shape all people's experience in this society, not just those who are disadvantaged (Andersen and Collins 2007).

Class also significantly differentiates group experience within given racial and gender groups. Latinos, for example, are broadly defined as those who trace their origins to regions originally colonized by Spain. The ancestors of this group include both White Spanish colonists and the natives who were enslaved on Spanish plantations. Today, some Latinos identify as White, others as Black, and others by their specific national and cultural origins. The very different histories of those categorized as Latino are matched by significant differences in class. Some may have been schooled in the most affluent settings; others may be virtually unschooled. Those of upper-class standing may have had little experience with prejudice or discrimination; others may have been highly segregated into barrios and treated with extraordinary prejudice. Latinos who live near each other geographically in the United States and who are the same age and share similar ancestry may have substantially different experiences based on their class standing (Massey 1993). Neither class, race, nor gender, taken alone, can be considered an adequate indicator of different group experiences.

**The Race–Class Debate.** The relationship between race and class is much debated among sociologists. The Black middle class goes all the way back to the small numbers of free Blacks in the eighteenth and nineteenth centuries (Frazier 1957), expanding in the twentieth century to include those who were able to obtain an education and become established in industry, business, or a profession. Although wages for Black middle-class and professional workers never matched those of Whites in the same jobs, within the Black community the Black middle class has had relatively high prestige. Many sociologists conclude that the class structure among African Americans has existed alongside the White class structure, separate and different.

In recent years, both the African American and Latino middle classes have expanded, primarily as the result of increased access to education and middle-class occupations for people of color (Higginbotham 2001; Pattillo-McCoy 1999). Although middle-class

Blacks and Latinos may have economic privileges that others in these groups do not have, their class standing does not make them immune to the negative effects of race. Asian Americans also have a significant middle class, but they have also been stereotyped as the most successful minority group because of their presumed educational achievement, hard work, and thrift. This stereotype is referred to as the *myth of the model minority* and includes the idea that a minority group must adopt alleged dominant group values to succeed. This myth about Asian Americans obscures the significant obstacles to success that Asian Americans encounter, and it ignores the hard work and educational achievements of other racial and ethnic groups. The idea that Asian Americans are the "model minority" also obscures the high rates of poverty among many Asian American groups (Lee 1996).

Despite recent successes, many in the Black middle class have a tenuous hold on this class status. The Black middle class remains as segregated from Whites as the Black poor, and continuing racial segregation in neighborhoods means that Black middle-class neighborhoods are typically closer to Black poor neighborhoods than the White middle-class neighborhoods are to White poor ones. This exposes many in the Black middle class to some of the same risks as those in poverty. This is not to say that the Black middle class has the same experience as the poor, but it challenges the view that the Black middle class "has it all" (Pattillo-McCoy 1999; Lacy 2007) Furthermore, Black Americans are still much more likely to be working class than middle class; they are also more likely to be working class than are Whites (Horton et al. 2000).

**The Influence of Gender and Age.** The effects of gender further complicate the analysis of class. In the past, women were thought to derive their class position from their husbands or fathers, but sociologists now challenge this assumption. Measured by their own income and occupation, the vast majority of women would likely be considered working class. The median income for women, even among those employed full time, is far below the national median income level. In 2007, when median income for men working year-round and full time was $45,113, the median income of women working year-round, full time was $35,102 (DeNavas-Walt et al. 2008). The vast majority of women work in low-prestige and low-wage occupations, even though women and men have comparable levels of educational attainment.

Age, too, is a significant source of stratification. The age group most likely to be poor are children, 18 percent of whom live in poverty in the United States. This represents a change from the recent past when the aged were the most likely to be poor (see Figure 8.6). Although many elderly people are now poor (10 percent of those 65 and over), far fewer in this age category are poor than was the case not many years ago (DeNavas-Walt et al. 2008). This shift reflects the greater affluence of the older segments of the population—a trend that is likely to continue as the current large cohort of middle-aged, middle-class Baby Boomers grow older.

# Social Mobility: Myths and Realities

Popular legends extol the possibility of anyone becoming rich in the United States. The well-to-do are admired not just for their style of life but also for their supposed drive and diligence. The admiration for those who rise to the top makes it seem like anyone who is clever enough and works hard can become fabulously

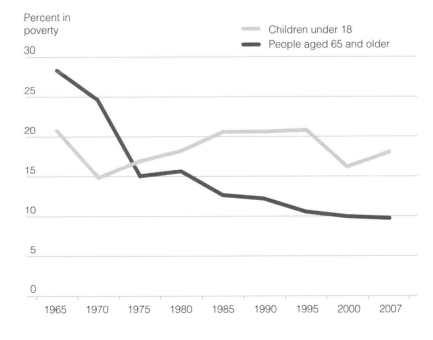

**FIGURE 8.6** *Poverty Among the Old and the Young, 1965–2007*

*Source:* DeNavas-Walt, Carmen, Bernadette Proctor, and Jessica C. Smith. 2008. *Income, Poverty, and Health Insurance Coverage in the United States: 2007.* Washington, DC: U.S. Census Bureau, #P60-235.

rich. The assumption is that the United States class system is a **meritocracy**—that is, a system in which one's status is based on merit or accomplishments, not other social characteristics. As the word suggests, in a meritocracy people move up and down through the class system based on merit, not based on other characteristics. Is this the case in the United States?

## Defining Social Mobility

**Social mobility** is a person's movement over time from one class to another. Social mobility can be up or down, although the American Dream emphasizes upward movement. Mobility can be either *inter*generational, occurring between generations, as when a daughter rises above the class of her mother or father; or *intra*generational, occurring within a generation, as when a person's class status changes as the result of business success (or disaster).

Societies differ in the extent to which social mobility is permitted. Some societies are based on *closed class systems,* in which movement from one class to another is virtually impossible. In a caste system, for example, mobility is strictly limited by the circumstances of one's birth. At the other extreme are *open class systems,* in which placement in the class system is based on individual achievement, not ascription. In open class systems, there are relatively loose class boundaries, high rates of class mobility, and weak perceptions of class difference.

## The Extent of Social Mobility

Does social mobility occur in the United States? Social mobility is much more limited than people believe. Success stories of social mobility do occur, but research finds that experiences of mobility over great distances are rare, certainly far less than believed. Most people remain in the same class as their parents. What mobility exists is typically short in distance, and some people actually drop to a lower status, referred to as *downward social mobility*. Research finds that rates of upward social mobility are highest among White men, followed by White women, then Black men, and finally, Black women (Mazunder 2008). Currently, half of all Americans say that they are not moving forward, and one-third say they have fallen further back (Acs and Zimmerman 2008). Evidence also suggests that mobility between generations may be becoming even more rigid than in the past (Sawhill and McClanahan 2006).

Social mobility is influenced most by factors that affect the whole society, not just by individual characteristics. Just being born in a particular generation can have a significant influence on one's life chances. The fears of today's young, middle-class people that they will be unable to achieve the lifestyles of their parents show the effect that being in a particular generation can have on one's life chances. In other words, when mobility occurs, it is usually because of societal changes that create or restrict opportunities, including such changes as economic cycles, changes in the occupational

structure, and demographic factors, such as the number of college graduates in the labor force (Beller and Hout 2006). But mobility in the United States is not impossible. Indeed, many have immigrated to this nation with the knowledge that their life chances are better here than in their countries of origin. And, the social mobility that does exist is greatly influenced by education. But, in sum, social mobility is much more limited than the American Dream of mobility suggests.

## Class Consciousness

Because of the widespread belief that mobility is possible, people in the United States, compared to many other societies, tend not to be very conscious of class. **Class consciousness** is the perception that a class structure exists along with a feeling of shared identification with others in one's class—that is, those with whom you share life chances (Centers 1949). Notice that there are two dimensions to the definition of class consciousness: the idea that a class structure exists and one's class identification.

There has been a long-standing argument that Americans are not very class conscious because of the belief that upward mobility is possible and because of the belief in individualism that is part of the culture. Images of opulence also saturate popular culture, making it seem that such material comforts are available to anyone. The faith that upward mobility is possible ironically perpetuates inequality since, if people believe that everyone has the same chances of success, they are likely to think that whatever inequality exists must be fair or the result of individual success and failure.

Class inequality in any society is usually buttressed by ideas that support (or actively promote) inequality. Beliefs that people are biologically, culturally, or socially different can be used to justify the higher position of some groups. If people believe these ideas, the ideas provide legitimacy for the system. Karl Marx used the term **false consciousness** to describe the class consciousness of subordinate classes who had internalized the view of the dominant class. Marx argued that the ruling class controls subordinate classes by infiltrating their consciousness with belief systems that are consistent with the interests of the ruling class. If people accept these ideas, which justify inequality, they need not be overtly coerced into accepting the roles designated for them by the ruling class.

Class consciousness in the United States has been higher at some times than others. Now, 46 percent of the public identifies as working class, 46 percent as middle class, 5 percent as lower class, and 3 percent as upper class (National Opinion Research Center 2004). There have been times when class consciousness was higher, such as during the labor movement of the 1920s and 1930s. Then, working-class people had a very high degree of class consciousness and mobilized on behalf of workers' rights. But now the formation of

*a sociological eye*
*on the media*

## Reproducing Class Stereotypes

The media have a substantial impact on how people view the social class system and different groups within it. Especially because people tend to live and associate with people in their own class, how they see others can be largely framed by the portrayal of different class groups in the media. Research has found this to be true and, in addition, has found that mass media have the power to shape public support for policies for public assistance.

To begin with, the media overrepresent the lifestyle of the most comfortable classes. It is the rare family that can afford the home decor and fashion depicted even in soap operas, ironically most likely watched by those in the working class. Media portrayals, such as those found on television talk shows as well as sports, tend to emphasize stories of upward mobility. When the working class is depicted, it tends to be shown as deviant, reinforcing class antagonism and giving viewers a sense of moral and "class superiority" (Gersch 1999).

Content analyses of the media also find that the poor are largely invisible in the media (Mantsios 2001). Those poor people who are depicted in television and magazines are more often portrayed as Black than is actually the case, leading people to overestimate the actual number of the Black poor. The elderly and working poor are rarely seen (Clawson and Trice 2000; Gilens 1996). Representations of welfare overemphasize themes of dependency, especially when the portrayal is of African Americans. Women are also more likely than men to be represented as dependent (Misra et al. 2003). And rarely are welfare activists shown as experts; rather, public officials are typically given the voice of authority (Ryan 1996). One result is that the media end up framing the "field of thinkable solutions to public problems" (Sotirovic 2000, 2001), but do so within a context that ignores the social structural context of social issues.

*Further resources*: See the film, *Class Dismissed: How TV Frames the Working Class*, Media Education Foundation. **www.mediaed.org**

*Sources:* Gersch, Beate. 1999. "Class in Daytime Talk Television." *Peace Review* 11 (June): 275–281; Sotirovic, Mira. 2001. "Media Use and Perceptions of Welfare." *Journal of Communication* 51 (December): 750–774; Sotirovic, Mira. 2000. "Effects of Media Use on Audience Framing and Support for Welfare." *Mass Communication & Society* 2-3 (Spring-Summer): 269–296; Bullock, Heather E., Karen Fraser, and Wendy R. Williams. 2001. "Media Images of the Poor." *The Journal of Social Issues* 57 (Summer): 229–246; Clawson, Rosalee A., and Rakuya Trice. 2000. "Poverty as We Know It: Media Portrayals of the Poor." *The Public Opinion Quarterly* 64 (Spring): 53–64; Gilens, Martin. 1996. "Race and Poverty in America: Public Misperceptions and the American News Media." *Public Opinion Quarterly* 60 (Winter): 515–541; Misra, Joy, Stephanie Moller, and Marina Karides. 2003. "Envisioning Dependency: Changing Media Depictions of Welfare in the 20th Century." *Social Problems* 50 (November): 482–504; Ryan, Charlotte. 1996. "Battered in the Media: Mainstream News Coverage of Welfare Reform." *Radical America* 26 (August): 29–41.

a relatively large middle class and a relatively high standard of living militates against class discontent. Racial and ethnic divisions also make strong alliances within various classes less stable. The growing inequality of today could result in a higher degree of class consciousness, but this has not yet developed into a significant class-based movement for change.

# Why Is There Inequality?

Stratification occurs in all societies. Why? This question originates in classical sociology in the works of Karl Marx and Max Weber, theorists whose work continues to inform the analysis of class inequality today.

## Karl Marx: Class and Capitalism

**Karl Marx** (1818–1883) provided a complex and profound analysis of the class system under capitalism—an analysis that, although more than 100 years old, continues to inform sociological analyses and has been the basis for major world change. Marx defined classes in relationship to *the means of production,* defined as the system by which goods are produced and distributed. In Marx's analysis, two primary classes exist under capitalism: the *capitalist class,* those who own the means of production, and the *working class* (or proletariat), those who sell their labor for wages. There are further divisions within these two classes: the *petty bourgeoisie,* small business owners and managers (those whom you might think of as middle class) who identify with the interests of the capitalist class but do not own the means of production, and the *lumpenproletariat,* those who have become unnecessary as workers and are then discarded. (Today, these would be the underclass, the homeless, and the permanently poor.)

Marx thought that with the development of capitalism, the capitalist and working class would become increasingly antagonistic (something he referred to as class struggle). As class conflicts became more intense, the two classes would become more polarized, with the petty bourgeoisie becoming deprived of their property and dropping into the working class. This analysis is still reflected in contemporary questions about whether the classes are becoming more polarized, with the rich getting richer and everyone else worse off, as we have seen.

In addition to the class struggle that Marx thought would characterize the advancement of capitalism, he also thought that capitalism was the basis for other social institutions. Capitalism is the *infrastructure* of society, with other institutions (such as law, education, the family, and so forth) reflecting capitalist interests. Thus, according to Marx, the law supports the interests of capitalists; the family promotes values that socialize people into appropriate work roles; and education reflects the interests of the capitalist class. Over time, capitalism increasingly penetrates society, as we can clearly see with the corporate mergers that characterize modern life and the predominance of capitalist values in society's institutions.

Why do people support such a system? Here is where ideology plays a role. **Ideology** refers to belief systems that support the status quo. According to Marx, the dominant ideas of a society are promoted by the ruling class. Through their control of the communications industries in modern society, the ruling class is able to produce ideas that buttress their interests.

Much of Marx's analysis boils down to the consequences of a system based on the pursuit of profit. If goods were exchanged at the cost of producing them, no profit would be produced. Capitalist owners want to sell commodities for more than their actual value—more than the cost of producing them, including materials and labor. Because workers contribute value to the system and capitalists extract value, Marx saw capitalist profit as the exploitation of labor. Marx believed that as profits became increasingly concentrated in the hands of a few capitalists, the working class would become increasingly dissatisfied. The basically exploitative character of capitalism, according to Marx, would ultimately lead to its destruction as workers organized to overthrow the rule of the capitalist class. *Class conflict* between workers and capitalists, he argued, was inescapable, with revolution being the inevitable result. Perhaps the class revolution that Marx predicted has not occurred, but the dynamics of capitalism that he analyzed are unfolding before us.

At the time Marx was writing, the middle class was small and consisted mostly of small business owners and managers. Marx saw the middle class as dependent on the capitalist class, but exploited by it, because the middle class did not own the means of production. He saw middle-class people as identifying with the interests of the capitalist class because of the similarity in their economic interests and their dependence on the capitalist system. Marx believed that the middle class failed to work in its own best interests because it falsely believed that it benefited from capitalist arrangements. Marx thought that in the long run the middle class would pay for their misplaced faith when profits became increasingly concentrated in the hands of a few and more and more of the middle class dropped into the working class. Because he did not foresee the emergence of the large and highly differentiated middle class we have today, not every part of Marx's theory has proved true. Still, his analysis provides a powerful portrayal of the forces of capitalism and the tendency for wealth to belong to a few, whereas the majority work only to make ends meet. He has also influenced the lives of billions of people under self-proclaimed Marxist systems that were created in an attempt, however unrealized, to overcome the pitfalls of capitalist society.

## Max Weber: Class, Status, and Party

**Max Weber** (1864–1920) agreed with Marx that classes were formed around economic interests, and he agreed that material forces (that is, economic forces) have a powerful effect on people's lives. However, he disagreed with Marx that economic forces are the primary dimension of stratification. Weber saw three dimensions to stratification:

- *class* (the economic dimension);
- *status* (or prestige, the cultural and social dimension); and,
- *party* (or power, the political dimension).

Weber is thus responsible for a *multidimensional view* of social stratification because he analyzed the connections between economic, cultural, and political systems. Weber pointed out that, although the economic, social, and political dimensions of stratification are usually related, they are not always consistent. A person could be high on one or two dimensions, but low on another. A major drug dealer is an example: high wealth (economic dimension) and power (political dimension) but low prestige (social dimension), at least in the eyes of the mainstream society, even if not in other circles.

Weber defined *class* as the economic dimension of stratification—how much access to the material goods of society a group or individual has, as measured by income, property, and other financial assets. A family with an income of $100,000 per year clearly has more access to the resources of a society than a family living on an income of $40,000 per year. Weber understood that a class has common economic interests and that economic well-being was the basis for one's life chances. But, in addition, he thought that people were also stratified based on their status and power differences.

*Status,* to Weber, is the prestige dimension of stratification—the social judgment or recognition given to a person or group. Weber understood that class distinctions are linked to status distinctions—that is, those with the most economic resources tend to have the highest status in society, but not always. In a local community, for example, those with the most status may be those who have lived there the longest, even if newcomers arrive with more money. Although having power is typically related to also having high economic standing and high social status, this is not always the case, as you saw with the example of the drug dealer.

Finally, *party* (or what we would now call power) is the political dimension of stratification. It is the capacity to influence groups and individuals even in the face of opposition. Power is also reflected in the ability of a person or group to negotiate their way through social institutions. An unemployed Latino man wrongly accused of a crime, for instance, does not have much power to negotiate his way through the criminal justice system. By comparison, business executives accused of corporate crime can afford expensive lawyers and, thus, frequently go unpunished or, if they are found guilty, serve relatively light sentences in comparatively pleasant facilities. Again, Weber saw power as linked to economic standing, but he did not think that economic standing was always the determining cause of people's power.

Marx and Weber explain different features of stratification. Both understood the importance of the economic basis of stratification, and they knew the significance of class for determining the course of one's life. Marx saw people as acting primarily out of economic interests. Weber refined the sociological analyses of stratification to account for the subtleties that can be observed when you look beyond the sheer economic dimension to stratification, stratification being the result of economic, social, and political forces. Together, Marx and Weber provide compelling theoretical grounds for understanding the contemporary class structure.

## Functionalism and Conflict Theory: The Continuing Debate

Marx and Weber were trying to understand why differences existed in the resources and power that different groups in society hold. The question persists of why there is inequality. Two major frameworks in sociological theory—functionalist and conflict theory—take quite different approaches to understanding inequality (see Table 8.2, p. 200).

**The Functionalist Perspective on Inequality.** Functionalist theory views society as a system of institutions organized to meet society's needs (see Chapter 1). The functionalist perspective emphasizes that the parts of society are in basic harmony with each other; society is characterized by cohesion, consensus, cooperation, stability, and persistence (Parsons 1951a; Merton 1957; Eitzen and Baca Zinn 2007). Different parts of the social system complement one another and are held together through social consensus and cooperation. To explain stratification, functionalists propose that the roles filled by the upper classes—such as governance, economic innovation, investment, and management—are essential for a cohesive and smoothly running society and hence are rewarded in proportion to their contribution to the social order (Davis and Moore 1945).

According to the functionalist perspective, social inequality serves an important purpose in society: It motivates people to fill the different positions in society that are needed for the survival of the whole. Functionalists think that some positions in society are more important than others and require the most talent and training. Rewards attached to those positions (such as higher income and prestige) ensure that people will make the sacrifices needed to acquire the training for functionally important positions (Davis and Moore 1945). Higher class status thus comes to those who acquire what is needed for success (such as education and job training). In other words, functionalist theorists see inequality as based on a reward system that motivates people to succeed.

**The Conflict Perspective on Inequality.** Conflict theory also sees society as a social system, but unlike functionalism, conflict theory interprets society as being held together through conflict and coercion. From a conflict-based perspective, society comprises competing interest groups, some with more power than others. Different groups struggle over societal resources and compete for social advantage. Conflict theorists argue that those who control society's resources also hold power over others. The powerful are also likely to act to reproduce their advantage and try to shape societal beliefs to make their privileges appear to be legitimate and fair. In sum, conflict theory emphasizes the friction in society rather than the coherence and sees society as dominated by elites.

From the perspective of conflict theory, derived largely from the work of Karl Marx, social stratification is based on class conflict and blocked opportunity. Conflict theorists see stratification as a system of domination and subordination in which those with the most resources exploit and control others. They also see the different classes as in conflict with each other, with the unequal distribution of rewards reflecting the class interests of the powerful, not the survival needs of the whole society (Eitzen and Baca Zinn 2007). According to the conflict perspective,

| table 8.2 | Functionalist and Conflict Theories of Stratification | |
|---|---|---|
| **Interprets** | **Functionalism** | **Conflict Theory** |
| *Inequality* | Inequality serves an important purpose in society by motivating people to fill the different positions in society that are needed for the survival of the whole. | Inequality results from a system of domination and subordination where those with the most resources exploit and control others. |
| *Class structure* | Differentiation is essential for a cohesive society. | Different groups struggle over societal resources and compete for social advantage. |
| *Reward system* | Rewards are attached to certain positions (such as higher income and prestige) as a way to ensure that people will make the sacrifices needed to acquire the training for functionally important positions in society. | The more stratified a society, the less likely that society will benefit from the talents of all its citizens, because inequality prevents the talents of those at the bottom from being discovered and used. |
| *Classes* | Some positions in society are more functionally important than others and are rewarded because they require the greatest degree of talent and training. | Classes exist in conflict with each other as they vie for power and economic, social, and political resources. |
| *Life chances* | Those who work hardest and succeed have greater life chances. | The most vital jobs in society—those that sustain life and the quality of life—are usually the least rewarded. |
| *Elites* | The most talented are rewarded in proportion to their contribution to the social order. | The most powerful reproduce their advantage by distributing resources and controlling the dominant value system. |
| *Class consciousness/ ideology* | Beliefs about success and failure confirm the status of those who succeed. | Elites shape societal beliefs to make their unequal privilege appear to be legitimate and fair. |
| *Social mobility* | Upward mobility is possible for those who acquire the necessary talents and tools for success (such as education and job training). | There is blocked mobility in the system because the working class and poor are denied the same opportunities as others. |
| *Poverty* | Poverty serves economic and social functions in society. | Poverty is inevitable because of the exploitation built into the system. |
| *Social policy* | Because the system is basically fair, social policies should only reward merit. | Because the system is basically unfair, social policies should support disadvantaged groups by redirecting society's resources for a more equitable distribution of income and wealth. |

inequality provides elites with the power to distribute resources, make and enforce laws, and control value systems; elites use these powers in ways that reproduce inequality. Others in the class structure, especially the working class and the poor, experience blocked mobility.

Conflict theorists argue that the consequences of inequality are negative. From a conflict point of view, the more stratified a society, the less likely that society will benefit from the talents of its citizens; inequality limits the life chances of those at the bottom, preventing their talents from being discovered and used. To the waste of talent is added the restriction of human creativity and productivity.

**The Debate Between Functionalist and Conflict Theories.** Implicit in the argument of each perspective is criticism of the other perspective. Functionalism assumes that the most highly rewarded jobs are the most important for society, whereas conflict theorists argue that some of the most vital jobs in society—those that sustain life and the quality of life, such as farmers, mothers, trash collectors, and a wide range of other laborers—are usually the least rewarded. Conflict theorists also criticize functionalist theory for assuming that the most talented get the greatest rewards. They point out that systems of stratification tend to devalue the contributions of those left at the bottom and to underutilize the diverse talents of all people (Tumin 1953). In contrast, functionalist theorists contend that the conflict view of how economic interests shape social organization is too simplistic. Conflict theorists respond by arguing that functionalists hold too conservative a view of society and overstate the degree of consensus and stability that exists.

The debate between functionalist and conflict theorists raises fundamental questions about how people

# what would they say now?

## Classical Theorists Reflect on Social Class and Sports

Suppose some of the classical theorists of sociology observed an American sports event? What might they say about social class and sports?

**Emile Durkheim:** Truthfully, my theories do not address social class that much because I am more interested in the cultural symbols and events that bind people together. So I notice that people wear a lot of sports symbols, like jerseys and hats, and they put a lot of these symbols on their cars! It certainly projects an identity to others that must make them feel part of some collective group. I can't help but wonder if some of these symbolic identities are connected to people's social class location. I mean, I don't see really rich people wearing NASCAR caps, but I do see them with various yacht club logos on their polo shirts and ties.

**Max Weber:** I think there is more than one dimension to this question of the connection between social class and sports. Everywhere I look I see class, power, and prestige all tangled up in sports. First, look at the class differences associated with different sports: Some seem to have much more prestige than others. But there is also a big connection to politics. Wow—during elections, there are politicians all over the place—at tailgate parties and hanging out in the expensive box seats. It just seems like sports are really embedded in the culture of this society, something especially suggested by the phrase an "All-American."

**Karl Marx:** I just see corporate profits and exploitation everywhere I look. My goodness, not only are the stadiums named for corporate sponsors, but I've even heard various plays labeled by a sponsor, like the "AT&T All-American Play of the Week!" And the money that is spent on the commercials! It makes me faint to think of how much is spent just to get the fans to buy a particular brand of beer! Social class is everywhere in sports, although the workers are often invisible. Sure, some of the athletes are very highly paid, but it's the working-class people holding this all together. Who do you think cleans up these stadiums after the fans leave, or cooks the food, and takes out all the trash? It's an amazing example of a capitalist social system!

**W.E.B. Du Bois:** There has been a strong tendency throughout U.S. history to use Black people as material resources that yield dividends for others. I am as thrilled as anyone else to see the incredible athletic accomplishments of my people, and it seems that sports are one place where the color line is at least blurred. But there are yet too many instances where racial prejudice rears its head. Black people will not be free in any context until the color line in sports, and elsewhere, is gone.

view inequality. Is it inevitable? How is inequality maintained? Do people basically accept it? This debate is not just academic. The assumptions made from each perspective frame public policy debates. Whether the topic is taxation, poverty, or homelessness, if people believe that anyone can get ahead by ability alone, they will tend to see the system of inequality as fair and accept the idea that there should be a differential reward system. Those who tend toward the conflict view of the stratification system are more likely to advocate programs that emphasize public responsibility for the well-being of all groups and to support programs and policies that result in more of the income and wealth of society going toward the needy.

# Poverty

Many people in the United States were shocked when, following the devastation of Hurricane Katrina in New Orleans and the Gulf Coast, thousands of poor, mostly African American people were seen on national TV in horrific circumstances, struggling to stay alive and visibly poor. Katrina uncovered one of the faces of poverty in the United States. For many people it was surprising to see conditions that are normally associated with poor, underdeveloped nations right here in the United States in one of our major and beloved cities.

The truth is that, despite the relatively high average standard of living in the United States, poverty afflicts millions of people. And the particulars of poverty are deeply related to the social structures of class, race, and gender. In New Orleans, for example, when Katrina hit, 28 percent of the population was poor—twice the national rate. Two-thirds of families headed by women in New Orleans were poor, twice the national rate (U.S. Census Bureau 2004). Although a disaster like Katrina can hurt anyone— and did harm people of differing social and economic statuses—natural disasters tend to have a particularly hard impact on the most vulnerable social groups, such as the poor. This shows that disasters are not just natural phenomena; they also have sociological dimensions (Bobo and Dawson 2006; Hartman and Squires 2006).

The poverty that Katrina unmasked was not, of course, news to social scientists who have long analyzed the extent of poverty in the United States and how it affects society's problems. Poor health care, failures in the education system, and crime are all related to poverty. Who is poor, and why is there so much poverty in an otherwise relatively affluent society?

The federal government has established an official definition of poverty used to determine eligibility for government assistance and to measure the extent of poverty in the United States. The **poverty line** is the amount of money needed to support the basic needs of a household, as determined by government; below this line, one is considered officially poor. To determine the poverty line, the Social Security Administration takes a low-cost food budget (based on dietary information provided by the U.S. Department of Agriculture) and multiplies by a factor of three, assuming that a family spends approximately one-third of its budget on food. The resulting figure is the official poverty line, adjusted slightly each year for increases in the cost of living. In 2007, the official poverty line for a family of four was $21,203.

Although a cutoff point is necessary to administer antipoverty programs, this definition of poverty can be misleading. A person or family earning $1 above the cutoff point would not be officially categorized as poor.

## Who Are the Poor?

There are now more than 37 million poor people in the United States, representing 12.5 percent of the population. After the 1950s, poverty declined in the United States; it increased sharply from about 1978 until the mid-1990s, declined, and has been on the rise again since 2000. Although the majority of the poor are White, disproportionately high rates of poverty are also found among Asian Americans, Native Americans, Black Americans, and Hispanics. One-third of Native Americans, 25 percent of African Americans, 22 percent of Hispanics, 10 percent of Asians and Pacific Islanders, and 8 percent of non-Hispanic Whites are poor (DeNavas-Walt et al. 2008). Among Hispanics, there are further differences among groups. Puerto Ricans—the Hispanic group with the lowest median income—have been most likely to suffer increased poverty, probably because of their concentration in the poorest segments of the labor market and their high unemployment rates (Tienda and Stier 1996; Hauan et al. 2000). Asian American poverty has also increased substantially in recent years, particularly among the most recent immigrant groups, including Laotians, Cambodians, Vietnamese, Chinese, and Korean immigrants; Filipino, Japanese, and Asian Indian families have lower rates of poverty (U.S. Census Bureau 2004; Lee 1994).

The vast majority of the poor have always been women and children, but the percentage of women and children considered to be poor has increased in recent years. The term **feminization of poverty** refers to the large proportion of the poor who are women and children. This trend results from several factors, including the dramatic growth of female-headed households, a decline in the proportion of the poor who are elderly (not matched by a decline in the poverty of women and children), and continuing wage inequality between women and men. The large number of poor women is associated with a commensurate large number of poor children. By 2007, 18 percent of all children (those under age 18) in the United States were poor, including 10 percent of non-Hispanic White children, 35 percent of Black children, 29 percent of Hispanic children, and 12 percent of Asian American children (DeNavas-Walt 2008).

One-third of all families headed by women are poor (see Figure 8.7). In recent years, wages for young workers have declined; since most unmarried mothers are quite young, there is a strong likelihood that their children will be poor. Because of the divorce rate and generally little child support provided by men, women are also increasingly likely to be without the contributing income of a spouse and for longer periods of their lives. Women are more likely than men to live with children and to be financially responsible for them. However, women without children also suffer a high poverty rate, compounded in recent times by the fact that women now live longer than before and are less likely to be married than in previous periods.

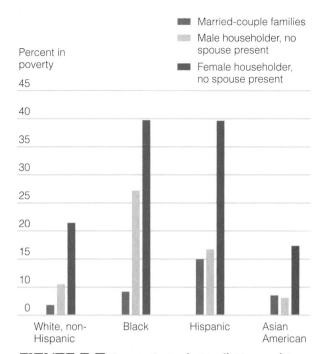

**FIGURE 8.7** *Poverty Status by Family Type and Race*

Source: U.S. Census Bureau. 2008. *Historical Income Tables Households,* Table POV-02.

## Debunking Society's Myths

**Myth:** Marriage is a good way to reduce women's dependence on welfare.

**Reality:** Although it is true that married-couple households are less likely to be poor than single-headed households, forcing women to marry encourages women's dependence on men and punishes women for being independent. Research indicates that poor women place a high value on marriage and want to be married, but also understand that men's unemployment and instability makes their ideal of marriage unattainable. In addition, large numbers of women receiving welfare have been victims of domestic violence (Scott et al. 2002; Edin and Kefalas 2005).

The poor are not a one-dimensional group. They are racially diverse, including Whites, Blacks, Hispanics, Asian Americans, and Native Americans. They are diverse in age, including not just children and young mothers, but men and women of all ages, and especially a substantial number of the elderly, many of whom live alone. They are also geographically diverse, to be found in areas east and west, south and north, urban and rural, although, as Map 8.2 shows, poverty rates are generally higher in the South and Southwest. One marked change in poverty is the growth of poverty in suburban areas to over 9 percent of all poverty. At the same time, half of the poor live inside central cities. But the focus on urban poverty should not cause you to lose sight of the extent of rural poverty as well.

Despite the idea that the poor "milk" the system, government supports for the poor are limited. Half of the poor receive no food stamps; 80 percent get no housing assistance; less than half receive Medicaid, which is the federal health care system for the poor (National Priorities Project 2007; U.S. Census Bureau 2008b). Budget reductions at the state and federal level also have an impact on poverty, especially among women who are more reliant than men on public sector jobs. All told, government support for poor women and their children is negligible, despite the fact that the system is reviled as overly generous and producing sloth and dependence.

Among the poor are the thousands of homeless. It is difficult to estimate the number of homeless people. Depending on how one defines and measures homelessness, the estimates vary widely. If you count the number of homeless on any given night, there may be about 444,000 to 842,000 homeless people (depending on the month measured), but measuring those experiencing homelessness over a period of one year, the estimates are about 3.5 million people (National Coalition for the Homeless 2008).

Whatever the actual numbers of homeless people, there has been an increase in homelessness over the past two decades, even without counting those displaced by Hurricane Katrina in 2005. Families are the fastest growing segment of the homeless—40 percent; children are 40 percent of the homeless.

map **8.2** *MAPPING AMERICA'S DIVERSITY*

## Poverty in the United States

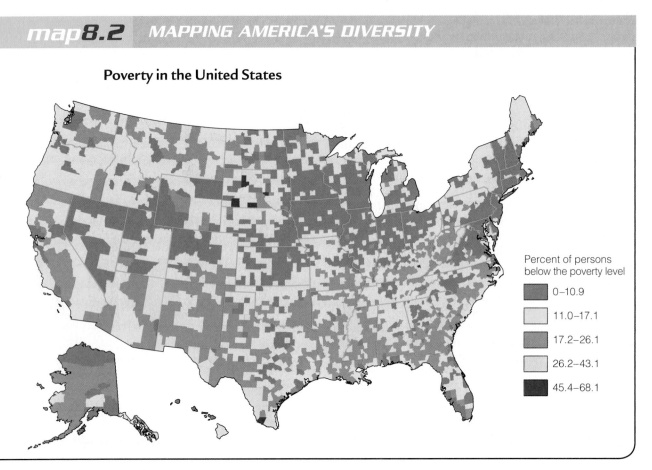

Percent of persons
below the poverty level

| | |
|---|---|
| ▨ | 0–10.9 |
| □ | 11.0–17.1 |
| ▨ | 17.2–26.1 |
| □ | 26.2–43.1 |
| ■ | 45.4–68.1 |

*This map shows regional differences in poverty rates (that is, the percentage of poor in different counties). As you can see, poverty is higher in the South (14.2 percent) than in the West (12 percent), Northeast (11.4 percent), and Midwest (11.1 percent). Various social factors explain different rates of poverty, including regional labor markets, the degree of urbanization, immigration patterns, and population composition, among other factors. What do you think the major causes of poverty are in your region?*
*Data:* U.S. Census Bureau. 2004. *American Fact Finder.* **www.census.gov.**

Moreover, half of the women with children who are homeless have fled from domestic violence (National Coalition Against Domestic Violence 2001; Zorza 1991). Among homeless people, about 40 percent are African American; another 40 percent are White; 13 percent, Hispanic; 4 percent, Native American; and 2 percent, Asian (National Coalition for the Homeless 2006).

There are many reasons for homelessness. The great majority of the homeless are on the streets because of the lack of affordable housing and an increase in poverty, leaving many people with no choice but to live on the street. Add to that problems of inadequate health care, domestic violence, and addiction, and you begin to understand the factors that create homelessness. Some of the homeless (about 16 percent of single, homeless adults) are mentally ill; the movement to get mental patients out of institutional settings has left many without mental health resources that might help them (National Coalition for the Homeless 2008).

## Causes of Poverty

Most agree that poverty is a serious social problem. There is far less agreement on what to do about it. Public debate about poverty hinges on disagreements about its underlying causes. Two points of view prevail: Some blame the poor for their own condition, and some look to social structural causes to explain poverty. The first view, popular with the public and many policymakers, is that poverty is caused by the cultural habits of the poor. According to this point of view, behaviors such as crime, family breakdown, lack of ambition, and educational failure generate and sustain poverty, a syndrome to be treated by forcing the poor to fend for themselves. The second view is more sociological, one that understands poverty as rooted in the structure of society, not in the morals and behaviors of individuals.

**Blaming the Victim: The Culture of Poverty.** Blaming the poor for being poor stems from the myth that success requires only individual motivation and ability. Many in the United States adhere to this view and hence have a harsh opinion of the poor. This attitude is also reflected in U.S. public policy concerning poverty, which is rather ungenerous compared with other industrialized nations. Those who blame the poor for their own plight typically argue that poverty is the result of early childbearing, drug and alcohol abuse, refusal to enter the labor market, and crime. Such thinking puts the blame for poverty on individual choices, not on societal problems. In other words, it blames the victim, not the society, for social problems (Ryan 1971).

The **culture of poverty** argument attributes the major causes of poverty to the absence of work values and the irresponsibility of the poor. In this light, poverty is seen as a dependent way of life that is transferred, like other cultural values, from generation to generation. The culture of poverty argument has now been adapted by many policymakers to argue that the actual causes of poverty are found in the breakdown of major institutions, including the family, schools, and churches.

Is the culture of poverty argument true? To answer this question, we might ask: Is poverty transmitted across generations? Researchers have found only mixed support for this assumption. Many of those who are poor remain poor for only one or two years; only a small percentage of the poor are chronically poor. More often, poverty results from a household crisis, such as divorce, illness, unemployment, or parental death. People tend to cycle in and out of poverty. The public stereotype that poverty is passed through generations is thus not well supported by the facts.

A second question is, Do the poor want to work? The persistent public stereotype that they do not is central to the culture of poverty thesis. This attitude presumes that poverty is the fault of the poor, that if they would only change their values and adopt the American work ethic, then poverty would go away. What is the evidence for these claims?

Most of the able-bodied poor *do* work, even if only part-time. Moreover, as we saw above, the number of workers who constitute the *working poor* has increased. You can see why this is true when you calculate the income of someone working full-time for minimum wage. Someone working forty hours per week, fifty-two weeks per year, at minimum wage will have an income far below the poverty line. This is the major reason that many have organized a *living wage campaign*, intended to raise the federal minimum wage to provide workers with a decent standard of living.

Current policies that force those on welfare to work also tend to overlook how difficult it is for poor people to retain the jobs they get. Prior to welfare reform in the mid-1990s, poor women who went off welfare to take jobs often found they soon had to return to welfare because the wages they earned were not enough to support their families. Leaving welfare often means losing health benefits, yet incurring increased living expenses. The jobs that poor people find often do not lift them out of poverty. In sum, attributing poverty to the values of the poor is both unproven and a poor basis for public policy (Albelda and Tilly 1996; Catanzarite and Ortiz 1996).

**Structural Causes of Poverty.** From a sociological point of view, the underlying causes of poverty lie in the economic and social transformations taking place in the United States. Careful scholars do not attribute poverty to a single cause. There are many causes. Two of the most important are the *restructuring of the economy,* which has resulted in diminished earning power and increased unemployment, and *the status of women in the family and the labor market,* which has contributed to women being overrepresented among the poor. Add to these underlying conditions the federal policies in recent years that have *diminished social support for the poor* in the form of welfare, public housing, and job training. Given these reductions in federal support, it is little wonder that poverty is so widespread.

## Debunking Society's Myths

**Myth:** Mothers on welfare have more children to increase the size of their welfare checks.

**Sociological perspective:** No causal relationship exists between the size of welfare benefits and the number of births by welfare recipients. The presence of "family cap" policies (those that prohibit welfare benefits with the birth of an additional child) are not associated with women's childbearing (Ryan et al. 2006).

The restructuring of the economy has caused the disappearance of manufacturing jobs, traditionally an avenue of job security and social mobility for many workers, especially African American and Latino workers (Baca Zinn and Eitzen 2007; Wilson 1996). The working class has been especially vulnerable to these changes. Economic decline in those sectors of the economy where men have historically received good pay and good benefits has meant that fewer men are the sole support for their families. Most families now need two incomes to achieve a middle-class way of life. The new jobs that are being created fall primarily in occupations that offer low wages and few benefits; they also tend to be filled by women, especially women of color, leaving women poor and men out of work (McCall 2001; Browne 1999; Andreasse 1997). Such jobs offer little chance to get out of poverty. New jobs are also typically located in neighborhoods far away from the poor, creating a mismatch between the employment opportunities and the residential base of the poor.

Declining wage rates caused by transformations taking place within the economy fall particularly hard on young people, women, and African Americans and Latinos, who are the groups most likely to be among the working poor. The high rate of poverty among women is also strongly related to women's status in the family and the labor market. Divorce is one cause of poverty, although minority women are more likely than White women to be poor even within marriage (Catanzarite and Ortiz 1996). Women's child-care responsibilities make working outside the home on marginal incomes difficult. Many women with children cannot manage to work outside the home, because it leaves them with no one to watch their children. More women now depend on their own earnings to support themselves, their children, and other dependents. Whereas unemployment has always been considered a major cause of poverty among men, for women low wages have a major role. Notice that the median income for all women ($27,337 in 2007) is not that far above the poverty line.

The persistence of poverty also increases tensions between different classes and racial groups. William Julius Wilson, one of the most noted analysts of poverty and racial inequality, has written, "The ultimate basis for current racial tension is the deleterious effect of basic structural changes in the modern American economy on Black and White lower-income groups, changes that include uneven economic growth, increasing technology and automation, industry relocation, and labor market segmentation" (1978: 154). Wilson's comments demonstrate the power of sociological thinking by convincingly placing the causes of both poverty and racism in their societal context, instead of the individualistic thinking that tends to blame the poor for their plight.

## Welfare and Social Policy

Current welfare policy is covered by the 1996 Personal Responsibility and Work Reconciliation Act (PRWRA). This federal policy eliminated the longstanding welfare program titled Aid to Families with Dependent Children (AFDC), which was created in 1935 as part of the Social Security Act. Implemented during the Great Depression, AFDC was meant to assist poor mothers and their children. It acknowledged that some people are victimized by economic circumstances beyond their control and deserve assistance. For much of its lifetime, this law supported mostly White mothers and their children; not until the 1960s did welfare come to be identified with Black families.

The new welfare policy gives block grants to states to administer their own welfare programs through the program called **Temporary Assistance for Needy Families (TANF).** TANF stipulates a lifetime limit of five years for people to receive aid and requires all welfare recipients to find work within two years—a policy known as *workfare*. Those who have not found work within two months of receiving welfare can be required to perform community service jobs for free.

In addition, welfare policy denies payments to unmarried teen parents under eighteen years of age unless they stay in school and live with an adult. It also requires unmarried mothers to identify the fathers of their children or risk losing their benefits (Hays 2003; Edin and Kefalas 2005). These broad guidelines are established at the federal level, but individual states can be more restrictive, as many have been. At the heart of welfare reform is the idea that public assistance creates dependence, discouraging people from seeking jobs. The very title of the new law, emphasizing personal responsibility and work, suggests that poverty is the fault of the poor. Low-income women, for example, are stereotyped as just wanting to have babies to increase the size of their welfare checks—even though research finds no support for this idea (Edin and Kefalas 2005).

Is welfare reform working? Many claim that welfare reform is working because, since passage of the new law, the welfare rolls have shrunk. But having

## Is It True?*

| | True | False |
|---|---|---|
| 1. Income growth has been greatest for those in the middle class in recent years. | | |
| 2. The average American household has most of its wealth in the stock market. | | |
| 3. Social mobility is greater in the United States than in any other Western nation. | | |
| 4. The majority of welfare recipients are African American. | | |
| 5. Poor, teen mothers do not have the same values about marriage as middle-class people. | | |
| 6. Old people are the most likely to be poor. | | |
| 7. Poverty in U.S. suburbs is increasing. | | |
| *The answers can be found on page 207. | | |

## Is It True? (Answers)

1. FALSE. Income growth has been highest in the top 20 percent of income groups; most others have seen their incomes remain relatively flat (DeNavas-Walt et al. 2008).

2. FALSE. Eighty percent of all stock is owned by a small percentage of people. For most people, home ownership is the most common financial asset (Oliver and Shapiro 2006).

3. FALSE. The United States has lower rates of social mobility than Canada, Sweden, and Norway and ranks near the middle in comparison to other Western nations (Beller and Hout 2006).

4. FALSE. The majority of those receiving welfare (TANF) are White (U.S. Census Bureau 2008).

5. FALSE. Research finds that poor, teen mothers value marriage and want to be married, but associate marriage with economic security, which they do not think they can achieve (Edin and Kefalas 2005).

6. FALSE. Although those over 65 years of age used to be the most likely to be poor, poverty among the elderly has declined; the most likely to be poor are children (DeNavas-Walt et al. 2008).

7. TRUE. Although most of the poor live inside metropolitan areas, poverty in the suburbs has been increasing (De Navas-Walt et al. 2008).

fewer people on welfare does not mean poverty is reduced; in fact, as we have seen, poverty has actually increased since passage of welfare reform. Having fewer people on the rolls can simply mean that people are without a safety net.

Many studies also find that low-wage work does not lift former welfare recipients out of poverty (Hays 2003). Critics of the current policy also argue that forcing welfare recipients to work provides a cheap labor force for employers and potentially takes jobs from those already employed. In the first few years of welfare reform, the nation was also in the midst of an economic boom; jobs were thus more plentiful. But in an economic downturn, those who are on aid or in marginal jobs are vulnerable to economic distress, particularly given the time limits now placed on receiving public assistance (Albelda and Withorn 2002).

Research done to assess the impact of a changed welfare policy is relatively recent. Politicians brag that welfare rolls have shrunk, but reduction in the welfare rolls is a poor measure of the true impact of welfare reform because this would be true simply because people are denied benefits. And because welfare has been decentralized to the state level, studies of the impact of current law must be done on a state-by-state basis. Such studies are showing that those who have gone into workfare programs most often earn wages that keep them below the poverty line. Although some states report that family income has increased following welfare reform, the increases are slight. More people have been evicted because of falling behind on rent. Families also report an increase in other material hardships, such as phones and utilities being cut off. Marriage rates among former recipients have not changed, although more now live with nonmarital partners, most likely as a way of sharing expenses. The number of children living in families without either parent has also increased, probably because parents had to relocate to find work. In some states, the numbers of people neither working nor receiving aid also increased (Lewis et al. 2002; Acker et al. 2002; Bernstein 2002).

The public debate about welfare rages on, often in the absence of informed knowledge from sociological research and almost always without input from the subjects of the debate, the welfare recipients themselves. Although stigmatized as lazy and not wanting to work, those who have received welfare actually believe that it has negative consequences for them, but they say they have no other viable means of support. They typically have needed welfare when they could not find work or had small children and were without child care. Most were forced to leave their last job because of layoffs or firings or because the work was only temporary. Few left their jobs voluntarily.

Welfare recipients also say that the welfare system makes it hard to become self-supporting, because the wages one earns while on welfare are deducted from an already minimal subsistence. Furthermore, there is not enough affordable day care for mothers to leave home and get jobs. The biggest problem they face in their minds is lack of money. Contrary to the popular image of the conniving "welfare queen," welfare recipients want to be self-sufficient and provide for their families, but they face circumstances that make this very difficult to do. Indeed, studies of young, poor mothers find that they place a high value on marriage, but they do not think they or their boyfriends have the means to achieve the marriage ideals they cherish (Hays 2003; Edin and Kefalas 2005).

Another popular myth about welfare is that people use their welfare checks to buy things they do not need. But research finds that when former welfare recipients find work, their expenses actually go up. Although they may have increased income, their expenses (in the form of child care, clothing, transportation, lunch money, and so forth) increase, leaving them even less disposable income. Moreover, studies find that low-income mothers who buy "treats" for their children (name-brand shoes, a movie, candy, and so forth) do so because they want to be good mothers (Edin and Lein 1997).

Other beneficiaries of government programs have not experienced the same kind of stigma. Social Security supports virtually all retired people, yet they are not stereotyped as dependent on federal aid, unable to maintain stable family relationships, or insufficiently self-motivated. Spending on welfare programs is also a pittance compared with the spending on other federal programs. Sociologists conclude that the so-called welfare trap is not a matter of learned dependency, but a pattern of behavior forced on the poor by the requirements of sheer economic survival (Hays 2003; Edin and Kefalas 2005).

# Chapter Summary

- **What different kinds of stratification systems exist?**

  *Social stratification* is a relatively fixed hierarchical arrangement in society by which groups have different access to resources, power, and perceived social worth. All societies have systems of stratification, although they vary in composition and complexity. *Estate systems* are those in which power and property are held by a single elite class; in *caste systems,* placement in the stratification is by birth, and in *class systems,* placement is determined by achievement.

- **How do sociologists define class?**

  *Class* is the social structural position groups hold relative to the economic, social, political, and cultural resources of society. It is highly significant in determining one's *life chances.*

- **How is the class system structured in the United States?**

  Social class can be seen as a hierarchy, like a ladder, where income, occupation, and education are indicators of class. *Status attainment* is the process by which people end up in a given position in this hierarchy. *Prestige* is the value assigned to people and groups by others within this hierarchy. Classes are also organized around common interests and exist in conflict with one another.

- **Is there social mobility in the United States?**

  *Social mobility* is the movement between class positions. Education gives some boost to social mobility, but social mobility is more limited than people believe; most people end up in a class position very close to their class of origin. *Class consciousness* is both the perception that a class structure exists and the feeling of shared identification with others in one's class. The United States has not been a particularly class-conscious society because of the belief in upward mobility.

- **What analyses of social stratification do sociological theorists provide?**

  Karl Marx saw class as primarily stemming from economic forces; Max Weber had a multidimensional view of stratification, involving economic, social, and political dimensions. Functionalists argue that social inequality motivates people to fill the different positions in society that are needed for the survival of the whole, claiming that the positions most important for society require the greatest degree of talent or training and are, thus, most rewarded. Conflict theorists see social stratification as based on class conflict and blocked opportunity, pointing out that those at the bottom of the stratification system are least rewarded because they are subordinated by dominant groups.

- *How do sociologists explain why there is poverty in the United States?*

  The *culture of poverty thesis* is the idea that poverty is the result of the cultural habits of the poor that are transmitted from generation to generation, but sociologists see poverty as caused by social structural conditions, including unemployment, gender inequality in the workplace, and the absence of support for child care for working parents.

- *What current policies address the problem of poverty?*

  Current welfare policy, adopted in 1996, provides support through individual states, but recipients are required to work after two years of support and have a lifetime limit of five years' support.

## Key Terms

## Online Resources

### *Sociology: The Essentials* Companion Website

**www.cengage.com/sociology/andersen**

Visit your book companion website where you will find more resources to help you study and write your research papers. Resources include web links, learning objectives, Internet exercises, quizzing, and flash cards.

 **is an easy-to-use online resource that helps you study in less time to get the grade you want NOW.**

**www.cengage.com/login**

Need help studying? This site is your one-stop study shop. Take a Pre-Test and Cengage NOW will generate a Personalized Study Plan based on your test results. The Study Plan will identify the topics you need to review and direct you to online resources to help you master those topics. You can then take a Post-Test to determine the concepts you have mastered and what you still need to work on.

Chapter nine
CHAPTER NINE
Chapter

# Global Stratification

Global Stratification

Theories of Global Stratification

Consequences of Global Stratification

World Poverty

Globalization and Social Change

Chapter Summary

[ **"It takes a** village to raise a child," the saying goes. But it also seems to take a world to make a shirt—or so it seems from looking at the global dimensions of the production and distribution of goods. Try this simple experiment: Look at the labels on your clothing. (If you do this in class, try to do so without embarrassing yourself and others!) What do you see? "Made in Indonesia," "Made in Vietnam," "Made in Malawi," all indicating the linkage of the United States to systems of production around the world. The popular brand Nike, as just one example, has not a single factory in the United States, although its founder and chief executive officer is one of the wealthiest people in America. Nike products are manufactured mostly in Southeast Asia.

Taking your experiment further, ask yourself: Who made your clothing? A young person trying to lift his or her family out of poverty? Might it have been a child? In many areas of the world, one in five children under age 15 works (International Labour Organization 2002). What countries benefit most from this system of production? Answering these questions reveals much about the interconnection among countries in the global stratification system, a system in which the status of the people in one country is intricately linked to the status of the people in others. Recall from Chapter 1 that C. Wright Mills identified the task of sociology as seeing the social forces that exist beyond the individual. This is particularly important when studying global stratification.

*continued*

nine

CHAPTER NINE

CHAPTER NI

The person in the United States (or western Europe or Japan) who thinks he or she is expressing individualism by wearing the latest style is actually part of a global system of inequality. The adornments available to that person result from a whole network of forces that produce affluence in some nations and poverty in others. Dominant in the system of global stratification are the United States and other wealthy nations. Those at the top of the global stratification system have enormous power over the fate of other nations. Although world conflict stems from many sources, including religious differences, cultural conflicts, and struggles over political philosophy, the inequality between rich and poor nations causes much hatred and resentment. One cannot help but wonder what would happen if the differences between the wealth of some nations and the poverty of others were smaller. In this chapter we examine the dynamics and effects of global stratification.

# Global Stratification

In the world today, there are not only rich and poor people but also rich and poor countries. Some countries are well-off, some countries are doing so-so, and a growing number of countries are poor and getting poorer. There is, in other words, a system of **global stratification** in which the units we are considering are countries, much like a system of stratification within countries in which the units are individuals or families. Just as we can talk about the upper-class or lower-class individuals within a country, we can also talk of the equivalent upper-class or lower-class countries in this world system. One manifestation of global stratification is the great inequality in life chances that differentiates nations around the world. Simple measures of well-being, including life expectancy, infant mortality, and access to health services, reveal the consequences of a global system of inequality. And, the gap between the rich and poor is sometimes greater in nations where the average person is least well off. No longer can these nations be understood without considering the global system of stratification of which they are a part.

The effects of the global economy on inequality have become increasingly evident, as witnessed by public concerns about jobs being sent overseas. A coalition of unions, environmentalists, and other groups has also emerged to protest global trade policies that they believe threaten jobs and workers' rights in the United States, as well as contributing to environmental degradation. Such policies also encourage further McDonaldization (see Chapter 6). Thus, popular stores such as The Gap and Niketown often have been targets of political protests because they symbolize the expansion of global capitalism. Protestors see the growth of such stores as eroding local cultural values and spreading the values of unfettered consumerism around the globe. Protests over world trade policies also have emerged in a student-based movement against companies that manufacture apparel with college logos.

The relative affluence of the United States means that U.S. consumers have access to goods produced around the world. A simple thing, such as a child's toy, can represent this global system. For many young girls in the United States, Barbie™ is the ideal of fashion and romance. Young girls may have not just one Barbie, but several, each with a specific role and costume. Cheaply bought in the United States, but produced overseas, Barbie is manufactured by those probably not much older than the young girls who play with her and who would need all of their monthly pay to buy just one of the dolls that many U.S. girls collect by the dozens (Press 1996: 12).

The manufacturing of toys and clothing are examples of the global stratification that links the United States and other parts of the world. When companies export jobs, workers in the United States lose them. For example, note that in 1973, more than 56,000 U.S. workers were employed in toy factories. Now, even though the market has become glutted with the latest popular items, only 27,000 U.S. workers are employed in toy factories. The companies that make the toys amass profits, but U.S. workers lose jobs and then blame foreign workers for taking them. Major toy manufacturers have adopted policies that prohibit the exploitation of child labor, but clearly it is more profitable for companies to take their labor overseas where workers are paid far less and get fewer benefits than many workers in the United States.

## Rich and Poor

One dimension of stratification between countries is wealth. Enormous differences exist between the wealth of the countries at the top of the global stratification system and the wealth of the countries at the bottom. Although there are different ways to measure the wealth of nations, one of the most common is to use the per capita **gross national income (GNI).** The GNI measures the total output of goods and services produced by residents of a country each year plus the income from nonresident sources, divided by the size of the population. This does not truly reflect what individuals or families receive in wages or pay; it is simply each person's annual share of their country's income, should, in theory, the proceeds be shared equally. But you can use this measure to get a picture of global stratification (see Map 9.1).

Per capita GNI is reliable only in countries that are based on a cash economy. It does not measure informal exchanges or bartering in which resources are exchanged without money changing hands. These noncash transactions are not included in the GNI

*Global stratification often means that consumption in the more affluent nations is dependent on cheap labor in other less affluent nations.*

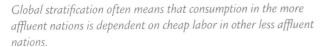

## VIEWING SOCIETY IN GLOBAL PERSPECTIVE

**Rich and Poor**

GNI per capita, 2003

- Low-income countries ($765 or less)
- Lower middle-income countries ($766–3,035)
- Upper middle-income countries ($3,036–9,385)
- High-income countries ($9,386 or more)
- No data

*Most nations are linked in a world system that produces wealth for some and poverty for others. The GNI (gross national income), depicted here on a per capita basis for most nations in the world, is an indicator of the wealth and poverty of nations.*

*Source:* World Bank Atlas 2007. © 2007 by World Bank. Reprinted by permission. **www.worldbank.org**

*Many common products marketed in the United States are produced in a global economy.*

United States is 419 times wealthier than an average citizen of Burundi. In Afghanistan, the GNI was estimated to be $875 or less (World Bank 2009), indicating the relative affluence of people in the United States.

Which are the wealthiest nations? Figure 9.1 lists the ten richest countries in the world measured by the annual per capita GNI in 2007. Luxembourg is the richest nation in the world on a per capita basis; the United States, seventh. Of course, Luxembourg has a tiny population compared with the United States. Note that most of the wealthy countries are in western Europe. They are mostly industrialized countries (or support such countries through such businesses as banking), and they are mostly urban. These countries represent the equivalent of the upper class—even though many people within them are poor.

Now consider the ten poorest countries in the world, also shown in Figure 9.1, and again using per capita GNI as the measure of wealth. Not every country reports reliable statistics on poverty, so there may be other extremely poor nations, but we do know that most of the world's poorest countries are in eastern or central Africa. These countries have not become industrialized, are largely rural, have high fertility rates, and still depend heavily on subsistence agriculture. These countries rank at the bottom of the global stratification system.

Clearly, many countries in the world are very poor, whereas other countries are rich. This does not mean that all people in rich countries are rich or that all people in poor countries are poor. But on average, people in poor countries are much worse off than people in rich countries. In many poor countries, the life of an average citizen is desperate; these countries also have the largest populations. In a world with a population

calculation, but they are more common in developing countries. As a result, measures of wealth based on the GNI, or other statistics that count cash transactions, are less reliable among the poorer countries and may underestimate the wealth of the countries at the lower end of the economic scale.

The per capita GNI of the United States, which is one of the wealthier nations in the world (though not the wealthiest on a per capita basis), was $46,040 in 2007. The per capita GNI in Burundi, one of the poorest countries in the world, was $110. Using per capita GNI as a measure of wealth, the average person in the

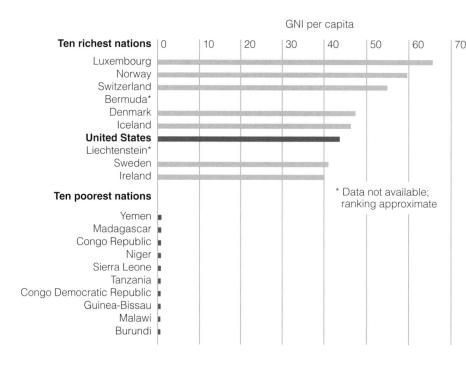

**GNI per capita**

**Ten richest nations**

|  | |
| --- | --- |
| Luxembourg | |
| Norway | |
| Switzerland | |
| Bermuda* | |
| Denmark | |
| Iceland | |
| **United States** | |
| Liechtenstein* | |
| Sweden | |
| Ireland | |

**Ten poorest nations**

|  | |
| --- | --- |
| Yemen | |
| Madagascar | |
| Congo Republic | |
| Niger | |
| Sierra Leone | |
| Tanzania | |
| Congo Democratic Republic | |
| Guinea-Bissau | |
| Malawi | |
| Burundi | |

\* Data not available; ranking approximate

**FIGURE 9.1** *The Rich and the Poor: A World View\**

\*GNI per capita, measured in U.S. dollars.

*Source:* World Bank Atlas 2002, p. 18-19. Copyright © by World Bank. Reprinted by permission. **www.worldbank.org**

*Global stratification means that enormous differences exist not only in the relative well-being of different countries but also within nations. Large numbers of people live in poverty such as in this refugee camp at Mazar-i-Sharif in Afghanistan—one of the poorest nations in the world.*

of nearly six billion, more than three billion—more than half the world's population—live in the poorest forty-five countries. Often poor nations are rich with natural resources but are exploited for such resources by more powerful nations. We will look more closely at the nature and causes of world poverty later in this chapter.

## Global Networks of Power and Influence

Global stratification involves nations in a large and integrated network of both economic and political relationships. **Power**—meaning the ability of a country to exercise control over other countries or groups of countries—is a significant dimension of global stratification. Countries can exercise several kinds of power over other countries, including military, economic, and political power. The **core countries** have the most power in the world economic system. These countries control and profit the most from the world system, and thus they are the "core" of the world system. These include the powerful nations of Europe, the United States, Australia, and Japan.

Surrounding the core countries, both structurally and geographically, are the **semiperipheral countries** that are semi-industrialized and, to some degree, represent a kind of middle class (such as Spain, Turkey, and Mexico). They play a middleman role, extracting profits from the poor countries and passing those profits on to the core countries. At the bottom of the world stratification system, in this

model, are the **peripheral countries.** These are the poor, largely agricultural countries of the world. Even though they are poor, they often have important natural resources that are exploited by the core countries. This exploitation, in turn, keeps them from developing and perpetuates their poverty. Often these nations are politically unstable, and, though they exercise little world power, political instability can cause a crisis for core nations that depend on their resources. Military intervention by the United States or European nations is often the result.

This categorizing system emphasizes the power of each country in the world economic system. Another way that these countries are sometimes labeled is as first-, second-, and third-world nations. This language grows out of the politics of the Cold War and reflects the political and economic dimensions of global stratification. **First-world countries** consist of the industrialized capitalist countries of the world, including the United States, New Zealand, Australia, Japan, and the countries of western Europe. They are industrialized and have a market-based economy and a democratically elected government. The **second-world countries** are socialist countries, which include the former Soviet Union, China, Cuba, North Korea, and, prior to the fall of the Berlin Wall, the eastern European nations. During the Cold War, these countries had a communist-based government and a state-managed economy, as some still do. Although less developed than the first-world countries, the second-world countries tried to provide citizens with services such as free education, health care, and low-cost housing, consistent with the principles of socialism, but poverty often prevented them from doing so. Moreover, their governments were not democratically elected. **Third-world countries** in this scheme are the countries that are poor, underdeveloped, largely rural, and with high levels of poverty. Many of the governments of the third-world countries are autocratic dictatorships (ruled by one person with absolute authority), though not all. Although these countries are generally poor, wealth is concentrated in the hands of only a few elite.

Because this system of categorization was based on the logic of the Cold War, it has changed. For instance, the oil-rich countries of the Middle East are not part of the first or second world, according to this scheme, but they also do not belong in the same category as the poor countries of Africa and Asia because they have considerably more wealth. The collapse of the Soviet Union and the change in the governments of eastern Europe has led to the transformation of almost all the second-world countries. Although some countries still have a communist-based government, many of them, including China, are moving toward a market economic system. Still, like the terms *core* and *periphery,* the terms *first-, second-,* and *third-world* are useful in denoting the power differences of nations within global stratification.

# >doing sociological research

## Servants of Globalization: Who Does the Domestic Work?

*Research Question:* International migration is becoming an increasingly common phenomenon. Women are one of the largest groups to experience migration, often leaving poor nations to become domestic workers in wealthier nations. What are these women's experiences in the context of global stratification? This is what Rhacel Salazar Parreñas wanted to know.

*Research Method:* Parreñas studied two communities of Filipina women, one in Los Angeles and one in Rome, Italy, conducting her research through extensive interviewing with Filipina domestic workers in these two locations. She supplemented the interviews with participant observation in church settings, after-work social gatherings, and in employers' homes. The interviews were conducted in English and Tagalog—sometimes a mixture of both.

*Research Results:* Parreñas found that Filipina domestics experienced many status inconsistencies. They were upwardly mobile in terms of their home country but were excluded from the middle-class Filipino communities in the communities where they lived. Thus, they experienced feelings of social exclusion in addition to being separated from their own families.

*Conclusions and Implications:* The women Parreñas studied are part of a new social form: *transnational families*—that is, families whose members live across the borders of nations. These Filipinas provide the labor for more affluent households while their own lives are disrupted by these new global forces. As global economic restructuring evolves, it may be that more and more families will take this form as they adapt to changing economic and social conditions.

### Questions to Consider

1. Are there domestic workers in your community who provide child care and other household work for middle- and upper-class households? What is the race, ethnicity, nationality, and gender of these workers? What does this tell you about the division of labor in domestic work and its relationship to global stratification?

2. Why do you think domestic labor is so underpaid and undervalued? Are there social changes that might result in a reevaluation of the value of this work?

*Source:* Parreñas, Rhacel Salazar. 2001. *Servants of Globalization: Women, Migration and Domestic Work.* Stanford, CA: Stanford University Press.

## SEE *FOR YOURSELF*

### *THE GLOBAL ECONOMY OF CLOTHING*

Look at the labels in your clothes and note where your clothing was made. Where are the products bearing your college logos manufactured and sold? Who profits from the distribution of these goods? What does this tell you about the relationship of *core, semiperipheral,* and *peripheral* countries within world systems theory? What further information would reveal the connections between the country where you live and the countries where your clothing is made and distributed?

## Race and Global Inequality

Along with class inequality, there is a racial component to world inequality, which can be seen in several ways. The rich core countries, those that dominate the world system, are largely European, with the exception of the United States and Japan. In Europe and the United States, the population is mostly White; in the poor countries of the world, mostly in Africa, Asia, or South America, the populations are largely people of color. On average, there are vast differences in life chances and lifestyle between the countries of the world with White populations and the countries of the world with Black populations.

Exploitation of the human and natural resources of regions populated by people of color has characterized the history of Western capitalism, with people of color being dominated by Western imperialism and colonialism. The inequities that have resulted are enormous. Patterns of malnutrition and hunger show these inequities. More than one billion people in the world suffer from malnutrition and hunger. The vast majority of these people are people of color—that is, those not of European descent (Uvin 1998).

How did this racial inequality come about? On the surface, global capitalism is not explicitly racist, as were earlier forms of industrial capitalism. Yet, in fact, it is the rapid expansion of the global capital system that has led to the increase in racial inequality between nations. In the new capitalist system, a new **international division of labor** has emerged that is not tied to place but can employ cheap labor anywhere. Cheap labor is usually found in non-Western countries. The exploitation of cheap labor has created a poor and dependent workforce that is mostly people of color. The profits accrue to the wealthy owners, who are mostly White, resulting in a racially divided world. Some have argued further that multinational corporations' exploitation of the poor peripheral nations has forced an exodus of unskilled workers from the impoverished nations to the rich nations. The flood of third-world refugees into the industrialized nations is thereby increasing racial tensions, fostering violence, and destroying worker solidarity (Sirvananadan 1995).

South Africa, the United States, and Brazil each developed different sets of racial categories. Although all three countries have many people of mixed descent, race is defined differently in each place. In South Africa, the particular history of Dutch and English colonialism led to strongly drawn racial categories that defined people in four separate categories: "White," "coloured" (including indigenous Khoi and San people, as well as people of mixed descent), "Black," and "Indian." Except for Black South Africans, who had no political representation under apartheid, there were three separate parliaments—one for each of the other groups. In the United States, given its history of slavery, the "one drop" rule was used, which defined anyone with any African heritage as Black, thus ruling out any category of mixed race.

Brazil is yet a different case. The Brazilian elite declared Brazil a racial democracy at the early stages of national development. Racial differences were thought not to matter. Yet, instead of creating an egalitarian society free of racism, Afro-Brazilians were still of lower social status and Euro-Brazilians remain at the highest social status, suggesting that color itself stratifies people—a sociological phenomenon sometimes referred to as "colorism" (Marx 1997; Frederickson 2003; Telles 2004).

# Theories of Global Stratification

How did world inequality occur? Sociological explanations of world stratification generally fall into three camps: modernization theory, dependency theory, and world systems theory, each explained here (see Table 9.1).

## Modernization Theory

**Modernization theory** views the economic development of countries as stemming from technological change. According to this theory, a country becomes more "modernized" by increased technological development, and this technological development is also dependent on other countries. Modernization theory was initially developed in the 1960s to explain why some countries had achieved economic development and why some had not (Rostow 1978).

Modernization theory sees economic development as a process by which traditional societies become more complex and differentiated. For economic development to occur, modernization theory predicts, countries must change their traditional attitudes, values, and institutions. Economic achievement is thought to

| table9.1 | Theories of Global Stratification | | |
|---|---|---|---|
| | **Modernization Theory** | **Dependency Theory** | **World Systems Theory** |
| *Economic Development* | Arises from relinquishing traditional cultural values and embracing new technologies and market-driven attitudes and values | Exploits the least powerful nations to the benefit of wealthier nations that then control the political and economic systems of the exploited countries | Has resulted in a single economic system stemming from the development of a world market that links core, semiperipheral, and peripheral nations |
| *Poverty* | Results from adherence to traditional values and customs that prevent societies from competing in a modern global economy | Results from the dependence of low-income countries on wealthy nations | Is the result of core nations extracting labor and natural resources from peripheral nations |
| *Social Change* | Involves increasing complexity, differentiation, and efficiency | Is the result of neocolonialism and the expansion of international capitalism | Leads to an international division of labor that increasingly puts profit in the hands of a few while exploiting those in the poorest and least powerful nations |

derive from attitudes and values that emphasize hard work, saving, efficiency, and enterprise. These values are said by the theory to be found in modern (developed) countries but are lacking in traditional societies. Modernization theory suggests that nations remain underdeveloped when traditional customs and culture discourage individual achievement and kin relations dominate.

As an outgrowth of functionalist theory, modernization theory derives some of its thinking from the work of Max Weber. In *The Protestant Ethic and the Spirit of Capitalism* (1958/1904), Weber saw the economic development that occurred in Europe during the Industrial Revolution as a result of the values and attitudes of Protestantism. The Industrial Revolution took place in England and northern Europe, Weber argued, because the people of this area were hardworking Protestants who valued achievement and believed that God helped those who helped themselves.

Modernization theory is similar to the argument of the culture of poverty, which sees people as poor because they have poor work habits, engage in poor time management, are not willing to defer gratification, and do not save or take advantage of educational opportunities (see Chapter 8). Countries are poor, in other words, because they have poor attitudes and poor institutions.

Modernization theory can partially explain why some countries have become successful. Japan is an example of a country that has made huge strides in economic development, in part because of a national work ethic (McCord and McCord 1986). But the work ethic alone does not explain Japan's success. In sum, modernization theory may partially explain the value context in which some countries become successful and others do not, but it is not a substitute for explanations that also look at the economic and political context of national development. It also rests on an arrogant perspective that the United States and other more economically developed nations have superior values compared to other nations. Critics point out that this perspective blames countries for being poor when other causes of their status in the world may be outside their control. Whether a country develops or remains poor may be the result of other countries exploiting the less powerful. Modernization theory does not sufficiently take into account the interplay and relationships between countries that can affect a country's economic or social condition.

Developing countries, modernization theory says, are better off if they let the natural forces of competition guide world development. Free markets, according to this perspective, will result in the best economic order. But, as critics argue, markets do not develop independently of government's influence. Governments can spur or hinder economic development, especially as they work with private companies to enact export strategies, restrict imports, or place embargoes on the products of nonfavored nations.

## Dependency Theory

Although market-oriented theories may explain why some countries are successful, they do not explain why some countries remain in poverty or why some countries have not developed. It is necessary to look at issues outside the individual countries and to examine the connections between them. Drawing on the fact that many of the poorest nations are former colonies of European powers, another theory of world stratification focuses on the processes and results of European colonization and imperialism. This theory, called **dependency theory,** focuses on explaining the persistence of poverty in the world. It holds that the poverty of the low-income countries is a direct result of their political and economic dependence on the wealthy countries. Specifically, dependency theory argues that the poverty of many countries is a result of exploitation by powerful countries. This theory is derived from the work of Karl Marx, who foresaw that a capitalist world economy would create an exploited class of dependent countries, just as capitalism within countries had created an exploited class of workers.

Dependency theory begins by examining the historical development of this system of inequality. As the European countries began to industrialize in the 1600s, they needed raw materials for their factories, and they needed places to sell their products. To accomplish this, the European nations colonized much of the world, including most of Africa, Asia, and the Americas. **Colonialism** is a system by which Western nations became wealthy by taking raw materials from colonized societies and reaping profits from products finished in the homeland. Colonialism worked best for the industrial countries when the colonies were kept undeveloped to avoid competition with the home country. For example, India was a British colony from 1757 to 1947. During that time, Britain bought cheap cotton from India, made it into cloth in British mills, and then sold the cloth back to India, making large profits. Although India was able to make cotton into cloth at a much cheaper cost than Britain, and very fine cloth at that, Britain nonetheless did not allow India to develop its cotton industry. As long as India was dependent on Britain, Britain became wealthy and India remained poor.

Under colonialism, dependency was created by the direct political and military control of the poor countries by powerful developed countries. Most colonial powers were European countries, but other countries, particularly Japan and China, had colonies as well. Colonization came to an end soon after the Second World War, largely because of protests by colonized people and the resulting movement for independence. As a result, according to dependency theory, the powerful countries turned to other ways to control the poor countries and keep them dependent. The powerful countries still intervene directly in the affairs of the dependent nations by sending troops or, more often, by imposing economic or political restrictions and sanctions. But other methods, largely economic, have been developed to control the dependent poor countries, such as price controls, tariffs, and, especially, the control of credit. Indeed, the level of debt that some nations accrue is a major source of global inequality.

The rich industrialized nations, according to dependency theory, are able to set prices for raw materials produced by the poor countries at very low levels so that the poor countries are unable to accumulate enough profit to industrialize. As a result, the poor, dependent countries must borrow from the rich countries. However, debt creates only more dependence. Many poor countries are so deeply indebted to the major industrial countries that they must follow the economic edicts of the rich countries that loaned them the money, thus increasing their dependency. This form of international control has sometimes been called **neocolonialism,** a form of control of the poor countries by the rich countries but without direct political or military involvement.

**Multinational corporations** are companies that draw a large share of their profits from overseas investments and that conduct business across national borders. They play a role in keeping the dependent nations poor, dependency theory suggests. Although their executives and stockholders are from the industrialized countries, multinational corporations recognize no national boundaries and pursue business where they can best make a profit. Multinationals buy resources where they can get them cheapest, manufacture their products where production and labor costs are lowest, and sell their products where they can make the largest profits.

Many critics fault companies for perpetuating global inequality by taking advantage of cheap overseas labor to make large profits for U.S. stockholders.

Companies are, in fact, doing what they should be doing in a market system: trying to make a profit. Nonetheless, dependency theory views the practices of multinationals as responsible for maintaining poverty in the poor parts of the world.

One criticism of dependency theory is that many poor countries were never colonies, for example, Ethiopia. Some former colonies have also done well. Two of the greatest postwar success stories of economic development are Singapore and Hong Kong. Both of these countries were British colonies—Hong Kong until 1997—and clearly dependent on Britain, yet they have had successful economic development precisely because of their dependence on Britain. Other former colonies are also improving economically, such as India.

## World Systems Theory

Modernization theory examines the factors internal to an individual country, and dependency theory looks to the relationship between countries or groups of countries. Another approach to global stratification is called **world systems theory.** Like the dependency theory, this theory begins with the premise that no nation in the world can be considered in isolation. Each country, no matter how remote, is tied in many ways to the other countries in the world. However, unlike dependency theory, world systems theory argues that there is a world economic system that must be understood as a single unit, not in terms of individual countries or groups of countries. This theoretical approach derives to some degree from the work of the dependency theorists and is most closely associated with the work of Immanuel Wallerstein in *The Modern World System* (1974) and *The Modern World System II* (1980). According to this theory, the level of economic development is explained by

*The gap between the rich and poor worldwide can be staggering. At the same time that many struggle for mere survival, others enjoy the pleasantries of a gentrified lifestyle.*

*Guest workers programs provide immigrant labor in many nations of the world. Here Indian immigrant workers stage a hunger strike in Washington, DC to protest the treatment of immigrant workers helping to restore New Orleans in the aftermath of hurricane Katrina.*

understanding each country's place and role in the world economic system.

This world system has been developing since the sixteenth century. The countries of the world are tied together in many ways, but of primary importance are the economic connections in the world markets of goods, capital, and labor. All countries sell their products and services on the world market and buy products and services from other countries. However, this is not a market of equal partners. Because of historical and strategic imbalances in this economic system, some countries are able to use their advantage to create and maintain wealth, whereas other countries that are at a disadvantage remain poor. This process has led to a global system of stratification in which the units are not people but countries.

World systems theory sees the world divided into three groups of interrelated nations: core or first-world countries, semiperiperial or second-world countries, and peripheral or third-world countries. This world economic system has resulted in a modern world in which some countries have obtained great wealth and other countries have remained poor. The core countries control and limit the economic development in the peripheral countries so as to keep the peripheral countries from developing and competing with them on the world market; thus the core countries can continue to purchase raw materials at a low price.

Although world systems theory was originally developed to explain the historical evolution of the world system, modern scholars now focus on the international division of labor and its consequences. This approach is an attempt to overcome some of the

shortcomings in world systems theory by focusing on the specific mechanism by which differential profits are attached to the production of goods and services in the world market. A tennis shoe made by Nike is designed in the United States; uses synthetic rubber made from petroleum from Saudi Arabia; is sewn in Indonesia; is transported on a ship registered in Singapore, which is run by a Korean management firm using Filipino sailors; and is finally marketed in Japan and the United States. At each of these stages, profits are taken, but at very different rates.

## *thinking sociologically*

What are the major industries in your community? Find out in what parts of the world they do business, including where their product is produced. How does the *international division of labor* affect jobs in your region?

World systems theorists call this global production process a **commodity chain,** the network of production and labor processes by which a product becomes a finished commodity. By following a commodity through its production cycle and seeing where the profits go at each link of the chain, one can identify which country is getting rich and which country is being exploited.

World systems theory helps explain the growing phenomenon of international migration. An international division of labor means that the need for cheap labor in some of the industrial and developing nations draws workers from poorer parts of the globe. International migration is also the result of refugees seeking asylum from war-torn parts of the world or from countries where political oppression, often against particular ethnic groups, forces some to leave. The

*Public debates over immigration policy have mobilized many who point out that immigration has long been a part of our national heritage.*

development of a world economy, however, is resulting in large changes in the composition of populations around the globe. **World cities,** that is, cities that are closely linked through the system of international commerce, have emerged. Within these cities, families and their surrounding communities often form *transnational communities,* communities that may be geographically distant but socially and politically close. Linked through various communication and transportation networks, transnational communities share information, resources, and strategies for coping with the problems of international migration.

International migration, sometimes legal, sometimes not, has radically changed the racial and ethnic composition of populations not only in the United States but also in many European and Asian nations (Rodriquez 1999; Light et al. 1998). Some of those who migrate internationally are professional workers, but many others remain in the lowest segments of the labor force where, although their work is critical to the world economy, they are treated with hostility and suspicion, discriminated against, and stereotyped as undeserving and threatening. In many nations, including the United States, this has led to numerous political tensions over immigration, even while the emergence of migrant groups in world cities is now a major feature of the urban landscape (White 1998).

There are a number of criticisms of world systems theory. Certainly, it is useful to see the world as an interconnected set of economic ties between countries and to understand that these ties often result in the exploitation of poor countries. For one, countries that were once at the center of this world system no longer occupy such a lofty position—England, for example. Peripheral countries can also improve their standard of living with investment by core countries, although the benefits do not accrue equally to groups within such nations. Low-wage factories may benefit managers, but not the working class. Even core countries can be hurt by the world system, such as when jobs

move overseas. Who benefits from this world system is differentiated—in all countries—by one's placement, not just in the world class system but in the class system internal to each country within this global system. Also, low-wage sweatshops are found in all nations, not just the peripheral countries. Despite these criticisms, world systems theory has provided a powerful tool for understanding global inequality.

# Consequences of Global Stratification

It is clear that some nations are wealthy and powerful and some are poor and powerless. What are the consequences of this world stratification system? Table 9.2 shows some of the basic indicators of national well-being for selected nations. You can see that there are considerable differences in the quality of life in these different places in the world.

## Population

One of the biggest differences in rich and poor nations is population. The poorest countries comprise three billion people—over half the world's population (World Bank 2007). The poorest countries also have the highest birthrates and the highest death rates. The total *fertility rate,* how many live births a woman will have over her lifetime at current fertility rates, shows that in the poorest countries women on average have almost five children. Because of this high fertility rate, the populations of poor countries are growing faster than the populations of wealthy countries; these countries therefore also have a high proportion of young children.

In contrast, the richest countries have a total population of approximately one billion people—only 15 percent of the world's population. The populations of the richest countries are not growing nearly as fast

| table9.2 | Quality of Life: A Comparative Perspective | | | | |
| --- | --- | --- | --- | --- | --- |
| | Life Expectancy (years) | Infant Mortality (per 1000 births) | Adult Literacy (percent of population over 15) | Child Malnutrition (percent underweight) | Access to Safe Water (percent of population) |
| Afghanistan | 45 yrs | 165 | 29% | n/a | 40% |
| Iran | 71 | 32 | 77 | n/a | 94 |
| Iraq | 61 | 115 | 60 | 12% | 81 |
| Mexico | 75.1 | 22.6 | 91 | n/a | 97 |
| United States | 77.9 | 6.9 | 95 | 1 | 100 |

n/a, not available.

*Source:* World Bank. 2007. **www.worldbank.org;** U.S. Census Bureau. 2006. *Statistical Abstract of the United States.* Washington, DC: U.S. Department of Commerce.

as the populations of the poorest countries. In the richest countries, women have about two children over their lifetime, and the populations of these countries are growing by only 1.2 percent. Many of the richest countries, including most of the countries of Europe, are actually experiencing population declines. With a low fertility rate, the rich countries have proportionately fewer children, but they also have proportionately more elderly, which can also be a burden on societal resources. Different from the poorest nations, the richest ones are largely urban.

Rapid population growth as a result of high fertility rates can make a large difference in the quality of life of the country. Countries with high birthrates are faced with the challenge of having too many children and not enough adults to provide for the younger generation. Public services, such as schools and hospitals, are strained in high-birthrate countries, especially because these countries are poor to begin with. However, very low birthrates, as many rich countries are now experiencing, can also lead to problems. In countries with low birthrates, there often are not enough young people to meet labor force needs, and workers must be imported from other countries.

Although the data clearly show that poor countries have large populations and high birthrates and rich countries have smaller populations and low birthrates, does this mean that the large population results in the low level of wealth of the country or that high fertility rates keep countries poor?

Scholars are divided on the relationship between the rate of population growth and economic development (Cassen 1994; Demeny 1991). Some theorize that rapid population growth and high birthrates lead to economic stagnation and that too many people keep a country from developing, thus miring the country in poverty (Ehrlich 1990). However, other researchers point out that some countries with very large populations have become developed (Coale 1986). After all, the United States has the third largest population in the world at 281 million people, yet it is one of the richest and most developed nations in the world. China and India, the two nations in the world with the largest populations, are also showing significant economic development. Scholars now believe that even though in some situations large population and high birthrates can impede economic development, in general fertility levels are affected by levels of industrialization, not the other way around. That is, as countries develop, their fertility levels decrease and their population growth levels off (Hirschman 1994; Watkins 1987).

## Health and Environment

Significant differences are also evident in the basic health standards of countries, depending on where they are in the global stratification system. The high-income countries have lower childhood death rates, higher life expectancies, and fewer children born

underweight. People born today in wealthy countries can expect to live about seventy-seven years, and women outlive men by several years. Except for some isolated or poor areas of the rich countries, almost all people have access to clean water and acceptable sewer systems.

In the poorest countries the situation is completely different. Many children die within the first five years of life, people live considerably shorter lives, and fewer people have access to clean water and adequate sanitation. In the low-income countries, the problems of sanitation, clean water, childhood death rates, and life expectancies are all closely related. In many of the poor countries, drinking water is contaminated from poor or nonexistent sewage treatment. This contaminated water is then used to drink, to clean eating utensils, and to make baby formula. For adults, waterborne illnesses such as cholera and dysentery sometimes cause severe sickness but seldom result in death. However, children under age 5, and especially those under the age of 1, are highly susceptible to the illnesses carried in contaminated water. A common cause of childhood death in countries with low incomes is dehydration brought on by the diarrhea contracted by drinking contaminated water.

Degradation of the environment is a problem that affects all nations, which are linked in one vast environmental system. But global stratification also means that some nations suffer at the hands of others. Overdevelopment is resulting in deforestation. The depletion of this natural resource is most severe in South America, Africa, Mexico, and Southeast Asia (World Bank 2007). On the other hand, the overproduction of "greenhouse gas," emission of carbon dioxide from the burning of fossil fuels, is most severe in the United States, Canada, Australia, parts of western Europe and Russia, and, increasingly, China—places that use the most energy.

Although high-income countries have only 15 percent of the world population, together they use more than half of the world's energy. The United States alone uses one-quarter of the world's energy, though it holds only 4 percent of the world's population (see Figure 9.2). Safe water is also crucial; more than a

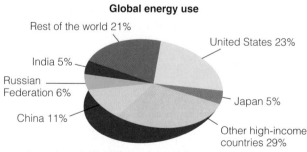

**FIGURE 9.2** *Who Uses the World's Energy?*

billion people do not have access to safe water. Moreover, water supplies are declining, a problem that will only be exacerbated by population growth and economic development. The World Bank has, in fact, warned that one-half of the world's population will face severe water shortage by the year 2025 (World Bank 2004). Clearly, global stratification has some irreversible environmental effects that are felt around the globe.

## Education and Illiteracy

In the high-income nations of the world, education is almost universal, and the vast majority of people have attended school at least at some level. Literacy and school enrollment are now taken for granted in the high-income nations, although people in these wealthy nations who do not have a good education stand little chance of success. In the middle- and lower-income nations, the picture is quite different. Elementary school enrollment, virtually universal in wealthy nations, is less common in the middle-income nations and even less common in the poorest nations.

How do people survive who are not literate or educated? In much of the world, education takes place outside formal schooling. Just because many people in the poorer countries never go to school does not mean that they are ignorant or that they are uneducated. Most of the education in the world takes place in family settings, in religious congregations, or in other settings where elders teach the next generation the skills and knowledge they need to survive. This type of informal education often includes basic literacy and math skills that people in these poorer countries need for their daily lives.

The disadvantage of this informal and traditional education is that although it prepares people for their traditional lives, it often does not give them the skills and knowledge needed to operate in the modern world. In an increasingly technological world, this can perpetuate the underdeveloped status of some nations.

## Gender Inequality

The position of a country in the world stratification system also affects gender relations within different countries. Poverty is usually felt more by women than by men. Although gender inequality has not been achieved in the industrialized countries, compared with women in other parts of the world women in the wealthier countries are much better off.

The United Nations is one of the organizations that carefully monitors the status of women globally. Their reports indicate mixed news with regard to women's status around the world. On the one hand, women's poverty has declined in some of the nations where it has been extreme, particularly in India, China, and some parts of Latin America. But in sub-Saharan Africa, women's poverty has increased. And though women's share of representation in governments has increased, they still hold only 16 percent of parliamentary seats worldwide. Also, although women have achieved near equity in levels of primary education, there are large gaps in the status of women and men in secondary and higher education—a fact that has huge implications for the work women do in a global economy that increasingly demands educational attainment (United Nations 2005a).

Perhaps most distressing is the global extent of violence against women. Violence takes many forms, including violence within the family, rape, sexual harassment, sex trafficking and prostitution, and state-based violence, among other things. The United Nations has concluded that "violence against women persists in every country in the world as a pervasive violation of human rights and a major impediment to achieving gender equality" (United Nations 2006a: 9). Several factors put women at risk of violence, ranging from individual level risk factors (such as a history of abuse as a child and substance abuse) to societal level factors, such as gender roles that entrench male dominance and societal norms that tolerate violence as a means of conflict resolution (see Table 9.3). Clearly, the inequalities that mark global stratification have particularly deleterious effects for the world's women.

## War and Terrorism

The consequences of global stratification are also found in the international conflicts that bring war and an increased risk of terrorism. Although global inequality is certainly not the only cause of such problems, it contributes to the instability of world peace and the threat of terrorism. Global stratification generates inequities in the distribution of power between nations. Moreover, globalization has created a world-based capitalist class with unprecedented wealth and power. This is a class that now crosses national borders, thus some have defined it as a "transnational capitalist class" (Langman and Morris 2002). Coupled with the enormous poverty that exists, the visibility of this class and its association with Western values leads to resentment and conflict. Furthermore, attempts by wealthier nations to control access to the world's natural resources, such as oil, generate much political conflict. Thus, the same power and affluence that makes the United States a leader throughout the world makes it a target by those who resent its dominance.

In the Middle East, for example, oil production has created prosperity for some and exposed people in these nations to the values of Western culture. When people from different nations, such as those in the Middle East, study at U.S. universities and travel on business or vacations, they are exposed to Western values and patterns of consumption. As one commentator has noted, "Even those who have remained at home have not escaped exposure to Western culture.

| table9.3 | Risk Factors for Violence Against Women: A Global Analysis |
|---|---|

The United Nations has studied the frequent use of violence against women in the world and identified the factors that put women at risk. These factors are found at various levels.

*Individual Level:*
- Frequent use of alcohol and drugs
- Membership in marginalized communities
- History of abuse as a child
- Witnessing marital violence in the home

*Community Level:*
- Women's isolation and lack of social support
- Community attitudes that tolerate and legitimate male violence
- High levels of social and economic inequality, including poverty

*Family/Relationship Level:*
- Male control of wealth
- Male control of decision making
- History of marital violence
- Significant disparities in economic, educational, or employment status

*Societal Level:*
- Gender roles that entrench male dominance and women's subordination
- Tolerance of violence as a means of conflict resolution
- Inadequate laws and policies to prevent and punish violence
- Limited awareness and sensitivity on the part of officials and social service providers

*Source:* United Nations. 2006a. *In-Depth Study on All Forms of Violence Against Women.* New York: United Nations.

In most of the countries of the modern Middle East western cultural influences are pervasive. They see western television programs, they watch western movies, they listen to western music, frequently wear western clothes and visit western web sites. Even western foods are locally available. McDonald's are now found in many of the major cities" (Bailey 2003: 341). Moreover, the sexual liberalism of Western nations and the relative equality of women also add

*Global conflicts, including war, can result from the inequality that global stratification produces..*

to the volatile mix of nations clashing (Norris and Inglehart 2002).

As a result, some traditional leaders, including religious clerics, define Western culture as a source of degeneracy. Countries such as the United States, where consumerism is rampant, then become the target of those who see this as a threat to their traditional way of life (Ehrlich and Liu 2002). In this sense, global stratification and the dominance of Western culture are inseparable (Bailey 2003). Understood in this way, terrorism is not just a question of clashing religious values (although that is a contributing factor) but also stems from the global dominance of some nations over others. This is why those who commit atrocious acts, like flying jets into the World Trade Center towers, can believe themselves as fighting for a righteous cause.

**Terrorism** can be defined as premeditated, politically motivated violence perpetrated against noncombatant targets by persons or groups who use their action to try to achieve their political ends (White 2002). Terrorism can be executed through violence or threats of violence and can be executed through various means—suicide bombs, biochemical terror, cyberterror, or other means. Because terrorists operate outside the bounds of normative behavior, it is very difficult to prevent. Although rigid safeguards can be put in place, such safeguards also threaten the freedoms that are characteristics of open, democratic societies. The fact that terrorism is so difficult to stop contributes to the fear that it is intended to generate.

Inequality is also connected to the context in which terrorism emerges. A study of Al Qaeda terrorists finds that the leaders tend to come from middle-class backgrounds, though they often use those who are young, poorly educated, and economically disadvantaged to carry out suicide missions. Families of suicide bombers often receive large cash payments; at the same time they can feel they have served a sacred cause (Stern 2003). The fact that one-third of Iraqis now live in poverty—a change from having a thriving, largely middle-class economy in the 1970s and 1980s—helps explain the high rates of violence within Iraq now (United Nations News Center 2007). This also suggests that improving the lives of those who now feel collectively humiliated could provide some protection against terrorism.

# World Poverty

One fact of global inequality is the growing presence and persistence of poverty in many parts of the world. There is poverty in the United States, but very few people in the United States live in the extreme levels of deprivation found in some of the poor countries of the world, as seen in Map 9.2.

In the United States, the poverty level is determined by the yearly income for a family of four that is considered necessary to maintain a suitable standard of living. Twelve and a half percent of Americans live in poverty (DeNavas-Walt et al. 2008). This definition of poverty in the United States identifies **relative poverty:** The households in poverty in the United States are poor compared with other Americans, but when one looks at other parts of the world, an income at the U.S. poverty line of $21,203 would make a family very well off.

The United Nations measures world poverty in two ways. **Absolute poverty** is the situation in which people live on less than $1 per day. **Extreme poverty** is defined as the situation in which people live on less than $275 a year, that is, on less than 75 cents a day. There are six hundred million people in the world who live at or below this extreme poverty level.

However, money does not tell the whole story because many people in the poor countries do not always deal in cash. In many countries, people survive by raising crops for personal consumption and by bartering or trading services for food or shelter. These activities do not show up in calculations of poverty levels that use amounts of money as the measure. As a result, the United Nations Development Program also defines what it calls the human poverty index.

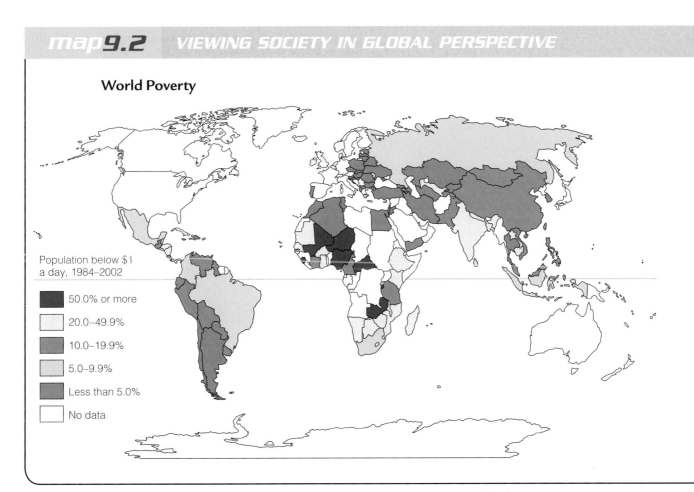

**map 9.2  VIEWING SOCIETY IN GLOBAL PERSPECTIVE**

**World Poverty**

Population below $1 a day, 1984–2002

- 50.0% or more
- 20.0–49.9%
- 10.0–19.9%
- 5.0–9.9%
- Less than 5.0%
- No data

*Source:* From World Bank Atlas 2007. Copyright © 2007 by World Bank. Reprinted by permission. **www.worldbank.org**

The **human poverty index** is a multidimensional measure of poverty, meant to indicate the degree of deprivation in four basic dimensions of human life: a long and healthy life, knowledge, economic well-being, and social inclusion. Different specific indicators of these different dimensions are used to measure poverty in the industrialized and developing countries because what constitutes these different dimensions of life can vary substantially in such different environments. In developing countries, the indicators are

- the percentage of people born not expected to live to age 40;
- the adult illiteracy rate;
- the proportion of people lacking access to health services and safe water; and,
- the percentage of children under age 5 who are moderately or severely underweight.

In industrialized countries, the human poverty index is measured by

- the proportion of people not expected to live to age 60;
- the adult functional illiteracy rate;
- the incidence of income poverty (because income is the largest source of economic provisioning in industrialized countries); and,
- long-term unemployment rates.

Figure 9.3 compares the human poverty index in select developing and industrialized nations (United Nations 2006c).

## Who Are the World's Poor?

Using the United Nations' definition of absolute poverty (those whose level of consumption falls below $1 per day), one billion people, about one-fifth of the world's population, live in poverty. Another 1.5 billion live on $1–$2 per day, resulting in more than 40 percent of the world's population forming what the United Nations calls a *global underclass*. The good news is that the number of people living in poverty is declining, with most of the reduction attributable to progress in East Asia, particularly in the People's Republic of China. At the same time, poverty in other areas is increasing, including in eastern Europe and central Asia. Sub-Saharan Africa has the highest incidence of poverty of anywhere in the world, despite the rich natural resources of this region. Almost half of the population in this region live in poverty. As a result, infant mortality here is high, life expectancy is low, school enrollment is low, and there are very high death rates due to AIDS (United Nations 2005b).

The character of poverty differs around the globe. In Asia, the pressures of large population growth leave many without sustainable employment. And, as manufacturing has become less labor intensive with more mechanized production, the need for labor in certain industries has declined. Even though new technologies provide new job opportunities, they also create new forms of illiteracy because many people have neither the access nor the skills to use information technology. In sub-Saharan Africa, the poor live in marginal areas

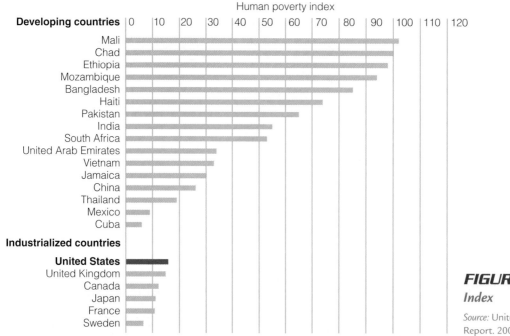

**FIGURE 9.3** *Human Poverty Index*

*Source:* United Nations Human Development Report. 2006. **www.undp.org**

where poor soil, erosion, and continuous warfare have created extremely harsh conditions. Political instability and low levels of economic productivity contribute to the high rates of poverty. Solutions to world poverty in these different regions require sustainable economic development, as well as an understanding of the diverse regional factors that contribute to high levels of poverty.

## Women and Children in Poverty

There is no country in the world in which women are treated as well as men. As with poverty in the United States, women bear a larger share of the burden of world poverty. Some have called this *double deprivation*—in many of the poor countries women suffer because of their gender and because they disproportionately carry the burden of poverty. For instance, in situations of extreme poverty, women have the burden of taking on much of the manual labor because in many cases the men have left to find work or food. The United Nations concludes that strengthening women's economic security through better work is essential for reducing world poverty (United Nations 2005a).

Because of their poverty, women tend to suffer greater health risks than men. Although women outlive men in most countries, the difference in life expectancy is *less* in the countries in poverty. This is explained by several factors. For one, fertility rates are higher in poor countries. Giving birth is a time of high risk for women, and women in poor countries with poor nutrition, poor maternal care, and the lack of trained birth attendants are at higher risk of dying during and after the birth.

High fertility rates are also related to the degree of women's empowerment in society—an often neglected aspect of the discussion between fertility and poverty. Societies where women's voices do not count for much tend to have high fertility rates as well as other social and economic hardships for women, including lack of education, job opportunities, and information about birth control. Empowering women through providing them with employment, education, property, and voting rights can have a strong impact on reducing the fertility rate (Sen 2000).

Women also suffer in some poor countries because of traditions and cultural norms. Most (though not all) of the poor countries are patriarchal, meaning that men control the household. As a result, in some situations of poverty the women eat after the men, and boys are fed before girls. In conditions of extreme poverty, baby boys may also be fed before baby girls because boys have higher status than girls. As a result, female infants have a lower rate of survival than male infants.

A distressing number of children in the world are also poor (see Figure 9.4). Children in poverty do not have the luxury of an education. Schools are usually few or nonexistent in poor areas of the world, and families are so poor that they cannot afford to send their children to school. Children from a very early age are required to help the family survive by working or performing domestic tasks such as fetching water. In extreme situations, children at a young age work as beggars, young boys and girls are sold to work in sweatshops, and young girls are sold into prostitution by their families. This may seem unusually cruel and harsh by Western standards, but it is difficult to imagine the horror of starvation and the desperation that many families in the world must feel that would force them to take such measures to survive. In poor countries, families feel they must have more children for their survival, yet having more children perpetuates the poverty. The United Nations estimates that there are 211 million children between age 5 and 14 in the paid labor force throughout the world. Most of the children, 127 million, are in Asia, and 48 million are in sub-Saharan Africa (International Labour Organization 2002). Many of these children work long hours in difficult conditions and enjoy few freedoms, making products (soccer balls, clothing, and toys, for example) for those who are much better off.

Another problem in the very poor areas of the world is homeless children (Mickelson 2000). In many situations, families are so poor that they can no longer care for their children, and the children must go without education out on their own, even at young ages. Many of these homeless children end up in the streets of the major cities of Asia and Latin America. In Latin America, it is estimated that there are thirteen million street children, some as young as six years old. Alone, they survive through a combination of begging, prostitution, drugs, and stealing. They sleep in alleys or in makeshift shelters. Their lives are harsh, brutal, and short.

## Debunking Society's Myths

**Myth:** There are too many people in the world, and there is simply not enough food to go around.

**Sociological perspective:** Growing more food will not end hunger. If systems of distributing the world's food were more just, hunger could be reduced.

## Poverty and Hunger

How can you live on less than $1 a day? The answer is that you cannot, or at least you cannot live very well. Malnutrition and hunger are growing problems because many of the people in poverty cannot find or afford food. The World Health Organization estimates that about eight hundred million people in the world are malnourished, which leads to disease (World Health Organization 2000).

Hunger results when there is not enough to eat to feed a designated area (such as a region or country). It may be that there is an inadequate supply of food or that households simply cannot afford to purchase enough food to feed themselves. Hunger stifles the mental and physical development of children and leads to disease and death. The trend in the world has been a reduction in the number of malnourished people, with the number of malnourished people expected to drop to under six hundred million by the year 2015. This is encouraging, but it is also short of the goal for reducing hunger that the World Health Organization has hoped for (World Health Organization 2000). Although the food supply is plentiful in the world, and is actually increasing faster than the population, the rate of malnutrition is still dangerously high.

Why are people hungry? Is there not enough food to feed all the people in the world? In fact, plenty of food is grown in the world. The world's production of wheat, rice, corn, and other grains is sufficient to adequately feed all the people in the world. Much grain grown in the United States is stored and not used. The problem is that the surplus food does not get to the truly needy. The people who are starving lack what they need for obtaining adequate food, such as arable land or a job that would pay a living wage. In many cases, in the past people grew food crops and were able to feed themselves, but today much of the best land has been taken over by agribusinesses that

# [understanding *diversity*

## War, Childhood, and Poverty

"In 2003, surgeons were forced to amputate both of Ali Ismaeel Abbas's arms after an errant U.S. bomb slammed into his Baghdad home during the opening phase of the Iraq war. Pictures of the twelve-year-old, who lost his parents in the attack, soon appeared on TV screens and in newspapers around the world. Since then, Abbas, who was treated in Kuwait, has come to represent a grim reality: All too often the victims of war are innocent children" (McClelland 2003: 20).

In the past ten years alone, UNICEF estimates that over two million children have died in war, with even more injured, disabled, orphaned, or forced into refugee camps (Machel 1996). One estimate is that of all the victims of war, 90 percent are civilian—half of those, children (McClelland 2003).

In the aftermath of war children are also highly vulnerable to outbreaks of disease. In Iraq, following the war in 2003, many children died of diseases such as anemia and diarrhea—diseases that can be prevented. Children in Iraq were already living under extreme hardship under the regime of Saddam Hussein. Economic sanctions against Iraq during his regime also produced high infant mortality because of food shortages.

The United Nations has passed resolutions prohibiting the use of children under age 18 in combat. It has linked the threats to children from violence with high rates of poverty around the world. Although reducing poverty would not eliminate the threat of war, it would go a long way toward improving children's lives in war-torn regions.

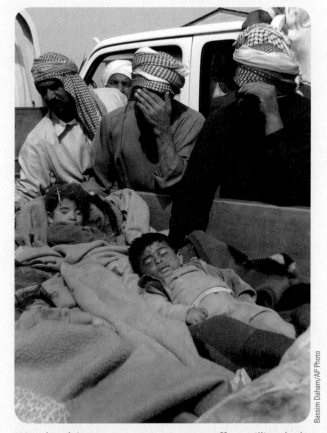

*War, though it may seem remote to some, affects millions both in the United States and in war-torn countries. Many of those most affected are children. Here relatives mourn the death of children killed during a U.S. raid in Tikrit, Iraq in 2006.*

Bassim Daham/AP Photo

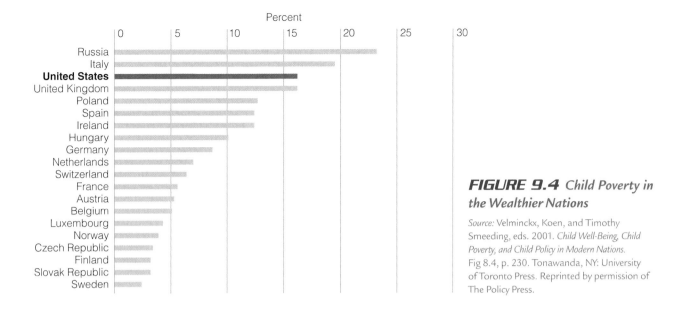

**FIGURE 9.4** *Child Poverty in the Wealthier Nations*

*Source:* Velminckx, Koen, and Timothy Smeeding, eds. 2001. *Child Well-Being, Child Poverty, and Child Policy in Modern Nations.* Fig 8.4, p. 230. Tonawanda, NY: University of Toronto Press. Reprinted by permission of The Policy Press.

grow cash crops, such as tobacco or cotton, and subsistence farmers have been forced onto marginal lands on the flanks of the desert where conditions are difficult and crops often do not grow.

## Causes of World Poverty

What causes world poverty, and why are so many people so desperately poor and starving? More to the point, why is poverty decreasing in some areas but increasing in others? We do know what does *not* cause poverty. Poverty is not necessarily caused by too rapid population growth, although high fertility rates and poverty are related. In fact, many of the world's most populous countries, India and China, for instance, have large segments of their population that are poor, but even with very large populations these countries have begun to reduce poverty levels. Poverty is not caused by people being lazy or uninterested in working. People in extreme poverty work tremendously hard just to survive, and they would work hard at a job if they had one. It is not that they are lazy; it is that there are no jobs for them.

Poverty is a result of a mix of causes. For one, the areas where poverty is increasing have a history of unstable governments or, in some cases, virtually no effective government to coordinate national development or plans that might alleviate extreme poverty and starvation. World relief agencies are reluctant to work in or send food to countries where the national governments cannot guarantee the safety of relief workers or the delivery of food and aid to where it should go. Food convoys may be hijacked or roads blocked by bandits or warlords.

In many countries with high proportions of poverty, the economies have collapsed and the governments have borrowed heavily to remain afloat. As a condition of these international loans, lenders, including the World Bank and the International Monetary Fund, have demanded harsh economic restructuring to increase capital markets and industrial efficiency. These economic reforms may make good sense for some and may lead these countries out of economic ruin over time, but in the short run, these imposed reforms have placed the poor in a precarious position because the reforms also called for drastically reduced government spending on human services.

Poverty is also caused by changes in the world economic system. Although poverty has been a long-term problem and has many causes, increases in poverty and starvation in Africa and Latin America can be attributed in part to the changes in world markets that favored Asia economically but put sub-Saharan Africa and Latin America at a disadvantage. As the price of products declined with more industrialization in places such as India, China, Indonesia, South Korea, Malaysia, and Thailand, commodity-producing nations in Africa and Latin America suffered. In Latin America, the poor have flooded to the cities, hoping to find work, whereas in Africa they did the opposite, fleeing to the countryside hoping to be able to grow subsistence crops. Governments often had to borrow to provide help to their citizens. Many governments collapsed or found themselves in such great debt that they were unable to help their own people. This has created massive amounts of poverty and starvation.

An often unrecognized cause of poverty is war. War disrupts the infrastructure of a society—its roads, utility systems, water, sanitation, even schools. For countries already struggling economically, this can be devastating. Food production may be disrupted and commerce can be threatened as it may be difficult, even impossible, to move goods in and out of a country. And the loss of life and major injury can mean that there are fewer productive citizens who can work, thus threatening family and community well-being (Pathways to Peace 2009). Moreover, the billions of dollars spent each year on military struggle rob societies of the resources that could be used to address humanitarian needs. Add to this the fact that wars are more likely to occur in nations that are already poor and you see the impact that war has on world poverty.

In sum, poverty has many causes. It is a major global problem that affects the billions who are living in poverty, but also affects all people in one way or another. In some areas, poverty rates are declining as some countries begin to improve their economic situation; however, in other areas of the world, poverty is increasing, and countries are sinking into financial, political, and social chaos.

# Globalization and Social Change

Globalization is, in some ways, not a new thing. Nations have long been engaged through a global system of trade, travel, and tourism. But what is new about globalization is the extent to which it permeates daily life for people all over the world and the pace with which globalization is developing. New technologies now allow for extraordinarily fast transactions across tremendous distances, both linking people together in new ways and transferring goods, cultural symbols, and communication systems in ways that were unimaginable not that long ago (Eitzen and Baca Zinn 2006).

Globalization is thus ushering in social changes—some good, some not—that will continue to evolve in the years ahead. As we have seen, globalization has meant that many countries in the world are becoming better off, but many countries remain persistently poor, some very poor. Is the world getting better or worse? What will happen in the future?

There is some good news. In some areas of the world, particularly east Asia, but also in Latin America, many countries have shown rapid growth and are emerging as stronger nations. These countries are sometimes called the **newly industrializing countries (NICs),** and they include South Korea, Malaysia, Thailand, Taiwan, and Singapore. In these countries, the governments have invested in social and economic development, often with outside help from other nations and corporations. Because some of the NICs have large populations, their success demonstrates that economic development can occur in heavily populated countries. China, for example, has embarked on an aggressive policy of industrial growth, and India is also improving economically.

Yet for all the success stories that globalization has generated, many nations are not making it. These include nations on all continents. In many cases, governments have collapsed or are corrupt, the economy is bankrupt, the standard of living is poor, and people are starving. In many areas of the world ethnic hatred has led to mass genocide and forced millions from their homes, creating huge numbers of refugees. In Darfur in the western region of Sudan, over 400,000 civilians have been murdered and millions have lost their homes, creating an international outcry demanding that Western governments intervene to stop the violence and provide massive humanitarian aid.

Globalization has also brought the expansion of the system of capitalism, including to nations once hostile to capitalist economics, such as China. This has opened new markets, increased global trade, but also expanded the reach of multinational corporations. The development of such world financial markets may bring prosperity and wealth to many nations and individuals, and it can allow some formerly poor countries to share in the world's wealth. But economic prosperity does not usually filter down to the people at the lower levels of society, and it can force nations into huge amounts of debt, thus allowing poverty and hunger to continue—or even worsen. Thus, while market economies create opportunities for some to become wealthy, both individuals and nations, many nations and individuals do not benefit from this global transformation.

Globalization is a strong force that will continue to shape the future of most nations. Some see globalization simply as the expansion of Western markets and culture into all parts of the world. Western civilization brings positive new values (including democracy and more equality for women), but it can also bring values that may not be seen as positive changes—such

*In an increasingly global world, it is easier for people to become aware of international conflict and human rights abuses, thus generating social movements to advocate for more humane treatment.*

Don Emmert/AFP/Getty Images

as increased consumerism or a change in the nation's sexual mores. Globalization certainly brings new products to remote parts of the world (movies, clothing styles, and other commercial goods), but some see this as a form of imperialism—that is, the domination of Western nations. Resistance to Western globalization and imperialism produces some of the international problems now dominating United States and world history, as evidenced in the hostility felt by militant fundamentalist Islamic groups toward the United States.

Globalization has created great progress in the world—including trade, migration, the spread of diverse cultures, the dissemination and sharing of new knowledge, greater freedom for women, travel, and so forth. Moreover, globalization has not simply extended the values and knowledge of Western culture. Many of the things we now take for granted in our culture originated in non-Western cultures. For example, the decimal system—fundamental to modern math and science—originated in India between the second and sixth centuries and was soon further developed by Arab mathematicians. Western societies certainly get credit for the development of science and technology, but the credit is not theirs alone (Sen 2002).

It is no doubt true that globalization is contributing to the inequality between nations and to the exploitation of some nations and groups by others. Perhaps the solution is not in resisting globalization, but in working so that the benefits of the global economy, global technology, and knowledge reach parts of the world in less exploitative ways. As long as great disparities in standards of living, human rights and basic freedoms, environmental quality, and so forth persist, world conflict is likely to be the result.

# Chapter Summary

• **What is global stratification?**

*Global stratification* is a system of unequal distribution of resources and opportunities between countries. A particular country's position is determined by its relationship to other countries in the world. The countries in the global stratification system can be categorized according to their per capita gross national product, or wealth. The world's countries can also be categorized as *first-, second-,* or *third-world* countries, which describe their political affiliation and their level of development. The global stratification system can also be described according to the economic power countries have.

• **How do systems of power affect different countries in the world?**

The countries of the world can be divided into three levels based on their power in the world economic system. The *core countries* are the countries that control and profit the most from the world system. *Semiperipheral countries* are semi-industrialized and play a middleman role, extracting profits from the poor countries and passing those profits on to the core countries. At the bottom of the world stratification system are the *peripheral countries,* which are poor and largely agricultural, but with important resources that are exploited by the core countries. Most of these nations are populated by people of color, perpetuating racism as part of the world system.

• **What are the theories of global stratification?**

*Modernization theory* interprets the economic development of a country in terms of the internal attitudes and values. Modernization theory ignores that the development of a country may be due to its economic relationships with other more powerful countries. *Dependency theory* draws on the fact that many of the poorest nations are former colonies of European colonial powers that keep colonies poor and do not allow their industries to develop, thus creating dependency. *World systems theory* argues that no nation can be seen in isolation and that there is a world economic system that must be understood as a single unit.

• **What are some of the consequences of global stratification?**

The poorest countries have more than half the world's population and have high birthrates, high mortality rates, poor health and sanitation, low rates of literacy and school attendance, and are largely rural. The richest countries have low birthrates, low mortality rates, better health and sanitation, high literacy rates, high school attendance, and largely urban populations. Although women in the wealthy countries are not completely equal to men, they suffer less inequality than do women in the poor countries.

- *How do we measure and understand world poverty?*

  *Relative poverty* means being poor in comparison to others. *Absolute poverty* describes the situation where people do not have enough to survive, measured as having the equivalent of $1 per day. *Extreme poverty* is defined as the situation in which people live on less than 75 cents a day. The United Nations has developed a *human poverty index*—a multidimensional measure that accounts for life expectancy, knowledge,

economic well-being, and social inclusion. Poverty particularly affects women and children. Children in the very poor countries are forced to work at very early ages and do not have the opportunity for schooling. Street children are a growing problem in many cities of the world. Starvation is also a consequence of the global stratification system.

- *What is the future of global stratification?*

  The future of global stratification is varied and depends on the country's position within the world economic system. Some countries, particularly those in east Asia—commonly referred to as *newly industrializing countries*—have shown rapid growth and emerged as developed countries. Many nations, though, are not making it. Governments collapse, countries suffer economic bankruptcy, the standard of living plummets, and people starve.

## Key Terms

## Online Resources

### Sociology: The Essentials Companion Website

www.cengage.com/sociology/andersen
Visit your book companion website where you will find more resources to help you study and write your research papers. Resources include web links, learning objectives, Internet exercises, quizzing, and flash cards.

 **is an easy-to-use online resource that helps you study in less time to get the grade you want NOW.**

www.cengage.com/login
Need help studying? This site is your one-stop study shop. Take a Pre-Test and CengageNOW will generate a Personalized Study Plan based on your test results. The Study Plan will identify the topics you need to review and direct you to online resources to help you master those topics. You can then take a Post-Test to determine the concepts you have mastered and what you still need to work on.

# 10

## Chapter ten
### CHAPTER TEN

# Race and Ethnicity

[
**You might expect** a society based on the values of freedom and equality, such as ours, not to be deeply afflicted by racial conflict, but think of the following situations:

- When Hurricane Katrina struck New Orleans and the Gulf Coast in 2006, hundreds of thousands of people were displaced and billions of dollars of property destroyed. Although the hurricane affected the lives (and deaths) of many, African Americans—many of them poor—were disproportionately killed or left homeless. Millions of Americans were shocked by the images of poor people desperate to survive but left without federal or state governmental help for a long time.

- In 2009, James von Brunn, an eighty-eight year-old self-proclaimed white supremacist, gunned down and killed a security guard at the U.S. Holocaust Memorial Museum in Washington, DC. James von Brunn was known by federal authorities to be affiliated with various hate groups. The shooter left an anti-Semitic letter in his car, parked outside the Museum, charging that "Obama was created by Jews." The guard who was shot and killed, Stephen T. Johns, a thirty-nine year old, African American guard who worked at the Museum. Von Brunn, shot and wounded by other security guards, was charged with murder.

- Derogatory labels, which reinforce prejudice and racism, have been applied throughout American history to persons of color, and despite minimal improvements in race relations, they persist only slightly diminished right up to the present: Blacks (niggers, coons, jigaboos, spades, sambos, jungle bunnies), Hispanics (spics, greasers, wetbacks, beaners), and Asians (slants, slopes, chinks, Japs, flips).

*continued*

Michael Newman/PhotoEdit

ten Chapter ten CHAPTER TE